The Concept of RASA

With Special Reference to Abhinavagupta

The Concept of RASA

With Special Reference to Abhinavagupta

Edited by
S.C. Pande

Indian Institute of Advanced Study
Shimla

Aryan Books International
New Delhi

THE CONCEPT OF RASA

ISBN: 978-81-7305-384-9

Published in **2009** by

Indian Institute of Advanced Study
Rashtrapati Nivas, Shimla-171 005

and

Aryan Books International
Pooja Apartments, 4B, Ansari Road, New Delhi-110 002 (India)
Tel.: 23287589, 23255799; Fax: 91-11-23270385
E-mail: aryanbooks@gmail.com
www.aryanbooks.com

Computer Typeset and Printed in India by
ABI Prints & Publishing Co., New Delhi

Preface

Rasa (aesthetic pleasure) is accepted as the highest value of poetry (*kāvya*), hence it is called the soul of *kāvya* (वाक्यं रसात्मकं काव्यम्). The *rasa* is a vey old concept and is found in the Upaniṣad wherein it is equated with or the synonym of Brahman, the highest bliss. (रसो वै सः। रसं ह्येवायं लब्ध्वानन्दी भवति। तैत्तिरीय-उपनिषद् II/7). In the field of dramaturgy, Bharata the author of the *Nāṭyaśāstra* is the first known Āchārya of the *rasa* theory and Abhinavagupta is his commentator. Āchārya Abhinavagupta has been one of the most profound thinkers of India in the 10th century AD. He hailed from Kashmir and was a prolific writer. Though mainly a Kashmir Shaiva philosopher, his contribution in the field of literary criticism is remarkable. He was the celebrated author of two commentaries – *Abhinavabhāratī* on the *Nāṭyaśāstra* and *Locana* on the *Dhvanyāloka*. In both the commentaries he has presented a scholarly and philosophical exposition of the *rasa* experience in the light of the *Dhvani* theory of Ānandavardhana. There is undercurrent of spirituality in all his writings. According to him the *rasa* experience (रसास्वाद) though never identical with but similar to Brahmāsvāda because at the time of *rasa* realisation the aesthete or the connoisseur goes beyond the limitations of the ego-centric experiences. Abhinavagupta's theory of *rasa*, though not accepted in toto by some of the later writers on poetics particularly the anti-*dhvani* theorists, still holds ground.

So keeping in view the importance of the *rasa* theory and Abhinavagupta, Prof. G.C. Pande, the then chairman of the governing body of the Indian Institute of Advanced Study, Shimla thought of making a fruitful discussion on this important subject. He asked me to organise a seminar by inviting the scholars of literary criticism from different states of India, as far as possible. The present book is the outcome of that seminar.

I express my deep sense of gratitute to Prof. G.C. Pande and Prof. Mrinal Miri, the then Director of IIAS, who provided all the facilities for the smooth conduct of the seminar. I am also grateful to the present dynamic director Prof. Peter R. deSouza and also Dr. Debarshi Sen, the Publication Officer and Mr. Ashok Sharma, the PRO at the IIAS, for expediting the long awaited publication of the book.

S.C. Pande
Editor

Contents

Introduction

The Indian Institute of Advanced Study, Shimla, organized a three-day National Seminar on "The Concept of *Rasa* with Special Reference to Abhinavagupta" on June 7, 8 and 9, 1999. About thirty Sanskrit scholars from different states of India were invited but only seventeen could ultimately participate. The seminar was marked by insightful presentation by the speakers and lively and enthusiastic participation by the audience.

S. Ranganath presented his paper on "Abhinavagupta's Concept of *Śāntarasa* in the Light of his Commentary on the *Bhagavadgītā*". After giving Abhinavagupta's justification of the *Śāntarasa*, he quoted eight stanzas of the *Bhagavadgītā* wherein Abhinavagupta justified the *Śāntarasa* as the supreme *Rasa* and concluded with the statement that *Śānta* as a *Rasa* runs throughout the *Bhagavadgītā* if the commentary of Abhinavagupta be studied carefully.

Kamalesh Datta Tripathi in "*Rasa* and *Bhāvānukīrtana* Complementarity of two concepts" said, "*Nāṭyaśāstra* offered the central concept of Indian Aesthetics, i.e. *Rasa* in its sixth chapter and another concept of *Bhāvānukīrtana*, compatible to it appears even before it in the first chapter. Both the concepts are complementary to each other and form one grand theory." He made special effort for understanding the concept of *Bhāvānukīrtana* as distinguished from the concept of *anukīrtana*. He concluded by saying that *Rasa* expericence in the spectator depends upon the glorious re-telling of *bhāva*. Traditionally Indian theatre and in fact the entire traditional work of art, may be ultimately defined as *Bhāvānukīrtana* in terms of creative process and it may be seen as *Rasa* in terms of aesthetic experience. The interdependence of each other explains the complementary nature of both the concepts.

Radhavallabh Tripathi in his paper "Theory of *Rasa*: A Secular Approach" said that *Rasa* originated from *Atharvaveda*, which has preserved various traditions belonging to the tribes in India. *Rasa* is basically linked with such traditions and also two types of worldview as delineated through the myths of Indra and Varuṇa imbued in the aesthetics of *Rasa*. All *Rasa*s do not culminate into the same invariable experience. *Rasas* like *Bībhatsa*, *Raudra* and *Bhayānaka* require aesthetics quite different from *Śṛṅgāra*, *Adbhuta*, etc. Owing to their monistic outlook, *ācāryas* like Abhinavagupta and Viśvanāth overlooked the plurality and diversity of creative process and aesthetic experience.

V.N. Jha in his paper "Epistemology of *Rasa* Experience" says that, "The universe of our experience is partly given by God and partly created by man. A tree is given, a chair is created, the mud is given, a pitcher is created, flowers are given, garland is created, voice is given, music is created and language is given, poetry is created." The literary artist gives an aesthetic shape to the given world through a beautiful arrangement and rearrangement and thus transforms an ordinary world into a world of art. It is clear that Bhaṭṭanāyaka and Abhinavagupta take the help of Advaita philosophy to explain the *Rasa* theory, but the comparison does not go too far. The *rasa* experience cannot be equated with the experience of the ultimate reality – the *Brahman* – because the aesthetic experience is by a connoisseur who has not transcended his jīvahood whereas the experience of the *Brahman* is when the experience has transcended the jīvahood too. *Rasa* can be a *viṣaya* of experience but the *Brahman* cannot. Hence, *Rasāsvāda* is not *Brahmāsvāda* but *Brahmāsvāda-sahodara*.

In 'आचार्य अभिनवगुप्त निरूपित रसप्रक्रिया' Dashrath Dwivedi discussed in detail the nature of *Rasa* experience and process of *Rasa*-realization as expressed by Abhinavagupta in his *Abhinavabhāratī* and *Locana* commentaries. The paper indicated that

Dwivedi had sufficient command over the text of the commentaries of Abhinavagupta. While tracing the history of the *rasa* theory right from the *Nāṭyaśāstra*, Bhāmaha, Rūdraṭa, Daṇḍi, Udbhaṭa, he threw light on the question as to how the concept of *rasa* developed in the work of Bhaṭṭanāyaka and culminated in the commentaries of Abhinavagupta and was brought to the area of Kashmir Śaivism.

Rajendra Mishra in his insightful paper entitled 'आनन्दवर्धन की रसदृष्टि के व्याख्याकार आचार्य अभिनवगुप्त' explained many passages of the *Locana* and *Abhinavabhāratī* pertaining to the *rasa* theory very critically and meticulously with many illustrations, and gave his own interpretations wherever necessary. He emphasized Abhinavagupta's viewpoint that *rasa* is the real and ultimate sense of the poetry which pervades throughout the body of the aesthete like the fire spreading all over the dried wood. So the capacity of the learned aesthete to enjoy the poetry, i.e., सहृदयता is the prerequisite for *rasa* experience. *Rasa* as interpreted by Abhinavagupta is basically experienced in drama but it can also be experienced in poetry provided it is properly dramatized by the aesthete in his mind while reading it. Apart from *rasa*, Mishra also referred to भावध्वनि, भावप्रशम, भावोदय, as is explained by Abhinavagupta, and critically examined all the minute points relating to *rasa* experience as referred to in the commentaries of Abhinavagupta.

Anupa Pande in her erudite paper "The Indian Aesthetic-Tradition and Abhinavagupta – Concept of *Rasa*" described the various stages of the development of aesthetic ideas in ancient India. While pointing out the importance of Bharata's *Nāṭyaśāstra*, she said that it sums up the sacred and popular notions of the Vedic and Janapada ages which had developed out of Vedāṅgas and the Upavedas and which included the science of music, drama, sculpture and architecture. According to her, *Nāṭyaśāstra* recapitulates the traditional notion of the sacred and invisible or transcendental value of art forms and activities and at the same time formulates the notion of art as entertainment and enjoyment. In Bharata, human reality has its focus in *bhāva* and dramatic representation is its *anukaraṇa* or *anukīrtana*. Aesthetic experience is called *Rasa*, a unity of entertainment and enlightenment. The philosophical interpretation which Abhinavagupta gave of *Rasa* as संविद्विश्रान्ति or चमत्कार underplayed the essentiality of the specific roles of different media and techniques in the different arts and converted *Rasa* into a universal aesthetic category comparable to beauty. The emphasis on beauty suggests something objective and hence promotes the danger of seeking it exclusively in specific art forms. *Rasa*, on the other hand, clearly emphasizes the subjectivity of art experience. The distinction of *Rasa* from any other psychological experience is clear in Abhinava where *Rasa* is transcendental, the return of consciousness to its own innate and universal but immediate ecstatic nature. By the philosophical genius of Abhinavagupta, *Rasa*, thus became the comprehensive principle of Indian, aesthetics.

Prakash Pandey in his article on 'अभिनवगुप्त का स्वातन्त्र्यवाद एवं साधारणीकरण की उनकी अवधारणा' started with the assertion that the process of universalization (साधारणीकरण), the prerequisite for the *Rasa* experience, has been explained by three *ācāryas* in their own way. The first explanation is by Bhaṭṭanāyaka, the second one is by Abhinavagupta and the third by Paṇḍitarāja Jagannātha, the great Advaita Veḍāntin. He after going deep into the important philosophical texts of Kashmir Śaivism has interpreted the concept of साधारणीकरण in the light of the स्वातन्त्र्यवाद of Abhinavagupta. He successfully tried to solve all the problems and objections raised against the theory of universalization in the context of *Rasa* realization and established the fact that साधारणीकरण is intimately connected with aesthetic enjoyment.

Damodar Ram Tripathi in his paper 'रसस्य अलौकिकत्वम्', took into account almost all the prominent commentators in general and Abhinavagupta's commentaries in particular to present a clear picture of *Rasa* realization and its supra-mundane nature. His paper was mainly based on numerous Sanskrit commentaries. He gave his own interpretation wherever he disagreed with the commentators. Thus, his paper was entirely text-based and critical.

V. Kutumba Sastry's paper is entitled "The Problem of *Śāntarasa*". He started with the observation that *Śāntarasa* has been subjected to a great deal of discussion. It comprises several problems within it: (i) the textual problems concerned with the question of authenticity of passage relating to *Śāntarasa*, found in the *Nāṭyaśāstra* of Bharatamuni, (ii) practical problems concerned with the enactment of *Śāntarasa* on the stage and its appeal to the people, (iii) problem with regard to its *Sthāyibhāva*, (iv) doctrinal problems concerned with the explanation of the process of *rasa* realization, and

(v) problems related with the illustrations of *Śāntarasa* in Sanskrit literature. He discussed the last two problems in detail. His arguments were absolutely convincing and hence appealed to the audience. He concluded with the statement that Abhinavagupta made a sincere attempt to put experience of *Rasa* at par with *Savikalpasamādhi* of Patañjali. Thus, he quotes Bhagavān Patañjali extensively. If this parallelism between *Rasa* realization and *Savikalpasamādhi* is accepted, then acceptance of *Śāntarasa* as the ninth and primordial *rasa* cannot be challenged. Seen from his philosophical background, it appears that Abhinavagupta's treatment of *rasa* theory and his arguments in favour of *Śāntarasa* are mutually supportive and interdependent.

Rekha Jhanji in her paper on "*Śivarasa* and *Nāṭyarasa:* Sources of Aesthetic Experience in Abhinavagupta" highlighted the philosophical thoughts of Abhinavagupta vis-à-vis his aesthetic principles. While working on the *Nāṭyaśāstra,* she realized that Abhinavagupta in his commentary gives interpretations that are not necessarily warranted by the text of the *Nāṭyaśāstra.* It is because of the fact that Abhinavagupta's comments originate from his larger philosophical and spiritual interests. Thus, to understand Abhinavagupta's aesthetics, it is necessary to understand his metaphysics because that permeates into his entire conception of *kāvya.* Art objects can be looked upon from vantage points: (i) from the side of the creator and (ii) from the side of the beholder. From both these dimensions, Abhinava's reflections are saturated with his metaphysics. *Śivarasa* is the essence of all cosmic creation and *Nāṭyarasa* is the essence of drama and poetry. The rejection of the objective dimension of *Rasa* seems to highlight the parallel between *Nāṭyarasa* and *Śivarasa.* In mundane life detachment can be achieved only through different forms of *Sadhanā.* Thus, what happens quite easily in theatre on account of साधारणीकरण is achieved with great difficulty in the spiritual realism. However, despite this difference both the aesthetic experience and the spiritual experience are inherently enjoyable. The influence of Abhinava's tantric framework on his aesthetics has another fascinating dimension. This concerns his attitude towards the sensuous experience. It is interesting to note that even though Abhinava's metaphysical works are replete with examples from experiences of sensuous enjoyment, equanimity seems a continued preoccupation with him. He asserts his belief in *Śāntarasa* by proclaiming that the culmination of enjoyment of all

Rasas lies in turning away from all stimulants and realization of equanimity within oneself. Such a view could not have been possible without metaphysics blending into his aesthetic experience.

Ramakant Sharma Angiras in his paper entitled 'आचार्य अभिनवगुप्तप्रणीत स्तोत्रों में रससाधना का दर्शन' started with the thought-provoking statement that right from Bharata up to Abhinavagupta the treatment of *Rasa* based on various analogies has gone astray from the real path of *Rasa* realization and hence in the present paper an attempt is made to unfold the real view of *Rasa* on the basis of the poetical works of Abhinavagupta. The learned scholar said that the twin forms of Śiva and Śakti, not different from the संवित् शिव, are ultimately one and that one is Śiva. Śiva with his *vimarśa* power is playing in the सृष्टि and his play is itself the Drama. For the devotees of Śiva the whole world is a theatre. Lord Śiva is the supreme actor and the manifestation of actor's self is the supreme bliss. When the *Sādhaka* contemplates the संवित् शिव and is in complete union with him and sees all the manifestations of sentiments as various forms of Śiva, he begins to enjoy the *Rasa*.

Navjivan Rastogi, specialist in Kashmir Śaivism and a keen observer of the philosophical background of Abhinavagupta's *Rasa* theory, in 'रसानुभूति प्रतिमान के रूप में' enumerated in the beginning many words expressing the *Rasa* used by Abhinavagupta. The words are आस्वाद, संविद्विश्रान्ति, रसना, चमत्कार, भोग and चर्वणा. There are two reasons for explaining the *Rasa* experience in so many words. First, the historian wants to encompass all the different earlier aesthetic traditions; secondly, the process and the nature of *Rasa* realization is multidimensional and hence cannot be expressed by one single word. Out of many technical terms used in the context of *Rasa* realization, the learned scholar selected one term, *Pratibhāna* (intuitive perception), and dealt with it in detail to see as to which aspect of *Rasa* is highlighted by this term. While explaining the *Rasasūtra* of Bharata, Abhinavagupta used the word *'Pratibhāna'* in different senses so much so that there was apparent contradiction in its various meanings. Prof. Rastogi with his keen penetrative insight and analyzing acumen presented a good synthesis and fine explanation of *Pratibhāna* in the context of *Rasa* experience, keeping in view the deep philosophical thought of Abhinavagupta. His philosophical discussion made the concept of हृदयसंवाद and तन्मयीभाव absolutely clear.

Uma Deshpande in her paper "Abhinavagupta's Rasa Theory and his Commentary on the *Bhagavadgītā*" starts with the presentation of the brief profile of Abhinavagupta and then deals with the topics like concept of *Kāvya* and *Rasa* in Sanskrit literature, *Śāntarasa* and Abhinavagupta's philosophy of poetry and his Commentary of the *Gītā* on the basis of his *Rasa* theory. "Abhinavagupta's Commentary on *Bhagavadgītā*," she said, "is more like an epitome of the text than the elucidation of every verse". For Abhinavagupta the *Bhagavadgītā* is a *Kāvya* and since a *Kāvya* like *Bhagavadgītā* is linked with *Puruṣārtha* directly, it depicts *Śāntarasa* culminating into the cessation of all momentary and ephemeral miseries. In his commentaries on the *Dhvanyāloka* and the *Nāṭyaśāstra*, Abhinavagupta has stressed the significance of *Śāntarasa* and evolved a new philosophy of the *Rasa* theory applicable not only to the literary forms like the *Bhagavadgītā* but also to the human life, making it more meaningful and interesting. Thus, the contribution of Abhinavagupta to the field of poetics and philosophy is both pioneering and epoch making.

Hariram Mishra in 'रससिद्धान्त की प्रेरणा शब्दब्रह्मवाद' highlights the influence of the philosophy of grammar on the theory of *Rasa*. Mishra being himself a grammarian and a scholar of aesthetics could very well explain his views on grammar and its relation to the *Rasa* theory. Bhartṛhari, the grammarian philosopher, is of the opinion that to know a thing in its correct perspective the knowledge of all the *Śāstras* is essential because by going through all the *Śāstras* the knower develops the faculty of differentiating between right and wrong. The rhetoricians have accepted this view fully and hence Abhinavagupta points out that to know the *Rasa* theory one has to take into account the विज्ञानवाद, स्फोटवाद, सत्कार्यवाद and अद्वैतवाद. With his wide and intensive study of the difficult grammatical texts, Mishra presented a clear picture of रसब्रह्मवाद and शब्दब्रह्मवाद.

Amiya Kumar Mishra in his paper 'रससंख्या निर्धारण' says that when Bharata says that the number of *Rasas* is eight, he is only referring to his earlier tradition of ब्रह्मा or द्रुहिण. It is Abhinavagupta who tried to establish the fact that nine *Rasas* were acceptable to Bharata on the basis of some other recension containing different reading of the *Nāṭyaśātra*. Mishra following the viewpoint of many other scholars holds the view that the number of *Rasas* according to Bharata is only eight. The number started increasing in the works of later rhetoricians; first the *Śāntarasa* by Abhinavagupta, then *Preyān* by Rudraṭa and later on *Mṛgayārasa, Dyūtarasa, Udāttarasa, Uddhatarasa, Vatsalyarasa, Laulyarasa* and *Bhaktirasa.* Rūpa Goswāmi, the Vaiṣṇava Ācārya, was the great exponent of the *Bhaktirasa*. He held the view that it was wrong to say that *Bhakti* is only a *bhāva.* In reality *Bhakti* is the main *Rasa* and all other *Rasas* one subsidiary to it.

The *Rasa* theory, according to H.N. Chatterji Shastri, took a new turn towards the end of the sixteenth century because of the special influence of Chaitanya and Chaitanyism. The *Rasa Śāstra* of Bharata and Abhinavagupta turned out to be a philosophical-cum-psychological affair, new in its design, unheard of before. The contribution of Rūpa Goswāmi, Jīva Goswāmi, Madhusūdana and Kavi Karṇapūra was highlighted and the concept of *Cittadruti, Vasana, Vasanabhasa, Kāntāprema* in the context of *Rasaśāstra* was explained. In the paper only a passing reference has been made about his observations regarding *Bhakti* and *Bhaktirasa.*

Biswanarayan Shastri in his paper "Metaphysical and Psychological Approach to *Rasa* by Abhinavagupta and Viśvanātha" observed that the causation theory of *Nyāya-Vaiśeṣika,* the transformation of *Sāṁkhya* and monism of *Vedānta* and *Śivādvaita* had their influence on postulation of *Rasa* theory and arriving at the conclusion. After critically analyzing the *Rasa* theories of Bharata's commentators, the author threw some new light on the two terms, i.e., *Sādhāraṇīkaraṇa* and *Camatkāra* and brought out the minute points of difference in the views of Abhinavagupta, Viśhvanātha and Mahimabhaṭṭa relating to *Rasa* realization.

Kalanath Shastri in 'रसाभास का यथार्थ और वास्तविक क्षेत्र' equates रसाभास with the concept of 'Pathetic Fallacy' of Western literary criticism. He first raised a very important question regarding the acceptance of रसाभास as the first rate poetry. The question is if रसाभास is based on the lack of propriety why then is it treated as good as any other ध्वनिकाव्य. Shastri finds a very convincing solution to this problem and discusses in detail quoting the relevant passages from the nature description of *Kumārasaṃbhavam* and the amorous expressions of Rāvaṇa before Sītā, etc. The paper indicates the depth of thought and critical acumen of the learned author.

Rahasbihari Dwivedi in his paper 'Rasāsvādaḥ' discusses the nature of *Rasa* realization. He presented a brief survey of the *Rasa* and the process of *Rasa* realization right from the Vedas up to the modern thinkers. He observed that the concept of *Rasāsvāda* and its practice was prevalent even in the Vedic times. He quoted several vedic hymns to substantiate his view. He critically explained the theory ofAbhinavagupta that *Mahārasa* is only one which takes the various forms on account of the variety of the Vibhavādi. All elements of drama are directed towards *Rasa* only. He also examined critically the views of *Dhvani* theorists and the *Mīmāṃsakas* regarding *Rasa* realization. Not only the rhetoricians but the poets like Kālidāsa and Bhavabhūti have also indirectly referred to the *Rasāsvāda* in their works. In the end he has referred to his unpublished work काव्यतत्त्वमीमांसा wherein he maintains that all the beautifying elements of poetry like *Alaṃkāra, Rasa, Rīti, Dhvani*, and *Vakrokti* lead us to *Āhlāda* (आह्लाद) like all the rivers flowing towards ocean. He said that some new *Rasas* should also be accepted. They are प्रक्षोभरस and राष्ट्रभक्तिरस, and some new forms of poetry like प्रगतिशीलकाव्य, उपन्यास, नभोनाटक (Radio Drama), and हास्यव्यङ्ग्य काव्य may be taken into consideration.

Rewa Prasad Dwivedi in "The Text of Bharata's *Rasasūtra*" raises an important problem about a reading in the Bharata's *Rasasūtra*. The word is *sthāyi*. The problem is that in the famous *Rasasūtra*, the word स्थायी does not occur except in some passages like:

1. विभावानुभावव्यभिचारिसंयोगाद्रसनिष्पत्तिः (N.S. Baroda edn., p. 272)
2. विभावानुभावव्यभिचारिपरिवृतः स्थायी रसनाम (रसता) लभते (N.S. Baroda edn., p. 349).

The other problem is about the basis of difference between *sthāyi* and *vyabhicāri* because ultimately *sthāyi* also being a mental state is momentary.

The learned scholar with his keen penetrative insight and critical acumen has discussed these important problems of the *Nāṭyaśāstra* meticulously taking into account the views of many important rhetoricians like Mammaṭa, Hemacandra, Bhoja, and Paṇḍitarāja Jagannātha, etc. His deep study of Bharata and Bhoja will certainly attract the attention of the scholars of aesthetics. He concludes that *Rasasūtras* of different canons have been mingled in the *Nāṭyaśāstra* since long and the *sūtra* containing *sthāyi* is a later development of the first one not containing *sthāyi*. So far as Abhinavagupta is concerned, he followed the first but could not leave aside the latter.

Vidya Niwas Mishra, the renowned Sanskrit scholar in his paper "Theoretical Foundation of *Rasa* Theory of Abhinavagupta", observed that the *Rasa* theory is not the revelation of Bharata or Abhinavagupta. It is rather an adumberation of the idea of re-enactment of the first movement, of release of the seed or rather of fulfilment of the singleness in allness of a reintegration through disintegration. *Rasa* means the latent essence. *Rasa* is the most desired flavour as well as experience of immortality. *Rasa* is something which flows as well, hence it forms a process of liquidification of whatever is solid till at last it remains in the form of essence. *Rasa* derives its meaning of supreme bliss from the juice of *soma,* the divine and exhilarating drink. Transcendental experience of *Rasa* may be repeated time and again but the experience is everything, something new and unique because it is unlike the nature of usual production. *Rasa* experience, though a sensate experience, is such an essence of that experience which can transform the sensate experience into aesthetic experience. After critically examining the various meanings of *Rasa,* he goes deep into the concept of *Vāk* and finds therein the source of *Rasa* theory. The *Vāk* concept has four components – *Vāk* is the creative energy, *Vāk* is an epitome of the creative process itself, *Vāk* is the first act of speech articulation, and *Vāk* is an exchangeable item with *soma,* the divine juice.

Dr. Mishra dealt upon the Vedic foundation of the *Rasa* theory. His treatment of the concept of *Rasa* in this context is absolutely original, deep and thought provoking.

Sushma Kulshrestha in her presentation 'करुणविप्रलम्भ परिशीलन (अभिनवगुप्त एवं कामदशा के विशेष आलोक में)' has extensively and meticulously dealt with the theory and practice of करुणविप्रलम्भ. Though विप्रलम्भ is a form of शृंगाररस but करुणविप्रलम्भ touches the limits of करुणरस. The difference of करुण and विप्रलम्भशृङ्गार is based on their *Sthāyibhāvas*. The *Sthāyibhāva* of करुण is शोक and that of विप्रलम्भ is Rati. In विप्रलम्भशृङ्गार death enumerated as the final कामदशा is only व्यभिचारिभाव but when it transforms into a permanent mood it transgresses the limits of शृङ्गार and hence becomes करुण. करुणविप्रलम्भ is a step between करुण and विप्रलम्भशृङ्गार. Kulshrestha has taken into account the views of almost all the important rhetoricians in this context. She after discussing the passage relating to रतिविलाप and अजविलाप in Kālidāsa has come to the conclusion that करुणविप्रलम्भ is only a beautiful and attractive form of विप्रलम्भशृङ्गार.

S.C. Pande

Keynote Address

तदिव्यमव्ययं धाम सारस्वतमुपास्महे। यत्प्रसादाद्विलीयन्ते मोहान्धतमसश्छटा:।।

स्थायी प्रबुद्धविषये व्यभिचारिभूत: कामाकुलासु जनतासु महानुभाव:।
अन्तर्विभावविषयो रसमात्रमूर्ति: श्रीमान् प्रसन्नहृदयोऽस्तु मम त्रिणेत्र:।।

The word रस literally means 'essence' or 'taste'. In the *Chāndogyopniṣad* it is taken as essence.

एषा भूतानां पृथिवी रस:। पृथिव्या आपो रस:। अपाम् ओषधयो रस:।
ओषधीनां पुरुषो रस:। पुरुषस्य वाग् रसो वाच ऋग् रस: ऋचां साम रस:,
साम्न: उद्गीथो रस:, स एष रसानां रसतम: परम: परार्धोऽष्टमोऽयमुद्गीथ:।
छान्द. १/१/२-३

In the context of Indian poetics and dramaturgy, the *Rasa* denotes the essence of aesthetic pleasure. In the words of K.C. Bhattacharya, "The artistic sentiment is not merely a feeling among feelings but the feeling par excellence."

According to Abhinavagupta, the *Rasa* is the essence or the soul of poetry:

तेन रस एव वस्तुत: (काव्यस्य) आत्मा वस्त्वलंकारध्वनी तु सर्वथा रसं प्रति पर्यवस्येते।
(*लोचन* on *ध्वन्या.* I/5)

It is not only the highest value of *kāvya* but also the means to achieve the highest पुरुषार्थ, i.e., the मोक्ष.

ततस्त्रिवर्गात्मकप्रवृत्तिधर्मविपरीतनिवृत्तिधर्मात्मको मोक्षफल: शान्त:।
तत्र स्वात्मावेशेन रसचर्वणेत्युक्तम्। (*अभिनवभारती*)

In the *Taittirīyopaniṣad,* the *Rasa* is equated with *Ānanda* or *Ātmā*:

रसो वै स: रसं ह्येवायं लब्ध्वानन्दी भवति।
.... एष ह्येवानन्दयति यदा ह्येवैष एतस्मिन्
अदृश्ये अनात्म्ये अनिरुक्तेऽनिलयेऽअभयं प्रतिष्ठां विन्दते।
अथ सोऽभयं गतो भवति। (II/7)

The propounder of the *Rasa* theory is Bharata, the author of the *Nāṭyaśāstra* – the first ever treatise on Indian dramaturgy and musicology. According to him, *Rasa* is all-pervading and gives meaning to drama नहि रसादृते कश्चिदर्थ: प्रवर्तते because for a person devoid of aesthetic taste, drama or poetry has no meaning.

सवासनानां तु नाट्यादौ रसस्यानुभवो भवेत्।
निर्वासनास्तु रङ्गान्तर्वेश्मकुड्याश्मसंभवा:।।

The famous four commentators of the *Rasasūtra* of Bharata, i.e., Bhaṭṭalollata, Śrīśaṅkuka, Bhaṭṭanāyaka and Abhinavagupta have dealt with the process of *Rasa* realization and the nature of *Rasa* in every possible detail according to the tenets of their own philosophical schools. It is only Abhinavagupta who has refuted the *Rasa* theories of his earlier commentators of *Rasasūtra.* Though he, after rejecting the *Bhoga* theory of Bhaṭṭanāyaka with all humility, says that actually he has not refuted or found fault with the theories of his predecessors but has only improved upon them or has modified them.

तस्मात् सतामत्र न दूषितानि मतानि तान्येव तु शोधितानि।
पूर्वप्रतिष्ठापितयोजनासु मूलप्रतिष्ठाफलमामनन्ति।।

(हिन्दी *अभिनवभारती*, पृ. 469)

This humility of Abhinavagupta is due to the fact that he holds Bhaṭṭanāyaka in high esteem, though being a *Dhvani* theorist he is at loggerheads with Bhaṭṭanāyaka who was an *anti-Dhvani* theorist.

It is Bhaṭṭanāyaka who revolutionized the concept of *Rasa* by explaining it on purely philosophical level and equating it with संविद्विश्रान्ति and ब्रह्मास्वाद and for realizing this highest form of aesthetic pleasure or supreme bliss, the विभावादि, the means to such realization, have to be absolutely impersonal or universalized. This process of universalization (साधारणीकरण) is nothing but the aesthetic contemplation of the object of art or विभावादि in the context of poetry. In this process not only the object of joy but the subject or the aesthete (सहृदय) has also to be universalized, i.e., the personal sentiment *sthāyibhāva* undergoes a change and becomes impersonal. In addition to the concept of universalization (साधारणीकरण), Bhaṭṭanāyaka's greatest contribution in the context of poetry and drama is that he regards it as व्यापारप्रधान and not शब्दार्थप्रधान because the aesthetic enjoyment is in the form of mental operation, action or aesthetic contemplation and not an experience of some accomplished thing. He says व्यापारप्राधान्ये काव्यधीर्भवेत् (*लोचन ध्व.* I/5). It is because of this operativeness of the aesthetic enjoyment the words of the poetry do not lose their significance after conveying their meaning only but they are to be read again and again by the aesthete or the enjoyer of poetry. Abhinavagupta says –

> काव्यात्मकशब्द निष्पीडनेनैव तच्चर्वणा दृश्यते। दृश्यते हि तदेव काव्यं पुनः पुनः पठन् चर्व्यमाणश्च सहृदयो लोकः, न तु काव्यस्य तत्र 'उपादायापि ये हेया' इति न्यायेन कृततप्रतीतिकस्य अनुपयोग एवेति।
>
> (*लोचन ध्व.* I/ 18).

Abhinavagupta following Bhaṭṭanāyaka defines *Rasa* as

> संविदानन्दचर्वणाव्यापाररसनीयरूपो रसः। स काव्यव्यापारैकगोचरो रसध्वनिः।
>
> (*लोचन ध्व.* I/ 4).

> विभावादिजः प्रतीतिविशेषो रसनाक्रिया इति व्यपदिष्टः।
>
> (हिन्दी *अभिनवभारती*, पृ. 499)

In Bharata the aesthetic experience or रसानुभूति was mostly confined to drama. Abhinavagupta, following Bharata, also says that the *Kāvya* or poetry has to be dramatized for *Rasa* realization.

> न नाट्य एव रसा: काव्येऽपि नाट्यायमान एव रस। काव्यार्थविषये हि प्रत्यक्षकल्पसंवेदनोदये रसोदय इत्युपाध्याया:। यदाहु: काव्यकौतुके प्रयोगत्वमनापन्ने काव्ये नास्वाद संभव:। तेन नाट्य एव रसा न लोक इत्यर्थ:। काव्यं च नाट्यमेव (हिन्दी *अभिनवभारती*, पृ. 504)

Abhinavagupta has used two words very often, हृदयसंवाद and तन्मयीभवन, as the precondition for *Rasa* realization. हृदयसंवाद means tallying of heart, i.e., with reference to poetry, means that the enjoyer (सहृदय) and the poet be in the same wavelength. It is possible only when the object, i.e., विभावादि and the subject, i.e., enjoyer are completely transformed and hence universalized (साधारणीकृत). In the process of तन्मयीभवन the subject after losing its limitations is completely object-immersed and enjoys the sentiment *sthāyi* aroused and thus attains a unique form of experience which is supra mundane and such aesthetic pleasure cannot be compared with any worldly pleasure but can only be compared to the ब्रह्मानन्द, i.e., the supreme bliss ब्रह्मास्वादभिवानुभावयन्नलौकिकचमत्कारी शृङ्गारादिको रस:। (*का.प्र.* IV)

Here I would like to ask some questions:

First, can *Rasa* be compared with *Brahman* or can *Rasānanda* be compared to *Brahmānanda?* It is true that in simile the two things, i.e., *Upameya* and *Upamāna* are similar but never identical (तद्भिन्नत्वे सति तद्गतभूयोधार्मवत्वं सादृश्यम्). The *Upamāna* is placed in juxtaposition to the *Upameya* in order to make the image of the *Upameya* more clear and glaring just as the beauty of the lady's face is compared to a lotus because the lotus is invariably beautiful and is already well perceived by everyone. So, while comparing the lotus with the face, the image of the beautiful face becomes clearer and more artistic and glaring. But in the case of comparing *Rasānanda* to the *Brahmānanda*, the situation is quite different. The *Upameya Rasānanda* has been well experienced by every *sahṛdaya* because *Rasa* is only an object of मानस प्रत्यक्ष or साक्षात्कारात्मिका अनुभूति, i.e., a perceptual feeling and not an imaginary experience but the *Upamāna Brahmānanda* has never been the object of our experience so how can a feeling beyond our experience make the image of the *Rasa* more clear. For those liberated persons (जीवन्मुक्त) who have experienced the *Brahmānanda* the simile can be appropriate. But was Bhaṭṭanāyaka – the propounder of *Brahmāsvād* theory – a जीवन्मुक्त? If not, he has only based his theory of *Brahmāsvādasavidha* on *Āgamapramāṇa* and not on *Pratyakshapramāṇa*. K.C. Bhattacharya in his 'Concept of Rasa' says "the conception of Rasa or aesthetic essence may be interpreted entirely in terms of feeling without any reference to the intellectual ideal or the spiritual ideal."

Abhinavagupta while refuting the अनुकरणवाद of Śrisaṅkuka says that how can one feel that the actor Rama is imitating the real Rama, i.e., the अनुकार्यराम because none has ever seen the real Rama:

न च रामगतां रतिमुपलब्धपूर्विणः केचित्।
एतेन 'रामानुकारी नटः' इत्यपि निरस्तः प्रवादः। (हिन्दी *अभिनवभारती*, पृ. 451)

If the actor Rama cannot imitate the real Rama because he has not seen him, how can we compare *Rasānanda* with *Brahmānanda*, which we have never experienced.

Second, should not the *Śāntarasa* be traced somewhere in the Śramaṇa tradition. In my opinion, the first mention of *Śāntarasa* occurs in the *Anuyogadvārasūtra* of Aryarakṣita, a Jain work belonging to the 3rd century AD.

Third, what is the nature of विभावादि? Whether they are द्रव्यरूप or भावरूप? Rewa Prasad Dwivedi has raised this problem and discussed in detail to prove that they are भावरूप only.

Fourth, can *Śānta* be accepted as *Rasa* in the drama and poetry both?

Fifth, who is the real enjoyer of *Rasa* – the original character (अनुकार्य) poet, actor (*naṭa*) or the spectator (*prekṣaka*)? If we accept that the *Rasa* is neither realized by the original character or the actor then how will we explain the following statement of Bhavabhūti in the *Uttararāmacaritam*.

पुटपाकप्रतीकाशो रामस्य करुणो रसः।

Here obviously 'Rama' stands for the original character (अनुकार्य) only. This view of Bhavabhūti is in conformity with that of Bhaṭṭalollaṭa who says:

मुख्यया वृत्त्या रामादावनुकार्ये तद्रूपतानुसन्धानान्नर्तकेऽपि प्रतीयमानो रसः।
(का.प्र. IV–28)

But these views of Bhavabhūti and Bhaṭṭalollaṭa are quite opposed to that of Dhananjaya, the author of *Daśarūpaka*, who says that *Rasa* is never realized by the original character as he is the thing of the past only:

> रसः स एव स्वाद्यत्वाद्रसिकस्यैव वर्तनात्।
> नानुकार्यस्य वृत्तत्वात् काव्यस्यातत्परत्वतः।।
>
> (दशरूपक IV/28)

Bharata clearly mentions that *Rasa* is enjoyed by the spectator only. He says in the *Nāṭyaśāstra* –

> स्थायिभावानास्वादयन्ति हर्षादींश्चाधिगच्छन्ति (*ना.शा.* VI)

Abhinavagupta says that the *Rasa* is experienced by the *sahṛdaya*.

The poet also becomes like a spectator when he enjoys it though the original seat of *Rasa* is the heart of the poet only:

> मूलबीजस्थानीयः कविगतो रसः। कविर्हि सामाजिकतुल्य एव।
>
> (*अभि.भा.* VI)

Sixth, whether the *Rasa* is only आनन्दरूप or it is सुखरूप and दुःखरूप both. Bharata takes in the form of both सुख and दुःख because while defining the प्रेक्षक he says:

> यस्तुष्टौ तुष्टिमायाति शोके शोकमुपैति च। (*ना. शा.*)

But Abhinavagupta's view is quite different. He maintains that the *Rasa* experience is in the form of highest pleasure only. The pain can never be thought of in this context.

> अस्मन्मते तु संवेदनमेव आनन्दघनमास्वाद्यते का तत्र दुःखाशङ्का।
>
> (हिन्दी *अभि. भा.*)

Over and above these problems we must also discuss as far as possible the views of the modern critics like Ācārya Rama Chandra Shukla, Krishna Chandra Bhattacharya, M. Hiriyanna, Kanti Chandra Pande, Govind Chandra Pande, etc. in the context of the *Rasa* theory.

Krishna Chandra Bhattacharya in the chapter 'The Concept of Rasa' of his book *Studies in Philosophy*, Vol. I says:

> *Rasa* means either aesthetic enjoyment or that which is aesthetically enjoyed. The significance of the concept is best

> interpreted by the orientation of aesthetic enjoyment in reference to the feeling. As will be explained presently the artistic sentiment is not merely a feeling among feelings but the feeling par excellence standing as it does on a new grade or level altogether as compared with other feelings. The conception of *Rasa* or aesthetic essence may thus be interpreted entirely in terms of feeling without any reference to the intellectual ideal or the spiritual ideal.

M. Hiriyanna in the *Indian Conception of Values* says:

> *Rasa* experience is the outcome more of a reconstruction than of remembrance. The whole theory is based on the recognition of an affinity of nature between the poet and the reader of poetry; and on the basis of this affinity, it is explained that appreciation of poetry is essentially the same as the creation of it.

Acharya Ram Chandra Shukla, one of the greatest critics of Hindi literature, in his book *रसमीमांसा* (pp. 88-89) disagreeing with the views of Sanskrit rhetoricians in regard to the description of nature as only the *Uddīpana Vibhāva* (stimulants) of *śṛṅgāra* only, says that these descriptions of forests, gardens, seasons of nature are not only the *Uddīpana* of *śṛṅgāra* because the poets have in fact not made such descriptions as accessories of sentiment *(Uddīpana Vibhāva)* but they are independently the आलम्बन विभाव of our sentiments.

साहित्य के आचार्यों की दृष्टि में वन, उपवन, ऋतु आदि श्रृंगार के उद्दीपनमात्र हैं ... पर सोचने की बात है कि क्या प्राचीन कवियों ने इनका वर्णन इसी रूप में किया है? क्या विश्वहृदय वाल्मीकि ने वनों और नदियों का वर्णन इसी उद्देश्य से किया है? क्या महाकवि कालिदास ने *कुमारसंभव* के आरम्भ में ही हिमालय का जो विशद वर्णन किया है वह श्रृंगार के उद्दीपन की दृष्टि से ही है? कभी नहीं। ये वर्णन पहले तो प्रसंग प्राप्त हैं अर्थात् आलम्बन की परिस्थिति को अंकित करने वाले हैं। इनके बिना आश्रय और आलम्बन शून्य में खड़े मालूम पड़ते हैं। ... प्राकृतिक वर्णन केवल अंगरूप से हमारे भावों के आलम्बन नहीं हैं, स्वतन्त्ररूप से भी हैं। जिन प्राकृतिक दृश्यों के बीच हमारे आदिम पूर्वज रहे और अब भी अधिकांश भाग जो नगरों में नहीं आया है, रहता है, उनके प्रति प्रेमभावपूर्ण साहचर्य के प्रभाव से संस्कार या वासना के रूप में हमारे अन्तःकरण में निहित हैं। उनके दर्शन या काव्यादि में प्रदर्शन से हमारी भीतरी प्रकृति का जो अनुरंजन होता है वह अस्वीकृत नहीं किया जा सकता। इस अनुरंजन को केवल दूसरे भावों का उत्तेजक कहना अपनी जड़ता का ढिंढोरा पीटना है। जो प्राकृतिक दृश्यों को केवल कामोद्दीपन की सामग्री समझते हैं उनकी रुचि भ्रष्ट हो गई है और संस्कार

सापेक्ष है। मैंने पहाड़ों में या जंगलों में घूमते हुए ऐसे साधु देखें हैं जो लहराते हुए हरे-भरे जंगलों, स्वच्छन्द शिलाओं पर चांदी से ढलते हुए झरनों, चौकड़ी भरते हिरनों और डालियों पर कलरव कर रहे विहंगों को देख मुग्ध हो गए हैं। काले मेघ जब अपनी छाया डालकर चित्रकूट के पर्वतों को नीलवर्ण कर देते हैं तब नाचते हुए नीलकण्ठों को देखकर सभ्यताभिमान के कारण शरीर चाहे न चाहे पर मन अवश्य नाचने लगता है। इसमें कोई सन्देह नहीं कि ऐसे दृश्यों को देखकर हर्ष होता है। हर्ष एक संचारी भाव है। इसलिए मानना पड़ेगा उसके मूल में रतिभाव वर्तमान है और वह रतिभाव उन दृश्यों के प्रति है।

Govind Chandra Pande in the last chapter of his book, *भक्तिदर्शनविमर्श:*, while describing the nature of *Rasa* realization, says that *Rasa* is neither a feeling of recreation or amusement nor an experience of imaginary pleasure nor the real experience of the supreme consciousness and bliss (चिदानन्द) nor the feeling of mental enjoyment arising out of mundane things; but it *(Rasa)* is the experience of the Truth suggested by the feeling or it is the apparent experience of Ātman.

रसो न मनोरंजनमात्रं काल्पनिकसुखास्वादो वा, लौकिकभावानुसारिणा वा मनसा तद्विषयास्वाद:, स्वाभाविकस्य वा चिदानन्दस्य आस्वाद:। स हि भावव्यङ्ग्यसत्यसाक्षात्कार: आत्मावभासो वा। (पृ. 112)

He further says that in our Indian tradition, the learned thinkers analyzing the duality of pleasure and pain have accepted the *Śānta* (शान्त) or *Bhakti* (भक्ति) as the highest form of *Rasa*, while in Western literature those dramas are generally popular which have *Hāsya* (हास्य) or *Karuṇa* (करुण) as the dominant *Rasa*. While highlighting the two alternatives and various aspects of *Rasa* realization, he says:

> रस स्वरूपमप्यत्र संक्षेपेण विचारमर्हति। अत्र द्वौ पक्षौ एव प्रमुखौ भावास्वाद एव रस:, भावोपहितविशेषा संविदेव रस इति च। पुनश्च आनन्दात्मको रस: सुखदु:खात्मको वेत्यपि विप्रतिपति:। केचिच्च रसं व्यवहारिकं नाट्यीयं भक्तिगतं ब्रह्मानन्दात्मकं चेति चतुर्धेव निर्दिशन्ति।
>
> (*भक्तिदर्शनविमर्श:* पृ० 110)

S.C. Pande

1

Epistemology of Rasa-Experience

V.N. Jha

The universe of our experience is partly given by God and partly created by man. A tree is given, a chair is created; the mud is given, a pitcher is created; cotton is given, a thread is created; flowers are given, garland is created; voice is given, music is created; language is given and poetry is created. There is something which is given to man which he has not created and there is something which he creates out of the given. Therefore, our world of experience consists of both the given and the created.

THE GIVEN

The philosophers of our past have thoroughly analyzed this given world. For example, the analysis presented by the Indian logicians (*Nyāya Vaiśeṣikas*). For them, the world is a *padārtha* or an entity which can be a referent of a linguistic term (*padasya arthaḥ*). Such an entity can be either positive (*bhāva*) or negative (*abhāva*). Thus, a tree is an entity and the absence of that tree elsewhere is also an entity.

A positive entity is classified in six sets of entities such as substances (*dravya*), quality (*guṇa*), action (*karman*), universal (*sāmānya*), particular (*viśeṣa*), and inherence (*samavāya*). Each one of these sets is further divided into sub-sets. Thus, substance is of nine kinds, viz., earth (*pṛthvi*), water (*āp*), fire (*tejas*), air (*marut*), ether (*ākaśa*), time (*kāla*), space (*dik*), soul (*ātman*), and mind (*manas*). Qualities are twenty-four: colour (*rūpa*), taste (*rasa*), smell (*gandha*), touch (*sparśa*), number (*saṃkhyā*), measure (*parimāṇa*), contact (*saṃyoga*), division (*vibhāga*), separateness (*pṛthaktva*), moisture (*sneha*), heaviness (*gurutva*), fluidity (*dravatva*), remoteness (*paratva*), nearness (*aparatva*), knowledge (*buddhi*), happiness (*sukha*), unhappiness (*duḥkḥa*), desire (*icchā*), hatred (*dveṣa*), volition (*prayatna*), merit (*dharma*), demerit (*adharma*), impression (*saṁskāra*), and sound (*śabda*).

Actions are of five kinds, viz., going upward (*ūrdhvagamana*), going downward (*adhaḥpatana*), shrinking (*ākuñcana*), spreading (*prasārṇa*), and going (*gamana*).

Class property or generic property or universal (*sāmānya*) is only one, like potness, treeness and so on.

Particulars (*viśeṣa*) are endless and they are found in all permanent substances. These particulars distinguish one permanent substance from the other permanent substance.

Inherence (*samavāya*) is a single permanent relation, which is accepted in the following five cases:

(a) Between a quality and its locus;
(b) Between an action and its locus;
(c) Between a universal and its locus;
(d) Between a whole and its parts; and
(e) Between a particular (*viśeṣa*) and its locus.

Absence (*abhāva*) is broadly of two kinds, mutual absence (*anyonyābhāva*) and absolute absence (*atyantābhāva*). Absolute absence is further divided into three types: pre-absence (*pragabhāva*), relational absence (*saṃsargābhāva*), and destruction (*dhvaṃsa*). This is our given world with which we behave. But behaviour presupposes knowledge of that with which we behave. Naturally, we would like to know how do we know this given world. Therefore, the Indian logicians took up the issue of the process of knowing the world. This is what is known as epistemology. The logicians arrived at the conclusion after analysis that there are four ways of knowing the world: Perception (*pratyakṣa*), Inference (*anumāna*), Analogy (*upamāna*), and Language (*śabda*). Let us see briefly how these instruments of knowing work.

We are given five external sense-organs made of five primordial elements (*pañca-mahābhūtas*) to have direct access to the external world, and the sixth sense-organ called mind to volition, happiness, unhappiness, hatred, love, kindness, merit (*puṇya*), demerit (*pāpa*) and our impressions left behind by our experience.

It is not the case only that we have access to the world, both external and internal, only when it is in direct contact with these six sense-organs. We can know them even if sometimes the world is beyond the reach of a sense-organ. The instrument, or the process of knowing in such a situation, is inference. Inference works on the basis of an invariable relation (*vyāpti*) between the ground (*hetu*) on the basis of which we want to know the world (*sādhya*).

We know the world through language. But the understanding of language depends on the knowledge of the relationship between a sign and what a sign stands for. The tradition has discussed that issue in detail and has discovered various ways of knowing this relationship between a word and its meaning. The following verse presents a list of such means of knowing that relationship:

> शक्ति-ग्रहो व्याकरणोपमान-कोशाप्तवाक्यव्यवहारतश्च।
> वाक्यस्य शेषात् विवृतेर्वदन्ति सान्निध्यतः सिद्धपदस्य वृद्धाः।।

Śakti here means the primary relationship between a word or, to be very precise, between a morpheme and its referent.

One can know that relationship by grammar, *Upamānapramāṇa*, dictionary, sentence of a reliable person, elder's usage, scriptural description paraphrase, and the proximity of a known word.

It may be noted that *Upamānapramāṇa* is one of the means of knowing the relation between a morpheme and its referent.

Similarly, language is one of the means to know the world.

The *Prācīna-Nyāya* tradition has presented a beautiful analysis in this context. Gautama defines *pratyakṣa* as follows:

> *indriyārtha-sannikarṣotpannam jñānam avyapadeśyam*
> *avyabhicāri vyavasāyātmakam pratyakṣam.*

A cognition which is produced out of the contact between a sense organ and an object and which is not expressible in language, which is not erroneous, and which is determinate in charater is *pratyakṣa*.

While interpreting the clause *avyapadeṣyam*, the Bhāṣyakāra Vātsyāyana writes:

यावदर्थं वै नामधेयशब्दास्तैरर्थसम्प्रत्ययः अर्थसम्प्रत्ययाच्च व्यवहारः
तत्रेदमिन्द्रियार्थसन्निकर्षादुत्पन्नमर्थज्ञानं रूपम् इति वा,
रस इत्येवं वा भवति रूपरसशब्दाश्च विषयनामधेयम्।
तेन व्यपदिश्यते ज्ञानम्-रूपमिति जानीते, रस इति जानीते।
नामधेयशब्देन व्यपदिश्यमानं सत् शाब्दं प्रसज्येते।
अत आह - अव्यपदेश्यमिति। (*वा.भा.* 1.1.4)

This analysis amounts to saying that language comes to play only after a cognition has arisen. In other words, a speaker encodes his cognition after it has arisen. Thus, a cognition can arise prior to language. Obviously, this is the refutation of the view that no cognition is possible without language, which has found expression later on in the following verse of Bhartṛhari, the celebrated author of the *Vākyapadīya*:

न सोऽस्ति प्रत्ययो लोके यः शब्दानुगमादृते।
अनुविद्धमिव ज्ञानं सर्वं शब्देन भासते।। I/123

This implies that a speaker first acquires his knowledge or cognition and then verbalizes it by encoding it in a language known to him. This gives rise to the following model of analysis:

World	Knowledge of the World	Encoding of the Knowledge	Verbalization

Once the verbalization has taken place through the utterance or writing of a sentence, it reaches a hearer or reader and another process begins: that is the process of decoding. This process of decoding is called the *śabdabodha* (understanding of the sentence meaning). A sentence, when decoded, results into verbal understanding or knowledge. The following is the process discovered by the *Mīmāṃsaka*s and the Indian logicians:

Stage I : reception of a sentence (*padajñāna*)
Stage II : remembering the referent of each morphemic constituent of that sentence (*padārtha-smaraṇa*)
Stage III : interring the intention of the speaker (*tātparyajñāna*)
Stage IV : relating the remembered meanings (*padārtha-anvaya*)
Stage V : understanding the relations among the remembered referent (*śabdabodha*)

Suppose there is a sentence (a+b+c+d) consisting of four morphemes – a, b, c and d. The following will arise with regard to the process of verbal understanding:

```
Step I      a + b + c + d
Step II     a + b + c + d
            |   |   |   |
           'a' 'b' 'c' 'd'
```

where 'a', 'b', 'c', and 'd' are the referents remembered from a, b, c, and d through a relation indicated by the vertical line above. Sometimes it may so happen that any of the elements of the sentence may remind of two referents, say a 'a' a" when both 'a' a" are not intended by the speaker. This will be settled in the next step by knowing the intention of the speaker and thereby eliminating either 'a' or a". Thus,

```
Step III    a + b + c + d
            |   |   |   |
           'a' 'b' 'c' 'd'
```

where a' has been eliminated after knowing the intention of the speaker.

```
Step IV     a + b + c + d
            |   |   |   |
           'a' 'b' 'c' 'd'
```

where relations among 'a', 'b', 'c' and 'd' have been identified.

```
Step V      a' – b' – c' – d'
```

where the rectangular box is the resultant knowledge or verbal understanding of the sentence meaning (*anvayabodha*).

This knowledge of the hearer or reader is expected to be identical with the knowledge of the speaker or writer for establishing rapport between them. Unless this happens, there can be no rapport between a speaker and hearer and consequently no communication can take place. This model of communication can be presented as follows:

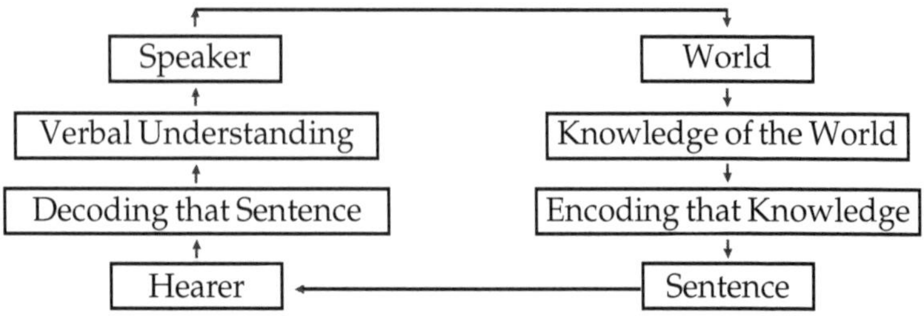

This is the story of communicating through ordinary language with the ordinary given world of our ordinary experience. With this analytic background, we shall now turn to the analysis of the world of literary art, aesthetic experience of that world of art, language of art appreciation of an art form and finally establishing a rapport between an artist and a connoisseur.

THE CREATED

As against the given world of our experience, there is the created world of experience. An art form, be it music, or dance, or painting, or sculpture or a literary art form like drama, poetry, short story, novel, and the like is created by human being unlike the ordinary world of our experience, which is given by God and not created by any human being.

That the world of literary art is created by a literaly artist is clearly stated in following oft-quoted verse:

> अपारे काव्यसंसारे कविरेकः प्रजापतिः। यथास्मै रोचते विश्वं तथेदं परिवर्तते।
> शृङ्गारी चेत् कविः काव्ये जातं रसमयं जगत्।।
> स एव वीतरागश्चेत् नीरसं सर्वमेव तत्।।

Here काव्य means literary art form, काव्य संसार means the world of literary art. कवि stands for a literary artist and he is the creator (प्रजापति) of the world of his literary art form. विश्व here stands for the ordinary world of our experience. An artist's creation is conceived here as transformation of the given. Thus, it is clear that an artist does not create from nothing; rather he transforms the given into his world of art. He creates his world of art out of the experience of the given world. As a matter of fact, there is transformation at all levels and components. We can easily conceptualize the model of this transformation as follows:

कवि	– काव्यसंसार	– काव्यसंसारानुभव	– काव्यभाषा	– सहृदय
↑	↑	↑	↑	↑
वक्तृ	– विश्व	– विश्वानुभव	– भाषा	– श्रोतृ

A literary artist (कवि) is a transformed state of an ordinary speaker (वक्तृ); काव्यसंसार is the transformation (परिवर्तन) of the given world (विश्व); aesthetic experience (काव्यसंसारानुभव) is again a transformation of the ordinary experience (विश्वानुभव); the language of literary art is also prepared out of the ordinary language, and the listener or reader of literary art (सहृदय) is also not an ordinary listener (श्रोतृ), but a transformed listener, i.e., a connoisseur (सहृदय).

Thus, creation is transformation. Now the question is how does this transformation take place? The Indian traditional philosophers of art are quite clear about this, when they discuss the causal factors in the process of materializing a literary art form (काव्यहेतु). Mammaṭa puts it as follows:

शक्तिर्निपुणता लोकशास्त्रकाव्याद्यवेक्षणात्।
काव्यज्ञशिक्षयाभ्यास इति हेतुस्तदुद्भवे।। *का.प्र.* I/3

An ordinary speaker attains the state of a literary artist (कवि) due to various factors like प्रतिभा, अभ्यास, etc. His encyclopaedic knowledge, philosophy of life and world-view coupled with the most prominent factor called the कारयित्री प्रतिभा, bring about the desired transformation or elevation from an ordinary speaker (वक्तृ) to a literary artist (कवि).

These very factors coupled with the faculty of sensitivity (भावयित्री प्रतिभा) bring about the desired transformation even in an ordinary listener or reader elevating him or her to the level of a connoisseur (सहृदय).

The literary artist (कवि-प्रजापति) gives an aesthetic shape to the given world through a beautiful arrangement and rearrangement, and thus transforms an ordinary world into a world of art. Thus, his creation is nothing more than a beautiful arrangement and thus transforms an ordinary world of art. Thus, his creation is nothing more than a beautiful arrangement and rearrangement of the given.

A literary artist is both an ordinary speaker as well as a literary artist. He is already born with the capacity of encoding his ordinary experience of an ordinary world and when he creates a world of art, he extends this capacity to encode an aesthetic experience into language. He finds difficulty in encoding the aesthetic experience into an ordinary language and thus he also creates a language of literary art by transforming again the ordinary language into the language of art. Here too he brings about the desired transformation through various arrangements and rearrangements giving rise to various ornaments of speech (*alaṃkāra*), modes and dicta (गुणवृति, etc.), which can give joy to a sensitive connoisseur (सहृदय).

As an ordinary language is required to encode an ordinary experience of an ordinary world of our experience, so a literary language is required to give expression to an aesthetic experience of the world of art. This distinction was clearly known to the Sanskrit poeticians.

Bhāmaha defined *kāvya* as शब्दार्थौ सहितौ काव्यम् and said that it is the वक्रोक्ति of both *śabda* (form) and *artha* (content) that makes the literary art palatable and charming. He cannot think of any other mode that attributes charm to a literary form. He says:

वक्रशब्दाभिधेयोक्तिः रिष्टा वाचामलङ्कृतिः (काव्या. I/36)

implying thereby that it is only the aesthetic arrangement of both *śabda* and *artha* that gives rise to the decoration of that arrangement and says:

कोऽलङ्कारोनया विना (*काव्या.* II/85)

He is very clear about the distinction between ordinary language and literary language, when he says,

गतोऽस्तमर्कः भातीन्दुः यान्ति वासाय पक्षिणः।
इत्येवमादि किं काव्यं वार्तामेनां प्रचक्षते।। (*काव्या.* II/87)

Thus, Bhāmaha knows that language of mere report, i.e., the language of ordinary communication is different from the language of aesthetic communication.

We find the same definition of काव्य of भामह, which is taken for elaboration by कुन्तक in his वक्रोक्तिजीवित. It runs as follows:

शब्दार्थौ सहितौ वक्रकविव्यापारशालिनि।
बन्धे व्यवस्थितौ काव्यं तद्विदाह्लादकारिणी।। (व.जी. I/7)

While elaborating on सहितौ, he observes that it is true that *śabda* and *artha* always remain together but that togetherness is meaningful so far as it is an ordinary language. Hence, that is not intended in the case of literary language. Not only the togetherness (साहित्य) is different here, but both *śabda* and *artha* are also not the ordinary *śabda* and ordinary *artha*. He says:

वाच्योऽर्थो वाचकः शब्दः प्रविद्धमिति यद्यपि।
तथापि काव्यमार्गेऽस्मिन् परमार्थोऽयमेतयोः।। (व. जी. I/8)

शब्दो विवक्षितोऽर्थैकवाचकोऽन्येषु सत्स्वपि।
अर्थः सहृदयाह्लादकारिस्वस्पन्दसुन्दरः।। (व. जी. I/9)

while paraphrasing काव्यमार्गे in his वृति. He writes अस्मिन्नलौकिके काव्यमार्गे indicating thereby that literary art form is not an ordinary form.

And then he turns to the concept of साहित्य and says:

साहित्यमनयोः शोभाशालितां प्रति काप्यसौ।
अन्यूनातिरिक्तत्व-मनोहारिण्यवस्थितिः।। (व. जी. I/17)

Again the word अलौकिक (not ordinary) is employed in the वृति of this verse. It runs as under:

सहितयोः भावः साहित्यम्। अनयोः शब्दार्थयोः कापि अलौकिकी चेतनचमत्कारकारितायाः कारणम् अवस्थितिः विचित्रैव विन्यासभङ्गी। कीदृशी-अन्यूनातिरिक्तत्वमनोहारिणी परस्परस्पर्धित्व-रमणीया। यस्यां द्वयोः एकतरस्यापि न्यूनत्वं निकर्षो न विद्यते, नापि अतिरिक्तत्वमुत्कर्षो वा अस्तीति।

One may also mark here the phrase विचित्रैव विन्यासभङ्गी, which is at the root concept with regard to the creation of a literary art form.

The वृति over the same verse continues to clarify the word *śabda*. It says,

शोभा सौन्दर्यमुच्यते। तया शालते श्लाघते यः स शोभाशाली,
तस्य भावः शोभाशालिता, तां प्रति सौन्दर्यशालिताम्प्रति इत्यर्थः।

सैव सहृदयाह्लादकारिता। तस्यां स्पर्धित्वेन यासौ अवस्थितिः
परस्परसाम्यसुभगम् अवस्थानं सा साहित्यमुच्यते।

As a matter of fact even a slight imbalance either in the arrangement of *śabda* or that of *artha* will destroy, which is the ground for enjoyment of charm.

The वृत्ति further says,

परमार्थतः पुनः उभयोरपि एकतरस्य साहित्य-विरहोऽन्यतरयापि पर्यवस्यति। तथा च अर्थः समर्थवाचकाभावे स्वात्मना स्फुरन्नपि मृतकल्प एवावतिष्ठते। शब्दोऽपि वाक्यप्रयोगि-वाच्यासम्भवे वाच्यान्तरवाचकः सन् वाक्यस्य व्याधिभूतः प्रतिभाति।

Thus, what is required is both, the form and the content should be arranged in such a way that the desired effect of rendering joy to a connoisseur manifests automatically:

उभावेतालङ्कार्यौ तयोः पुनरलङ्कृतिः।
वक्रोक्तिरेव वैदग्ध्यभङ्गीभणितिरुच्यते।। (*व. जी.* I/10)

The वृत्ति says,

कासौ वक्रोक्तिरेव। प्रसिद्धाभिधानव्यतिरेकिणी विचित्रैव अभिधा।

It is an expression which is different from the ordinary mode of expression.

Ācārya Ānandavardhana too underlines this distinction between the given and the created when he categorically says that the *śabda* of a literary form is different from that of an ordinary language and same is the case with the meanings that constitute the world of art. To put it in his words:

सोऽर्थस्तदुक्तिसामर्थ्ययोगी शब्दश्च कश्चन।
यत्नतः प्रत्यभिज्ञेयौ तौ शब्दार्थौ महाकवेः।। (*ध्वन्यालोक* I/8)

The वृत्ति over it makes further explicit by saying:

व्यङ्ग्यव्यञ्जकाभ्यामेव हि सुप्रयुक्ताभ्याम् महाकवित्वलाभो महाकवीनाम्, न वाच्यवाचकरचनामात्रेण।

With all this what I wanted to demonstrate is that the world of art is different (अलौकिक) from ordinary world and it is created by the artist not from any vacuum but from the very ordinary world of his experience, and this he does by bringing about transformations. He keeps on searching various modes of transformations with full vigilance. *Dhvanyāloka* 1.9 says:

आलोकार्थी यथा दीपशिखायां यत्नवान् जनः।
तदुपायतया तद्वद् अर्थे वाच्ये तदादृतः।।

Once the lamp is in his hand, he does not require any other lamp to illumine the lamp in his hand.

Here I conclude the discussion on the philosophy of creating a literary art form with the following statement of the 9th-century logician Jayantabhaṭṭa:

कुतो वा नूतनं वस्तु वयमुत्प्रेक्षितुं क्षमाः।
वचो विन्यासवैचित्र्यं केवलमवधार्यताम्।। (*न्यायमञ्जरी*, Āhnika-1)

EPISTEMOLOGY OF A *RASA* EXPERIENCE

Let us now turn to the other issue of our theme, viz., the philosophy of appreciation of a literary art form.

We have already seen that the appreciation of a literary art form can be done only by a सहृदय. A सहृदय is one who is equal in all respects with the creator. He is with an appreciative genius (*bhāvayitrī pratibhā*). He is not an ordinary श्रोतृ. He is a transformed श्रोतृ. He alone is capable of visiting the world, which is being shown by the creator. He alone has access to the world of art because he alone is capable of knowing the relationship between a literary language and its relation to the world of art. He alone is capable of understanding the symbols, metaphors and imageries employed by the creator artist to bring about the desired transformation. This is the reason that the Sanskrit poeticians always say that the art form should be सहृदयाह्लादकारी or तद्विदाह्लादकारी.

Since we are concerned here with the literary art form, the process of appreciation has to begin from decoding the sentence and understanding the sentence-meaning. Here the process of decoding will remain the same as that of decoding an ordinary sentence. We might require additional relations between a unit of a sentence and its intended referent. As we need to know the intention of the speaker, to know the meaning of his sentence, here we will require to know the purpose or ultimate intention of the literary artist to properly grasp the meaning of his art-form.

What is most important is to have rapport with the artist. This is possible only when the understanding of the connoisseur matches the aesthetic experience of the artist.

Creation of an art form is an intentional act and the creator must therefore have some purpose behind his creation. Unless one is successful in understanding the intention of the artist, one cannot feel satisfied that he has understood the art form. There is no guarantee that if a particular understanding of an art form has been palatable to a connoisseur, he has understood the intended meaning of that art form. But logically seeing, the meaning of an art form has to be only that which is intended by an artist. The same is true with literary art form also. Whatever is intended by the artist is the meaning of his art and not all possible meanings of that art, because creation of a literary art is an intentional act. Therefore, the understanding of the सहृदय must match the aesthetic experience which the artist wanted to communicate through his art-form. A सहृदय must try hard to understand the intention of the artist by all means before he passes. The following diagram may make the point clear:

कवि → काव्यसंसार → काव्यसंसारानुभव → काव्यभाषा → सहृदय ┐
||
काव्यसंसारानुभव ← ┘

This position is required to be taken because otherwise we cannot explain rapport between an artist and the *sahṛdaya*.

Let us look into this entire analysis more closely. The *rasa* is an effect that emerges from *vibhāva* (say, the heroine), *anubhāva* (say, her amorous glances) and *vybhicāribhāva* (say, her passing moods). The experience of this *rasa* or aesthetic rapture is not an ordinary experience. But it is the transformation of an ordinary experience into *rasānubhāva*. This happens through the *vyāpāra* called *sādhāraṇikaraṇa*. This *vyāpāra* consists in the act of universalizing what is ordinarily individual. This aims at freedom from the consideration of 'mine' and 'thine'.

As per Bhaṭṭanāyaka, there are three aspects in the epistemology of an aesthetic experience, *abhidhā*, *bhāvanā* and *bhoga*. *Abhidhā* prepares the room for the operation of *bhāvanā* also called *bhāvakatva* and *bhoga*, also called *bhogikṛti* or *bhojakatva* or *carvaṇa*.

In the words of Bhaṭṭanāyaka:

ध्वनिर्नामापरो योऽसौ व्यापारो व्यञ्जनात्मकः।
तस्य सिद्धेऽपि भेदे स्यात् काव्येंऽशत्वं न रूपता।।

What Bhaṭṭanāyaka had in his mind can be made further clear from the following verse preserved in his commentary called *Kaumudi* on *Locana:*

व्यापारस्त्रिविधो बुधैरभिमतः काव्येऽभिधाभावना–
भोगोत्पादकतात्मना तदधिको नास्ति ध्वनिर्नाम नः।
सिद्धाद्या व्यवहारभूमिषु विभावाद्यर्थसाधारणी
कारात्मात्वपरा निरर्गलरसास्वादात्मिकेवान्तिमा।।

The first function is concerned with the verbal discourse, the second with rendering *vibhāva*, etc. universal and common to all, and the third is nothing but delectation.

The second step is quite interesting. It is *sādhāraṇikaraṇa* which transcends the boundaries of private and public, personal or individual. It raises all *vibhāva*s, etc. to a common and collective level so that they may be realized as *rasa*.

Any art form must terminate into the realization of this *rasa* or aesthetic pleasure.

Rasa according to Bhaṭṭanāyaka is originated in the hero mainly, shared by all the actors and relished by the spectators or audience. Abhinavagupta summarizes this as follows:

स च यद्यपि अनन्तविभावाद्यातगा तथापि सर्वेषां जनानां संविदि तस्याश्च भोक्तरि, भोक्तृ वर्गस्य च प्रधाने भोक्तरि पर्यवसानान्नायकाभिधा न भोक्तृविशेष स्थायि–

This mental state transcends the awareness of 'mine' or 'thine'.

सा च एकचित्तवृतिः स्वपरकीयमिति अनन्तचित्तवृत्तिशतविशेषिता।

By the function of universalization the audience or spectators start realizing that they too are in the same state.

It is because of this *sādharaṇikaraṇa* that the aesthetic rapture cannot be compared with any mundane experience. At this state the connoisseur is freed from personal ego and hence as in actual life, the emotions brought about by the entire dramatic effect neither results into grief when there is bereavement from the beloved nor into a feeling of aversion towards women.

This is what is the experience of *rasa*. Abhinavagupta further says:

भट्टनायकस्त्वाह-रसो न प्रतीयते, नोत्पद्यते, नाभिव्यज्यते स्वगतत्वेन हि प्रतीतौ करुणे दु:खित्वं स्यात्। न च सा प्रतीतिर्युक्ता। सीतादेरविभावत्वात्, स्वकान्तास्मृत्यसंवेदनात्।।

Thus, *rasa* cannot be said to be experienced by the spectator in him; neither is it produced in him nor is it revealed in him.

It cannot be accepted as personally experienced by the spectator because the actual reality like Sītā, etc., does not take part in it. Nor does one remember one's own wife under that situation. But people do have *rasa* experience. How does it happen?

Bhaṭṭanāyaka presents his own solution through his theory of universalization. He says:

तस्मात् काव्ये दोषाभावगुणालङ्कारमयत्वलक्षणेन, नाट्ये चतुर्विधाभिनयरूपेण निजनिबिडमोहसङ्कटकारिणा विभावादिसाधारणीकरणात्मनोऽभिधातो द्वितीयेनांशेन भावकत्वव्यापारेण भाव्यमानो रस:।

Thus, it is through the magic of *sādhāraṇikaraṇa*, a transformed or transcendental experience takes place. When the *sthāyibhāva*s get universalized, the enjoyer or experiencer also gets universalized.

As Śridhara, the commentator of *Kāvyaprakāṣa* puts it:

भावकत्वं साधारणीकरणम्। तेन हि विभावादय: स्थायी च साधारणीक्रियन्ते। साधारणीकरणं च एतदेव यत् सीतादि विशेषाणां (कामिनीत्वादिसामान्येन) उपस्थिति:।

Indeed, the enjoyer or knower has no limitation; it is already *vibhu*.

Here too one can see that there is transformation of ordinary experience to an aesthetic experience:

काव्यानुभव

↑

साधारणानुभव

This maintains the symmetry in the universal Indian model of art experience.

This aesthetic experience is different from ordinary experience, because it is transcendental in nature, because it liberates a connoisseur from the consideration of 'mine' and 'thine';

because it takes the connoisseur to his extended substratum; and because the *sahṛdaya* is elevated to a level which is beyond ordinary *sukha* and *duḥkha*.

Then, can this experience of *rasa* be treated as the experience of the *Brahman?*

Bhaṭṭanāyaka finds a very close similarity between the world of art and the world of our ordinary experience. The *saṁsāra* is *avidyāprasūta*, the same is the case with *kāvyasaṁsāra*: it is also based on false name (*nāman*) and form (*rūpa*). As the ordinary world is inexplicable (*anirvacanīya*), so is the world of art which is neither true nor false. As the ordinary false world leads to the attainment of ultimate goal of life, through *śravaṇa*, *manana* and *nididhyāsana*, so also the unreal world of art will lead to the attainment of liberation from the bondage of mine and thine, i.e., the aesthetic pleasure.

In the words of Abhinavagupta:

यथा हि कल्पनामात्रसारं तत एव अनवस्थितैकरूपं क्षणेन कल्पनाशतसहस्रसहं स्वप्नादिविलक्षणमपि सुष्ठुतरां हृदयग्रहनिदानत्यक्तस्वालम्बन-ब्रह्मकल्प-नटोपरचितं रामरावणादिचेष्टितम् असत्यं कुतोऽपि अभूताद्भुतवृत्या भाति। तथाभासमानमपि च पुमर्थोपायतामेति। तथा तादृगेव विश्वमिदम् असत्यनामरूपप्रपञ्चात्मकम्, अथ च श्रवणमननादिवशेन परमपुरुषार्थप्रापकमिति लोकोत्तरपरमपुरुषार्थसूचनेन शान्तरसाक्षेपोऽयं भविष्यति। (*अ. भा.* on *ना.शा.* I/1)

It is clear that Bhaṭṭanāyaka and Abhinavagupta take the help of *Advaita* philosophy to explain the *rasa* theory. But the comparison does not go too far. Jagannātha in his *Rasagaṅgādhara* records the views of new theoreticians who think that the analogy does not help much. The *rasa* experience cannot be equated with the experience of the Ultimate Reality, the Brahman, because aesthetic experience is by a connoisseur who has not transcended his *jīva*-hood. *Rasa* can be a *viṣaya* of an experience, but the *Brahman* cannot. Hence, *rasāsvāda* is not *Brahmāsvāda* but *Brahmāsvāda-sahodara*, very similar to *Brahmāsvāda*, as rightly characterized by the art theoreticians.

2

Concept of Rasa as Presented by the Vaiṣṇava Theologicians and Ālaṅkārikas of Bengal

*H.N. Chatterjee Sastri**

INTRODUCTORY NOTE

A special fealure of scholars in the field of Indology is, whatever may be the subject, they ultimately reach back to the stage where communion with the supreme self is contemplated as a final goal. In this respect, whatever may be the topic, it turns out to be a philosophical treatise, a *darśana*, in the real sense of the term – as indicated in the statement of the *Bṛhadāraṇyaka Upaniṣad* – *ātma vā, are draṣṭavyaḥ śrotavyaḥ, mantavyaḥ, nididhyāsitavyaḥ*. *Rasaśāstra* is no exception to this rule. The *śāstra* which was in its preliminary stage, so to say, was in design psychic in character and pleasure-yielding in nature, towards the end of the sixteenth century, because of the special influence of Caitanya, and Caitanyaism assumed a new turn and *Rasaśāstra* of Bharata and expounded by Abhinavagupta turned out to be a philosophical-cum-psychological

* The author could not send his complete article due to serious illness.

affair – new in its design, unheard of before. In this short paper an attempt is made to highlight some of the aspects of this *Rasaśāstra* of the Bengal *Vaiṣṇava*s, which have not yet received the attention even in the works of eminent scholars like Sushil Kumar De, P.V. Kane and S.P. Bhattacharya. I have concentrated principally on Madhusūdana's *Bhaktirasāyana* and the works of Gosvāmis of West Bengal and finally on Kavikarṇapūra. In that respect the paper, though short, may modestly claim to contain matters of *rasa* which demanded earlier attention of eminent scholars but which could not be effected, maybe, for the fact that most of the books were written in Bengali.

The advent of Sri Caitanya in Bengal made significant contribution not only towards the religious aspect of Vaiṣṇavism but also towards new attitude unto *Alaṅkāra* literature. Caitanya selected Sanātana and Rūpa for the highly difficult task of exposing his theology and its *Rasaśāstra* in which they were materially reinforced by the mystical metaphysical scholarship of their nephew Jīva Gosvāmi. They were men of great literary capacity, acute theologicians and passionate poets, as well as ascetic devotees. Their authoritative position as the fit and chosen disciples, specially instructed and commissioned for the exacting task, their austere and saintly character, their selfless devotion to the cause, and their laborious and life-long scholarship gave them a unique influence as the three authoritative Gosvāmis or teachers of the cult.

Of the two brothers, Sanātana and Rūpa and their nephew Jīva, whose literary activity and productions far outweigh those of other Gosvāmis in range, depth, quality and magnitude, there exists a more detailed and reliable record. Jīva, himself at the close of his *Laghutoṣaṇi* of Sanātana's commentary on the *Bhāgavata*, presents the genealogy of the family as well as a list of the principal works of Sanātana and Rūpa.

In the present paper we have analyzed the concept of *rasa* according to *Bhaktirasāyana* of Madhusūdana and *Kavi Karṇapūra*. He has referred to *cittadruti*, *vāsanā*, *kaṭhinatva*, *vāsanābhāsa* as also *kāntāprema*. The view of *Karṇapūra* has also been recorded here and Rūpa's *Bhaktirasāmṛtasindhu* has also been taken into consideration.

Special reference has been made to Abhinava's decision about the number of *rasa*s according to *Bhāgavata* as numbered as X.43.17.

This is as explained by *Bhaktimāṛtaṇḍa* and *Viśvanātha* and others have interestingly been studied with respect to the varieties of *rasa*s. In this way the Vaiṣṇavic concept of *rasa* has been pointed out to be original in their approaches for which they claimed distinctive studies.

3

Theoretical Foundation of Rasa Theory of Abhinavagupta

Vidya Niwas Mishra

Rasa theory is not a revelation of Bharata or Abhinavagupta. It is rather an adumberation of the idea of re-enactment of the first movement, of release of the seed or rather of fulfilment of the singleness in allness of a reintegration through disintegration (as described in the *Puruṣa Sūkta* to be the First Principles). If we go into the different connotations of the word *rasa*, the above point is made out more clearly. *Rasa* means the latent essence. This latent essence of everything is within the bounds of direct perception, sight, hearing, smell, touch and flavour. So there is a beautiful coinage in the word *jyotirasomamṛtam*. The primordial waters are described as illuminating juice of immortality. So *rasa* is the most desired flavour as well as experience of immortality. Immortality is a feeling of not dying, the refusal of death. It is a commitment to life. Another meaning of desire of *rasa* is to manifest and also the capacity to manifest. It is analogous to that stage of speech act, *vāk*, where there is a desire to enter into dialogue with one's other self. This desire can be likened to an intense humid heat which makes the seed split into a sprout. It is a precursor act of manifestation. So it is neither manifest nor unmanifest. It is a sudden flash before illumination.

Rasa is something which flows as well. It is also a process of liquidification of whatever is solid and whatever is gaseous. It, in turn, is also a process of melting a metal into liquid so that its impurities are burnt out and only its pure essence remains. So it can also mean a process of de-objectification of a sense object. *Rasa* derives its meaning of Supreme Bliss from the juice of *Soma*, the Divine exhilarating drink. This drink is prepared by crushing the leaves of the *Soma* creeper with a piece of stone in stone vessel. This juice is kept in the open and the Sun ferments it. The shining froth is the result of a complete act of sacrifice. This act is reflected into the digit by digit gradual disintegration of the Moon and into the final act of complete disappearance. It is that disappearing digit which is merged into the Sun or in a poetic language, reaches a point of consummation. It revives in a moment of approximation of death. This revival (rather rebirth) of the self (in other words, the resurrection of the spirit) is the goal of all life. Because such an experience is not only a complete annihilation of whatever goes by the name of spirit, it is self-seeking as well and it is also a transcendence into a realm where the desirer and the desired are both merged in the desire itself. This overpowering desire like a hungry wolf not able to find any victim, gnaws its own flesh and the desire is eaten by the desire itself. Such an act of transcendence is repeated time and again but the experience is every time something new, something unique because this is not of the nature of usual production. To quote Kālidāsa, "it is a happening in the recollection of the pure consciousness without involving any mental or supramental participation". So, this is beyond even imagination.

Rasa also means craving which even though withdraws one from the sense objects, keeps impression of sense object left in the sixth sense, namely, the mind and does not leave unless this craving is merged in a larger craving of the extra sensory experience of Pure Bliss. In other words, *rasa* is the abstraction of all sensate experiences transformed into perfume-like inseparable substance. From the above denotations and connotations of the word *rasa*, a theory could be easily formulated which emphasizes that:

1. *Rasa* experience though without denying a sensate experience, is such an essence of that experience which through words, colours, shapes and melodies can transform the sensate experience into aesthetic experience.

2. *Rasa* is a process of manifestation and for that is a self-effacing process, where experiencer runs the risk of self naughting, may be, for a split of a second; this manifestation is not of something new, something unique but in itself is a joy every time, afresh and unique.
3. *Rasa* is a transcendence for both the external and internal worlds. It is at the same time an internalization of the external and externalization of the internal.

Besides the intrinsic meaning of *rasa*, there is another source of *rasa* theory. The concept of *vāk* is the seed of all Indian theorization and so it is naturally the source of *rasa* theory also. The *vāk* concept has four components:

(i) *Vāk* is the creative energy and is the driving force of all creation inasmuch as it is a quantum of unreleased latent energy;
(ii) *Vāk* is an epitome of the creative process itself. It is, in fact, the first vibration immediately preceding the movement of creation. It is the first step light as well as the first ripple of a sound. It is a desire not only to be with the other but also to have an intimate dialogue with the other in order to find one part of the self into the so-called other part. In modern terms, it is a will to communicate with the other in order to understand the other.
(iii) *Vāk* is the first act of speech articulation and it is preceded by a long process of meditation so that the speech is pure and well meaning. This speech is itself held in high regard as human value.
(iv) *Vāk* is an exchangeable item with *Soma*, the divine juice. *Vāk* transformed into a cow is exchanged as barter or *Soma*. This exchange is an indicator of an internal relationship between a well wrought human creation and its equal Divine Bliss.

These four components of the concept of *vāk* form the foundation of the *rasa* theory inasmuch as this theory speaks of a state of mind which is free from all states of personal likes and dislikes, all states of sensuality, all states of pleasure and pain. The nature of *rasa* experience as delineated by Abhinavagupta as *rasa* is in many ways analogous to the process of creation. This can be illustrated by several Vedic passages describing creation and the role of *vāk* and *aditi* (the deity of totality, indivisibility) in creation and the legends pertaining to *vāk*.

This is an upshot of the Vedic foundation of the *rasa* theory.

4

Śiva-rasa and Nāṭya-rasa Sources of Aesthetic Experience in Abhinavagupta

Rekha Jhanji

This paper[1] attempts to explore the sources of aesthetic consciousness in Abhinavagupta's thought. Abhinavagupta was an exponent of *Śaivāgamas*; he gave a detailed exposition of Tāntric philosophy of the Śaiva tradition by writing texts like the *Tantrāloka* and *Parātrinśikāvivarṇa*. Before he set out to write commentaries on Ānandavardhana's *Dhvanyāloka* and the *Nāṭyaśāstra* of Bharata, he had devoted most of his attention to the analysis of consciousness. He saw the whole creation as the play or consciousness which according to him, is the *śakti* of Parama Śiva. He saw the ultimate reality (Śiva) in terms of *prakāśa* (light) and *vimarṣa* (consciousness). It is this eternal and transcendental monistic reality which turns itself into variegated forms by its own will. Thus, the whole world originates from one single source and each manifestation is internally connected with the other. As is stated in the *Vijñāna Bhairava*:

> The same self characterised by consciousness is present in all the bodies; there is no difference in it anywhere. Therefore a

> person realising that everything (in essence) is the same (consciousness) triumphantly rises above transmigratory existence.[2]

When I first started working on the *Nāṭyaśāstra* text, I realized that in his commentary on it, Abhinavagupta sometimes gives interpretations that are not necessarily warranted by the text. As I worked more on this text, I realized that many of his comments originate from his larger philosophical and spiritual interests. Thus, to understand Abhinavagupta's aesthetics, it is necessary to understand his metaphysics because that permeates into his entire concept of *kāvya:*[3] (poetry). This becomes evident if we look at his interpretation or both the *Nāṭyaśāstra* and *Dhvanyāloka*. In the course of this paper I will refer to some passages from both these texts to substantiate my viewpoint.

In his interpretation of the first *śloka* of the *Nāṭyaśāstra*, Abhinava refers to Bhaṭṭanāyaka's commentary on it to establish his point of view that Brahmā (or Paramātman according to Bhaṭṭanāyaka) created drama as a model for recognizing the insubstantiality of this world born of ignorance. It (*nāṭya*) is similar to (this world) which is essentially imaginary, incapable of being constant in any particular form, capable of undergoing hundreds and thousands of changes in an instant, different from dreams and the like. Despite this it is capable of captivating one's interest in the free Brahmā-like actors who render the Rāma-Rāvaṇa interaction by (their gestures); those actions appear untrue and yet marvellous. Despite being presented in this form, it becomes a means of pursuing the four goals of life (*purūṣārthas*). Similarly this world is an unreal manifestation of name and form. Even then it is capable of obtaining the *purūṣārthas* by hearing and pondering over (spiritual instruction). It can also bring about *śāntarasa* through the highest *purūṣārthas*. As is said that all the *rasas* originate from *śāntarasa*. Thus, by *brahmaṇā yadudāhṛtam* is also indicated the ultimate objective (*pāramārthika prayojana*). This is the interpretation given by Bhaṭṭanāyaka in *Sahṛdaya Darpaṇa*. Abhinava further quotes an invocatory verse from the above text:

> Salutation to the great poet Śambhu, the creator of the three worlds because sensitive people (*rasika*s) enjoy every moment of this worldly theatre created by him.[4]

Abhinava considered this an appropriate interpretation of the origin of *Nāṭyaśāstra*. Although on many issues Abhinava expresses his disagreernent with Bhaṭṭanāyaka, here he quotes him to endorse the latter's attempt to seek a metaphysical justification for the practice of theatre. This kind of metaphysical justification is clearly not necessary if one takes Bharata's *sūtra* on its face value. There are many more passages in the text of the *Abhinavabhāratī* but this opening passage played an important role in inspiring one to look into Abhinavagupta's other philosophical works for a better understanding of his aesthetics.

Art objects can be looked upon from two vantage points:

(i) from the viewpoint of the creator, and
(ii) from the viewpoint of the beholder.

From both these dimensions Abhinava's reflections are saturated with his metaphysics. We have already seen that in the *Nāṭyaśāstra*, Brahmā is the great *naṭa* (actor) who creates this imaginary spectacle which entirely owes its existence to his will. If he wished, it could have been different. In *Dhavanyāloka* also, Ānandavardhana quotes a *śloka* (from *Agni Purāṇa*) which compares the poet with Prajāpati (the creator):

> In the boundless realm of poetry, the poet alone is the creator, and as it pleaseth him, so doth this world revolve. If the poet be intent upon the erotic sentiment in his poem, the whole world will be suffused with that sentiment. But if he be void of emotion (in his poem), the world too will be devoid of sentiment. A good poet will freely design even insentient objects to act as sentient ones and sentient objects to act as insentient ones.[5]

Abhinavagupta gives an interesting interpretation of this passage in his *Locana*. He translates *apāre* as endless. He contends that, *śṛṅgāri* in this context implies the gustation of *śṛṅgāra* in terms of *vibhāva* (determinants), *anubhāvas* (consequents) and *vyabhicāribhāvas* (transitory states), not a womanizer. Quite as Bharatamuni says that *anubhāva* renders the emotions which lie deep in the psyche of the poet and thus projects the poetic meaning. In all these statements, the poet is given the most prominent place. The *śṛṅgāra* (erotic sentiment) actually denotes *rasa* in this passage. Till such time that there is a *rasika* (connoisseur) that entire emotive experience only provides the range of worldly emotions of pain and pleasure. Without the poet's sublimation of it, it does not become capable of aesthetic enjoyment.[6]

From these two passages it seems clear that Abhinavagupta sees the poet in the light of the divine creator. Just as the creator playfully creates this entire world from one single intention, similarly the poet creates the dramatic world through his aesthetic intention. The creator is not judgemental about his creation; whatever the nature of the created object, he derives pleasure from it. And the true *rasika* is that who can decode this aesthetic intention by imaginatively entering into the poet's world and listening to his *hṛdaya saṁvāda* (a phrase quite commonly used by Abhinava) rendered in terms of different sentiments and emotions. Quoting Bharata, Abhinava holds *rasa* to be central to poetic meaning (*na hi rasādṛte kascidarthaḥ pravartate*, N.S. VI, 32). Without *rasa* the entire dramatic work will lose its unity. The experience of *rasa* evokes a sense of wonder (*camatkāra*) in the spectator. This term again draws its significance from spiritual experience. As Gnoli points out:

> In the Spanda School (Vasugupta etc.) an idea very like to that expressed by *Camatkāra* is conveyed by the word *Vismaya*, astonishment. The general idea underlying these words ... is that both the mystical and aesthetic experience imply the cessation of a world, the *Saṁsāra* – and its sudden replacement by a new dimension or reality.[7]

Bharata has given cues for an elaborate discussion of the relationship between *rasa*s and *bhāva*s. Despite the different *bhāva*s which would be usually thought of as the elements of *rasa*, there could be even subsidiary *rasa*s that may become elements for the main *rasa* of a work. The term used for this main *rasa* is '*mahārasa*'. Abhinava sees a *mahārasa* as a running thread that connects all the different elements in it. This *mahārasa* would be like the soul of a poem or a play, just as Parama Śiva is the reality behind the world of appearance. Abhinava says in *Tantrasāra*:

> This atman is the form of light and is absolutely free. It covers its form and then suddenly reveals it. In this way it absolutely hides and reveals by turns the Śiva-rasam.[8]

Śiva-rasa is the essence of all cosmic creation and *nāṭya rasa* is the essence of drama and poetry. In fact *rasa* alone is *nāṭya*. And *rasa* (in art) is not given, it has to be experienced. This is how Abhinava distinguishes his concept of *rasa* from his predecessors like Bhaṭṭa, Lollaṭa, Śaṅkuka and Bhaṭṭanāyaka. He distinguishes *rasa* from *sthāyībhāvas* and also emphasizes its experiential character. He states:

> ... the determinants are not the causes of the production (*niṣpatti*) of *Rasa*; otherwise, *Rasa* should continue to exist even when they no longer fall under cognition. Nor are they the cause of its cognition (*jñapti*) (if they were, they would have to be included among the means of knowledge (*pramāṇa*) because *Rasa* is not an objective thing (*siddha*), which could function as a knowable object... the expressions 'determinants' do not designate any ordinary thing, but what serves to realize the gustation (*carvaṇopayogi*).[9]

This rejection of the 'objective' dimension of *rasa* again seems to highlight the parallel between *nāṭya-rasa* and *Śiva-rasa*. Abhinava holds that like the *rasa* in art which depends on the *rasika*, the Parama Śiva can be experienced only by freeing oneself of all the *malas* (impurities) that one has collected due to identifying oneself with one's limited being, for He hides himself in his creation and cannot be seen in terms of ordinary ways of cognition.

In theatre the *rasika* transcends his limitations by *sādhāraṇīkaraṇa* (generalization) because the emotions and sentiments rendered in it get depersonalized. For, in a certain sense these emotions do not belong to any particular person and yet are experienced by all those who participate in the theatrical work. But *sādhāraṇikaraṇa* also presupposes imaginative participation. This participation is possible only because at some deeper level there is an inherent interconnection of all living beings. Abhinava does not thinks that a spectator can identify himself only with a person similar to him. He says:

> that no being (animal or deity) exists with which man has no affinity of nature. The *saṁsāra* is beginningless and every man, before being that which he actually is, has been all the other beings as well. The consciousness of the spectator thus possesses (in other words, is varied by ...) the latent impressions of all the possible beings and he is therefore susceptible of identitying himself with each of them.[10]

Thus, to understand the nuances of the concept of *sādhāraṇīkaraṇa* it would be useful to see it in the light ofAbhinava's inherent belief in the unity of all creation.

Freedom from involvement is facilitated in theatre because of *abhinaya* with *gīta* (song) and *vādya* (music), for these theatrical accessories help in creating aesthetic distance in the spectator. The 'unreality' of theatre saves the spectator from under-distancing. In mundane life detachment can be achieved only through different forms of *sādhanā*. Thus, what happens quite easily in theatre is achieved with great difficulty in the spiritual realm. However, despite this difference of effortlessness and effort, both the aesthetic experience and the spritual experience are inherently enjoyable. It is interesting to note that while for understanding the notion of *nāṭyarasa*, the *Śiva-rasa* provides the backdrop, aesthetic joy seems to become an exemplar for the mystic. As the *Śiva sūtra*s state:

nartaka Śiva (3/9) *raṅgo anaratmā* (3/ 10)[11]

Aesthetic enjoyment gives a clue to the mystic to treat the whole creation as the stage for the play of consciousness. Here it seems that Abhinava's aesthetics and his metaphysics chase one another to capture his idea of the experience of the transfiguration of consciousness.

The influence of Abhinava's Tāntric framework on his aesthetics has another fascinating dimension; this concerns his attitude towards the sensuous experience. Sensuous experience acquires a central position in all our aesthetic enjoyment. For without becoming sensitive to the details of the sensuous experience, no artistic creation or appreciation is possible. One becomes a true *sahṛdaya* only when one is sensitive to the nuances of images and emotions associated with any experience. Abhinava is so sensitive to sensuous images that they flow even into his metaphysical works. But it is interesting to note that even though Abhinava's metaphysical works are replete with examples from experiences of sensuous enjoyment, equanimity seems a continued preoccupation with him. He contends that the real joy of any sensuous experience lies in the moment after the fulfilment of a desire when one has reached a state of tranquility. He asserts his belief in *śāntarasa* by proclaiming that the culmination of enjoyment of all *rasa*s lies in the turning away from all stimulants and realization of equanimity within oneself.[12] He seems to echo the following verse of the *Vijñāna Bhairava*:

> When the yogi mentally becomes one with the incomparable joy of song and other objects, then of such a yogi, there is, because of the expansion of his mind, identity with that (i.e. with the incomparable joy) because he becomes one with it.[13]

Such a view could not have been possible without Abhinava's metaphysics blending into his aesthetic reflections.

NOTES AND REFERENCES

1. I express my deep gratitude to my friend and Sanskritist colleague Dr. Dharmananda Sharma under whose able guidance I could read some part of the text of *Abhinavabhāratī* and some of the *stotras* of Abhinavagupta.
2. *Vijñāna Bhairava* or *Divine Consciousness*, Sanskrit text with English tr. by Jaideva Singh, Motilal Banarsidass, Delhi, 198, verse 100, p. 91.
3. For Abhinavagupta, *Kāvya* also includes *Nāṭya* because a sympathetic reader (*sahṛdaya*) can imaginatively recreate the whole play even without all the accessories (*upakaraṇas*).
4. *Abhinavabhāratī* Ch. I, 2, 6 Sanskrit text translated into Hindi with commentary by Ācārya Viśveśvara, Hindi Dept., Delhi University, 1973, p. 36. I have provided a free English translation of the above.
   नमस्त्रैलोक्यनिर्माणकवये शम्भवे यत:। प्रतिक्षणं जगन्नाट्यप्रयोगरसिको जना:।।
5. *Dhvanyāloka of Ānandavardhana*, critically ed. by K. Krishnamorthy, Karnatak University, Dharwar, 1974, III. 42, p. 251.
   अपारे काव्यसंसारे कविरेक: प्रजापति। यथास्मै रोचते विश्वं तथेदं परिवर्तते।।
   श्रृंगारी चेत् कवि: काव्ये जातं रसमयं जगत्। स एव वीतरागश्चेन्नीरसं सर्वमेव तत्।।
   भावानचेतनानपि चेतनवच्चेतनानचेतनवत्। व्यवहारयति यथेष्टं सुकवि: काव्ये स्वतन्त्रतया।।
6. *Dhvanyāloka Locana*, p. 498, Chaukhamba edition.
7. R. Gnoli, *The Aesthetic Experience According to Abhinavagupta*, Chaukhamba Sanskrit Series, Varanasi, p. XLVI.
8. *Tantrasāra*, p. 25.
   एष प्रकाशरूप आत्मा स्वच्छन्दो ढौकयति निजरूपम्।
   पुन: प्रकटयति झटिति अथ क्रमवशादेष परमार्थेन शिवरसम्।।
9. R. Gnoli, op. cit., pp. 84-85.
10. Ibid., 58-89 n.
11. *The Aphorisms of Śiva* (*Śivasūtra*) wilh commentary by Bhaskarācārya, tr. with exposition notes by Mark Dyczkowski, Varanasi, 1991, pp. 105, 107.
12. तत्र सर्वरसानां शान्तप्राय एवास्वादो न विषयेभ्यो विपरिवृत्त्या तन्मुख्यतालाभात्। हिन्दी अभिनवभारती, p. 635.
13. गीतादिविषयास्वादा: समसौख्यैकतात्मन:। योगिनस्तन्मयत्वेन मनोरूढेस्तदात्मता।। *VB* Verse 73, p. 69.

5

Abhinavagupta's Concept of Śāntarasa in the Light of his Commentary on the Bhagavadgītā

S. Ranganath

I

In India, aesthetics, poetics and metaphysics have always been integrated intrinsically into one discipline. For example, the concept of *ānanda* is common to aesthetics as well as metaphysics:

ānando brahmeti vyajānāt

Viśwanātha in his *Sāhityadarpaṇa* points out as Brahmānanda Sahodaraḥ. This expression, *brahmānanda sahodaraḥ*, brings together the bliss of Brahman and the enjoyment of literature together as brothers. M. Hiriyanna, who has written authoritatively on Indian aesthetics as well as metaphysics, points out that the ultimate aesthetic experience is giving up of the ego and the self so that it can merge into the individual Absolute Self. He also points out that *jīvanmukti* is the ultimate goal of both *kāvyānanda* through *rasaniṣpatti* and intellectual realization through metaphysics. Thus, the concept of *jīvanmukti*, which is associated in the present context with *śāntarasa* as depicted in the *Bhagavadgītā* in the commentary of Abhinavagupta, makes this a bridge between aesthetics and metaphysics, between *kāvya* and *smṛti*. Indeed, the *Bhagavadgītā* can also be dealt with at the level of literature, from the point of view of modern Western theories of linguistics and stylistics. In the various English commentaries on the *Bhagavadgītā* this is clear. However, as it is outside the scope of present discussion, it is enough to mention it as a link between literature and *Smṛti*. We have in our concept of literature pointed out that the purpose of literature is fundamentally similar to the purpose of *Śruti*, the *Smṛti* and the *Purāṇa*. What is said by way of do's and don'ts in an authoritative manner by the *Śruti* as *Prabhu Sammita*, is turned into pleasant request in literature as *Kāntāsammita*. Again, the connection between Abhinavagupta's other works, which are generally considered as pure literary criticism, can be connected with the commentary on the *Bhagavadgītā*. In fact, Abhinavagupta's name is so famous in informed Western critical circles that an astute critic like Muriel C. Bradbrook of Cambridge not only mentions him approvingly but applies his thought to literatures other than Indian like Japanese and British. Taking a cue from this, it is possible to interpret Western texts in the context of Abhinavagupta. This makes us curious about the life and works of Abhinavagupta who is one of the greatest intellectuals Indian has ever produced.

II. LIFE AND WORKS OF ABHINAVAGUPTA

We get a brief sketch of Abhinavagupta's descent and social conditions in the concluding portions of his two works, namely, the *Tantrāloka* and *Parātrimśikā vivaraṇa*. This sketch, when coupled with information gathered from the stray references to his life in the vast literature that he, his pupils, his commentators and the followers of his theories have produced, gives us more or less connected information, though still incomplete, about his life. His father Narasimhagupta, who was of great intellectual calibre, had equal proficiency in all the *śāstras* and was a great devotee of Śiva. The name of his mother was Vimalakala. She was a very pious and religious lady. Thus, the family atmosphere was thoroughly religious and scholarly. He had nearly twenty teachers under whom he learnt almost all branches of learning like grammar from his father Narasimhagupta, *dvaita tantras* from Varṇanātha, *brahmavidyā* from Bhutiraja, Śaivism from Bhutirajatanaya, *karma* and *trika darśanas* from Lakshmaṇagupta, *dhvani* from Bhaṭṭenduraja, dramaturgy from Bhaṭṭaṭauta and so on.

Works

Nearly forty-four works written by Abhinavagupta have been authenticated. *Bodha Pancadaśika, Mālinī Vijaya, Vārtika, Parātriṃśikā Vivṛti, Tantrāloka, Tantrasāra, Tantrāvatadhanika, Dhvanyālokalocana, Abhinavabhāratī, Paramārthasāra, Iśvarapratyabhijña Vivṛti, Vimarśinī, Paryanta Pancaśikā, Ghaṭakarparakulaka Vivṛti, Kramastotra, Parmārtha Dwādaśikā, Paramārtha Carcā, Mahōpadeśa Vimśatikā, Anuttāṣtika, Anubhava Nivedana, Rahasya Pancadaśikā, Tantroccaya Pururavō Vicāra, Kramakeli, Śivadṛṣtyālocana, Purvapañcikā, Padārtha Praveśa Nirṇayaṭīka, Prakīrṇatāvivaraṇa, Prakirṇavivaraṇa, Kathāmukhatilaka, Laghvī Prakriyā, Bhedavāda Vidāraṇa, Devi stotra Vivaraṇa, Tattvādhva Prakāśika, Śiva Śaktyavinābhāva Stotra, Bimbapratibimbavāda, Paramārthasaṅgraha, Anuttara Śataka, Prakaraṇa Stotra, Nāṭyalocana, Anuttara Tattva Vimarśiṇī Vṛtti, Bhagavadgītārtha Saṅgraha,* and so on. The last mentioned is my present concern in this paper.[1]

Thus, his works could be broadly divided into three periods namely Alaṅkara period, Tāntric period and Vedāntic period.

III. A Note on *Śāntarasa* in the Background of *Rasa*

It is well known that the *rasa* theory has been developed in Sanskrit right from very early times. *Rasa* is that which should be experienced:

rasyate āsvādyate iti rasaḥ.

The word *rasa* occurs in *Taittirīyopaniṣad: raso vai saḥ. rasam hyevāyam labdhvānandī bhavati.*[2] The *rasa* theory was very effectively formulated by Bharata in his *Sūtra: Vibhāvānubhāva vyabhicāri saṁyogāt rasaniṣpattiḥ.*[3]

This *rasa* theory could also be very effectively applied to Western literature, both ancient and modern, which has resulted in a new and original interpretation of Western classics. For example, the concept of *karuṇa rasa* (pathos) can be applied to Marlow's *Doctor Faustus,* Shakespeare's *King Lear,* Milton's *Samson Agonistics* and Eliot's *Murder in the Cathedral.* Similarly, *hāsyarasa* can be applied to several comedies including several Western comedies like Shakespeare's *Tempest*. It is, indeed, very rewarding to apply *śāntarasa* to Shakespeare's *Hamlet* and understand the so-called inaction of Hamlet. While most Western critics think that this is a defect, in fact it is the tragic flaw in *Hamlet*. From our point of view, it is actually a virtue as can be seen in our present discussion of the concept of action in the *Gīta*. Essentially the problem of Hamlet is the same as that of Arjuna. Hamlet is disgusted with the world and thus he has *jugupsā*. V. Raghavan in his *Number of Rasas* rightly remarks:

> Truth whose realisation is salvation is of the nature of Self which is *ātman*. It has to be realised by piercing the veil of things which are *anātman* and which shroud the *ātman*. Things which are *anātman* must be loathed and this loathing and *anātman* led to the *jugupsā* view. The *rati* view is closely related to *jugupsā* view for when *anātman* is loathed *ātman* has to be loved. This love of *ātman* or *ātmarati* is the *sthāyin* of *śānta*. When one realises *ātman* everywhere, his love floods the universe; then *jugupsā* flies away, for there is none besides or beyond *ātman* to be shunned.[4]

This is what the sixth stanza of *Iśopaniṣad* states:

yastu sarvāṇi bhutāni ātmanyevānupaśyati,
sarvabhuteṣu cātmānaṃ tato na vijugupsate.[5]

This *ātmarati* is the *sthāyin* of *śānta*, since the final state of *mokṣa* is one of *ānanda* and the Self which is realized is itself of the form of bliss. *Gīta* III.17 highlights this thought as follows:

yaścātmaratireva syāt atmaṭṛptaśca mānavaḥ,
ātmanyeva ca sanṭṛptaḥ tasya kāryaṃ na vidyate.[6]

Abhinavagupta holds that *tattvajñāna* or *ātmasvarupa* itself is the *sthāyin* of *śānta*. He states in his *Abhinavabhāratī*:

> *kastarhi atra sthāyī? ucyate-iha tattvajñānameva tāvan mokṣa sādhanamiti tasyaiva mokṣe sthāyitā yuktā. tattvajñānañca nāma atmajñānameva.*[7]

The above-mentioned *jugupsā* view by Raghavan results in an attitude of *vairāgya* towards all action especially the one of taking revenge, which is the height of *rājasa guṇa*. Indeed, the *guṇa* theory as explained in the *Guṇatrayavibhāga Yoga* of the *Gītā* is most useful in understanding the Western texts. Thus, when Western critics are puzzled about the inaction of Hamlet, we can easily understand it as the problem of *sāttvika svabhāva*, which is asked to perform the action of *rājasika* nature. In fact, Hamlet is so philosophical a character which is seen in his soliloquies that he craves for liberation –*mumukṣutva*. This is the reason why he tells Horatio that he worships him and places him in his heart of hearts because Horatio is not 'A passion slave'. No further comment is necessary in the present context and it has been brought out to show that the work of Indian critics like Abhinavagupta can be profitably applied to our understanding of not only our literature, but the literature in many languages, while talking about *śāntarasa* in the Western context we have to make a distinction between the 'Peace that passeth understanding', 'calm of mind all passions spent' thus indicating that *śāntarasa* is not the latter. It is not quietude because of lack of strength. In the context of Buddhism the eyes of Lord Buddha in the expression therein are considered a perfect representation of *śāntarasa*. Now let us turn to Abhinavagupta's view on *śāntarasa*.

IV. ABHINAVAGUPTA'S JUSTIFICATION OF *ŚĀNTARASA*

Śānta is accepted as a *rasa* by Abhinavagupta and he recognizes it in the poetry and drama and treats it as the basic *rasa*. The treatment of *śāntarasa* in *Abhinavabhāratī* is quite long. However, we may give here some important points about the nature of *śānta* from the point of view of Abhinavagupta who criticizes the scholars who do not accept *śānta* as a *rasa*.

There are four main aims of human life (*puruṣārthas*), namely, *dharma*, *artha*, *kāma* and *mokṣa*. Like Smṛti and Itihāsa, literature also presents them through poetry and drama. The first three, namely, *dharma*, *artha* and *kāma* are presented on the stage by turning *rati*, etc., to be aesthetically relished as *sṛṅgāra*, *vīra*, etc., "Why should it not be possible to present similarly the mental state (whatever that may be) responsible for attaining *mokṣa*", asks Abhinavagupta to the opponents of *śānta*. If well presented, it would arouse the aesthetic relish in such spectators who possess aesthetic susceptibility. Hence there is no force in saying that *śāntarasa* does not exist.

What then is the basic mental state or the *sthāyibhāva*, we may ask. To this, Abhinavagupta replies – realization of the ultimate *tattvajñāna* to which we have referred to earlier and hence it is not taken up here.

Bhāvas like *rati*, etc. are spoken as *sthāyin* because they are comparatively more stable than *vyabhicārins* inasmuch as they affect the Self so long as *vibhāvas* responsible for their rise persist. But, they cannot stand independently. They are to the Self what the picture is to the canvas. The Self as such is the most permanent of all the *sthāyins* and relegates all other *sthāyins* to the position of *vyabhicārins*. The permanence of the *ātman* is real and natural and not comparative. It is, therefore, not necessary to mention it separately in the list of *sthāyibhāvas*.

The *sthāyibhāva* can be aesthetically appreciable, not in the fashion in which *rati*, etc. are appreciated, but in quite a distinct manner. Bharata calls it *śama* (tranquility) and not *ātman*. *Śama* is not a distinct state of mind but the Self itself. Hence, *tattvajñāna* and the *śama* mean the Self itself. Thus, *ātmajñāna* is the *sthāyin* of *śānta*. All the *anubhāvas* coupled with *yama* and *niyama* will form its *anubhāva*, as also those which are termed by Bharata as *svabhāvābhinaya*. They are called *svabhāvābhinaya* for *śānta* only in their sphere. *Vibhāvas* are grace of God, etc. Love for humanity, etc. form the *vyabhicārins*.

For a man who has realized the true nature of the Self, all his efforts are doing good to others. This is *dayā* which is intimately connected with *śānta*. Therefore, some term *śāntarasa* as *dayāvīra* or *dharmavīra* because of the hero's enthusiasm even to sacrifice his body for others which is a *vyabhicāri* in *śānta*. Abhinavagupta has rightly quoted the example of Jīmutavāhana from *Nāgānandam* to quote the point in hand.[8]

Abhinavagupta states the nature of aesthetic experience of *śānta* in the following words:

> Just as the white string whereon gems of different kinds are loosely and thinly strung, shines in and through them, so does the pure self through the basic mental states such as *rati*, *utsāha*, etc. which affect it. The aesthetic experience of *śānta* consists in the experiences of the self as free from the entire set of painful experience which are due to the external expectations and therefore is a blissful state of identity with the Universal Self. It is the experience of Self in one of the stages on the way to perfect realisation. Such a state of Self when presented, either on the stage or in poetry and therefore universalised, is responsible for the arousal of a mental condition which brings the transcendental bliss.[9]

Abhinavagupta quotes the following stanzas to substantiate his view:

mokṣādhyātmanimittaḥ tattvajñānārthahetusamyuktaḥ
niḥśreyasadharmayutaḥ śānto raso nāma vijñeyaḥ
svaṃ svaṃ nimittamāsthāya śāntadutpadyate rasaḥ
punarnimittāpāye tu śānta eva pratīyate.

Sāntarasa is to be known as that which arises from desire to secure liberation of the Self, which leads to the knowledge of truth and is connected with the property of highest bliss. Various feelings, due to their particular respective causes, arise from *śānta* and when these causes disappear, they melt back into *śānta*.

Śānta is thus the basic *rasa*, all other *rasas* being only its variations due to superimposition of different *sthāyibhāvas*. It is interesting in this context to note that Abhinavagupta in his *Abhinavabhāratī* refers to some manuscripts of *Nāṭyaśāstra* where *Śāntarasa* section is found treated just before the *sṛṅgāra rasa* to indicate that it is the *prakṛti* of all the *rasas*.

In this background, having established *śānta* firmly, it becomes imperative to look at the concept of *śāntarasa* in *Bhagavadgītā* as commented by Abhinavagupta by taking only eight stanzas at random as a sample survey.

V

(i) *II.71*

vihāya kāmān yaḥ sarvān pumānscarati nispṛhaḥ
nirmamo nirahaṅkāraḥ sa śāntimadhigacchati

Who so forsaketh all desires and goeth onwards free from yearnings, selfless and without egoism, he goeth to peace.[10]

The statement *śāntimadhigacchati* in the above stanza has been explained by Abhinavagupta as follows:

Sa yogi sarvakāmasanyāsitvāt śāntirūpam mokṣameti[11] – that *yogin* will be in eternal peace because he has overcome all his desires.

In the real sense, one who has overcome the sense of 'I' and 'mine' can only be a *sanyāsin* according to the following statement of Kullūkabhaṭṭa, a reputed commentator on *Manusmṛti:*

ahaṅkāramamakāratyāga eva sanyāsaḥ natu kāṣāyavāsaḥ.

Everyone in common parlance speaks, 'I am this', 'This is mine' *Ahamidam mamedam iti naisargikoyam lokavyavahāraḥ*[12] and gets into bondage and suffers life's tribulations, but, only a person who remains unattached to the worldly objects can be in his original Self. Such detachment of Self is explained in the *Bhagavadgītā* on the analogy of the lotus leaf detached from the water of the lotus pond. (*padmapatramiva ambhasā*.)

(ii) *IV.18*

karmaṇyakarma yaḥ paśyet akarmaṇi ca karma yaḥ
sa buddhimān manuṣyeṣu sa yuktaḥ kṛtsnakarmakṛt

He who seeth in-action in action, and action in in-action, he is wise among men, he is harmonious even while performing all action.[13]

Here, Abhinavagupta makes a special remark on the word *karma*.

He says that a *jñānin* can be in his original state of eternal peace because he would have transgressed all *karma* having performed it without any expectations:

ato asya kena karmaṇa phalam deeyatāmiti upadśāntattve
tu kṛtsnāni karmāṇi kṛntati chinatti.[14]

Here, Abhinavagupta seems to have the following statement of *Muṇḍakopaniṣad* in his mind:

bhidyate hṛdayagranthiḥ chidyante sarva samśayāḥ
kṣīyante cāsya karmāṇi tasmin dṛṣte parāvare.[15]

When a *jñānin* has realized himself, his knot of mind stands cut, all his doubts stand dispelled and all actions cease to exist.

(iii) *VI.7*

jitātmanaḥ praśāntasya paramātmāsamāhitaḥ
śītoṣṇasukha duḥkheṣu tatha mānāpmānyoḥ.

The higher self of him who is Self controlled and peaceful is uniform in cold and heat, pleasure and pain as well as in honour and dishonour.[16]

Abhinavagupta says:

jitamanasaḥ jitātmanaḥ praśāntasya parātmasu samāpannaḥ,
nirahaṅkāraḥ praśāntaḥ jñānam abhrāntabuddiḥ yasya.[17]

One who has conquered his mind will be in his eternal calmness, which is the nature of his original Self as he will have no illusions regarding the ultimate knowledge (eternal knowledge).

The word *jitātmanaḥ* is very important here because it is always the mind which is responsible for the bondage or the release as the Upaniṣad puts it:

mana eva manuṣyāṇām kāraṇam bandhamokṣayoḥ

The mind which is fickle has been compared to that of a bee by Chandrasekhara Bharati Mahaswamigal of Sringeri Sarada Peetham in his *Ācārya Padāvalambana Stuti* as follows:

kimanyato dhāvasi cittabḥṛnga
prayāhi tatraiva ramasva nityam.[18]

The art of mind control has been discussed at length by Sadaśiva Brahmendra in his works like *Yoga Sudhākara*, which is a learned commentary on the *Yogasūtra of Patañjalī* and *Manoniyamanam* – a short treatise on the art of mind control. To control the mind he has suggested a remedy, *brahmaṇi mānasa sancare.*[19]

(iv) *XI.55*

matkarmakṛnmatparamo madbhaktaḥ saṅgavarjitaḥ
nirvairaḥ sarvabhuteṣu yaḥ sa māmeti pāṇḍava.

He who doeth actions for Me, whose supreme good I am, My devotee, freed from attachment, without hatred of any being, he cometh unto me, O, Pāṇdava.[20]

Abhinavagupta offers a revealing remark on the word *matkarmakṛt* here:

matkarmakṛditi sakala upasamharānte parama
praśānta rūpam brahma tattva sthitim dadāti.[21]

One who has done action in the name of God would be in the state of Brahmanhood which is characterized by total equanimity of mind and eternal peace from which he cannot be disturbed.

This *parama praśāntattva* and *brahmatattva sthiti*, which Abhinavagupta could be evinced in the life of Sadaśiva, discusses Brahmendra and Ramana with the following illustrations:

> *śāntāhaṅkṛti doṣaḥ susamāhita mānasaḥ kopi*
> *pūrṇendu śiṣirabhāvaḥ rājatyānanda cidrasikaḥ.*[22]

> One who is in his state of quietude, one who is totally devoid of ego, one who has an equanimity and coolness of mind, like a full moon, is abiding in his supreme bliss.

In fact, this statement of Sadaśiva Brahmendra appears as though it is a statement of direct personal experience: *anubhava vākya*.

About the personality of Ramana, his most loved pupil Kāvyakanta Gaṇapathi Muni remarks:

> *śaktimantamapi śānti saṃnyutam bhaktimantamapi bhedavarjitam*
> *vīitarāgamapi lokavatsalam sādhubhāvamapi namraceṣṭitam.*[23]

Though Ramana had physical strength, still, he did not give up mental peace; though he had a devotion, it was without duality; though he was cut off from the worldly bondage, still, he was there to guide the humanity at large; though he appeared to be meek, still, he was firm in his stance.

This reminds us of the following statement of Śaṅkarācārya in *Vivekacūḍāmaṇi*:

> *śāntā mahānto nivasanti santaḥ vasantaval lokahitamcarantaḥ.*[24]

> Great men will be quiet and doing good to humanity at large just as the spring season brings about good to everyone.

(v) *XII.12*

> *śreyo hi jñanam abhyāsāt jñānād dhyānaṃ viśiṣyate*
> *dhyānāt karmaphalatyāgaḥ tyāgat śāntiranantaram.*

> Better indeed is wisdom than constant practice. Meditation is better than wisdom. Renunciation of the fruit of action is better than meditation and peace follows renunciatiorn.[25]

Here, Abhinavagupta makes his observations on the word *karmaphalatyāga:*

karmaphalatyage ca ātyantikī śāntiḥ.[26]

One who has not bothered about the Fruit of action will have eternal peace. Here, Abhinavagupta seems to have the following stanza of *Bhagavadagītā* in his mind;

karmaṇyevādhikāraste ma phaleṣu kadācana.[27]

Thy business is with the action only, never with the Fruits.

The word *ātyantiki śāntiḥ* in the opinion of Abhinavagupta is nothing but emancipation or self-realization, which all the orthodox systems of Indian philosophy are striving for. This state of self realization is possible only by resorting to the four-fold means such as:

(i) *nityānitya vāstu vivekaḥ*
(discrimination between eternal and non-eternal things)

(ii) *ihāmutaraphalabhāgavirāgaḥ*
(renunciation of this worldly as well as other worldly pleasures) as could be evinced through the character of Naciketā in *Kathopaniṣad.*

(iii) *śamādi ṣaṭka sampatti*
(having total control over external senses, internal senses, etc., and

(iv) *Mumukṣutva* (the intense desire for liberation).
Self is to be realized, reflected and pondered over, says Yājñavalkya to Maitreyi in *Bṛhadāraṇyakopniṣad.*

atmā va are draṣṭavyaḥ, śrotavyo mantavyo nididhyāsitavyaḥ.[28]

(vi) *XIII.13*

adveṣṭa sarvabhūtānām maitraḥ karuṇa eva ca
nirmamo nirahankāraḥ samaduḥkhasukhaḥ kṣamī

He who beareth no ill will to any being, friendly and compassionate without attachment and egoism, balanced in pleasure and pain and Forgiving.[29]

On this stanza, the remark of Abhinavagupta is

satataṃ yogi vyavahārāvasthāyāmapi praśānta antaḥ kāraṇatvāt.[30]

> *Yogin* is one who even in his day-to-day activities will keep up his equanimity of mind.

This statement of Abhinavagupta could be seen with the following stanza of *Bhagavadgītā:*

> *duḥkheṣvanudvignamanāḥ sukheṣu vigataspṛhaḥ*
> *vītarāga bhayakrodhaḥ sthitadhīr munirucyate.*[31]

> He whose mind is free from anxiety amid pains, indifferent amid pleasures, fear and anger, is called a sage of stable mind.

(vii) *XV.4*

> *tataḥ padam tat parimārgitavyam yasmin gatā na nivartanti bhūyaḥ*
> *tameva cādyaṃ puruṣam prapadye yataḥ pravṛttiḥ praṣṛtā purāṇī*

> That path beyond may be sought treading which there is no return. I go indeed to that primal man where the ancient energy streamed forth.[32]

Here on the word *tat padam*, Abhinavagupta states

> *tat padam praśāntam, avyayaṃ padam tadeva.*[33]

Indeed, the final path is that from where there is no return to this mortal world and to know that Yama was catechized by Naciketā in the *Kaṭhopaniṣad* and ultimately sought the eternal knowledge of the self from Yama, which could be seen in *Kaṭhopaniṣad* as well as the second chapter of *Bhagavadgītā*:

> *ya enam vetti hantāraṃ yascainaṃ manyate hatam*
> *ubhau tau na vijānītau nāyam hanti na hanyate.*[31]

> He who regardeth this as slayer, and he who thinketh he is slain, both of them are ignorant. He slayeth not, nor is he slain.

> *na jāyate mṛyate vā kadācin nāyam bhūtvā bhavitā vā na bhūyah*
> *ajo nityaḥ śāśvatoyam purāṇo na hanyate hanyamāne śarīre.*[35]

> He is not born, nor doth he die, not having been, ceaseth he anymore to be; un-born, perpetual, eternal and ancient, he is not slain when his body is slaughtered.

The word *tat* in the statement of Abhinavagupta's *Tatpadam* is the abode of Brahman and if this *jīva* realizes that he would be in communion with God which is nothing but *tat tvam asi*.[36] That thou art – the famous dictum propounded by the father Āruṇi to his son Śvetaketu in the chapter six of *Chāndogyopaniṣad* with the help of nine illustrations: *navahkṛtvobhyāsaḥ* – wherein the latter returned home after twelve years of *gurukulavāsa* with a great deal of arrogance.

(viii) *XVII.24*

tasmāt omityudāḥṛtya yajñadānatapaḥkriyāḥ
pravartante vidhānoktāḥ satatam brahmavādinām.

> Therefore, with the pronouncing of *om*, the acts of sacrifice, gift and austerity, as laid down in the ordinances, are always commenced by the knowers of the eternal.[37]

On the word *om*, Abhinavagupta remarks: *omityanena samupaśānta samastaprapañcam*[38] – with the chanting of *om* the world will come to a standstill.

The word *om* is a sacred syllabic, which is as great as Brahman himself as it seems to have emerged from the throat of Brahman:

oṅkārascātha śabdaśca dvāvetau brahmaṇaḥ purā
kaṇṭham bhitvā viniryātau tasmān māngalikā vubhau.[39]

The words *om* and *atha* seem to have directly emerged from Brahman and hence both are auspicious.

The word *om* has the following seven connotations, remarks Mankha in his Koṣa:

abhyudāne abhyupāgame tūṣṇīm bhāve samarcane
dāna pratigrahāduu ca omkārepi ca mangale.[40]

> *Om* could be chanted on the occasions of honouring someone, while receiving something, while one is maintaining silence (this is what we need in the present context), while one is offering worship, while giving charity and receiving charity and on all auspicious occasions.

CONCLUSION

Thus, it could be concluded that *śānta* as a *rasa* runs throughout the *Bhagavadgītā* and if the commentary of Abhinavagupta is studied carefully, this aspect becomes clear not only in the eight illustrations that have been chosen here which directly deal with the *śāntarasa*, but elsewhere also. However, in the interest of brevity, only a selection has been made here.

NOTES AND REFERENCES

1. K.C. Pandey, *Abhinavagupta: A Historical and Philosophical Study*. The Chaukhamba Sanskrit Series, Varanasi, 1963, pp. 27-28.
2. *Taittirīyopaniṣad*, II.7.
3. *Bhrata's maxim* of *rasa*.
4. V. Raghavan, *The Number of Rasas*, Adyar Research Centre, Madras, III revised edn., 1975, p. 92.
5. *Iśopaniṣad*, sixth *mantra*.
6. *Bhagavadgītā*, III.17.
7. *Abhinavabhāratī of Abhinavagupta*, ed. Dr. Nagendra, Delhi, 1960, p. 623.
8. G.T. Deshpande, *Abhinavagupta*, Sahitya Akademi, Delhi, 1989, pp. 97-99.
9. K.C. Pandey, *Indian Aesthetics*, pp. 249-50.
10. M.W. Burnway, *Bhagavadgītā*, Asian Publication Service, New Delhi, 1981, p. 151.
11. *Abhinavagupta's Commentary on Bhagavadgītā*, II.71, Nirṇayasāgar Press, Bombay, 1936.
12. *Śaṅkarācārya's Commentary on Adhyāsa Bhāṣya of Brahmasūtras*.
13. *Bhagavadgītā*, IV, 14, M.W. Burnway's translation.
14. *Abhinavagupta's Commentary*, op. cit., IV.14.
15. *Muṇḍakopaniṣad*, II.2.9.
16. *Bhagavadgītā*, IV.14, Burnway's translation.
17. *Abhinavagupta's Commentary*, op. cit., VI.7.
18. Chandrasekhara Bharati Mahasvamigal, *Ācārya Padāvalambana Stuti*.
19. *Sadāśiva Kīrtanāni*.
20. *Bhagavadgītā*, XI. 55. Burnway's translation.
21. *Abhinavagupta's Commentary*, op. cit., XI.55.
22. Sadāśiva Brahmendra, *Ātmavidyāvilāsa*, Stanza 20, Vani Vilas Press. Srirangam, 1908.
23. *Ramanagita*.
24. *Vivekachūḍāmaṇi* of Śankarācārya, Stanza 30.
25. *Bhagavadgita*, XII.12. Burnway's translation.
26. *Abhinavagupta's Commentary*, op. cit., XII.12.
27. *Bhagavadgītā*, 11.47.
28. *Bṛhadāraṇyakopaniṣad*, 11.4.5.
29. *Bhagavadgītā*, XII.13. Burnway's translation.
30. *Abhinavagupta's Commentary*, op. cit., X11.13.
31. *Bhagavadgītā*, 2.5 6.
32. *Bhagavadgītā*, XV.4. Burnway's translation.
33. *Abhinavagupta's Commentary*, op. cit., XV.4.
34. *Bhagavadgītā*, II. 19.
35. *Bhagavadgītā*, II. 20.
36. *Chāndogyopaniṣad*, VI chapter.

37. *Bhagavadgītā*, XVII.24. Burnway's translation.
38. *Abhinavagupta's Commentary*, op. cit., XVll.24.
39. *Ratnaprabha Commentary* on the Sutra *athātho brahmajijñāsā* of Bādarāyaṇa's *Brahmasūtras*.
40. *Mankhakoṣa*.

BIBLIOGRAPHY

Abhinavagupta, *Abhinavagupta*.
Bhagavadgītā, edited by M.W. Burnway.
Brahmendra, Sadasiva, *Ātmavidyavilasa*.
Bṛhadāraṇyakopaniṣad.
Chāndogyopaniṣad.
Deshpande, G.T., *Abhinavagupta*.
Gītārthasangraha, Abhinavagupta's commentary on *Bhagavadgītā*.
Iśopaniṣad.
Maṅkhakosa.
Muṇḍakopaniṣad.
Pandey, K.C., *Abhinavagupta: A Historical and Philosophical Study*.
——, *Indian Aesthetics*.
Ramangita.
Raghavan, V., *The Number of Rasas*.
Ratnaprabha, *Commentary on the Sutra: athātho brahmajyñāsā* of Bādarāyaṇa Vyāsa.
Śaṅkarācārya, *Vivekachūḍāmaṇi*.
Sadaśiva Kīrtanani.
Śānkarabhaṣya on Brahmasūtras.
Swamigal, Chandrasekhara Bharathi, *Ācārya Padavalambanastuti*.
Tattirīyopaniṣad.

6

The Indian Aesthetic Tradition and Abhinavagupta: Concept of Rasa

Anupa Pande

Several stages may be distinguished in the development of aesthetic ideas in ancient India. In the earliest or Vedic phase, it is divinity which is conceived as the primary artist endowed with creative vision, the world being his creation. Thus, the *Chāndogya Upaniṣad*[1] says:

> *Sadeva Somya idamagra āsīdekamevādvitīyam ...*
> *tadaikṣata bahusyām prajāyeya iti.*
>
> *Sa ya eṣo 'ṇimā aitadātmyamidam sarvam*
> *tat satyam sa ātmā tattvamasi,*[2]

"O Saumya! In the beginning was being alone, one without a second. It thought, may I be many, may I be born."

"Now, this subtle essence, this is the self of all this. That is the truth, that is the self that thou art." *Rūpam rūpam pratirūpo babhūva*[3] declares that consciouness has assumed all the diverse forms of the world. Then again, *Kavirmanīṣī paribhūḥ svayambhūḥ yāthātathyatorthān vyadadhācchāśvatībhyaḥ samābhyaḥ,*[4] i.e., "From eternal times, He has created meanings in accordance with their essential reality." *Kavirekaḥ Prajāpatiḥ*[5] declares Ānandavardhana. The original Being is the creator and creation is by becoming many different forms. All the forms contain the creative essence. They are the manifestations of the creative consciousness itself. This theory applies to the human poet or artist also, who creates forms as manifestations of his own consciousness.

Human art imitates the divine. *Veda* is the creative *Logos* (*Kṛti*). *Nāṭya*, also known as *Nāṭyaveda*, is *anukṛti*, endowed with creativity at the secondary level. The sculptor and architect follow the paradigmatic measures, drama re-enacts the sacred myths, dance presents divine and cosmic rhythms, sacred music seeks to relate itself to the radiant effluence of the sun and the outpourings of the Soma. This is not to say that these sacred forms and notions of art were unconnected with popular folk forms and notions of art. The *Nāṭyaśāstra* of Bharata may be said to constitute a watershed. It sums up the sacred and popular notions of the Vedic and Janapada ages, which had developed out of the *Vedāṅgas* and the *Upavedas* and which include the sciences of music, drama, sculpture and architecture. It recapitulates the traditional notion of the sacred and invisible or transcendental (*adṛṣṭa*) value of art forms and activities and at the same time formulates the notion of art as entertainment (*rañjana*) and enjoyment (*rasa*).

The famous *Rasa Sutra* of Bharata declares: *vibhāvānubhāva-vyabhicārisaṃyogād rasaniṣpattiḥ*.[6] It is worth noting here that the terms *vibhāva*, *anubhāva* and *vyabhicāribhāva* refer to stage representations, not to the realities of life. It follows, therefore, that the *rasa* they produce must also be a stage effect rather than some aspect of real life. That is why the *rasas* are called *nāṭya-rasas*. *Vibhāvas*, *anubhāvas* and *vyabhicāribhāvas* are represented through *abhinaya* on stage – *yo'yam svabhāvo lokasya sukhaduḥkhasamanvitaḥ/ so'ṅgādyabhinayopeto nāṭyamityabhidhīyate*.[7] Abhinava explains: *Evam dayāratyādirūpānukaraṇabhūto nāṭyalakṣaṇo'rthaḥ katham pratītigocarībhavatītyāḥa-aṇgāditi ye'bhinayāḥ āṅgikādyaḥ na ca te liṅgasaṅketādirūpāḥ*.[8] The ensemble (*saṃyoga*) of the representations (*vibhāvādi*) induces a characteristic experience in the spectators (*rasaniṣpatti*). This experience is a union of subjective and objective aspects. Its subjective aspect is shown by the description of *nāṭya* as providing distraction from affliction (*vinodajananam*) and rest from weariness (*viśrāmajananam*). This kind of subjective effect may be seen in such pure arts as music, but drama presents an objective spectacle of the vicissitudes of life (*lokānukaraṇam, bhāvānukīrtanam*) and is able to instruct (*upadeśajananam*) and give fortitude in suffering (*sthairyam duḥkhārditasya ca ... dhṛtirudvignacetasām*). This instruction is of a moral nature since it affects emotional organization. The experience of the spectators, thus, is neither purely emotional and subjective nor purely cognitive and objective. Its entertainment is not unstructured, such as provided by mere juggling or merely rhythmic dancing. Nor is its instruction merely conceptual or mediate, such as any *śāstra* may provide. It recognizes the emotions by presenting the quintessential wisdom of life as a spectacle. The uniqueness of the dramatic experience or *rasa* is, thus, evident in Bharata. It is not mere excitement or sentimentality, for drama is described as a way to wisdom, the fifth Veda.

Thus, if we consider the concept of *rasa* in the context of the general dramatic theory of Bharata, we see that it is not a merely descriptive or psychological category. It is, rather, an evaluative or aesthetic category. The reasons for this may be succintly stated thus: (a) *Rasas* are described as *nāṭya rasas*, and thus distinguished as such from what belongs to *loka*. As something belonging distinctly to dramatic performance and experiences, *rasa* is already *alaukika* by implication in Bharata. (b) *Rasa* is brought about by *vibhāva, anubhāva* and *vyabhicāribhāvas*. The first two are clearly conceived as belonging primarily to the stage, not to reality. Although *vyabhicāribhāvas* may be said to belong to pyschological reality, their combination (*saṃyoga*) with *vibhāva* and *anubhāva* suggests that *vyabhicāribhāvas* here denote the stage intimations of psychological factors that would also make the interpretation of *saṃyoga* quite simple. It will denote the combination of diverse stage representation into one unified spectacle. (c) Drama represents the vicissitudes of life through the use of *pāṭhya, gīta* and *abhinaya*. *Rasas* are mentioned besides these three as a fourth constituent. *Rasa* could thus be different from a mere technical factor of representation and could be interpreted to be the characteristic aesthetic effect, tone or mood of the whole as apprehended by the spectators. (d) *Rasa* and *bhāva* are clearly distinguished in the *Nāṭyaśāstra*. The *bhāvas* are effective psychic states while *rasa* is achieved by the spectator through the dramatic intimation of *bhāvas*. Just as in music, a procession of notes in certain combinations reveals a characteristic melodic whole or *raga*, similarly, it seems that the representation of *bhāvas* reveals *rasa* as an aesthetic whole.

Although *rasa* is used by Bharata to indicate the peculiar flavour or quintessential quality of a dramatic performance and its experience, he does not give any philosophical analysis of the problems involved. Human reality, dramatic representation and aesthetic experience need to be related in an adequate manner. In Bharata, human reality has its focus in *bhāva* and dramatic representation is its *anukaraṇa* or *anukīrtana*. Aesthetic experience is called *rasa*, a unity of entertainment and enlightenment, and is classified into eight, in relation to the gamut of *bhāvas*.

The notion of imitation is itself a puzzling one. What is the congnitive status of the apprehension of dramatic representation, is another puzzle. How the experience of life is transformed into an aesthetic experience needs to be explained. In the dicussion of these problems, later commentators elaborated the notions of imagination, intution, aesthetic distance, subjective universality, self-revelation mediated by feeling, and of the tranquility, illumination and beautitude of aesthetic experience. At the same time, the notion of *rasa* was formally generalized beyond drama into poetry and other arts. The number of *rasas* become nine as they include the *śāntarasa* also.

The development of the theory of *dhavni* in poetry brought about the inherently dramatic character of poetry and enabled the concept of *rasa* to cover both drama and poetry. The connection of *rasa* with music is also quite clear. Although pure music does not have an *ālambana vibhāva* corresponding to *Nāṭya*, its evocative power (*uddīpana*, *vyañjaka*) is undoubted. What it evokes may not be a defined emotion but it does help the manifestation of feeling as shown by *sāttvika bhāvas*. It manifests *rasa* as ecstatic delight by purifying, intensifying and interiorizing consciousness. Similarly, acting suggestive of *rasa* was part of *nṛtya* or expressive dancing, The *Citrasūtra* clearly establishes the connection of painting with *bhāva* and *rasa*. The paintings of Ajanta are dramatic as well as *rasa*-oriented. The Buddha sculptures of Mathura and Sarnath epitomize the *śāntarasa*. It is thus clear that drama, dance, music, painting and sculpture shared a common aesthetic tradition, which aimed at the expression of feeling through the creation of a vivid form.

The most important interpretations are those of Bhaṭṭa Lollaṭa, Śaṅkuka, Bhaṭṭanāyaka and Abhinavagupta himself.[9] Bhaṭṭa Lollaṭa represented the most ancient view. Abhinava says that his interpretation was the one generally accepted by the older scholars. On this interpretation, *vibhāva*, *anubhāva* and *vyabhicāribhāvas* have their primary focus in the characters of real life. In particular situations they are combined with the innate or instinctive attitudes called *sthāyibhāva*. These are thus developed and become *rasas*. This *rasa* is apprehended by the spectators through the agency of the actors, their gestures and enactments. *Rasa*, thus, becomes something objective, which the play communicates to the spectator.

We have here, on the one hand, a psychology of emotional attitudes. Under certain situations, certain trains of emotions are generated and developed into intense experiences. The persons who are the objects of emotions are called *ālambana vibhāva*, i.e., objective causes. The situation itself in terms of time, place, etc., which serves to arouse feelings, is called *uddīpana vibhāva*. The physical expression of emotioinal reactions, such as tears or trembling, etc., are called *anubhāva*. Transient feelings such as worry, humility, etc., are called or *sañcārī bhāvas*. Thus, when Duṣyanta catches sight of Śakuntalā being bothered by the bee in the *āśrama* of Kaṇva and regrets his own inability to pursue his own desire, we have Śakuntalā as *ālambana vibhāva*, the situation in the *āśrama* as *uddīpana vibhāva*, the sighing of the king as *anubhāva*, and the immediate feelings of the king as *vyabhicāribhāvas*. We have, thus, a situation in which the latent *sthāyibhāva* of *rati* in the king is developed and manifested. This is a situation in real life, a situation of actually felt emotional flow. On the stage, the real life situation is imitated and enacted by the actors. Viewing the actors on stage, the spectators believe that they are viewing the real life situation. Thus, through the force of *anusandhāna* they apprehend (*pratīti*) the *sthāyibhāva* of Duṣyanta, developed by *vibhāva*, etc.; and thus developed and apprehended, this *sthāyibhāva* is *rasa*. This interpretaion is in close agreement with common sense, according to which the spectators see the real life through its enactment and apprehend its emotions in the process.

While the identification of *rasa* with *sthāyibhāva*, through the functioning of *vibhāva*, etc., follows the text of Bharata and is unquestionable, the interpretation of Lollaṭa suffers from inadequate attention to the manner in which the actors on the stage represent reality and succeed in communicating it, as also in the neglect of the spectator and his experience. Besides, it is not clear why the view of the real life emotion should entertain or instruct the spectators.

Śaṅkuka attacks the theory at several points. If the *sthāyibhāva* is already real before combining with the *vibhāvas*, etc., why does it need them? On the other hand, if it is not real on stage, how can it combine with anything? If one proposes numerous gradations of the *sthāyibhāva* in the process of development, it will be too vague and mutable a thing to be classified in the manner in which the *ācāryas* have done it. From this, Śaṅkuka concludes that the *sthāyibhāva* of the real characters cannot be identified with *rasa* either in itself or conceived in terms of any programme of development. For Śaṅkuka, when the *sthāyibhāva* of the character is imitated by the actor through the presentation of the *vibhāvas*, etc., then it becomes *rasa* for the spectators. The natural causes, consequences and auxilliaries of the *sthāyibhāva*, when presented on the stage, are called *vibhāva*, *anubhāva*, and *vyabhicāribhāvas*. Perceiving and understanding these, the spectator is able to infer the *sthāyibhāva* in the actor playing the role of the real character. Such an inferred and imitated *sthāyibhāva* is *rasa*. The resultant apprehension of the spectators is not like anything in actuality. It is neither true cognition, nor false cognition, nor doubt, nor is it the cognition of similarity. The spectator neither identifies nor distinguishes the actor from the character, nor does he see the one like the other, nor is he in a state of doubt. Nevertheless, he has a vivid experience which is unquestionable. This experience is explained by Śaṅkuka on the basis of the imitation of reality on the stage and a peculiar inferential apprehension of it by the spectator. The example of the picture horse (*citra-turaga*) has been brought up to illustrate the situation. The painted horse is not perceived to be real or unreal or merely as a likeness or a case of doubt. Its lines, colours, etc. enable the viewer to reach a peculiar inferential apprehension, which is nevertheless vivid and unique.

The account of Śaṅkuka rightly emphasizes the nature of drama as an imaginative spectacle, which is apprehended in its own right. Neither is the apprehension cognitive nor is its content natural. The experience is unique and imaginative. At the same time, Śaṅkuka seems to connect the spectacle with reality through imitation and the discernment of what is imitated through inference. This seems to produce a contradiction. If the spectacle imitates reality, how can its appprehension not be the apprehension of *sādṛśya?* If the apprehension is gained through inference, how can it avoid being cognitive? The theory of Śaṅkuka, thus, is a curious blend of two different notions. On the one hand, it is the notion of drama as an imitation where the primary theme of the imitation of *sthāyibhāva* is a matter of inference. On the other hand, drama is conceived as an imaginative spectacle which forms the subject of a unique experience.

The characterization of *rasa* experience in its specific nature is carried forward by Bhaṭṭanāyaka. He distinguishes between three different functions and levels through which aesthetic experience is generated and declares the last of these to be the enjoyment of *rasa*. The first stage is constituted by the presentation of the simple meaning or situation, which is called *abhidhā* or denotation in the case of words used in poetry. This, however, is accompanied by a peculiar process of generalization called *bhāvakatva* or *vibhāvanā* or *sādhāraṇīkaraṇa*. This is really the imaginative transformation of reality into a spectacle which is lifted out of actual space, time or social relations. This is followed by a peculiar subjective experience where the mind is in a state of luminous peace and withdrawal into its own pure nature. This is called *bhojakatva*. Viewed thus, *rasa* is the subjective enjoyment of the *sthāyibhāva* within a generalized or universalized context. The *sthāyibhāva* which is here enjoyed is not to be identified with any specific or actual feeling whether of the real character or the actor or the spectator. It is rather the focal element in an ideal situation, apprehended within a concrete or imaginative subjective vision. Drama or any art presents the ideal truth of feelings and felt experiences imaginatively, thereby creating a generalized context which remains at the same time something concrete and directly experienceable. Bhaṭṭanāyaka is, thus, able to expound the nature of *rasa* within the category of what may be called a subjective universal, a notion which is analogous to that of Kant.

It will be admitted on all hands that Abhinavagupta was the greatest thinker in the Indian tradition of aesthetics. He was not only a saint but also philosopher, musician, poet and critic. He has interpreted the concept of *rasa* in the light of the theory of *dhvani* and the spiritual metaphysics of the Pratyabhijñā school of Kashmir Śaivism. For him, the world presented by a dramatic or poetic or any art work is imaginative and quite distinct from the actual world. It is, therefore, described by him as *alaukika*. The actual world is based on causal forces. The representations in art are only ideal and consist of images and meanings. That is why the *vibhāva*, etc. are *alaukika* and are not to be confused with the real causes, auxiliaries and consequences of emotions in real life. Feelings are not presented or represented through any imitation on the stage. They are apprehended in terms of an immediate and subjective experience brought about by the evocative power of acting or words. The generalization to which Bhaṭṭanāyaka alludes, transforms not merely the object of aesthetic experience and the relation of the spectator to it, but also the subjectivity or self-awareness of the spectator. Now, the self of the spectator as of any other human being consists of pure consciousness which has the innate capacity of self-expression. The whole universe is of the nature of such consciousness. All particular experiences arise out of this foundational consciousness or *saṃvit*, through specific determinations of subjectivity and objectivity. As a result, all experiences end up as the content of a moment of self- consciousness. This moment of resting in the inward nature of consciousness (*samvidviśrānti*) constitutes a beatific moment. It is the peculiar virtue of aesthetic experience that by detaching the self from its natural or habitual determinations, leads it to a moment of inner experience, mediated by feelings and images. *Rasa*, thus, has to be understood as a kind of mediated and transitory self-experience. At this point it is not difficult to see how aesthetic experience at once moves and enlightens. It is described in terms of a vivid imaginative self-realization. Such an experience has a peculiar illuminative intensity. It is this quality which is designated as *rasa*.

Abhinava admits that there has been a development in understanding and his own views depend on the contribution of earlier scholars. The first point emphasized is that Bharata himself has stated *rasa* to be the meaning of the poetic work (*kāvyārtha*). The proper reader of poetry or spectator of drama gathers from the words or acting something more than the obvious presentation. Such a reader has to be an *adhikārī*, i.e., duly qualified. His heart must be capable of pure intuition (*nirmala pratibhāna*). Such a person, on hearing the sentences or watching the actors, attains mental intuition where the specific time and place of the direct meanings are disregarded. Thus, in the presentation of fear, neither the object, nor the subject of fear are apprehended in relationship to any specific actuality. That is why the idea of fear is vividly experienced without the spectator being overcome by fear. The generalization which is effected in this process of aesthetic experience is not a limited one. All limitations of space, time and causality belonging to the actual world are disregarded in favour of a world created by imagination. All the spectators share a common experience, despite as their individual differences, they share a common structure of instincts. The unobstructed contemplative consciousness is ecstatic (*camatkāra*). *Rasa* is *bhāva* grasped in a such a state of intuitive contemplation.

The philosophical interpretation which Abhinava gave of *rasa* as *samvid-viśrānti* or *camatkāra* underplayed the essentiality of the specific roles of different media and techniques in the different arts and converted *rasa* into a universal aesthetic category comparable to beauty. The emphasis on beauty suggests something objective and hence promotes the danger of seeking it exclusively in specific art forms. *Rasa*, on the other hand, clearly emphasizes the subjectivity of art experience. Bhaṭṭnāyaka had already brought out the universal character of this subjectivity. The distinction of *rasa* from any merely psychological experience is clear in Abhinava, where *rasa* is transcendental, the return of consciousness to its own innate and universal but immediate ecstatic nature.

Whether it is music or dance, poetry or drama, the first effect is to attract and focus the mind and thus reduce distraction and dullness. The next effect is to induce a generalized consciousness which is distant from the actual ego-subject or actual objects given in nature. In poetry and drama, there is an apprehension of the essential nature of feelings through images. In the apprehension of these suggested or evoked feelings, conciousness is no longer subordinated to action or reaction as in the behavioural world. The image of the world, instead, is the content reflective of consciousness itself. So the last effect of art is to lead consciousness to a deepening lucid intuition of itself. Consciousness creates the world, even as an artist does. And the perennial function of art is to lead consciousness back from the world to itself.

Such a theory of *rasa*; and by implication the theory of art, was made possible by the philosophical genius of Abhinavagupta. It was not matched again till the seventeenth century when the Vaiṣṇava *ācāryas* reared a new metaphysical structure for understanding Bhakti as *rasa*.

NOTES AND REFERENCES

1. *Chāndogya Upaniṣad*, Ch. 6, II, III section.
2. Ibid., Ch. 6, XIV section.
3. *Ṛk Saṃhitā*, 6.47.18.
4. *Īśopaniṣad*, Verse 8.
5. *Dhvanyāloka* (Benares, 1940), p. 498.
6. *Nāṭyaśāstra*. 6.31-2.
7. Ibid., 1.121.
8. *Abhinavabhāratī*, Ibid.
9. *Nāṭyaśāstra*. Ch. 6.

7

Rasa and Bhāvānukīrtana – Complementarity of Two Concepts

Kamalesh Datta Tripathi

Completion of the publication of *Nāṭyaśāstra* with *Abhinavabhāratī* from Baroda in 1964 coincides with a fresh interest of Indian scholars and artists in *Nāṭyaśāstra* and in traditional art forms available throughout the length and breadth of the country. The search for unity, continuity and identity in art-tradition finds a new impetus in the discovery of *Abhinavabhāratī*. Structural unity of the Sanskrit theatre continuing in the amazing variety of traditional theatre forms, in an unbelievably vast span of time and space rediscovered in the studies of *Nāṭyaśāstra* and *Abhinavabhāratī*, in recent years has resulted in an emphatic assertion of identity of Indian theatre tradition.[1] What has been discovered in the realm of traditional threatre was already felt in the field of traditional music. *Abhinavabhāratī* revealed a theoretical basis of this identity enshrined in the *Nāṭyaśāstra* of Bharata.

Nāṭyaśāstra offers the central concept of Indian aesthetics, i.e., *rasa* in its Sixth Chapter and another concept of *bhāvānukīrtana*, compatible to it, appears even before in the first chapter. Both the concepts are complementary to each other and form one grand theory.

But unfortunately traditional Sanskrit poetics confined itself to the sixth and seventh chapters and the chapters devoted to the nature and structure of poetic text of Sanskrit drama and showed scant interest in the question of ontological nature of *nāṭya* as well as the question of creative process seminally presented in the first chapter of *Nāṭyaśāstra* and elaborated in the commentary – *Abhinavabhāratī* – thereon. Although *Matsyapurāṇa* recognized the significance of the concept of *anukīrtana*[2] and refers to it in the context of arts and some modern scholars have noticed this fact,[3] yet, strangely enough, works on poetics and dramaturgy ignored this invaluable notion highlighted by Abhinavagupta in his celebrated commentary on *Nāṭyaśāstra*. Gnoli, a modern Italian scholar, drew our attention for the first time and translated a fragment of *Abhinavabhāratī* explaining the concept of *bhāvānukīrtana*,[4] but a close analysis of first and sixth chapters and the related portions of the entire *Nāṭyaśāstra* dealing with the aforesaid question of inter-relation of *rasa* and *bhāvānukīrtana* is still wanting.

With this view, the present paper discusses these two central concepts and their complementarity as gleaned from *Nāṭyaśāstra* and *Abhinavabhāratī*. It lays special effort for understanding the concept of *bhāvānukīrtana* as distinguished from the concept of *anukaraṇa*.

ANUKARAṆA AND ANUKĪRTANA

The myth of the origin of *nāṭya* and story of the first dramatic performance occuring in first chapter of the *Nāṭyaśāstra* are important from this angle. In particular, the failure of the first performance whose theme was the defeat of *daityas* (demons) is significant.

Angry as they were, *asuras* and *dānavas* (demons) caused troublesome interruptions during the first dramatic performance. The objection against the performance raised by Virupākṣa, together with the host of the *daityas* and *vighnas* (obstacles), had deep implications. The *daityas* said to Brahmā, "This knowledge of theatre which your Lordship has created at the behest of gods, has humiliated us. Oh *pitāmaha* of the entire world, this ought not to have been done by you in this way" (*NŚ*, I-103-3-1/2, Baroda edn. pp. 33-34).

The first performance was the nature of *anukīrti*, or *anukaraṇa* (imitation), and it is apparent that the *daityas* took *anukīṛti* too literally. Brahmā tried to remove the misgivings of demons about the nature of *nāṭya* by describing it as *trailokyasya sarvasya nāṭyam bhāvānukīrtanam* (the glorious retelling of the *bhāvas*, or the emotive states of the entire triple universe).[5]

Although Bharata defines drama as *anukaraṇa* elsewhere also,[6] Abhinavagupta emphasizes that *nāṭya* is essentially *anukīrtana* (retelling) of the *bhāvas* (emotive states) and not *anukaraṇa*, i.e., imitation. Abhinavagupta raises deeper ontological and aesthctic questions when he asks whether there is a comprehension of *nāṭya* as reality (*tattva*) or as similarity to it (*sādṛśya*), as in the case of a twin or as an error (*bhrānti*) as in the case of silver mistakingly recognized as such in a piece of mother of pearl. Or theatrical reality is the superimposition (*āropa*) as in the case of viewing the face of the beloved as moon, or as identification (*adhyavasāya*) as when one says: "This man from the land of *vāhika* is a bull." Or can we say that reality in theatre is a metaphoric supposition (*utprekṣyamāṇatva*) as when moon is fancied as the face of night or it is a replica (*pratikṛti*) as in the case of painting or a model, or as imitation or reproduction (*anukaraṇa*) as in the case of the intense desire of the pupil to recite the words of the Vedas as they are taught to him by his teacher. Or can we explain it as a sudden creation (*tātkālika-nirmāṇa*) as in the case of magic, or as an appearance of something (*tadābhāsa*) reproduced by tricks as in the case of the illusion created by a sleight of hand? Abhinavagupta offers a number of options mentioned above to explain ontologically the nature of *nāṭya*[7] and denies all such hypotheses for the following reasons:

First, if we take *nāṭya* as real or in the form in any such option as stated above, the spectator (*draṣṭṛ*) would lose his interest in the theatrical spectacle, for a spectator cannot be expected to have interest in that which does not concern him. How can the spectator have an interest in the 'real Rama' being present on the stage unless there is some common ground which relates both, i.e., the spectator and the 'real Rama'. What is true in the case of hypothesis of taking *nāṭyas* as 'real', is also true in case of other hypotheses. If the theatrical persona is taken to be 'real' or in absolute likeness to the real or in any other way mentioned above, there would be no scope for 'depersonalization' or 'universalization' (*sādhāraṇīkaraṇa*), of the dramatic characters and environment in which the characters have been placed in drama and the 'emotive states' represented in it. Moreover, there would be no possibility of relishing *rasa*, due to the lack of 'depersonalization' or 'universalization'.

Secondly, when a poet has been bound to a description tied by any of these aspects, poetry is likely to suffer, for if a poet/playwright or an artist takes theatre as reproduction of reality, or even something similar to it, he is not able to chisel out the flawless piece of art due to the very 'fixity' of the nature of the objects to be represented in theatre and other art forms. The very freedom of the poet, playwright, and artist is severely delimited, if we take 'art' as an 'imitation' or as 'superimposition', etc.

Thirdly, the performer's vision of art, which is essential to theatre, would not find its accomplishment, for he (the performer) would be involved in the most basic of the actual feelings of ordinary life, such as rage or indulgence, etc., as it usually happens at the sight of a couple engaged in love making (the onlooker may be filled with a sense of indignation or indulgence, etc.). And if so, the performer engrossed with his own personal experience would not be able to represent the reality of life. The fault of *daityas* lies in the fact that they took the *nāṭya* as identical with anyone of the hypotheses stated above.[8]

Abhinavagupta raises the objections from the angle of aesthetic experience of the spectator or connoisseur of the art, from the angle of playwright as well of an actor (second and third arguments have been put forward from the viewpoint of creative process) and singles out the concept of *anukaraṇa* in his brilliant analysis, for *anukaraṇa* appears to be basis for all other hypotheses in one way or the other and argues that imitation (*anukaraṇa*) amounts to be a farcical and comic copy of the 'real'. Therefore, it is essentially a distortion (*vikaraṇa*). It makes the indifferent one simply laugh and may cause indignation in those who belong to the side of the imitated one.[9]

Moreover, the reproduction of figures like Rāma, who belong to a hoary past, is simply impossible. Neither can someone similar to Rāma be produced because no one existed at the time of the actual event who is supposed to have seen Rāma nor can the actor reproduce his own sorrow just like that of Rāma, because it is absolutely absent in him. If it were actually present in him, his performance would fail to be a reproduction. Thus, the theory of *anukaraṇa* stands totally rejected.[10] If principal *prima facie* view of *anukaraṇa* is rejected, then all such similar views are automatically rejected.

Nāṭya is, therefore, an *anukīrtana* of the *bhāvas*. It is not a 'reproduction' in a strict sense; rather, it is a representation in the form of 'retelling'. This retelling is not of an actual event. On the contrary, it is retelling of the *bhāva* (emotive state) underlying that particular event.

Abhinavagupta does not elaborate the concept of *anukīrtana*. We have no option except understanding it through the etymological meaning of the term *kīrtana*.

The term *anukīrtana* means 'retelling' or 'renarrating', rather than 'imitating', 'making' and 'reproducing' things or emotive states. It is in no way an exercise for creating an illusion of the real. This creative aspect of retelling the *bhāvas* entails endless ways of the describing (*varṇanā*) the life and the world (*trailokya-svabhāva*), for *kīrtana* means repeated telling, reciting, and describing.

Secondly, the act of reverberating the *bhāvas* (emotive states), *lokasvabhāva* (the internal and external nature and behaviour of men, women and all beings), and *trailokya* (the triple universe) belongs to the order of extolling them. It is not merely re-stating the real. It is the retelling of the real, in order to glorify it. This act of retelling or *anukīrtana* captures the essential meaning of the original more powerfully than the 'imitation'.

Thirdly, it is the creative act of the artist/poet/dramatist and of the performer exercising his freedom to avoid whatever he deems fit to be avoided (*anucita*, i.e., wrong, evil) and to incorporate what is to be adopted (*ucita*, i.e., right, good).[11]

Kīrtana etymologically includes all the three meanings but the most important is the idea that it is not an imitational reproduction, but a reverberative representation. An artist does not recreate 'reality', at best, he 'retells' it in a glorious way. *Kīrtana*, in course of time, acquired another more specific meaning, that of 'raising a temple or a monument' in order to celebrate an auspicious or favourable occasion.[12] This sense of celebration is abundantly present in the meaning of *anukīrtana*.

Here one may be a bit careful: Though *anukīrtana* may be rendered here as a 'representation' or imaging or mimicking, there is some qualification which makes us realize the immense underlying difference between the Aristotelian and Indian concepts.

The concept of *anukīrtana* is deeply rooted in the Agamic idea of *vāc*.[13]

Nāṭyaśāstra derives this illuminating idea of 'glorious retelling' (*anukīrtana*) of 'affective emotions' (*bhāva*) from the Vedic and Agamic view of *vāc* and thus explains the exclusive nature of not only Indian theatre, rather, for that matter, the nature of entire Indian literature and art forms.

We may confine ourselves, for facilitating the present discussion, to *nāṭya*, which has been specifically defined as *abhinaya* of *rasa* and *bhāva*.[14] Etymologically the term *abhinaya* is derived from the root *nī* to carry, with the prefix *abhi* in the sense of towards. Thus, *abhinaya* is the theatrical action expressive of *rasa* and *bhāva* carrying it to the spectator.

Śārṅgadeva, a medieval exponent of dance and music, therefore, defines *nāṭya* quite in consonance with the concept of Bharata and Abhinava, primarily as *rasa* and secondarily as *abhinaya*.[15] Thus, Sanskrit drama has all along been viewed in terms of *prayoga* or performance and in terms of *kriyā* or practice. Moreover, whatever is extrinsically *abhinaya*, it is intrinsically *rasa*. Thus, *nāṭya* is ultimately *rasa*. Yet in order to make the *sahṛdaya* experience the *rasa* through *bhāva*, *prayoktā* or the performer is required to delineate *bhāvas* [emotive states-lasting (*sthāyin*) as well as the fleeting ones (*sañcārins*), through the *vibhāvas* (the stimuli), a person with reference to whom a sentiment arises (*ālambana*) and the natural and necessary connection of a sentiment with the cause which excites it (*uddīpana*), (*anubhāvas* – the facial and bodily, expressions consequential to emotive states)]. Thus, *abhinaya* is made possible. This is the reason why after the exposition of the *rasa* and *bhāvas*, exposition of *abhinaya* takes place in *Nāṭyaśāstra*.

Since *nāṭya* is primarily a body-language, hence *āṅgika* comes first. A very broad treatment has been given to *āṅgikābhinaya*. The *āṅgika* is loaded with several layers of contextual meaning which can be understood in terms of the whole spectrum of the Indian tradition from the mystical and the speculative to the ritualistic and the purely physical. This contextual framework of Bharata is an essential prerequisite for understanding the seemingly simple and arbitrary aphoristic, classification of the body and their 'uses' and 'usages' for expressing the emotions and situations.

After clearly defining the relationship of the 'expressive' and 'expressed' of the corporeal language based on movement and rest in the chapters 8 to 12, *Nāṭyaśāstra* takes up the question of putting up this language into practice in chapters 22 and 25. Abhinavagupta very clearly expounds the significance of these two aspects in *Abhinavabhāratī* thereon.[16]

As in our life, the emotive states as well as the stimuli and the environment are almost intertwined, so does it happen in the realm of *abhinaya*. Although the complementary nature of the *sāmānya* and *citrābhinaya* may be clearly seen in any excellent performance of traditional *nāṭya* or *nṛtya*, the three-fold *sāmānyābhinaya* – particularly the *sāttvikābhinaya*, the *sūcā*, the *aṅkura* and the other kinds of *aṅgika sāmānyābhinaya* – is predominantly employed in expressing the *bhāvas*. *Sāmānyābhinaya* is employed for the portrayal of *bhāva* and *citrābhinaya* is the technique for the delineation of *vibhāva*.[17]

Thus, in our traditional *nāṭya*, *abhinaya* may be seen as *anukaraṇa* of the entire universe, which ultimately transcends the mimetic representation and attempts at 'metacreation' through the imagination on the basis of the conceived form and behaviour in order to 'retell' the *bhāva* (*anukīrtana* of *bhāva*). Therefore, traditional theatre may be better defined in terms of 'telling' rather than 'doing'.

In fact, *anukaraṇa* and *bhāvānukīrtana* may be viewed as functionally parallel to *abhidhā* and *vyañjanā*, some imitative reproduction based on and similar to *vācya-vācaka bhāva* (denotational relationship) is needed as the first step in dramatic performance.

But, if it is too similar to the real, it will appear too gross and create, at best, an illusion of the real. Such an attempt in art may be seen as corresponding to a matter-of-fact statement in ordinary life. On the other hand, retelling of the real through gestures, colours, lines, curves, notes and so on may be seen as parallel to *vyañjanā*. Pt. K.P. Narayana Pisharoti, translator of *Nāṭyaśāstra* in Malayalam, explained this fact to this author a few years ago.

THE PERVASIVENESS OF THE CONCEPT AND ITS CULMINATION INTO RASA

This idea of *anukīrtana* of *bhāva* is a pervasive one and permeates the entire universe of Indian arts including dance, drama, literature, sculpture, paintings, architecture and music, etc. This *anukīrtana*, as the delineation of stimuli, situation and the emotions, culminates into the ultimate *rasa*. It is a journey from temporal and spatial to that which goes beyond time and space. It starts with the vivid delineation of relationship and then transcends it. In other words, it is transcending the multiplicity and merging into the unfragmented 'whole'. Entire traditional Indian philosophy strives for a leading from discursive knowledge (*vikalpa*) to a non-discursive one (*nirvikalpa*). Indian arts do the same, but in a different and a more spontaneous way.

Sanskrit *nāṭya* has been a means of realizing most intense, immediate, direct and concrete aesthetic experience, i.e., *rasa* through the *anukīrtana* of *bhāva*. This *anukīrtana* of *bhāva* in theatre is a holistic art-process, hence, it requires both music as well as dance as its integral elements in order to infuse delight (*rañjana*) and beauty (*śobhā*). The effect of the music may be seen in an instant and immediate experience of delight while dance instils certain amount of stylized beauty in the visual action and behaviour. The manner in which the performer elaborates the *bhāva* and the surroundings given in the theatrical text through movement, gesture, facial expression, songs and music, lies at the heart of *rasa*-aesthetic system. The difference betweem Indian and Western modes of presentations has been brilliantly analyzed in the following statement:

> Rather than acting out on stage an important action as is usual in Western drama – the death of a character, for example – in Sanskrit practice the character is shown reacting to that action. The performer mirrors in ever more elaborate patterns the chain of emotional responses which an action triggers. Dramatic form and theatrical technique, it could be said, are designed to reveal and to express emotional states, and it is the audience response to those emotional states that is Rasa.[18]

In fact, poetry or drama springing from the awareness that the primary human impulse is to imitate, emerging from the ontological postulation that our universe is the universe of duality or multiplicity and the basic concept of time as a linear and irreversible one, definitely stresses action, character, situation and above all conflict. It also stresses the ultimate and creative experience as being of the nature of 'understanding' the self and the forces of change in life. It is not accidental that the Western thought of theatre assumes new height in the Brecht's concept of theatre, where theatre becomes a vehicle of not only knowing life, but knowing for the sake of changing it. His idea of theatre helps achieve this objective of 'understanding'. On the other hand, there is the traditional Indian view of arts and aesthetics of *rasa*. In spite of the social and historical changes reflected in the Sanskrit plays and in spite of its dynamism, Sanskrit drama could preserve its essential nature and its links with the Sanskrit theatre traditions till the first half of the nineteenth century.

Although *nāṭya* as *kriyā* is creative *anukīrtana* of the *bhāva*, yet Bharata, at the same time, views *nāṭya* as the *anukaraṭa* of the 'three-fold universe' and the seven continents (*sapta-dvīpa*). But this Indian concept of *anukaraṇa* may be distinguished from the Greek concept of 'mimesis' in terms of its capacity to create a new world, whereas mimesis represents the world. In the Indian concept of *anukaraṇa*, "the model is forgotten as soon as the creation is complete".[19]

Abhinava upholds the view of his celebrated teacher, Bhaṭṭatauṭa that no recreation of the original historical 'Rāma' is possible as the actor only retells the historical or the present reality in traditional Indian theatre in a glorious way. Moreover, *nāṭya* is the celebration of reality.

Thus, *nātya* may be viewed experientially as *rasa*. While *anukīrtana* of the *bhāvas* is a creative act in the sense of *kriyā*, *rasa* is an experience (*anubhāva*) of the 'Self, as *vimarśaṇa* ('I' consciousness), the subtlest, the most intrinsic, indivisible, fundamental, fullest and purest aspect of the *kriyā* (activity) as *śakti* potentiality lying dormant in our consciousness.

All particular experiences in our ordinary life subjectively and objectively arise out of the foundational consciousness (*saṃvit*) through specific ideational determinations (*adhyavasāya* or *vikalpa*). Therefore, all the experiences in arts, at the outset delineate the same ordinary life and relationship, yet ultimately culminate in the *rasa*-experience which is the same foundational and aesthetic 'I' consciousness. Moreover, Bharata defines *nāṭya* as expressive of *kāvyārtha* (poetic meaning), i.e., *rasa*, and distinguishes it from 'pure' *nṛtya* (dance), which is independent of *kāvyārtha*. It is in this sense that *nṛtta* may be termed as 'non-representational' art form and *nāṭya* as a 'representational' one.

Bharata declares, "Nothing proceeds on the stage without reference to *rasa*."[20] He and his commentators emphasize that when all the components of the drama beginning with *vibhāva* (the cause of the 'emotive states' and the environment in which they take place), *anubhāva* (the 'consequents' expressive of those 'emotive states'), etc., are presented, the realization of *rasa* manifests itself in the spectator. Similarly, when any element required for the manifestation of *rasa* is missing, the *rasa* realization is rendered difficult, indirect, or incomplete.

Since cosmic multiplicity was created through the primordial act of sacrifice, therefore, unity may be regained through the same sacrificial act, freeing the self from its spatial and temporal limitations. The same creative act takes place in the sphere of aesthetic experience. The *sahṛdaya* (aesthete) of traditional Indian art, literature and theatre attains repose in his deeper 'Self' (*ātmaviśrānti*) for a moment and experiences *rasa* after having transcended the duality of relationship seen in temporal and spatial differentiations. It is an experience in which we move beyond ordinary temporality and spatiality, an experience which begins with the awareness of the 'relationship', but ultimately transcends it. However, the experience of Western art form is confined to the awareness of either affirmation or negation of a specific relationship, and is therefore entirely different from its Indian counterpart.

Art forms in which one has to transcend the temporal and spatial differentiations manifested in the world of relationship offer a very different aesthetic experience. Although in such art forms, one begins with the delineation of the *vibhāvas*, *anubhāvas* as well as *sañcāribhāva*s (relatively fleeting emotions), and the *sthāyibhāvas* (lasting or permanent emotions), the point of culmination is *sādhāraṇīkaraṇa* (de-personalization, universalization) in which these *vibhāvas*, etc. neither appear belonging or not belonging to the aesthete, nor belonging or not belonging to others (either an enemy or a friend or someone quite different), for there is neither affirmation nor negation of the specific relationship at the stage of universalisation.

It is an *anuvyavasāya* (re-perception and recognition). *Rasa* is, thus, awareness of the unfragmented Self or *ātmaviśrānti*, repose in the Self. Hence, it is wonderful. It is known by such synonyms as relishing (*rasa*, *rasana*, *āsvādana*), mastication (*carvaṇā*), flash of wonder (*camatkāra*), immersion (*nirveśa*), and enjoyment (*bhoga*).[21]

Ancient Indian culture experienced an integral view of creativity and aesthetic experience in this concept of theatre, that has its basis in the holistic view of the universe and in the circular concept of time.

It is not ultimately imitating and repeating the 'other'; rather it is retelling the 'becoming'.

COMPLEMENTARITY OF THE TWO CONCEPTS OF BHĀVĀNUKĪRTANA AND RASA

The complementarity of the two concepts may be made clear from the fact that Bharata offers two different analogies of the 'concept of *rasa*'. The first analogy of *sādava rasa*[22] illustrates the process of *vibhāvānubhāva vyabhicārisaṃyoga* giving rise to a unique and new experience, i.e., *rasa* which is manifested in the heart of the spectator of drama, whereas second analogy of 'seminal *rasa*' (*bījasthānīyah kavigato rasaḥ*)[23] and the *rasa* as emerging into a tree and offering its fruit illustrates the unity of experience from poet to the spectators through the play.

The creative process emerges from the *rasa*-experience of the poet/artist and is concretized in the *anukīrtana* of *bhāva* through the delineation of *vibhāva*, *anubhāva*, etc. in the dramatic text or the work of art-poetry, paintings, sculpture, etc. But the emergence of *rasa* in the heart of connoisseur of art depends upon the 'delineation of *vibhāva*', etc. It can never be brought about 'denotatively through just citing the term *śṛṅgāra* and so on.

Thus, *rasa* experience in the spectator depends upon the 'glorious retelling of *bhāva*'.

This inter-dependence of each other explains the complementary nature of both the concepts.

Such an understanding of *rasa* not only embraces all the aspects needed for a complete aesthetic theory which explains satisfactorily the questions of the ontological nature of work of art, the creative process and the aesthetic experience, but presents a profound and pervasive vision of Indian aesthetics. Dhvanivadins visualized all these aspects present seminally in *Nāṭyaśāstra* and developed it in their works in the light of philosophy of grammar on one hand and Trika philosophy on the other. Abhinava's interpretation is a testimony to this fact in the dramatic text or the work of art, i.e., poetry, paintings, sculpture, etc. But the emergence of *rasa* in the heart of connoisseur of art depends upon the 'delineation of *vibhāva*'. It can never be brought about denotatively through just citing the term *śṛṅgāra* and so on.

Traditional Indian theatre and, in fact, the entire traditional work of art, may be ultimately defined as '*bhāvānukīrtana*' in terms of creative process and it may be seen as *rasa* in terms of 'aesthetic experience'. The work of art is simultaneously 'a glorious retelling of emotive states'.

NOTES AND REFERENCES

1. Kamalesh Datta Tripathi, *Sanskrit Theatre*, Sriram Centre for Performing Arts, New Delhi, 1998, p. 17.
2. *Matsyapurāṇa*, Venkateshwar Press, Bombay, 1895, Colophon of Chapter 261 – *'iti mātsye mahāpurāṇe devatārccānukīrtana ...'*
3. Denabandhu Pandey, *Devatārccānukīrtana: Hindu Devapratimā-vijñāna*, Kishora Vidya Niketana, Varanasi, 1978, pp. 6-7.
4. Ranierio Gnoli, *The Aesthetic Experience According to Abhinavagupta*, Chaukhamba Sanskrit Series, Varanasi, 1995, pp. 88-101.
5. *Nāṭyaśāstra*, Baroda edn., 1956, Chapter I, Verse 107, p. 35.
6. Ibid., Ch. I, Verse 117, p. 42.
7. Ibid., p. 35.
8. Ibid., p. 35.
9. Ibid., p. 36.
10. Ibid., pp. 36-37.
11. *'Kaveśca niyata-varṇanīyatve Kāvyasyaivā sampatte-ranaucitya-Varjanāyogāt'*, ibid., p. 37.
12. Earliest reference to this meaning of *kīrtana* is found in Bāṇa. Vāsudeva Śaraṇa Agrawala has already drawn our attention to the significance of this notion. See *Kīrti, Kīrtimukha, Kīrtistambha, Kīrtana, Studies in Indian Arts*, Vishvavidyalaya Prakashan, Varanasi, pp. 241-48. Tradition has retained this meaning in the texts unfolding the purpose of making *mahanāgas* and *virāla siṁha* in order to protect *Kīrti*, See *Śilparatnakośa*, IGNCA, New Delhi, pp. 80, 84.
13. *Vākyapadīya*, the celebrated work of Vyākaraṇa Āgama, understands *vāc* as inherently present in all the knowledge (*jñāna*) and postulates *vāc* as *pratyavamarśinī* which is at the root of all the *śilpas* (crafts) and *kalās* (arts). See *Vākyapadīya*, Brahmakāṇḍa, verses 123, 124, 125 and auto commentary thereon, Sampurnanand Sanskrit University edn., 1998, Vol. I, pp. 183-88.

    Vāc is identified again with the 'conciousness' in all beings in the next verse. Traditions of *trika* and *traipura āgamas* unfold this philosophy in a brilliant way.
14. *Nāṭyaśāstra*, Chapter I, verse 119, Baroda edn., Vol. I, p. 42.
15. *'nāṭya-śabdo rase mukhyo, rasābhivyakti-kāraṇam, caturdhābhinayopetam, lakṣanāvṛttito budaiḥ. nartanam nāṭyam-ityuktam.'* Saṅgītaratnākara, Chapter VII, Nartanādhyāya, Verses 17-18.
16. *Nāṭyaśāstra*, Baroda edn., Vol. III, pp. 146-48.
17. Ibid., p. 264.
18. V. Raghavan, *Sanskrit Drama in Performance*, The University Press of Hawaii, Honololu, 1981, p. 44.
19. Bharat Gupta, *The Dramatic Concepts: Greek and Indian*, New Delhi, 1994, p. 98.
20. *Nāṭyaśāstra*, Baroda edn., p. 272.

21. Ibid., *Abhi.bha*. p. 37.
22. Ibid., Vol. I, pp. 287-90.
23. Ibid., Vol. I, p. 294, text and *Abhinavabhāratī;* thereon.

8

Metaphysical and Psychological Approach to Rasa by Abhinavagupta and Viśvanātha

Biswanarayan Shastri

Bharata's *Nāṭyaśāstra* is the earliest[1] available treatise on dramaturgy and literary criticism, which gives the definition of *rasa* or flavour. The definition of *rasa* runs: *"vibhāva anubhāva-vyabhicāri saṃyogad-rasa niṣpattiḥ."*[2] Though this definition of *rasa* appears to be simple and precise and has been accepted by all subsequent rhetoricians, they differ widely in providing meaning of the terms *saṃyoga*, contact or combination, and *niṣpatti*, realization or experience. One may render into English the above-mentioned Sanskrit *sutra* thus:

> *Vibhāva*, the exciting mood or the element which causes that mood, in combination with *anubhāva*, the accessary mood and *vyabhicārī*, the transient mood makes completion of *rasa*. Such a rendering is crude and does not reflect what the *sūtra* is intended to mean, observe the commentators.

The different interpretations given by different commentators and the stands taken by them have given rise to the presumption that *rasa* theory was conceived and discussed even prior to Bharata.[3] We are concerned with the post-Bharata position and particularly to Abhinavagupta's (c. 10th AD) doctrine of *rasa*.

Of the commentators on *Nāṭyaśāstra*, the theories propounded on *rasa* by Bhaṭṭalollaṭa (c. 9th AD), Śri Śaṅkuka (c. 9th AD), Bhaṭṭanāyaka (c. 9th AD) and Bhaṭṭatauṭa (c. 11th AD) have been quoted in *Abhinavabhāratī*, the commentary by Abhinavagupta. The works by the above-mentioned authors were lost and the scholars are totally dependent on what has been quoted in *Abhinavabhāratī*. It is not absolutely clear if Abhinava quoted them verbatim or expressed their views only, and scholars have not paid due attention to this aspect. A reference may be made to a piece of quotation in *Vivaraṇaṭīkā* on *Kāvyaprakāśa*, which differs from what is quoted in the *Abhinavabhāratī* as belongs to Śri Śaṅkuka. The gist of the statement is – when an actor plays Rāma and imitates the sentiment of Rāma, the spectators realize it as their own; the meaning of *rasa niṣpatti* is inference of *sthāyibhāva* as *rasa*.[4]

The views of the commentators could be understood in the prevailing philosophical doctrines, mainly *Mīmāṃsā*, *Sāṃkhya*, *Nyāya* and Kaśmīra Śaivism.

The causation theory of *Nyāya-Vaiśeṣika*, the transformation of *Sāṃkhya*, and monism of *Vedānta* and *Śivādvaita* had their influence on postulation of *rasa* theory and arriving at the conclusion. The discussion on the nature of aesthetic experience on reciting a *kāvya* or witnessing a dramatic performance resembles that of philosophical theories.

It is to be noted that Bharata's definition of *rasa* suggests that *rasa* is to be realized or experienced, that is in respect of dramatic performance where there are three entities, namely, the heroes of the theme, the actors and the spectators. In a *kāvya* these three are reduced to two, the heroes of the theme and the reader. If the dramatist comes to the scene, the dramatic performance has four entities and a *kāvya* has three, but the dramatist is not counted. Bharata's definition of rasa is in respect of drama, which, later on has been transferred to *kāvya*, and drama it seemed, was pushed to a secondary stage.

Bhaṭṭarūdraṭa (c. AD 850) states this tendency of shifting emphasis:

prāyo nāṭyam prati proktā bharatādyaiḥ rasasthitiḥ/
yathāmati mayāpyeṣā kāvyaṃ prati nigadyate//[5]

This provides a clue to the interpretation of *rasa* by Bhaṭṭalollaṭa, the foremost commentator of *Nāṭyaśāstra*. Bhaṭṭalollṭa posits, "where is *rasa* and where does it reside?" He states that *rasa* is not in the visual and verbal presentation of a theme by an author or an actor; *rasa* is an idea. What idea is represented? The real Rāma? The actor, who plays Rāma? Rāma, the described one? Or, the painted one? The reply is: it is an abstract idea of Rāma, which is conceived by the author or the actor. He identifies this idea for creating a condition in the mind which seems to be real and to drive home the point. Bhaṭṭalolloṭa's view may be presented like this – the *rasa* emerges in the mind of *anukārya* (who is imitated), meaning the dramatic personae. The actor imitates the sentiment of Rāma as has been described and he realizes or experiences *rasa*. Thus, *rasa* is experienced by *naṭa* and the spectators do not matter.

Utpalācārya (c. 9th AD), the author *Īśvarapratyabhijñā-kārikā*, mentions a term *pūrvābhāsa-yojanā* which conveys the sense of incipient-experience and refined sensibility to state the highest form of Śiva. Bhaṭṭalollaṭa uses the argument for experiencing aesthetic artistic presentation and its experience.

Bhaṭṭalollaṭa's views could be gathered in what is quoted by Abhinavagupta. Bhaṭṭalollaṭa, as quoted, says: *anubhāvāśca na rasajanyā atra vivakṣitā, teṣāṃ rasakāraṇatvena gaṇanārthatvāt api tu bhāvānāmeva*. This means *anubhāva* is not a cause for experiencing *rasa*; inconsistent emotiveness *vyabhicāri* makes *rasa* to emerge when associated with the permanent sentiment or *sthāyibhāva*.

Śri Śaṅkuka, the main opponent of Lollaṭa, criticizes Lollaṭa's theory on *rasa* and advances a new theory, which is known traditionally as *anumitivāda*, that *rasa* could be realized or experienced by inference. Śri Śaṅkuka utilizes arguments of logic relating to cause-effect theory. He says that if the *sthāyibhāva* is already existent, then the theory of causation does not arise, and if it is not existent then its association with *vibhāva* is impossible because two existent entities may combine. Thus, the causation theory stands refuted.

Śri Śaṅkuka's theory of *rasa* can be stated here briefly. The *sthāyibhāva* of the hero is imitated by an actor and he realizes the experience of the sentiment which is transferred to the spectators. He compares this experience with the experience that is gained on seeing a painted horse (*citra turaga*). That a painted horse is not a real horse, and not a non-horse, nor similar to a real horse. This is non-realization which is devoid of contact with the outside entities (*vedyāntara-sparśaśūnya*), a realization which is neither real, nor unreal, nor similar to the real. The same way when the spectators observe an actor playing Rāma, he realizes that he is neither Rāma nor non-Rāma nor similar to Rāma. In short, Rāma's emotion as imitated by the actor, which appears as *rasa* in the mind of the actor, is transferred to the spectators. He says the meaning of *rasaniṣpatti* is, *rasa* is inferred. Śri Śaṅkuka's theory has been opposed by Bhaṭṭanāyaka, Abhinavagupta and others. Bhaṭṭatauṭa, *guru* of Abhinava, has also advanced his views in *kāvyakautuka* on drama and its performance.

Abhinava rejects the theory of Śri Śaṅkuka on imitation by saying that it is impossible to imitate sentiment of the hero (*anukārya*) and it is also impossible that the spectators imitate the sentiment of the actor, because by imitating others one becomes a laughing stock.

> *para-ceṣṭānu-karaṇād hāsaḥ samudpajāyate*, says Bharata.

It is impossible to imitate *ālambanavibhāva* or *uddīpanavibhāva*. Moreover, what is imitated? Body movements are imitated. It is wrong. Love, anger, sorrow are the instincts or permanent sentiments of human being which cannot be imitated. No *cittavṛtti* of an entity could be an object for imitation. Nobody knows how Rāma expressed his sorrow on his separation from Sītā. Thus Abhinavagupta refutes the theory of Śri Śaṅkuka by shifting emphasis from the outward or visible aspect to the psychic sphere, and propounds his theory of experiencing *rasa*.

Bhaṭṭanāyaka advances a new theory of *rasa* which is known as *Bhojakatvavādu* in the traditional circle. He says that *rasa* is neither perceived nor caused nor manifested. It is to be enjoyed by the process of *bhāvakatva* and *bhojakatva-vṛttis*, which follow the *abhidhā-vṛtti* of works. His view is:

> first the words of literature and in the presentation of a drama appear as they are and understood. Then by the operation of *bhāvakatva-vṛtti* the entire episode appears as common to all human being, which is different from manifestation, feeling and remembrance. The process of *bhāvakatva* is not an ordinary psychological state.[6]

Bhojakatva-vṛtti, which makes rasa to be experienced, causes *sattva-guṇa* to appear prominently by suppressing the other two, *rajas* and *tamas*, and this is the condition for *rasa* realization. This is *bhogī-karaṇa* or *sādhāraṇikaraṇa*, i.e., rendering the sentiment universal, free from individual relation. This is like the realization of Brahmā, absolute. According to this view, realisation of *rasa* is not a psychological affair of an individual. Thus, Bhaṭṭanāyaka has stated that it cannot be said that *rasa* is perceived or cognized if *rasa* is caused to emerge or *rasa* is manifested. Bhaṭṭanāyaka's metaphysics clearly follows the monistic *Vedānta* and presents the world as a phenomenal one. It is seen that Abhinavagupta accepted the *sādhāraṇīkaraṇa* concept presented by Bhaṭṭanāyaka.

When such aesthetic discussion was going on in full swing, and the different views were vigorously propagated, there appeared Abhinavagupta (c. 10th AD), the towering personality with his deep knowledge of Kashmir, and Śaivism and Tāntrik practices. Abhinavagupta had the views of the commentators who preceded him and also the exposition on drama by his *guru* Bhaṭṭatauṭa, and senior contemporaries like Bhaṭṭainduraja and others. Abhinava's commentary on Ānandavardhana's *Dhvanyāloka* may be seen as an attempt to redefine the *Dhvani* theory, which was criticized and demolished by Bhaṭṭanāyaka. Though *Dhvanyāloka-locana* and *Abhinavabhāratī* survived, Bhaṭṭanāyaka's original work *Hṛdayadarpaṇa* was till date not available to us. Abhinavagupta has commented on all aspects of Bharata's *Nāṭyaśāstra*. However, we are concerned with his *rasa* theory as may be gathered from his comments on *Nāṭyaśāstra's rasaniṣpatti*. Abhinava with his deep knowledge of the *Vedānta* philosophy, practice of mystic Tantra and having faith in *Śivādvaita*, with the skill of a commentator and an insight of an art critic states that for perceptual individual experience, the perception of universal is absolutely necessary. Thus, Abhinava places the psychological individual experiences as the pivot for *rasāsvāda* which is a universal experience. The attempt to describe the theory of *rasa* by Abhinava in few pages appears to be an impossible proposition. However, Abhinava extends the principle of propounding a relation of self (*Jīva*) with the absolute or universe (*Brahma*) to the aesthetic pleasure. Though the absolute is self-luminous, it is not self-conscious. As against this, *Śivādvaita* doctrine admits that absolute (may be called Maheśvara) is not only self-luminous but self-conscious and dynamic also. In the commentary by Abhinava on *rasa* these two different principles, which do not agree, except the self-luminousness of absolute, could be seen.

Abhinavagupta states that after one understands the meaning of a *kāvya*, there appears something new, which is perceived by the mind. Such a perception is free from the limit of space and time and individuality, and this is a new perception. As it is free from limitation, the perception is perfect.

S.N. Dasgupta explains the process of universalisation as follows:

> The constitutive words of *kāvya* produce in the mind of the proper reader something novel, something that is over and above the meaning of the poem. After the actual meaning is comprehended there is an intuition by virtue of which the spatio-temporal reaction of particularity that is associated with all material events disappear and state of universalisation is attained.

Citing the instance of the deer in the hermitage of Kaṇva hotly chased by Duṣyanta with the bow fixed with an arrow, Abhinava says that the fear though has its root in the deer after its appearance as individual, it loses its individuality and becomes universal. Thus, the pure fear sentiment becomes completely different from the ordinary worldly fear sentiment of the individuals, because it is not mixed with other human sentiment. *"tathāvidhe hi bhaye nāṭyantam ātmā tiraskṛto na viśeṣatayā ullikhitaḥ."*

In this world, the incidents which are associated with an individual are linked with each other by some relation, or, one takes place following the other (*anusyūta*), and if the relation disappears causing fall of one or more incident, the entire system disappears from mind. The same way when the king Duṣyanta and the deer disappear, the resultant fear loses its character and it attains the universal character from the individual one. Thus, the fear psychic which is experienced by *sahṛdayas* is a common one, which is manifested after its association with the eternal desire of pleasure inherent in the mind of spectators or reciters.

It may be further said that *sādhāraṇīkaraṇa* or universal nature of a sentiment has two aspects, first the sentiment, say, fear as stated above appears as one, and the second the same in the mind of all the spectators or reciters as one common sentiment without any distinction, *"ata eva sarva-sāmājika-janānām ekaghanatayaiva pratipattiḥ-sutarām rasa-paripoṣāya sarveṣāmeva anādi-vāsanā-citrīkṛta-cetaṣāṃ vāsanā saṃvādāt."* Further, the common sentiment when mixed with eternal instinct does reach the stage of *rasa*-experience; it may be experienced or tasted when a new aesthetic consciousness arises. The new aesthetic experience is free from all limitations and causes. This consciousness is named *camatkāra*. This *camatkāra* is a new element in the *rasa* experience and has been defined differently. We may call it a particular condition of mind, that is aesthetic attitude of mind. *Camatkāra*, which is identical with the appearance of new aesthetic consciousness, is an action of mind. However, Abhinavagupta has not clearly stated what is the psychological state or how it exists in the mind. He says that this may be termed as perception, a kind of definite action (*niścayātmikā vṛtti*), an action of recollection, a resolute action, or simply an appearance (*sphūrti*). (*sa ca sākṣātkāra-svabhāvo mānasādhyavasāyo vā saṅkalpo vā smṛtir vā sākṣātkāra-svabhāvo'yam*).

Although this is an appearance but how appearance takes place cannot be explained or understood. If an attempt is made to describe the process, it relates to time, space and individual. Like ordinary happening it is neither of this world, nor false, nor can it be termed as beyond the description by words, etc. Abhinavagupta further says that in ordinary process the stream of thought is bound to face obstacle or hindrances and therefore not free from limitation in expression. In a *kāvya* or drama the thought (*bhāva*) is expressed freely without any interruption, hindrance or obstacle and turned into *rasa* which could flood the mind of the spectators, and that is the stage when *camatkāra* of *rasa* appears. He extends his argument further which explains the difference of ordinary perception and the perception that takes place on witnessing a drama. For a perception for instance, the sense perception needs an entity for cognition; here in the perception of *rasa*, mother entity disappears, the persons whose activity causes the perception are no more there and thus only *nirālamba* sense persist, which may be termed as universal ideal content. Thus, it does not depend on others for its existence, nor does it depend on the self who perceives. Thus, when all expected and usual impediments disappear, the new aesthetic sense appears in the *citta* and mixes with the eternal *vāsanā* and aesthetic pleasure is experienced (*hṛdaya samvādo lokasāmānya-vastuviṣayaḥ*). For experiencing an aesthetic pleasure no instrumentality of sense organs is needed; it is a function of mind, which is similar to spirituality.

Kapila Vatsyayana sums up the concept of *rasa* by Abhinavagupta:

> The aesthetic experience is *ānanda*, reechoing the Taittiryā Upanṣad's dictum of *raso vai saḥ*. Like the absolute it is self-luminous and self-conscions, devoid of all duality and multiplicity; it emerges from a single unified source which has the potency of multiplicity. The aesthetic experience is different from any ordinary experience as it is not based on objective perception, but is a subjective experience and realization. Its nature is *alaukika* (transmundane) and is akin or anologous to the mystic experience.[7]

This position of universalization can be stated by following Abhinava like this:

> An aesthetic composition by its very nature presents all aesthetic situation which is emotion, devoid of all its local characters. The other aesthetic character presents an universal character in manifestation in different minds. This mingles with the various subconscious or unconscious feeling lying dormant in the mind of spectators.

Vatsyayana further states that the term *camatkāra* is taken from Utpalācāraya's work by Abhinavagupta which he "elaborates on its metaphysical and aesthetic implication". *Camatkāra* is self-conscious of the self, free from all limitations and is also luminous; is not self-conscious.

Viśvanātha, a follower of Abhinavagupta and Ānandavardhana, shapes his *Sāhitya-darpaṇa* after the structure of Mammaṭa's *Kāvyaprakāśā*. He defines *rasa* that *sthāyibhāva* or the permanent sentiment such as love, etc., which after its proper association with *vibhāva*, *anubhāva* and *sañcāribhāva*, is mainfested as *rasa* in the mind of *sahṛdaya*.[9] Here he mentions *sthāyibhāva*, the permanent sentiment. Mammaṭa's *rasa* definition also mentions *sthāyibhāva*, which Viśvanātha imitates.[10]

He further clarifies his position by explaining what the word *vyakta* or manifestation means, that is experienced. Flavour is a kind something made manifest in different characters to which it is changed just as curd or the like consists of milk. He further supports his use of the word *vyakta*, that he does not mean to say that something previously completed and previously so extant like a pot which becomes visible in the light. The expression that *rasa* is being experienced is to be understood like the *odanam pacyate* and quotes Locanakāra Abhinavagupta, the commentator on *Dhvanyāloka*.

In short, Viśvanātha following Abhinavagupta states that when *rajas* and *tamas* – the two qualities of *citta* – are suppressed and *sattva* quality comes into prominence, at that stage the real *ātman* or consciousness becomes the only element, and this is identified with *ānandamaya* stage. At such a moment the sense of self disappears, one may realize *Brahma*, and the *rasa* realization is similar to this. It is to be noted that while Abhinavagupta following Śaiva *Pratyābhijñā* would call it omnipotent *aham*, i.e., Sadāśiva, Viśvanātha would perhaps call it universal entity, the absolute. Like Abhinavagupta he also raised the concept of *rasa* or precisely *rasasvādana* to the highest possible level of human conception. The observers will not miss the point that Viśvanātha uses the expression *sattvodreka*, i.e., exaltation of mind is main condition – precedent for association of permanent sentiment. The expression *sattvodreka* is first used by Bhaṭṭanāyaka and though his theory of *bhojakatva* has been rejected by Abhinavagupta, he has accepted Nayaka's theory of *'prakāś-ānandamaya-nijasaṃvid viśrāntih.'*

The meaning conveyed by this expression is that *rasa* is to be accepted as self-manifested one and it is by its inherent nature *ānandamaya* which can be realized or experienced by a self with his own intellect. How *ānanda* could be realized or experienced is not explained and Viśvanātha simply says it is conceived in the same manner as *Brahmopalabdhi* or realization of the absolute and he directs the questioners to those who advocate and establish *Brahmopalabdhi*. Viśvanātha says that the term permanent sentiment is mentioned not tautologically but in reliance of the maxim *'exceptio prabat regulam'* with a view to declaring that these sentiments are not necessarily main in other sentiments. Viśvanātha simplifies the meaning of the term *camatkāra* and he explains it as which could be used as the spirit of *rasa*. It has been defined as 'lighting flash' by Anandakumarasvami, and S.N. Dasgupta calls it 'self-flashing of thought' and the author mentions Narayana who defined *camatkāra*.

The objection raised by Mahimabhaṭṭa that if *rasa* is accepted as manifested one by *vyañjanā*, that *rasa* cannot be a self-luminous one. Viśvanātha treats this objection by saying that *rasa* is neither something that is created nor an object which could be made into manifestation. *Rasa* is a process of realization or enjoyment.

Viśvanātha is very clear in his definition of *rasa* and states that it neither belongs to self nor non-self. He has not stated how *sattvodreka* relates to mental perception and how non-self concept of knowledge could be defined, as objective or subjective sense.

NOTES AND REFERENCES

1. Bharata or Bharatamuni is credited with the authorship of *Nāṭyaśastra*. Some scholars are of the opinion that *Nāṭyaśastra* is not the product of one author. The date of Bharata is uncertain; he may be placed in the first century BC or first or second century AD.
2. *Nāṭyaśastra*, Chap. 6.
3. S.N., Dasgupta, *Kāvyavicāra*, (Beng.), p. 56.
4. Ibid., p. 65.
5. *Śṛṅgāratilaka*, 1.5.
6. *abhidhā bhāvanā cānyā tad bhogikṛtimeva ca/*
   tadbhogikṛta rūpena vyāpyate sidhimānnaraḥ//
   Bhaṭṭnāyaka quoted in *Abhinavabhāratī*.
7. Kapila Vatsyayan, *Bharata: The Nāṭyaśastra*, pp. 150-51.
8. Ibid.
9. *Sāhityadarpṇa*, 3.1.
10. *Kāvyaprakāśa*, 4.27, 28.

BIBLIOGRAPHY

Abhinavagupta, *Abhinavabhāratī* on *Nāṭyaśastra Locana*, a commentary of *Dhvanyāloka*.

Ānandavardhana, *Dhvanyāloka*.

Bhāmaha, *Kāvyalaṃkāra*, edited by B. Sarma and B. Upadhyaya, Chowkhamba Sanskrit Series, Varanasi.

Dandin, *Kāvyādarśa*, edited by N. Sastri.

Dasgupta, S.N., *Kavyavicar* (Beng), Chirayata Prakashan, Calcutta.

——, *A History of Indian Philosophy* (reprint 1996), Cambridge, 1960.

Dasgupta, S.N. and S.K. De, *A History of Sanskrit Literature*, Calcutta University, Calcutta.

De, S.K., *History of Sanskrit Poetics*, Firma K.L. Mukhopadhyaya, Calcutta, 1960.

Dhananjaya, *Dasurūpaka with Avaloka commentary*.

Gnoli, R., *The Aesthetic Experience According to Abhinavagupta*, Motilal Banarsidass, Delhi.

Induraja Bhaṭṭa, *Kāvya-kautuka-Sara-Sangraha*.

Keith, A.B., *The Aiteraya Ārṇyaka*, Ed. & Trans. Oxford, 1939.

Krishnamurthy. K., *Dhvanyāloka and its Critics*, Kavyalaya Publishers, Mysore, 1968.

Macdonell, A.A., *History of Sanskrit Literature*. Munshiram Manoharlal, Delhi, 1962.
Mahimabhaṭṭa, *Vyaktiviveka*, Chowkhamba, Varanasi.
Pandey, K.C., *Comparative Aethestics*, Vol. I & II, Chowkhamba Sanskrit Series, Varanasi.
Utpala-bhaṭṭa, *Iśvara-pratyabhijñā*.
Vatsyayana, Kapila, *Bharata: The Nāṭyaśāstra*, Sahitya Akademi, New Delhi, 1995.
Viśvanātha Kavirāja, *Sāhitya-Darpaṇa* with *Sanskrit Commentary*, Calcutta.
Mitra, P., *Sāhityadarpaṇa*, Eng. Trans., Calcutta.

9

The Problem of Śāntarasa

V. Kutumba Sastry

One of the most significant contributions of Abhinavagupta is his elaborate and scholastic development of the doctrine of *śāntarasa*. While Abhinavagupta is, by all standards, the brightest star in the galaxy of writers on Indian aesthetics and poetics, his doctrine of *śāntarasa* reaffirms the fact that the Indian mind-set always moves towards spiritualism in all aspects of human life. The establishment of *śānta* as the ninth *rasa* makes it clear that spiritualism in India influenced the domain of aesthetics also. *Śāntarasa* has been subjected to a great deal of discussion. The discussion took place in-between two extreme positions: some holding that *śānta* can never be accepted as *rasa* and others holding that *śānta* is the only *rasa* from which all *rasas*, indeed, do arise. The discussion of *śāntarasa* has a greater fallout – indeed greater than *śāntarasa* itself – in the form of a meticulous and minute analysis of the experience of *rasa*-realization. Indeed, subtle nuances of the theory of *rasa*-realization came out while discussing the *śāntarasa*. The problem of *śāntarasa* comprises more than several problems within it. For example:

(1) Textual problems concerned with the question of authenticity of passage related to *śāntarasa* found in the *Nāṭyaśāstra of Bharatamuni* by Abhinavagupta.

(2) Practical problems concerned with the enactment of *śāntarasa* on the stage and its appeal to the people.
(3) Problems with regard to its *sthāyibhāva*.
(4) Doctrinal problems concerned with the explanation of the process of *rasa*-realization.
(5) Problems related with the illustrations of *śāntarasa* in Sanskrit literature.

In this paper, an attempt is made to throw some light on the last two sets of problems, as the first two sets of problems have been more or less settled by the researchers and with regard to both of them, the champions of *śāntarasa* are compelled to be on defensive. The opinion of the majority of the researchers with regard to the portion of text related to *śāntarasa* in the *Nāṭyaśāstra* is in favour of holding it as an interpolation. There is, indeed, a possibility of saying that Abhinavagupta himself, who made the said text available for us, expressed doubt about its authenticity. Abhinavagupta employs weak and defensive arguments regarding the problem of its appeal to the sensitive spectator saying how does it matter. Also, he finds its unfitness for enactment in a loose way. The problem of *sthāyibhāva* is, at best, an ancillary one and can be solved somehow or the other.

Thus, greater support for establishment of *śāntarasa* is derived from the analysis of the process of *rasa*-realization and its prevalence in the works of established writers. There too, the second one, namely, the prevalence of *śāntarasa* in the literary works of reputed authors, is a source for building the argument which is simple, straightforward, non-controversial to a large extent and not easy to set aside. Indeed, the efforts of establishing *śānta* as the ninth *rasa* gathered momentum only from the time of Ānandvardhana, who had built up an unassailable theory that *śānta* was the main *rasa* (*aṅgirasa*) in the *Mahābhārata*. It is held to be one of the masterpieces of literary criticism and a standard paradigm for others to follow. Abhinavagupta, the foremost champion of *śāntarasa*, too, derived inspiration to build the doctrine of *śāntarasa* only from the above discussion of Ānandavardhana, in spite of his well-known leaning towards philosophy. It is needless to elaborate the point how greatly Abhinavagupta admires Ānandavardhana.

How large is the corpus of literature with *śānta* as its predominant sentiment? First of all, we can cite the large corpus in the form of the Upaniṣads. It is possible because many serious readers and critics of the Upaniṣads have expressed their admiration towards them as examples of inspirational poetry too, notwithstanding their mainly being works of metaphysical teachings. They are considered to be the out-pourings from the hearts of the sages in their ecstasy of enjoying the sublime basis of self-realisation. Again, at the end of the development of scholastic *rasa* theory, a parallelism has been struck between the self-realization and *rasa*-realiztion. The elaborate discussion of the theory of *rasa*-realization culminated in accepting that the sensitive spectator (*sahṛdaya*) enjoys the literature as it helps him to reveal his own self, which is of the nature of bliss and bliss alone. This position is nothing but the explicit endorsement of the Upanisadic statement: *na hi jāyāyāḥ kāmāya jāyā priyā bhavati, ātmanastu kāmāya jāyā priyā bhavati*, etc., wherein it is stated that all the worldly objects of enjoyment happen to be so only on the ground that they cause the enjoyment of one's own self Ānandavardhana, has shown the way of treating the same book as *śāstra* and *kāvya* from two different points of view. He treats *Mahābhārata* as *śāstra* from the point of view of, as he calls it, *śāstrāyaya*. He treats it as a piece of art from the point of view of *kāvyanaya*. Therefore, the Upaniṣads can also be treated as books concerned with the metaphysical teaching and pieces of literature as well.

Ānandavardhana took the responsibility of establishing a theory that *śānta* is the main *rasa* in the *Mahābhārata*, which is the largest literary work. He views it as *śāstra* as well as *kāvya*. The purport of the *Mahābhārata* is to establish temporality of all objects and to instil the sense of withdrawal from the world in the hearts of the sensible readers through the narration of miserable extinction of the Vṛṣṇi and Pāṇḍava races. The *Mahābhārata*, seen as a *śāstra*, aims at establishing the supremacy of *mokṣa* amongst all other *puruṣārthas*. Seen as a *kāvya*, it aims at establishing *śānta* as the supreme sentiment. Vyāsa declares in clear terms:

yathā yathā viparyeti lokatantramasāravat /
tatha tatha virāgo'tra Jāyate nātra saṁśayaḥ / /

Just (as much) as worldly pursuits
Turn out to be unavailing,
One's sense of aversion to them will become firm;
There is no doubt at all.

Ānandavardhana bases his argument mainly on the effort of Vyāsa to conclude the long story by narrating the total extinction of both the great dynasties, namely, Vṛṣṇis and Pāṇḍavas. He observes that such an effort will cause aversion and despair towards worldly objects in the hearts of sensible readers. He draws out the suggestion of the statement: *bhagavān vāsudevaśca kīrtyate'tra sanātanaḥ* (Herein, forsooth, will be glorified Lord Vāsudeva too, the eternal) as pointing towards the distasteful and miserable end of the exploits of the Pāṇḍavas and others which fall under the realm of ignorance and the fact that Bhagavān Vasudeva alone is truth, reality and eternal. This, in turn, instructs in a suggestive way: "to be devoted in heart only to that supreme lord; not to remain attached to empty pleasures and not to be too intent upon excellencies even like statesmanship, modesty and valour just for their own sake!" The suggestive word 'ca' in the sentence quoted above makes the utter futility of worldly existence very clear. Ānandavardhana repeatedly says that the elaborate description of heroic activities of Pāṇḍavas do have purport in creating sense of aversion, renunciation and withdrawal ultimately in the heart of the sensible reader.

On the basis of the above observation and clear-cut analysis of Ānandavardhana, we may, by way of applying the same principle, say that the main sentiment in the *Raghuvaṃśa* of Kālidāsa too is *śānta*. Here also the intention of Kālidāsa must be to instil the sense of aversion, despair, futility and withdrawal in the minds of his readers as he too has narrated the story of Raghus till Agnivarṇa who has been described as possessing all opposite qualities to the various qualities possessed by all the kings in the lineage. Agnivarṇa is an anti-climax character as portrayed by Kālidāsa. He is totally opposite to Dilīpa, Raghu, Śri Rāma, Kuśa, Atithi and several others. "Why Kālidāsa should culminate his *kāvya* with Agnivarṇa and why not with anyone before him in the long line of virtuous kings?" is a moot question. No proper reply is available except the one given by Ānandavardhana in the case of the *Mahābhārata*. Therefore, it will not be improper on our part to conclude that *śānta* is the main *rasa* in the *Raghuvaṃśa* and all other rasas are subsidiary to it as in the case of the *Mahābhārata*. The episodes of Dilīpa's service to the Cow, Nandanī, dialogue between Kautsa and Raghu, the grief of Aja, the veiling of Ayodhya, also help to build the sentiment *śānta*. While the introductory verses in the first canto portray the ideal kingly-hood on the basis of *śama* and *śānta*, Agnivarṇa's episode at the end portrays the impermanence and non-eternality of the entire world.

The presence of the element of *śāntarasa* in the greatest romantic masterpiece, namely, the *Abhijñāśākuntala* cannot be brushed aside easily. The impact of *śama* on each and every character of the drama is conspicuous. Except a small portion of the story of V and VI acts, the entire story takes place only in the serene atmosphere of hermitages. The tranquility and holiness of hermitages of sage Kaṇva, more so of sage Marīca leave behind indelible impressions of quietude in the minds of sensible spectators. Kālidāsa's portrayal of the emotional communication between trees, plants, rivers and other natural elements with the innocent inmates of the hermitages builds it up. While verbal descriptions such as *śāntamidamāśrama-padaṃ śamapradhāneṣu tapodhaneṣu*, express the sentiment *śānta*, *tejodvayasya yugapadvyasanodayābhyāṃ loko niyamyata ivātmadarśāntareṣu*, etc., highlight the mutability and impermanence of the worldly objccts. The Śārṅgarava's

> *abhyaktamiva snātaḥ śuciraśucimiva prabuddha iva suptam/*
> *baddhamiva svairagatirjanamiha sukhasaṅginamavaimi//*

portrays the *śānta* disposition beyond doubt.

Though it is ridiculous to say that *śānta* is the main *rasa* of the *Abhijñānaśākuntalam*, nonetheless, its presence throughout the drama cannot be ignored. The sentiment of love is delineated on the background of *śānta* by Kālidāsa. It is not far-fetched to interpret the verse *āparitoṣādviduṣām* as an expression of the doubt of Kālidāsa with regard to the success of his new and rare feat of mixing *śānta* with *śṛṅgāra*, which are held to be mutually opponent. It is this rare experiment which he alludes by saying *prayogavijñānam*. Similarly, the heroic poem, *Kumārasaṃbhava*, also has the element of *śāntarasa* in it. Lord Śiva himself is held to be the embodiment of *śānta*. The burning of Cupid, the two-tier penance of Pārvatī, the dialogue between the Brahmacārin and Pārvatī, help to build the sentiment *śānta* in the poem. The *Buddhacaritam* of Aśvaghoṣa and the *Nāgānandam* of Śriharṣa, of course, are excellent examples of *śāntarasa*. The *Vairāgyaśataka* of Bhartṛhari should not miss our attention.

Apart from these conventional examples of *kāvya*, *śānta* can be cited as the predominant or ancillary sentiment in the vast literature in the form of Purāṇas, and equally vast literature of *bhakti* and the spiritual *stotras*. Works like the *Yogavāsiṣṭha* can be understood only when we accept *śāntarasa*, and when they are viewed from the *kāvya* point of view.

Therefore, no one can close his eyes to the experience of *śānta* sentiment in the vast amount in Sanskrit literature. Once it has been shown as experienced in the literature, the theorists are obliged to accommodate it as one of the *rasas*. This compulsion is well experienced by the Indian theorists of poetics as more or less every-one after Ānandavardhana and Abhinavagupta has conceded it to be a *rasa* even though Bharata's text on it is not well received even by them.

One more observation needs to be made at this point. Few writers on Indian poetics have made an attempt to raise the case of *bhakti*, *vātsalya* and other *rasas*. Among them the case of *bhakti* is very strong and it also has a vast amount of literature. Illustrative literature stands as a sort of compulsion to concede more rasas and *bhāvas*. The theorists have to oblige the illustrative literature and modify their theories accordingly. But, writers need not oblige theorists and compose poems according to their canons. In spite of this fact, the case of *bhakti* received a setback as it has got love (*rati*) as its *sthāyibhāva* which is the *sthāyibhāva* of *śṛṅgāra* too. Therefore, theorists made a kind of *vyavasthā* that love between hero and heroine alone is to be held as attaining *rasa*-hood whereas love between any other persons is to be held as *vyabhicārin* only.

But such an escape is not possible with regard to *śānta* as its *sthāyibhāva;* it is not common to any other accepted *rasas*, whether it is *śama*, or *tṛṣākṣayasukha*, *nirveda* and so on. However, if we accept the theory of Kohala, *utsāha* is also cited as one of the possible *sthāyibhāvas* of *śānta*. Then it becomes common for *vīra* and *śānta*. But, no serious writer of *śānta* entertained it. Even if it is accepted, we can distinguish between the two *utsāhas*. *Utsāha*, the *sthāyin* of *vīra*, is of the nature of *nivṛtti*, and *utsāha* as *sthāyin* of *śānta* is of the nature of *nivṛtti*. Śaṅkarabhagavatpāda in his famous introductory passage of the *Gītābhāṣya*, makes an elaborate discussion highlighting the mutual opposition between *pravṛtti dharma* and *nivṛtti dharma* from various aspects. Therefore, one cannot be included in the other though the *sthāyin* is the same. The case of love is not the same as there is no mutual opposition.

We will now examine the theories of *rasa*-realization to know how far these theories support the case of *śānta*. The entire discussion owes its indebtedness to Abhinavagupta, the greatest personality in the domain of literary criticism in India. Whether it is the theory of Lollaṭa, Śaṅkuka or Bhaṭṭanāyaka, the source of all of them is the fragmentary restatement of Abhinavagupta in his elaborate commentaries on the *Nāṭyaśāstra* and *Dhvanyāloka*. The entire burden of systematization of *rasa* theory fell on the shoulders of Abhinavagupta.

The theories of Lollaṭa, Śaṅkuka, Bhaṭṭanāyaka and others are well known. I will make some general observations with regard to the development of the theory of *rasa*, which eventually reveal the basis for accepting *śāntarasa*. It is a fact that people derive pleasure and joy when they see a drama or read a poem. It is an experience that cannot be denied. The human experiences are classified under several heads, such as, perceptual, inferential, verbal and Śāstric, imaginative, extra sensory-perceptual, etc. Similarly, it is also a fact that people derive pleasure or joy or a kind of satisfaction or fulfilment when they come into contact with the sensory objects. An important question arises at this point as to whether the nature of experience of pleasure too differs on account of the difference of the means through which it is derived or remains the same even though the means differ. To cite an example: there is pleasure when one eats and relishes good food of his choice. There is also pleasure in wearing good and new clothes of one's choice and in applying various types of cosmetics. The question is whether there is difference in the nature of experience of pleasure in both the cases or does it remain the same. To say that it differs is not easy as we do not, indeed, differentiate the experience of pleasure *per se*. At the same time if we say that it remains the same, we may face the difficulty of answering questions like: "Why then a person should look for various kinds of means of joyful experience?" Neither are we convinced to accept that the experience of pleasure in each and every case is different. This may eventually lead to accept innumerable varieties of pleasures. We may, therefore, concede that while the goal in the form of experience of pleasure remains the same in all the cases, everyone tends to show a kind of preference to derive it through a particular set of means on account of his personal attitude, tastes and habits.

Coming back to the classification of experiences as cited above, we may group them mainly into three kinds on the basis of three different forms of the body we possess. Needless to remind that no experience is possible without a contact with one form or the other of the body (*ātmano bhogāyatanaṃ śarīram*). The three forms of bodies are gross (*sthūla*), subtle (*sūkṣma*) and causal (*kāraṇa*) as explained in the Upaniṣads and the Vedāntic texts. We can identify them with the body of flesh and blood, mind and the self or soul or *ātman*, respectively. Accordingly, we can classify the human experiences as physical, mental and spiritual. These are, however, not watertight compartments. They are classified only on the basis of predominance of the particular form of the body.

If we observe the historical development of the theory of *rasa*, we can see gradual development from the physical plane to the spiritual one. Bharatamuni places the aesthetic pleasure at par with the pleasure of relishing food. In fact, most of the technical terms of *rasa* theory are common with the terms used to signify the relish of food. For example: The very word *'rasa'* means taste and relishment and aesthetic pleasure as well. Terms like *carvaṇā*, *āsvādana*, *bhukti*, *bhoga*, etc. also support this view. Bharatamuni has drawn similarity between the experience of relishing food and experiencing all aesthetic joy in Chapter Six of the *Nāṭyaśāstra* in the first line of his famous *rasasūtra:*

> *ko dṛṣṭāntah? atrāha - yathā hi nānāvyañjanauṣadhidravyasamyogāt rasaniṣpattih bhavati yathā hi guḍādibhiḥ dravyaiḥ vyañjanaiḥ oṣadhibhiśca ṣāḍavādayo rasā nivartante tathā nānābhāvopagatā api sthāyino bhāvā rasatvamāpnuvanti.*

He quotes two verses of his predecessors:

yathā bahudravyayutairvyañjanairyutam/
āsvādayanti bhuñjānā bhaktaṃ bhaktavido janāḥ//
bhāvābhinayasaṃbaddhān sthāyibhāvāṃstathā budhāḥ/
āsvādayanti manasā tasmānnāṭye rasāsmṛtāḥ//

Lollaṭa may also be grouped with Bharatamuni as he holds perception as the means of cognition in experiencing the *rasa* realization.

Śaṅkuka and Bhaṭṭanāyaka place the experience of *rasa* on a mental plane. Śaṅkuka holds that inference is the means of cognition with regard to the experience of *rasa*. Bhaṭṭanāyaka speaks about *bhāvakatva* or *sādhāraṇīkaraṇa* which is certainly a mental activity. Abhinavagupta gives it a further elevation to the spiritual plane by bringing in the concepts of *āvaraṇabhaṅga* and revelation of *śuddhacaitanya*, etc. He says all the activities of dramatic personalities are aimed at making the *satvaguṇa* gain its supreme predominance and through that to break the veil that covers the self-luminous *ātman*, which is of the nature of *sat* (existence), *cit* (consciousness) and *ānanda* (bliss).

There is no doubt that the theory of *rasa*-realization reached its culmination in its treatment by Abhinavagupta. But, even after Abhinavagupta's treatment, the theories of Lollaṭa, Śaṅkuka and Bhaṭṭanāyaka need not be set aside as irrelevant. For, on account of one's own attitude, taste, refinement and mood, one may relish the aesthetic pleasure at any of the three levels mentioned above. Otherwise, the enjoyment of an ordinary man of the scenes in a drama or movie, where *āṅgikābhinaya* (physical gestures) predominates *sāttvikābhinaya* (display of emotions), becomes inexplicable. Pleasure is possible even without one's identification with the character represented by the actors. Efforts of Abhinavagupta and others are only aimed at the scaling of its sublimity.

This basic understanding solves several problems faced in accepting *śānta* as the ninth *rasa*. The question of its unsuitability to the presentation on stage, its presentable *sthāyibhāva*, and its uncommonness are all posed from the point of view of first two levels of *rasa*-realization. Since Abhinavagupta holds *rasa*-realization on spiritual plane, it becomes irresistible for him to champion the cause of *śānta*. Seen from his point of view, these questions become insignificant and that is how he answered them all at great length in his *Abhinavabhāratī*.

As Abhinavagupta holds that the experience of *rasa* is none other than the revelation of one's own self, it remains the same for him in respect of any *rasa*. This position impressed upon him to accept that *śānta* is the only *rasa* which is primordial from which all other *rasas* originate on account of the difference in their causal aggregate:

tatra sarva rasānām śāntaprāya evāsvādaḥ, viṣayebhyo viparivṛtyā/
tanmukhyatālābhaḥ kevalaṃ vāsanāntaropahitaḥ iti//

He also quotes a text of Bharata:

svaṃ svaṃ nimittamādāya śāntādutpadyate rasaḥ/
punarnimittāpāye tu śānta eva pralīyate//

Another important aspect of accepting *śāntarasa* is the realization that when there are eight *rasas* through which one can attain one or more of the three *puruśārthas* (goals of life), namely, *dharma, artha* and *kāma*, there is none to attain the last and most important of them, namely, *mokṣa*. Abhinavagupta says:

mokṣaphalatvena cāyaṃ paramapuruṣārthaniṣṭhatvāt sarvarasebhyaḥ pradhānatamaḥ/...

yathā iha tāvat dharmāditritayam, evaṃ mokṣo'pi puruṣārthaḥ śāstreṣu smṛtītihāsādiṣu ca prādhānyenopāyato vyutpādyata iti suprasiddham/ yathā ca kāmādiṣu samucitāscittavṛttayaḥ ratyādiśabdavācyāḥ kavinaṭavyāpāreṇa āsvādayogyatāprāpaṇadvāreṇa tathāvidha hṛdayasaṃvādavataḥ sāmājikān prati rasatvam śṛṅgāraditayā nīyante, tathā mokṣābhidhānaparamapuruṣārthocitā cittavṛttiḥ kimiti rasatvaṃ nānīyate iti vaktavyaṁ/

As we have made a reference to various kinds of experiences earlier, we may notice that there is a kind of extra-sensory perception or a kind of mystic experience well attested by the yogins. Patañjali has explained it in an elaborate way along with its lower *cittabhūmis* in the *Yogasūtras*. Abhinavagupta made a sincere attempt to put the experience of *rasa* at par with *savikalpasamādhi* of Patañjali. So he quotes Patañjali extensively in his *Abhinavabhāratī*. If this parallelism between the *rasa*-realization and *savikalpasamādhi* be accepted, the acceptance of *śānta* as the ninth and primordial *rasa* cannot be challenged.

Seen from this philosophical background, it appears that Abhinavagupta's treatment of *rasa* theory and his arguments in favour of *śānta* are mutually supportive and inter-dependent.

10

Theory of Rasa: A Secular Approach

Radhavallabh Tripathi

Describing the origin of *nāṭya* or theatre, Bharatamuni says that Brahmā culled different elements from the four Vedic *saṃhitas* and created *nāṭya*. *Rasa* is said to have come from *Atharvaveda*. Abhinavagupta has explained how and why *rasa* had to be derived from *Atharvaveda*. He has referred to some of the *abhicāras* or Tāntric practices in this connection.[1] *Atharvaveda* deals with such practices. Abhinavagupta seems to suggest that the man performing a Tāntric rite makes certain gestures. These gestures become the *anubhāvas*. He makes a person – be it a friend or a foe – as the subject of his rite. This person becomes *vibhāva*. This *vibhāva* is the cause of certain emotions. Thus, there is an amalgam of *vibhāvas*, *anubhāvas* and *sañcāri bhāvas* in Tāntric rites. There are several *sūktas* in *Atharvaveda* where *abhicāras* for attracting the love and attention of a lady are described. The state of mind while suffering the pangs of separation is described in such passages. Similarly, the bliss experienced at the time of union with the beloved is also described.[2] Thus, the theory of *rasa* was cultivated out of the Tāntrika rites or *abhicāras* as described in *Atharvaveda*. Such rites basically belonged to the tribal people. Tantra or *abhicāra* has two aspects. Basically it is performed for purely practical gains. But ultimately it is connected to something divine or other-worldly. In the terminology of Upaniṣads, the two *vidyās*, i.e., *parā* and *aparā* are interconnected and one has to know both of them together. In the same way, creativity leading to *rasa*-realization and the experience of *rasa* were basically viewed at purely empirical level. The idea of transcending the mundane reality or *ubhayadēśakālalyāga*, as Abhinavagupta puts it, has been introduced as a superstructure.

The Indian vision encompassing the two aspects of life – worldly and other-worldly and their invariable inter-relationship – has influenced our aesthetics or various concepts related to art. Amongst the Vedic deities, Indra and Varuṇa represent these two views.

In his famous *Asyavāmya Sūkta* in *Ṛgveda*, sage Dīrghatamas describes two birds residing on one and the same tree of *Aśvattha*. One of them is relishing the tasty fruit of the tree, while the other is not eating. He is simply seeing this one.[3]

Various interpretations have been offered to explain the symbolism behind this mantra. Obviously, the description of two birds here represents two different views. These can be termed as *pravṛtti* and *nivṛtti* in our tradition. The former stands for enjoying the pleasures of the world. The other one, however, stands apart; it visualizes the world with a different perspective.

In fact, Indra and Varuṇa are poles apart. Indra is the presiding deity of the *indriyas* or sense-organs. He is *ahalyājāra* or the paramour of Ahalyā. He represents the epicurian point of view. Varuṇa however does not stand for enjoying the world. He simply sees. He is the witness of good or bad deeds performed by men in this world. He regulates this world by observing *ṛta* – the universal law.[4] To Keith, Varuṇa represents the moral elevation in ancient India, which gradually disappears.[5] Deviprasad Chattopadhyay holds that Varuṇa was superceded by Indra and the concept of *ṛta* by that of *Brahman*, owing to the new features that eventually developed into the social life of Vedic people.[6] To him, it was the replacement of the 'primitive pre-class social organization of Vedic people that led to the loss of *ṛta*, the simple moral grandeur'. He has quoted VII. 28.4 of *Ṛgveda* to substantiate his theory, where the Vedic *ṛṣi* urges upon Indra to protect him from Varuṇa. The *ṛṣi* is apprehensive that Varuṇa has detected the *anṛta* amongst the followers of Indra, and he will punish them.

The idea of two different world-views is embedded in the very concept of *rasa*, particularly the theory of basic *rasas* and the subsidiary *rasas* postulated by Bharata. Bharatamuni in his *Nāṭyaśāstra* identifies four *rasas* as the original *rasas* – *śṛṅgāra*, *vīra*, *bībhatsa* and *raudra*. Out of each of these, four subsidiary *rasas* are generated. Thus, *hāsya* is born of *śṛṅgāra*, *adbhuta* comes of *vīra*, *bhayānaka* is produced by *bībhatsa*, and *karuṇa* by *raudra*.[7] Obviously, these *rasas* fall into two groups. There are *rasas* connected with pleasure and happiness which is derived from this mundane world. Then there are *rasas* which are basically connected with grief, fear or sad thought. It is in this background that the *ācāryas*, including Abhinavagupta, have viewed two types or *rasas* – *sukhātmaka* and *duḥkhātmaka*.[8] Ānandavardhana holds that all the *rasas* do not culminate into happiness.[9] *Rasa* is formed by the mixture of mixed feelings, *miśrīkṛtakramoraso vartate*. As Bhavabhūti says, *Sambhoga śṛṅgāra* alone is full of joy. Other *rasas* may have feelings of sadness and sorrow, *śṛṅgāra* and *bībhatsa* have totally opposite directions. How can they lead to a similar creativity and similar aesthetic delight? The experience of disaster, fear and contempt generated by *karuṇa*, *bhayānaka* and *bībhatsa rasas* will ultimately lead to sublimity and grandeur from the poet's point of view; the poetry imbued with such experience is born out of sublime and serene, a perspective comprising vastness or immensity, or *bhūmā* in the terminology of the Upaniṣads. In the creation and experience of *rasas* like *raudra*, *bībhatsa* and *bhayānaka*, this experience may be a result of terror or even hatred. To quote George Santayana:

> The vivid conception of great evils and that self assertion of the soul which gives the emotion of the sublime – Sublime depends upon the terror, terror makes us withdraw into ourselves, indifference comes as a rebound, and we have the emotion of detachment and liberation in which the sublime really consists.[10]

Varuṇa commands respect and unleashes terror but also stands for creativity leading to the comprehension of values.

Indra and Varuṇa thus represent two diverse stands of art creativity and art experience. There is a level of art activity where the mind is attached to physical charm. There is another level where it comprehends the reality. These two levels percolate in the layers of art experience too. Kant says:

> the satisfaction in the sublime does not so much involve a positive pleasure as admiration or respect which rather observes to be called negative pleasure.[11]

There is a level of affirmation, positivism and involvement in art creativity; and also, there is yet another level where the creator demolishes the existing reality, or negates it. For negating it, he has to stand apart and see, like Varuṇa.

Visualization and comprehension of reality presupposes duality. The idea of duality or the difference of the subject and the object in art experience was inherent in Lollaṭa and Śaṅkuka. Only Bhaṭṭanāyaka and Abhinavagupta entered into the arena of monism while interpreting the experience of *rasa*.

Bharata was aware of this duality or diversity of experience that different *rasas* will produce. Therefore, he said: "the connoisseurs get different feelings – pleasure, pain, etc., by seeing a performance."[12] The nature of aesthetic experience generated by each *rasa* is altogether different. The state of mind or *cittavṛtti* during the course of aesthetic experience in these *rasas* is also different. *Druti* (melting), *dīpti* (enlightening) and *vikāsa* (expansion) – these three different states of mind are said to result during the course of *rasa*-realization.[13] The effect of *śṛṅgāra* lies in producing *druti* whereas the *rasas* like *bībhatsa*, *raudra* or *vīra* will generate *dīpti* in the psyche of the connoisseur.

Thus, different outlooks can have their impact in creative process as well as the aesthetic experience. There is an objective view, leading the creator and the connoisseur to detachment and sublimity. There is also the subjective view, leading them towards involvement and enjoyment.

Bharata has also used the term *Nāṭyarasa* to denote this formalistic view of *rasa*. K. Krishnamurthy says:

> What deserves our special attention here (in Bharata) is the fact that the words *rasa* and *bhāva* are used in connection with the actor and the artists and not in connection with the spectator. Bharata's *Nāṭyaśāstra*, if studied in this background, will show how nowhere are the words *rasa* and *bhāva* confined to describe the spectator's exclusive experience. They are invariably used to refer to the activity of the artists. In other words, a historical approach to the concept of *rasa* and *bhāva* must admit that these two words describe the aesthetic situation, the art object outside, more than the subjective state of the critic.[14]

Bharatamuni basically viewed poetry and drama objectively. Bhaṭṭanāyaka and Abhinavagupta switched over to the subject of the *sahṛdaya*. They brought the inner world of the connoisseur into focus. To Bharata, both *rasa* and *bhāva* are parts of the *Nāṭyasaṅgraha* or the digest of theatre. *Bhāvas* in Bharata signify various physical or psychological states of the characters which create an environment on the stage. Some of these states can be temporal and some of them can be dominant. Barlingay understands *sthāyibhāva* in Bharata as *kāvyārtha* or the meaning of dramatic text or poetry.

> In the context of drama *sthāyībhāva* is the meaning of stage-symbol continuum; but the meaning is essentially the same as the meaning of (dramatic) poetry (*kāvya*) which is exibited on the stage. Thus the *kāvyārtha* can also be regarded as *sthāyibhāva*. Essentially the meaning of the poetry and the meaning of the staged poetry is the same. In one sense then we convert the poetic meaning of the stage symbolism though in another sense stage symbolism also yields meaning. The concept of *sthāyibhāva* then is not entirely a concept in drama, nor has it any fixed place, it is persistent meaning or sense connected with drama, poetry or any expression in ordinary language.[15]

To Bḩarata, *bhāva* meant the intention of the poet or the dramatist and also the expression of this intention. *Kaverantargataṃ bhāvaṃ bhāvayan bhāva ucyate* – *bhāva* is that which leads to the experience of the inner *bhāva* or the intension of the poetry – he says. *Bhāvika* – a figure of speech – has been conceived by Daṇḍin and others on the basis of this connotation of *bhāva*.[16] Thus, *bhāvika* is called so because it brings out the intention of the poet.

Ānandavardhana is very close to Bharata in his concept of *rasa* as a meaning suggested in poetry. *Pratīyamāna* or the suggested sense in the utterance of the poet is something different than the ordinary meaning, he says, implying that the suggested sense is a pan of the poetic structure. He also made it clear that when one is enjoying this suggested sense, the primary meaning invariably remains tagged with it:

Nahi vyaṅgyē pratīyamānē vācyabuddhirdūrībhavati

If *rasa* is *kāvyārtha*, then there is a subject to comprehend it. Therefore, the duality of the subject and object will have to be accepted at the time of *rasa*-realisation.

Following his guru Bhaṭṭatauṭa, Abhinavagupta postulated the theory of *śānta* as *mahārasa*, with *tattvajñāna* as its *sthāyibhāva*. Being an Advaitāite through and through, he perceived *śānta* as the ultimate in the process of *rasa*-realization. However, there is a dilemma in the theory. How can we term an experience as poetic or aesthetic experience when there is nothing except one and single consciousness? There has to be the duo of creator and the thing to be created in the creative process; and similarly there has to be the duo of the meaning of the poetry of a dramatic performance (*kāvyārtha*) on one hand and the cognizer (*pramātā*) on the other for the experience also. Interpreting the theory of Abhinava, Paṇḍitarāja Jagannātha says: *'vyaktiśca bhagnāvaraṇā cit'*– the expression of *rasa* lies in the pure consciousness, and *bhagnāvaraṇacidvisiṣṭo ratyārdisthāyibhāvo rasa iti sthitam, vastutastu ratyādyana-cchinnā bhagnāvaraṇā cidēva rasaḥ* – meaning that either the *sthāyibhāva* delimited by the unveiled consciousness is *rasa* of the consciousness itself, delimited by the *sthāyibhāva* can be called *rasa*. In this interpretation also, the consciousness (subject) and the *sthāyibhāva* (the object) are juxtaposed together. In the absence of either, there can be no experience. Jagannātha tries to resolve the dilemma by saying that from the point of view of consciousness, *rasa* is self-luminous (*svayamprakāśa*) and eternal (*nitya*); and from the point of view of *sthāyibhāva*, it is transitory (*anitya*) and likely to be enlightened (*itarabhāsya*). To distinguish it from the experience of Ultimate Reality or *brahmānanda*, he admits the existence of the subject (*vibhāvādiviṣayasaṃvalitacid-ānandālambanāt*). But even then the dilemma is not finally resolved. Paṇḍitarāja holds the consciousness realizing the *rasa* as aware of the process and the subject (*sākṣī*), and the subject of poetry as subjected by an aware consciousness (*sākṣibhāsya*). The difference between the seen and the thing to be seen thus remains at the time of *rasa*-realization.

The uniqueness of the creation of poetry and its experience lies in the fact that they always invariably encompass this physical world as the subject; and yet they also encompass the infinity, the divine and the other-worldly. In their enthusiasm to equate art-experience with the experience of divinity, *ācārya* as like Abhinavagupta treated aesthetic experience as something that is other-worldly or extrawordly, transcendental and manifesting beyond the framework of our time and space. To them it only takes place in the realm of literature and not in real life. They thus ignored the basic and fundamental reality of art-experience – its secular (*laukika*) base.

Contrary to Abhinavagupta's view, some of the *ācāryas* unequivocally hold the aesthetic experience of *rasapratīti* as *laukika*. Rāmcandra Guṇacandra, the authors of *Nāṭyadarpaṇa* and *Siddhicandragaṇi*, who wrote *Kāvyaprakāśakhaṇḍana*, take this stand. They also regard *rasa*-experience as an admixture of pleasure and pain.[17]

A secular approach to *rasa*-theory had always been there right from its inception in Bharata's *Nāṭyaśāstra*. Many of the *ācāryas* added new *rasas* to the list of eight or nine *rasas* from this point of view. Abhinavagupta himself has referred to the theory of *laulya rasa*, with *gardha* (greed) as its *sthāyin*. He does not altogether discard *laulya rasa*. He simply rules out the possibility of its independent existence. He says that the *sthāyin* of this so-called *laulya rasa* can[18] be incorporated either in *hāsa* or in *rati*.[19] The same logic is applicable to the theory of *bhakti* as an independent *rasa*.

Bhoja also does not strictly adhere to the theory of eight or nine *rasas*. He suggests some new *rasas*. One of these is *udātta*, with *mati* or wisdom as its *sthāyibhāva*. If *mati* is the prevailing mood, then again, there will be detachment and awareness in the experience of a poetic piece or a dramatic performance, rather than involvement or identification.

The theory of *laulya rasa*, which some of the predecessors of Abhinavagupta had postulated, subsequently comes back with a different name. Viśveśvara Pande of Almora, who flourished in the eighteenth century, came out with the theory of *māyā rasa* as a *prima facie* view (*pūrvapakṣa*).[20] The opponent argues that if *śanta* with *nivṛtti* as the dominating emotion can be accepted as *rasa*, *māyā rasa* with *pravṛtti* as the dominating force should also be accepted as a *rasa*. The traditions of Varuṇa and Indra have thus come along till our time in Sanskrit poetics.

Some of the *ācāryas* propounded the theory of two-fold *rasa*. *Rasa* is of two types – *laukika* (this-worldly) and *alaukika* (other-worldly). *Laukika rasa* is *svagata* (belonging to the character) and *alaukika rasa* is *paragata* (belonging to the connoisseur). Bhaṭṭanāyaka had stood against the theory of *svagata rasa*. But the other *ācāryas* continued to argue in favour of the other side of the *rasa* theory. They were standing on the solid ground which Bharatamuni himself had prepared. Defining *nāṭya* or theatre, Bharata had said: "The very nature of the people, invested with happiness and sorrow, when presented with fourfold *abhinaya*, becomes *nāṭya*."[20] Abhinavagupta identifies *nāṭya* as *rasa*. This way, he too accepts the empirical aspect of *rasa*. Viśvanātha in his *Pratatāparudrīya* says:

> *Rasa* in fact resides in the hero (or the character). But because of the delineation by an skilled actor, or by the hearing of a poem like that, the connoisseur also experiences it by perception, then *rasa* can be held as *paragata* and a cause of extreme delight.[21]

Ratnāpaṇa here comments that *rasa* is of two types – this wordly and other-wordly.[22] The former belongs to the *anukārya* or the character. Also Paṇḍitrāja Jagannātha added two new inter-relations to the theory of *rasa* in his *Rasagaṅgādhara*, i.e., *navyamata* and *paramata*. In both these interpretations, *rasa* is not an other-worldly experience.

Rasa is an experience of this life. The characters depicted in literature experience *rasa*. That is why Bhavabhūti says: *Rāmasya karuṇo rasaḥ* (*Uttararāmacarita*, III.1).

Hariprasāda, an author of late eighteenth century, who followed Paṇḍitarāja Jagannātha, propounded two varieties of *rasa* – *nitya* (eternal) *rasa* and *anitya* (transitory) *rasa*. The former is identical with the Spreme Being or Lord Kṛṣṇa Himself, whereas the latter is fragmentary, transitional and is evinced by the poet and the actor.[23]

G.C. Pande finds that Indian tradition imbibed three types of world-view – *pratyakṣavāda*, *vijñānavāda* and *ādhyātmavāda*. Historically speaking, they were reflected in the reverse order. Thus, Vedic tradition was dominated by *ādhyātmavāda* or spirituality, and subsequently the other views became conspicuous.[24] However, for the development of the concept of *rasa*, this order does not apply. We find that Bharatamuni had built up a theory that rested more on the empirical reality, and viewed *rasa* as an objective reality. The commentators and theorists who followed him laid more and more emphasis on the subjectivity, interpreting *rasa* as a psychic experience, and finally as pure or unveiled consciousness.

The whole structure of Ānandavardhana's theory crumbles down if the objective status of *rasa* is over-ruled. This happens in the thesis of Śrīvatsa Lāñchana Bhaṭṭācārya, an eminent rhetorician who flourished in 16th century. He has composed *Kāvyāmṛtam* in refutation to the *Kāvyaprakāśa* of Mammaṭa. The third *ullāsa* discusses the varieties of *dhvani* including *rasa*.

Owing to his Vedāntic outlook, Śrīvatsa accepts only four *rasas: śṛṅgāra, hāsya, vīra* and *adbhuta*. The other *rasas* have been rejected simply because they are imbued with pain (*duḥkha*). He also says that *rasa* is not *vyaṅgya* (expressed); it is *sākṣātkārya* (liable to be seen).[25] The author of *Parimala*, a commentary on Bhānudatta's *Rasamañjarī*, had earlier suggested a via media. Explaining the title *Rasamañjarī*, he raises the question: *rasa* is not contained in the *Mañjarī* then how is it that the work has been entitled as *Rasamañjarī?* He answers that *rasa* is something to be relished by a *sahṛdaya* and it is not a pan of a poem. But by *upacāra* or *lakṣaṇā*, the words are said to be imbued with *rasa*.[26]

Thus, the subjective view of *rasa* ultimately went to the extreme of rejecting it as an objective reality. Bharatamuni did not mean to pursue his theory to this extreme. *Rasa*, therefore, can also be held as an element embedded in the structure of a dramatic performance. But what about a literary piece? There also, *rasa* will be a pan of its structure. Rajendra Nanavati says:

> we can employ the term 'form' to translate *rasa*. *Rasa* is that form of the poet's emotion which resides in a generalised state in the poem. Abhinava describes it as of the nature of the permanent mental state of the hero, but that is because of the dramatic context of the statement.

Then he concludes: "There is no likelihood in incurring any mistake in identifying *rasa* with what we call Aesthetic Form in western poetics."[27]

Brahmanand Sharma has made an attempt to interpret the theory of *rasa* on Marxist lines. He identifies *rasānubhūti* as *satyānubhūti*, which is the experience of reality to him. This experience differs from the spiritual experience as there is imagery in it, whereas the spiritual experience tends to minimize and finally eradicate any image. *Lokasatya* or empirical reality is the basis of poetic creation. This reality also originates from *prāṇaśakti*, and *prāṇaśakti* rests on the economy. This economy is again based on *śrama* or work.[28]

The treatment of *rasa* ultimately as a singular, isolated and unique experience tends to make it inaccessible to a large number of readers or spectators, who are prone to go through a piece of literary work or dramatic performance with a contemplative feeling and not with *saundaryāveśa* or *rasāveśa* to adopt Abhinavagupta's terminology. Hence, there is need for other interpretations of *rasa* theory which may not subscribe to his theory.

NOTES AND REFERENCES

1. These practices have been termed as *prāṣṭuda* and *vaiṣṭuda*. Unfortunately, the reading of *Abhinavabhāratī* in (*COS* edn.) here is corrupt and lines have been mixed.
2. *Atharvaveda*, 6. 130. 2, 6.8,l.
3. *dvā suparṇā sayujā sakhāyā samānaṃ vṛkṣam pariṣaṣvajāte. tayōranyaḥ pippalaṃ svādvattyanaśnannanyo'bhicākaśīti*. (*Ṛgveda* 1.164.20; *Atharva*. IV 13.2).
4. *Ṛgveda*, 1.25; VII. 76.
5. A.B. Keith, *Religion and Philosophy of Vedas and Upanisads*, p. 33.
6. D.P. Chattopadhyay, *Lokāyata*, p. 635.
7. *śṛṅgārāddhi bhaveddhāsyō raudrācca karuṇō rasaḥ, virāccaivādbhutotpattirbībhatsācca bhayānakaḥ*. (*Nāṭyaśāstra*, VI.39).
8. *Abhinavabhāratī*, Vol. l, pp. 267, 292.
9. *yatra lakṣyē parikalpitaviṣayavyabhicārastadvirūpamevāstu. Dhvanyāloka, udyota* III, *vṛtti* on VI, Varanasi, 1965, p, 365.
10. George Santayana, *Sense of Beauty*, p. 181.
11. Kant, *Critique of Judgement*, p. 83.
12. *Sthāyibhāvamāsvādayanti sumanasaḥ prekṣakāḥ harṣādīścādhigacchanti. Nāṭyaśāstra*, Vol. I, p. 256, after VI 32-33.
13. *Daśarūpaka* IV.43.
14. K. Krishnamurthy, 'Traditional Indian Aesthetics in Theory and Practice', *Indian Aesthetic and Art Activity*, IIAS, Simla, 1968, p. 45.
15. S.S, Barlingay, 'Some Concepts of Bharata's Theory of Drama', in op. cit., p. 23.
16. *tad bhāvikamiti prāhuḥ prabandhaviṣayaṃ guṇam.*
    bhāvaḥ kaverabhiprāyaḥ kāvyesvāsiddisaṃsthitaḥ.
    parasparopakārivaṃ sarveṣāṃ vastuparvaṇām.
    viśēṣaṇānāṃ vyarthānāmakriyāsthānavarṇanā.
    vyaktiruktikramabalād gambhīrasyāpi vastunaḥ.
    bhāvāyattamidaṃ sarvamiti tad bhāvikaṃ viduḥ. (*Kāvyādarśa*, II, 364-66).
17. *Nāṭyadarpaṇa*, II. 37.
18. *eṣaiva ca gardhasthāyikasya laulyarasasya pratyākhyāne saraṇirmantavyā. Hāse vā ratau vānyatra paryavasānāt*. – *Abh*. Vol. 1, p. 341. Hemachandra, however, adopts this passage as follows: *tathā gardhasthāyikasya laulyarasasya Hāse vā ratau vā'nyatra vāntarbhāvo mantavyaḥ, evaṃ ca bhaktāvapi vācyamiti* – *Kāvyānuśāsana*, Vol. 1, Bombay, 1938, p. 106.
19. Viśveśvara, *Rasacandrikā*, Kashi Sanskrit Series-53, 1926, p. 68.
20. *yo 'yaṃ svabhāvō Lokasya sukhaduhkhasamanvitaḥ so'ṅgādyabhinayōpētō nāṭyamityabhidhīyatē* – *Nāṭyaśāstra*, 1. 119.
21. *tatra rasō nāyakāśraya eva. yadi paraṃ nipuṇanaṭacēṣṭayā tathāvidhakāvyaśravaṇabalēna ca sāmājikaiḥ sākṣād bhāvyatē tadā paragatasyāpi rasasya samyag bhāvanayā paratraniratiśayānanda-jananamaviruddham. Athavā mālatyādiśabdēbhyo yoṣinamātrapratītau ca*

smṛtyārūdhana tattadyōṣidviśeṣeṇa anukāryēṇa sāmājikāśrayatvam-apyaviruddham (*Pratāparudrīya*, p. 205).

22. *ayaṃ ca rasō laukikālokikabhedena dvividhaḥ tatrādyasyāśrayamāha-atrēti. rasō laukikō nāyakōnukāryō rāmādirāśrayō yasya sa tathōktaḥ. alaukikarasasyśrayamāha-athvēti.* (Ratnāpaṇa on above, p. 203).
23. *rasō hi dvi prakāraḥ – ānandaikapratītāvayavaḥ śamaśṛṅgārādi-bhēdaḥ, pūrṇānandaḥ śrīkṛṣṇākhyō nityastadanyaḥ ānanda-mayāvayavastu kavinaṭā-bhāṃ bhāvitaḥ aṃśabhēdēnānityaḥ. Kāvyālka,* Hariprasada, ed. Rama Gupta, Jaipur, 1989.
24. Govind Chandra Pande, *Saundaryadarśanavimarśaḥ*, p. 44.
25. Neeru Rani, *Śrīvatsalāñchana Bhaṭṭācārya kī kṛtiyon kā Adhyayana* (1993), pp. 3-9.
26. Ram Suresh Tripathi, ed., *Rasamañjarī* with *Parimala* and *Rasāmoda*, Aligarh, 1981, pp. 8-9.
27. Rajendra Nanavati, *Poetic Form in Kuntaka and Abhinava;* Proceedings of All India Oriental Conference, XXXII Session, Pune, 1987, p. 256.
28. Brahmanand Sharma, *Rasālocanam*, pp. 1-7.

11

रस संख्या निर्धारण

अमिय कुमार मिश्र

भरत ने रस संख्या केवल आठ मानी हैं:

> *श्रृंगारहास्यकरुणरौद्रवीरभयानका:।*
> *बीभत्साद्‌भुतसंज्ञौ चेत्यष्टौ नाट्ये रसा: स्मृता:।। ना.शा. 6.16।।*

अर्थात् श्रृंगार, हास्य, करुण, रौद्र, वीर, भयानक, बीभत्स, अद्‌भुत। यह संख्या निर्धारण भरत ने नहीं किया, वरन् उनसे पूर्व स्वयं ब्रह्मा अथवा द्रुहिण नाम के कोई प्राचीन महात्मा इस विषय में निर्णय दे चुके थे:

एते त्वष्टौ रसा: प्रोक्ता द्रुहिणेन महात्मना। (*6.17*)

भरत मुनि के समय में रसों की यह संख्या अत्यन्त प्राचीन परम्परा से चली आ रही थी। आगे चलकर भरत के प्रतिभावान् व्याख्याकार अभिनवगुप्त ने अपने मत के अनुकूल *नाट्यशास्त्र* के किसी अन्य पाठ के आधार पर यह सिद्ध करने का प्रयास किया कि भरत मुनि ने भी रस संख्या नौ ही मानी है और वे नौ होते हैं। परन्तु नाटक में शान्त रस को न मानने वाले तो 'बीभत्साद्‌भुतशान्ताश्च नव नाट्यरसा: स्मृता:' के स्थान पर 'बीभत्साद्‌भुतसंज्ञौ चेत्यष्टौ नाट्ये रसा: स्मृता:' इस रूप में 'अष्टौ' ऐसा पाठ मानते हैं। किन्तु यह उद्‌भावना प्रमाणित नहीं है। भरत ने उपर्युक्त 'रस संख्या वर्णन' प्रसंग में तो दो बार आठ रसों का उल्लेख किया है तथा उसके आगे भी स्थान-स्थान पर आठ रसों का ही स्पष्ट कथन है: जैसे कि उत्पत्ति, वर्ण और अधिदेवता के वर्णन में (*नाट्यशास्त्र,*

640-46) भावों के सन्दर्भ में जहां 8 स्थायी, 8 सात्त्विक और 33 संचारी भावों को मिलाकर कुल संख्या 49 मानी गयी है। इन सन्दर्भों से भी अभिनवगुप्त ने वैकल्पिक पाठों की ओर संकेत किया है, पर बात बनती नहीं है। अत: यह निश्चित है कि भरत ने रसों की संख्या केवल आठ ही मानी है। यह उनकी अपनी मान्यता नहीं थी, वरन् इसके पीछे प्राचीन परम्परा का सुदृढ़ आधार था।

भरत मुनि के बाद आचार्य दण्डी ने भी *काव्यादर्श* में केवल आठ रसों का ही उल्लेख किया है, *इह त्वष्टरसायत्ता रसवत्ता स्मृता गिराम्* (1.292) अर्थात् यहां रसवत् अलंकार में तो वाणी का आठ रसों से युक्त होना ही रसवत्ता माना गया है। किन्तु उनके थोड़े समय के बाद उद्भट् ने निर्भ्रान्त एवं सहज भाव से शान्त को मिलाकर नौ रसों का कथन किया है:

शृंगारहास्यकरुणरौद्रवीरभयानका:।
बीभत्साद्भुतशान्ताश्च नव नाट्ये रसा: स्मृता:।। 4.4।।

दण्डी और उद्भट के बीच और कोई विख्यात आचार्य नहीं हुआ, अत: विद्वानों का यह अनुमान है कि शान्त-रस की उद्भावना उद्भट ने ही की थी। किन्तु जिस प्रकार अनायास ही उद्भट ने शान्त-रस का उल्लेख किया है, उससे यह अनुमान होता है कि उन्होंने अपने समय में प्रचलित रस संख्या का ग्रहण मात्र किया है, अर्थात् शान्त रस उद्भट के समय तक रसशास्त्रियों में स्वीकृत हो चुका था। उद्भट ने केवल परम्परा का पालन किया है। एक सम्भावना यह भी हो सकती है कि उद्भट ने *नाट्यशास्त्र* के भाष्य में, जो आज उपलब्ध नहीं है, शान्त रस की तर्कपूर्वक स्थापना की हो। इन स्थितियों में केवल इतना ही मानना उचित होगा कि शान्त सहित नौ रस का प्रथम उल्लेख उपलब्ध ग्रन्थों में सबसे पहले उद्भट के 'काव्यालंकारसारसंग्रह' में ही मिलता है। वामन ने न रसों की संख्या का उल्लेख किया है और न सभी रसों के नाम ही दिए हैं। परन्तु रुद्रट ने स्वीकृत संख्या में प्रेयान् रस की वृद्धि कर दी है:

शृंगारवीरकरुणा बीभत्सभयानकाद्भुता हास्य:।
रौद्र: शान्त: प्रेयानिति मन्तव्या रसा: सर्वे।।12.3।।

यह प्रेयान् रस जिसका स्थायी भाव स्नेह है, शायद रुद्रट की ही अपनी कल्पना थी, परन्तु विद्वन्मण्डली से इसे मान्यता नहीं प्राप्त हुई, और इसका प्रमाण यह है कि रुद्रट के प्राय: समसामयिक रुद्रभट्ट ने भी अपने *शृंगारतिलक* में केवल नवरस का ही वर्णन किया है। वास्तव में, रुद्रट भी किसी एकाध रस-भेद की नवीन कल्पना के प्रति विशेष आग्रहशील नहीं थे, वे तो लोल्लट आदि कतिपय प्राचीन क्रान्तिकारी आचार्यों के अनुयायी थे, जो रसों की अनन्तता में विश्वास करते थे। उनकी अपनी धारणा यह थी:

रसनाद्रसत्वमेषां मधुरादीनामिवोक्तमाचार्यैः।
निर्वेदादिष्वपि तन्निकाममस्तीति तेऽपि रसाः।। 12.4।।

अर्थात् भरतादि आचार्यों ने स्थायिभावों को इसलिए रस माना है, क्योंकि इनमें मधुर, अम्ल आदि रसों की भांति आस्वाद है। यह आस्वाद्यता तो निर्वेदादि संचारी भावों में भी है, अतः वे भी रसत्व को प्राप्त होते हैं। यह निश्चय ही क्रान्तिकारी कल्पना थी, किन्तु परम्परा के प्रभाववश भोज के अतिरिक्त किसी अन्य आचार्य ने इसे स्वीकार नहीं किया। इनके उपरान्त आनन्दवर्धन के साथ ध्वनिकाल प्रारम्भ हो जाता है। आनन्दवर्धन की प्रवृत्ति विस्तार की अपेक्षा व्यवस्था की ओर अधिक थी, अतः उनसे रस संख्या में वृद्धि की आशा करना व्यर्थ है, उन्होंने नौ रसों की ही चर्चा की है। इस युग के जिन दो प्रमुख आचार्यों ने प्रस्तुत प्रसंग पर प्रकाश डाला है, वे हैं धनञ्जय तथा अभिनवगुप्त। वैसे तो महिमभट्ट, अग्निपुराणकार, मम्मट आदि ने भी रस को अत्यन्त महत्त्व दिया है, परन्तु रस संख्या के विषय में उन्होंने कोई विशेष बात नहीं कही। धनंजय ने आठ और नौ के विवाद का समाधान करते हुए यह व्यवस्था दी कि नाट्य में तो आठ रसों की सम्भावना है कुछ विद्वान् 'शम' स्थायी भाव और उसके परिपाक शान्त रस को भी स्वीकार करते हैं, परन्तु रूपकों में उसकी पुष्टि नहीं होती: *शममपि केचित्प्राहुः पुष्टिर्नाट्येषु नैतस्य।* (*दशरूपक* 4.35) इसकी व्यंजना यह हो सकती है कि काव्य में नवरस की स्थिति धनंजय को मान्य है, परंतु चूंकि उनका विवेच्य विषय रूपक है, अतः उनके लिए शान्त रस का वर्णन अप्रासंगिक है। धनञ्जय ने प्रेयान् तथा भक्ति रसों का खंडन किया है, उनके समय में या उनसे पूर्व एकाध विद्वान् ने मृगया रस तथा अक्ष (द्यूत) रस का भी उल्लेख किया था, किन्तु उन्होंने इन सभी का निराकरण किया है:

प्रीतिभक्त्यादयो भावा मृगयाक्षादयो रसाः।
हर्षोत्साहादिषु स्पष्टमन्तर्भावान्न कीर्तिताः।। 4.83।।

अर्थात् कुछ लोग प्रीति, भक्ति आदि को स्थायी भाव मानते हैं, तथा मृगया, जुआ आदि को रस मानते हैं। इनका समावेश हर्ष, उत्साह आदि स्थायी भाव में ही हो जाता है। अतः इनका पृथक् विवेचन करना ठीक नहीं समझा गया है। धनंजय के विपरीत अभिनवगुप्त ने अत्यन्त प्रबल शब्दों में सम्पूर्ण बुद्धिबल से शांत रस की नाट्य और काव्य दोनों में प्रतिष्ठा की है। उन्होंने इस सन्दर्भ में नाट्य और काव्य के भेद को भी स्वीकार नहीं किया। इस प्रकार, अभिनवगुप्त ने निर्भ्रान्त और निश्चित रूप में व्यवस्था दी है कि रस नौ ही होते हैं, न कम और न ज्यादा। परन्तु इसके साथ ही उन्होंने यह भी स्वीकार किया है कि कतिपय विद्वान् इन नौ प्रतिष्ठित रसों के अतिरिक्त और भी तीन रसों की स्थिति मानते हैं, जैसे (1) स्नेह रस (2) लौल्य रस और (3) भक्ति रस। किन्तु इनकी पृथक् सत्ता अन्ततः सिद्ध नहीं होती।

आर्द्रता रूप स्थायीभाव से युक्त स्नेह नामक दशम रस होता है, यह कहना उचित नहीं है। क्योंकि स्नेह एक प्रकार के आकर्षण का नाम है। वह (सब ही प्रकार का आकर्षण स्नेह) रति या उत्साहादि में ही समा जाता है। जैसे कि बालक का माता-पिता आदि के प्रति, युवकों का मित्रों के प्रति और लक्ष्मण आदि जैसे भाइयों के प्रति स्नेह का उदय, रति में समाविष्ट हो जाता है। इसी प्रकार वृद्धजनों का पुत्रादि के प्रति स्नेह (जिसको अन्य रसों के मानने वाले वात्सल्य रस नाम से कहते हैं) के विषय में समझना चाहिए (अर्थात् उसका भी अन्तर्भाव रति के भीतर ही हो जाता है)। गर्ध रूप स्थायीभाव वाले लौल्य रस के खंडन में यही पद्धति समझनी चाहिए, क्योंकि हास में अथवा रति में अथवा अन्य किसी रस में उसका अन्तर्भाव हो सकता है। इसी प्रकार भक्ति रस के विषय में भी समझना चाहिए। अर्थात् भक्ति रस अलग नहीं है। उसका भी रति में अथवा भाव में अन्तर्भाव हो सकता है।

(हिन्दी *अभिनव भारती, पृ. 641*)

रस संख्या का विस्तार सबसे अधिक भोज के *सरस्वतीकण्ठाभरण* और *शृंगारप्रकाश* में मिलता है। भोज की प्रवृत्ति संग्रहशील थी, अतएव उन्होंने अपने ग्रन्थों में प्राय: उपलब्ध सभी मतों का संकलन करने का प्रयास किया है। उन्होंने प्रसिद्ध नवरस के अतिरिक्त प्रेयान्, उदात्त और उद्धत-रसों का तो स्पष्ट वर्णन किया ही है।

...प्रेयांस: शान्तोदात्तोद्धता रसा:। सरस्वतीकण्ठाभरण ।।5.164

काव्यमाला संस्करण में 'शान्तोदात्तोद्धता रसा:' पाठ है, परन्तु जैसा कि डॉ. राघवन ने शृंगार प्रकार का उद्धरण देकर प्रमाणित किया है, ये नये रस नायक भेदों के अनुसार उद्‌भावित किये गये हैं। यथा –

प्रेयान् = धीरललित
उदात्त = धीरोदात्त
शान्त = धीरप्रशान्त
उद्धत = धीरोद्धत

अतएव, 'दान्त' पाठ अशुद्ध है। इनके अतिरिक्त भोज ने एक ओर स्वातन्त्र्य, आनन्द, प्रशम और पारवश्य और दूसरी ओर साध्वस, विलास, अनुराग तथा संगम रसों का भी उपर्युक्त दोनों ग्रन्थों में उल्लेख किया है। वस्तुत: भोज रसों के आनंत्य में विश्वास करते थे। रुद्रट तथा उनके टीकाकार नमिसाधु की भांति वे यह मानते थे, कि सभी भाव स्थायी, संचारी और सात्त्विक भी रसत्व को प्राप्त हो सकते हैं।

(देखिए : डॉ. राघवन की पुस्तक *'दि नम्बर ऑफ रसाज़'*, पृ. 124-125)

भोज के उपरान्त हेमचन्द्र ने भी *काव्यानुशासन* में अभिनवगुप्त के ही शब्दों का अनुवाद-सा करते हुए स्नेह, लौल्य तथा भक्ति रसों का उल्लेख एवं खण्डन किया है।

> एक-दूसरे से स्वतंत्र ये नौ ही रस हैं अतः आर्द्रतास्थायिक स्नेह को रस मानना ठीक नहीं है। इसी प्रकार युवाओं का मित्रों के प्रति स्नेह रति में, लक्ष्मण आदि का भ्रातृ-स्नेह धर्मवीर में तथा बालक का माता-पिता के प्रति स्नेह भय में अंतर्भुक्त हो जाता है। यही वृद्धजन के पुत्रादि-विषयक स्नेह के विषय में समझना चाहिए। ऐसे ही गर्धस्थायिक लौल्य रस का ह्रास या रति में अन्तर्भाव कहा जा सकता है। यही भक्ति के विषय में भी कहा जा सकता है।

(हेमचन्द्र, *काव्यानुशासन*, पृ. 106)

उधर, हेमचन्द्र के शिष्य रामचन्द्र-गुणचन्द्र ने भी प्रायः इसी प्रकार की चर्चा की है, किन्तु उन्होंने तीन अतिरिक्त रसों का भी उल्लेख किया है। ये हैं - व्यसन, दुःख और सुख।

किन्तु इनसे भिन्न और रस भी हो सकते हैं। जैसे, तृष्णा-रूप स्थायीभाव वाला व्यसन रस, अरति-रूप स्थायीभाव वाला दुःख रस और संतोष-रूप स्थायीभाव वाला सुख रस इत्यादि (अन्य रस भी हो सकते हैं)। कुछ लोग इनको रस तो मानते हैं, किन्तु इनका अन्तर्भाव पूर्वोक्त नौ रसों में ही कर लेते हैं।

(हिन्दी *ना.द.*, पृ. 306)

कविराज विश्वनाथ ने नवरस को स्वीकार कर लेने के बाद प्रायः स्पष्ट शब्दों में ही वात्सल्य रस को भी मान लिया है और उसका नियमित रूप से सांग वर्णन किया है: 'स्फुटं चमत्कारितया वत्सलं च रसं विदुः', प्रकट चमत्कारक होने के कारण वत्सल रस भी माना जाता है।

(*सा.द.* 3.251)

भानुदत्त कुछ और आगे बढ़ गये हैं। उन्होंने प्रारम्भ में तो रस के दो मौलिक वर्गों की कल्पना की है : स च रसो द्विविधः लौकिकोऽलौकिकश्चेति, अर्थात् रस दो प्रकार का होता है, लौकिक और अलौकिक। लौकिक सन्निकर्ष जन्य रस लौकिक हैं और अलौकिक सन्निकर्षजन्य रस अलौकिक हैं। लौकिक रस लौकिक सन्निकर्ष के माध्यम से छह इन्द्रियों के अनुसार छह हैं और अलौकिक रस अलौकिक सन्निकर्ष अर्थात् ज्ञान के तीन रूपों के अनुसार तीन हैं। ये हैं- (1) स्वाप्निक, (2) मानोरथिक और औपनायिक। इन अलौकिक रसों में, स्वप्न में प्राप्त रस स्वाप्निक है, मनोरथजन्य रस मानोरथिक है और ये दोनों ही सुख-दुःखमय हैं। अलौकिक रस का तीसरा भेद वह है जो काव्य के पद-पदार्थ अर्थात् शब्दार्थ और नाट्य से सिद्ध होता है, अर्थात् अलौकिक

रस-वर्ग के तृतीय भेद का नाम है काव्य या नाट्य रस। काव्य रस के अन्तर्गत सामान्यतः परम्परा-सम्मत नवरस को स्वीकार करने पर भी भानुदत्त ने वात्सल्य, लौल्य एवं भक्ति के अतिरिक्त कार्पण्य तथा माया, इन दो नवीन रसों का और उल्लेख किया है।

चित्तवृत्ति दो प्रकार की होती है। ये है प्रवृत्ति और निवृत्ति। निवृत्ति में जिस प्रकार शान्त रस होता है, उसी प्रकार प्रवृत्ति में माया रस की प्रतीति होती है। माया रस का निषेध नहीं किया जा सकता क्योंकि यदि निवृत्ति में शान्त रस की कल्पना संगत है, तो प्रवृत्ति में माया रस का निषेध कैसे किया जा सकता है ? यहां एक शंका यह हो सकती है कि माया रस स्वतन्त्र रस न होकर रति अर्थात् अनुरक्ति का ही एक रूप है। इसका उत्तर यह है कि यदि वह स्वतंत्र स्थायी न होकर केवल व्यभिचारी ही है तो किसका ? वास्तव में, माया की स्थिति तो परस्पर अनुकूल, प्रतिकूल सभी रसों में समभाव से है। कोई भी व्यभिचारी प्रतिकूल रसों में समभाव से संचरण नहीं कर सकता, अर्थात् ऐसा कोई भी व्यभिचारी नहीं है, जो विपरीत रसों में भी संचरण कर सके। अतः यह शंका उचित नहीं है। दूसरी शंका यह हो सकती है कि माया रस स्वतन्त्र रस न होकर सामान्य रस का ही पर्याय है, और शान्तेतर प्रसिद्ध आठ रस उसी के विशेष रूप या भेद हैं। इसका समाधान यह है कि यदि प्रवृत्तिरूपिणी माया रस का पर्याय है, तो उसका विपरीत रूप निवृत्तिमूलक 'शान्त' रस न रहकर रसाभास बन जाएगा। इसलिए माया स्वतंत्र रस ही है, व्यभिचारी नहीं। रति, हास, शोक आदि आठों भाव विद्युत् की तरह उसमें उत्पन्न और विलीन होते रहते हैं। अतः वे ही इसके व्यभिचारी हैं। माया रस का लक्षण इस प्रकार है– मिथ्याज्ञान की वासना ही प्रबुद्ध और उपचित होकर माया रस का रूप धारण कर लेती है। इसका स्थायीभाव है मिथ्याज्ञान, सांसारिक भोगों के उत्पादक धर्माधर्म विभाव हैं और पुत्र, कलत्र, विजय, साम्राज्य आदि अनुभाव हैं।

कार्पण्य रस : रस प्रसंग के आरम्भ में भानुदत्त ने वात्सल्य, लौल्य, भक्ति आदि के साथ एक नवीन रस का और उल्लेख किया है वह है कार्पण्य जिसका स्थायीभाव है स्पृहा, ''ननु वात्सल्यं, लौल्यं, भक्तिः कार्पण्यं जा कथं न रसः। आर्द्रताऽभिलाषश्रद्धास्पृहाणां स्थायिभावानां सत्त्वादिति''। किन्तु यह उल्लेख मात्र है। भानुदत्त को वात्सल्य, लौल्य और भक्ति के साथ-साथ कार्पण्य का रसत्व भी अग्राह्य है, क्योंकि आर्द्रता, अभिलाष, श्रद्धा के समान ही स्पृहा भी व्यभिचारी भाव मात्र है, स्वतन्त्र स्थायी नहीं है। वात्सल्य जिस प्रकार करुण रस का व्यभिचारी है उसी प्रकार भक्ति, शान्त का भी इसी प्रकार लौल्य के समान कार्पण्य भी हास्य का व्यभिचारीमात्र है।

इस प्रसंग में कदाचित् अन्तिम प्रयास किया वैष्णव आचार्य रूपगोस्वामी ने। उन्होंने काव्यशास्त्रियों के इस निर्णय का घोर विरोध किया कि भक्ति रस न होकर केवल भाव है और पूर्ण व्यवस्था के साथ भक्ति को प्रधान तथा शास्त्रीय रसों को गौण घोषित किया। उनके मतानुसार रस के दो प्रकार हैं:

1. मुख्य रस

शान्त भक्तिरस	शान्ति स्थायी
प्रीत भक्तिरस	प्रीति स्थायी
प्रेयान् भक्तिरस	सख्य स्थायी
वात्सल्य भक्तिरस	वात्सल्य स्थायी
मधुर भक्तिरस	मधुरा रति स्थायी

2. गौण रस

हास्य भक्तिरस	हासरति स्थायी
अद्‌भुत भक्तिरस	विस्मयरति स्थायी
वीर भक्तिरस	उत्साहरति स्थायी
करुण भक्तिरस	शोकरति स्थायी
रौद्र भक्तिरस	क्रोधरति स्थायी
भयानक भक्तिरस	भयरति स्थायी
बीभत्स भक्तिरस	जुगुप्सारति स्थायी

रस भेदों का विस्तार प्राय: यहीं पर समाप्त हो जाता है, इनके अतिरिक्त केवल एक नवीन रस 'व्रीडनक रस' का उल्लेख जैनों के *अनुयोगद्वारसूत्र* के आधार पर डॉ. राघवन ने किया है। व्रीडनक रस का स्थायी भाव व्रीडा या लज्जा है। उपर्युक्त सूत्र के टीकाकार मलधारी हेमचन्द्र (बारहवीं शती ई.) ने लिखा है कि कुछ विद्वान् व्रीडनक के स्थान पर भयानक रस की गणना करते हैं किन्तु भयानक तो अपने कारणभूत रस रौद्र का ही अंग है, अत: उसकी पृथक् सत्ता नहीं होती। भारतीय काव्यशास्त्र में सूत्रकार और भाष्यकार दोनों का ही कोई स्थान नहीं है, फिर भी केवल नवीनता की दृष्टि से ही व्रीडनक रस का उल्लेख मात्र कर देना असमीचीन नहीं है।

संस्कृत के अन्तिम मेधावी आचार्य हुए पंडितराज जगन्नाथ, जिन्होंने अत्यन्त प्रबल शब्दों में इस विस्तार प्रवृत्ति का खण्डन कर परम्परा की पुन: प्रतिष्ठा पर बल दिया, ''रसानां नवत्वगणना च मुनिवचननियन्त्रिता भज्येत, इति यथाशास्त्रमेव ज्याय:''। अर्थात् भक्ति आदि रसों का समावेश करने से मुनि द्वारा निर्धारित संख्या भंग हो जाएगी, अत: शास्त्र का अनुसरण करना ही श्रेयस्कर है। (*हि.रस.गं.*, पृ. 176)

12

अभिनवगुप्त प्रणीत स्तोत्रों में रस-साधना का दर्शन

रमाकान्त शर्मा आंगिरस

भरतमुनि के *नाट्यशास्त्र* से लेकर आज तक रस के स्वरूप को लेकर जितनी भी परिकल्पनाएं की गईं वे कहीं-न-कहीं किसी रूप में सादृश्यमूलक होकर मार्ग से भटक गईं। फलत: रस की बात साहित्य-समीक्षा या सौंदर्यबोध के गहन स्तरों के पास जाकर भी हाथों में से फिसल जाती है। अतएव रस को लेकर की जाने वाली चर्चा कहीं रुकने का नाम नहीं लेती। किसी सादृश्य के आधार पर की जाने वाली बात रसानुभूति को वाच्य बना देती है। परिणामत: लोल्लट चाहे किसी उत्पत्तिमूलक सादृश्य को लेकर अपनी व्याख्या दें, शंकुक अनुमितिवादी 'चित्रतुरग-न्याय' का आश्रय लेकर अपनी बात कहें, भट्टनायक भोगानुभव की समानता को लेकर भावकत्व के माध्यम से रस-भोग की बात कहें या फिर आचार्य अभिनवगुप्त की रस-सिद्धान्तपरक व्याख्या को 'अभिव्यक्ति-सादृश्य' के साथ जोड़कर देखें, बात सीधी होने की बजाए रसेप्सु के मन में अनेक शंकाओं और अनुत्तरित प्रश्नों को छोड़ जाती है। अत: प्रस्तुत अध्ययन में महामाहेश्वराचार्य अभिनवगुप्त की स्वरचित कुछ काव्यरचनाओं के आधार पर हम उनकी रसदृष्टि का उन्मेष करने का प्रयास करेंगे।

यह ठीक है कि वैदिक वाङ्मय में रस शब्द या उसके समानान्तर 'मधु', 'सोम', 'घृत', 'पयस्' आदि कुछ ऐसे पदों का स्थान-स्थान पर प्रयोग हुआ है, जिनके सेवन से मरा या सूखा-सड़ा-सा जीवन-प्राण फिर से उमग उठता है। *छान्दोग्योपनिषद्* में

प्राणविद्या अधिकरण में सत्यकाम ने व्याघ्रपाद के पुत्र गोश्रुति को मानवदेह में समस्त अंगों के रसभूत प्राण के रहस्य को देते हुए, अंत में यह कहा कि यदि इस प्राण के रहस्य को किसी सूखे ठूंठ के सामने भी कहा जाएगा तो उसमें फिर से शाखाएं फूट पड़ेंगी और कोंपलों के कोमल अंकुर उसमें उग आएंगे *''यद्येनत् शुष्काय स्थाणवे ब्रूयात् जायेरन् एव अस्मिन् शाखा: प्ररोहेयु: पलाशानि''* (*छान्दोग्योपनषिद्, 5.2.3*)।

उपनिषदों की यह चित्रमयी भाषा जो ऋचाओं के उद्‌गम के साथ ही जीवन की प्राणवत्ता को उसके उसी मूलरूप में मुखरित करती आ रही थी, वह सभ्यता के बोझिलपन से दूर संस्कृति की सारस्वत धारा थी। परवर्ती *आश्वलायन श्रौतसूत्र* (अ.3, पंचयज्ञ प्रकरण) में इस वैदिक ब्रह्मविद्या की तरलता, स्वादुता और सौष्ठव को एक वाक्य में उपसंहृत करते हुए कहा गया कि ऋचाओं के अध्ययन में दूध की धाराओं का रस, यजुर्वेद के मंत्रों के पाठ में उठती हुई घृत की सुरभियों का आस्वाद और ब्राह्मणग्रन्थ, कल्पसूत्र, गाथा, नाराशंसी, इतिहास, पुराण के अनुशीलन में अमृतपान की तृप्ति का आनन्द, ये सब इस अमृतावाक् के चर्वण का फल हो सकते हैं। यह अकृत्रिम संस्कृता वाक् नारद जैसे तत्त्वजिज्ञासु के प्रति जब सनत्कुमार के मुख से उपदिष्ट होगी तो यह सभी प्रकाश की उपासना में रत लोगों को जीवन के तमस् या अन्धकार के उस पार ले जाएगी, जिसे 'स्कन्द' कहा जाता है। जीवन की प्रथम रश्मियों का वह प्रवाह जहां एक बार झांक लेने के बाद जिंदगी की दैनन्दिन या रोजमर्रा की छोटी-छोटी वस्तुओं की ताक-झांक की वासना का सिलसिला समाप्त हो सकता है, क्योंकि वह स्कन्द उस पवित्रता और नैर्मल्य का नाम है, जिसके आसपास दूर-दूर तक कहीं कोई छिलका या आवरण-पात्र का नामोनिशान तक नहीं। उसी को कोई-कोई ''अमृतस्य परं सेतुं दग्धेन्धनमिवानलम्'' कहते हैं। वह धूमरहित वह विशोका समाधि है, जिसको एक बार छू लेने के बाद फिर रोज़-रोज़ मरना नहीं होता।

हिमालय के दक्षिण की ओर और समुद्र के उत्तर की ओर निष्पाप निवास करने वाली जिन जातियों या प्रजातियों के हाथ यह रहस्य लग गया उनकी पीढ़ियां इस रसानुभूति को किसी भी प्रकार से हाथ से न जाने देने के लिए विवश थीं। परवर्ती सभ्यताओं के बढ़ते हुए संघर्षों और उठते हुए कृत्रिम नैतिक मूल्यों के दबाव के अतिरिक्त उन लोगों ने कुछ ऐसे चैनल या सुरंगें बनाने का प्रयास बनाए रखा, ताकि धर्म, अर्थ और काम की बहती हुई त्रिवेणी के स्रोत ही न सूख जाएं। यह रसानुभूति का मानसर संभवत: शैवों के कैलाश से बहुत दूर नहीं था। महामाहेश्वराचार्य अभिनवगुप्त के प्राण इन्हीं हिमालय की उपत्यकाओं में मंडराते हुए जब मुखरित होते हैं तो उनके काव्य की मर्मस्पर्शिता उनके पाठकों को भी उस अनुत्तर पद का साक्षात्कार कराने लगती हैं और उनकी काव्य-प्रतिभा समाधि-काव्य की सृष्टि करने लगती है, जिसमें प्राणों का संचार स्वत: स्तब्ध होने लगता है। बन्ध और मोक्ष की शास्त्राभ्यास

या भोगाभ्यास से बनी हुई कल्पनाएं स्वत: ही निर्बन्ध होकर खुल जाती हैं। रज्जु में सर्प की भ्रान्ति या रात के अंधेरे में किसी छाया को पिशाच समझ बैठने की भ्रान्ति का आतंक स्वत: मिट जाता है तथा पदार्थों के ग्रहण एवं त्याग की अहंता का हिमखण्ड पिघलकर स्वस्थता में रूपान्तरित हो जाता है। इसलिए यह मानकर चलना होगा कि नाट्यशास्त्र पर *अभिनवभारती* नामक भाष्य लिखते हुए आचार्य अभिनवगुप्त की संवेदना अभिनवरूपा शक्ति और उस शक्ति में निगूहित जो महेश्वर हैं, उन दोनों के यामल रूप को आत्मसात् करके आचार्य शिवता की भूमि पर दृढ़ता से पैर जमा चुके थे। आचार्य की रचना *परमार्थचर्चा* पर विवरण आरम्भ करते हुए हरभट्ट कहते हैं:

अभिनवरूपा शक्तिस्तद्गुप्तो यो महेश्वरो देव:।
तदुभयामलरूपमभिनवगुप्तं शिवं वन्दे।।

शिव-शक्ति के इस यामलभाव को परमेश्वर की इच्छामात्र से कल्पित होने के कारण किसी भी रूप में संवित् शिव से भिन्न न होने से उनमें अद्वैतता कभी खण्डित नहीं होती। लगता है परवर्ती वैष्णव साहित्य में भी द्वैतता को अद्वैतता का ही रूप कल्पित करते हुए कहा गया है, ''लीलार्थं कल्पितं द्वैतमद्वैतादपि सुन्दरम्।'' परन्तु काश्मीर शैवाचार्यों ने लीला पद के स्थान पर परमेश्वर की स्वेच्छा और उसके उन्मुक्त स्वातन्त्र्य को ही क्रीडारस में उपयोगी बनाया। अभिनवगुप्त कहते हैं:

एष देवोऽनया देव्या नित्यं क्रीडारसोत्सुक:।
विचित्रान् सृष्टिसंहारान् विधत्ते युगपद् विभु:।।

अपनी ही विमर्श शक्ति से नित्य क्रीड़ा करते हुए शिव का सम्पूर्ण सृष्टि में और मानवचेतना के प्रत्येक केन्द्रीय धरातल पर प्रतिपल जो क्रीडन हो रहा है, वही तो नाट्यकला का मूल है। शिव की नाट्यक्रीड़ा में शिव स्वयम् ही नटराज की भूमिका करते हुए अज्ञान की ग्रन्थियों को तोड़ते हुए जब अपनी 'स्व-शक्ति' की अभिव्यक्ति करने लगते हैं, तो घनिष्ठता या गहनता की उस सान्द्र अनुभूति में आनन्दरूप मोक्ष उच्छल हो उठता है :

अज्ञानग्रन्थिभिदा स्वशक्त्यभिव्यक्तता मोक्ष:।

(*परमार्थसार*, 60)

काव्य एवम् काव्य की ही एक कला नाट्य के द्वारा इसी क्रीडारस को अपने सहृदयों के हृदय में जगाने के नैपुण्य को ही भरतमुनि ने अपने नाट्यशास्त्र का विषय बनाया है। कालान्तर में उस नाट्यशास्त्र की कुछ एक अपव्याख्याओं में ग्रन्थकारों के अपने-अपने बुद्धिभेद से किए गए अपकर्ष के कारण आचार्य अभिनवगुप्त ने शैवी

व्याख्या देकर अत्यन्त निगूढ केवल कुछ एक सहृदय लोगों द्वारा ही अपने अन्तरंग में स्फुरित होने वाली रस-संवित् को ठीक प्रकार से अभिव्यक्ति की दिशा देकर नाट्यशास्त्र की दृष्टि के अनुकूल रससूत्र की व्याख्या दी। कारण, संभवत: यही था कि महेश्वर के उपासक लोगों को यह पता था कि शिव नटराज हैं। यह विश्व, जो रंगशाला है, उसमें नटराज की आत्माभिव्यक्ति उनके आनंद के उच्छलन के अतिरिक्त क्या हो सकती है। अथवा यह स्व-स्वातन्त्र्य की अभिव्यक्ति क्या है ? वह अनुत्तर शिव के ही विश्व में परिपूर्ण अहंभाव के ही चमत्कार का उल्लास है।

अभिनवगुप्त की रचना *श्रीबोधपञ्चदशिका* के टीकाकार श्री हरभट्टशास्त्री श्लोक 14 की व्याख्या करते हुए कहते हैं कि शिव की अपनी स्वतन्त्र इच्छाशक्ति से ही क्रीडा-रसिक भगवान् महेश्वर इस विश्वरूपी नाट्य क्रीडा को प्रदर्शित करने के अभिप्राय से अन्तरात्मा के रंगमंच पर पृथक्-पृथक् भूमिका को लेकर विभाव और अनुभाव आदि से व्यंजित तथा सात्त्विक भावों के सहचारी पृथक्-पृथक् स्थायिभावों के द्वारा उद्घाटित या उद्भासित होकर अलौकिक, रस-सम्बन्धी चमत्कार का आस्वादन कराता है। जो लोग इस काव्य एवं नाटकजन्य अर्थ को नहीं समझ पाते या उसके परमार्थ ज्ञान से निम्नस्तरीय अपरा शक्तियों के बन्धन के कारण अपरिचित हैं उनका हृदय अविकसित या भीतर ही भीतर चल निकलने वाली अन्तस् की रस-लहरी से खिल नहीं पाता, "अन्त:स्रावविहीनानां सदा सन्तप्तचेतसाम्।" यह अन्त:स्राव अभिनवगुप्त के मत में संवित् या पराचेतना का वह प्रसाद या निर्मलता है, जो एक बार भैरव शिव की परा प्रतिभा में डुबकी लगा आने के बाद प्राप्त हो जाती है। जिसके बाद फिर किसी प्रकार के उपाय या प्रयत्न करने की आवश्यकता नहीं रहती। सहज ही में स्वप्रकाशता या उस रस की उपलब्धि होने लगती है, जिसे अध्यात्म की भाषा में शिव कहा जाता है। यथा-

उपायैर्न शिवो भाति भान्ति ते तत्प्रसादत:।
स एवाहं स्वप्रकाशो भासे विश्वस्वरूपक:।। तन्त्रालोक 3.63

आचार्य अभिनवगुप्त का यही शैव-काव्य का दर्शन है, जो *अभिनवभारती* आदि समीक्षा-निकषों के ललाट पर स्वर्ण रेखाओं के रूप में उद्भासित है। नाट्य आदि कलाओं में शैवी क्रीडा के अंगभूत विभाव, अनुभाव और संचारियों के सामरस्यमूलक संयोग से संवित् रूप शिव अथवा रस की अभिव्यक्तिपरक निष्पत्ति होती है।

काव्य-साहित्य या कला-समूह यदि जीवन का प्रतिनिधित्व करते हैं, तो जीवन की अनेकरूपा अभिव्यक्ति या परिणामशीलता विश्वमय और विश्वोत्तीर्ण के बीचो-बीच माननी होगी और जीवन की अभिव्यक्तियों को रसरूप शिवता के साथ जोड़कर देखना होगा। रस का वैलक्षण्य या लोकोत्तरता यही है कि वह विश्वमयता और विश्वोत्तीर्णता के शुक्र-शोणित में से उद्भूत होने पर भी स्वयं में नित्यनवीन है। ऋग्वेद संभवत: इसी

को अभिमुख बनाकर "नवो नवो भवति जायमान:" अर्थात् वह तत्त्वाग्नि उत्पन्न होने की प्रक्रिया को निमित्त बनाकर प्रतिपग एक प्रकार की नवीनता से दूसरे प्रकार की नवीनता में प्रवेश करता चलता है। बन्धन और मुक्ति की अवधारणाएं तब स्वयं ही द्रवित होकर उसी में समाविष्ट हो जाती हैं। इस शैवी अनुभव-साधना में जो घटित होता है, उसे आचार्य अभिनवगुप्त अपने सुप्रसिद्ध *अनुत्तराष्टिका स्तोत्र* काव्य में स्वरूपत: निरूपित करते हैं, कि राग-द्वेष या सुख और असुख वर्ग के भावों का उदय और अस्त होना, अहंकार एवम् दैन्य आदि जितना भी भावसमूह है, वे सब विश्ववपु शिव के ही भिन्न-भिन्न रूप होने के कारण स्वभावत: भिन्न नहीं होते। जब साधक या सिद्ध उस संवित् शिव की भावना या ऐक्यानुभव से सम्पन्न होकर उन समस्त भावों की विभिन्न अभिव्यक्तियों को शिवा की ही विभिन्न छवियों के रूप में देखने लगता है, तो उसे रसानुसन्धान होने लगता है। आधुनिक सन्दर्भ में महाप्राण निराला की अपने काव्य-कर्म की प्रौढ़ता के काल में श्याम की विभिन्न छवियां अपनी विभिन्नता को साथ लेकर भी ऐक्य-साधन करने लगी थीं और कवि की काव्य-संवित् शब्दात्मिका गीति के रूप में फूट निकली :

जिधर देखिए श्याम बिराजे
श्याम कुंज वन यमुना श्यामा श्याम गगन घन वारिद गाजे।
श्याम तामरस श्याम सरोवर श्याम अनिल छवि श्याम संवाजे।।
श्याम बलाका शालि श्याम है श्याम विजय बाजे नभ बाजे।
श्रुति के अक्षर श्याम देखिए दीपशिखा पर श्याम निवाजै।।

प्रस्तुत गीतिका की संवेदना की पराकाष्ठा सागर की एक ऊर्मि की तरह उस समय आकाश को छूने की ओर बढ़ती है जहा नीले मेघों के बीच वन्दनवार बनाकर एक लय के साथ उड़ी जा रही श्वेत वकपंक्ति या बलाका भी अपने रूप-रंग की पार्थिवता को छोड़कर श्यामा चेतना में बिना कुछ खोए तद्रूप हो उठती है। भारत के निगम और आगम की परम्परा के उपासकों की यही रस-संवित् जब भी उमड़ने लगती है, तो यह आधिभौतिक पदार्थों, आधिदैविक दृष्टियों और आध्यात्मिक अनुभूतियों के साथ बिना छेड़छाड़ किए या बिना विक्षिप्त या व्यथित किए ही एक नूतन अधिभूत, अधिदैवत एवम् अध्यात्म की सृष्टि करने लगती है। यही उसकी चिर-जीवन्तता और सनातनता का रहस्य रहा है। इसीलिए आचार्य अभिनवगुप्त अपने समाधि-काव्य की एक पंक्ति से संकेत करते हुए कहते हैं, "संविद्रूपमवेक्ष्य किं न रमसे तद्भावना निर्भर:" कि अरे भाई लोग उस परा संवित् को, जो अस्तित्व-अनस्तित्व, अभिधेयत्व-ज्ञेयत्व की प्रतीतियों और पदार्थों के भीतर से झांक रही है उसको एक बार आत्मसात् करके क्यों नहीं जी लेते ? यह जो माया है, अविद्या है यह आंख खुलने पर अद्वय चित् से अभिन्न

ही है। अतः उस अनुत्तर अनुभूति में पूजा, पूजक, पूज्य के भेद की कोई गुंजाइश ही नहीं अथवा शाक्तों की दृष्टि में 'ज्ञातृज्ञानज्ञेयानामभेदभावनम्' ही हो रहा हो तो सभी कुछ अपने स्व के अनुभव से स्वभाव में ही निर्मल हो उठता है। व्यर्थ के चिंतकों का वहां कोई प्रयोजन ही नहीं। क्योंकि वास्तव में अनेकत्व एकत्व का विरोधी नहीं है, अपितु वह स्वयंप्रकाश संवित् का ही वैभव है। इसलिए यहां न द्वैत है, न द्वैताद्वैत है, न विशिष्टाद्वैत है। चर्चा स्तोत्र में अभिनवगुप्त कहते हैं कि सृष्टि में ग्राह्य, ग्रहण एवम् ग्रहीता का विभाग शिवाभिन्न शक्ति के वैचित्र्य के कारण उसी का सहज सौन्दर्य बनकर स्फुरित होने लगता है। इसी द्वैत एवम् अद्वैत की ग्रन्थि को सुलझाने के लिए आचार्य अभिनवगुप्त अपने काव्य में कई बार जिन प्रतिमानों को उत्कीर्ण करते हैं उनमें एक है : 'मणिदर्पणविधि', जिसका उल्लेख आचार्य शंकर ने भी अपने *दक्षिणामूर्तिस्तोत्र* की प्रथम पंक्ति में किया है, ''विश्वं दर्पणदृश्यमाननगरी तुल्यं निजान्तर्गतम्।'' अभिनवगुप्त कहते हैं कि परमार्थता की दृष्टि खुलते ही शिव का जगत् से भेद, जीव का शिव से भेद अथवा शिव, जीव, जगत् को लेकर किए जाने वाले जितने भी भेदभाव हो सकते हैं, वे सभी अविरोधी होकर स्वच्छ संवित् रूपी मुकुर या दर्पण में ऐसे ही अन्वित हो जाते हैं, जैसे एक ही स्वच्छ प्रकाश वाले दर्पण में एक साथ ही बाह्य जगत् के प्रासाद-भवन, उन भवनों में स्थित हाथी, घोड़े, मेघ, समुद्र, पर्वत आदि विविध पदार्थ अपनी विविधता को बिना त्यागे एक साथ प्रतिबिंबित होते हुए प्रतिबिम्बों के रूप में उस दर्पण की ही विभूति होते हैं।

आदर्शकुक्षौ प्रतिबिम्बकारि सबिम्बकं स्याद्यदि मानसिद्धम्।
स्वच्छन्दसंविन्मुकुरान्तराले भावेषु हेत्वन्तरमस्ति नान्यत्।।
(*परमार्थचर्चास्तव, 5*)

क्रमस्तोत्र में आचार्य का कहना है कि एक बार शिवता के समावेश हो जाने पर पशुता के कारण दिखाई दे रही बन्धमयी सांसारिकता की स्थिति को शिवता के काव्य की आग्नेय ज्वाला से रसमय बनाकर जब समस्त भाव-दृष्टि को मैं पीने लगता हूं तो मैं परम सुख की अनुभूति से मदमत्त हो जाता हूं। क्योंकि उस समय मेरे स्व या आत्म के स्फार या उत्तरोत्तर बढ़ते हुए प्रसार से अनन्तवैचित्र्य की महिमा प्रकट होने लगती है:

विधुन्वानो बन्धाभिमतभवमार्गस्थितिमिमां
रसीकृत्यानन्तस्तुतिहुतवहप्लोषिताभिदाम्
विचित्रस्वस्फारस्फुरितमहिमारम्भरभसात्
पिबन्भावानेतान् वरद मदमत्तोऽस्मि सुखितः।। 5।। (*क्रमस्तोत्रम्, 5*)

वास्तव में, आचार्य अभिनवगुप्त की शिवसंवित्-साधना या रसानुभूति की प्रक्रिया जब आरम्भ होती है तो सहृदय के प्राण गणपति के रूप में, अपान बटुक के रूप में तथा समस्त इन्द्रियरूप देवियां अपने-अपने विषय भोगों की पूजा सामग्री लेकर हृदयकमल में स्थित आत्मलिंग चिन्मय भगवान् आनन्द भैरव का अभिपूजन करने आती हैं तो योगी का अवधान या ध्यान ही अपनी धी या धारणाशक्ति के बल से सद्गुरु बनकर शिवपथ का द्वार खोल देता है। बुद्धि अपने निश्चयरूप कुसुमों को लिए हुए ब्रह्माणी शक्ति बनकर आनन्दभैरव-भैरवी के आराधन के लिए पहुंच जाती है। अहंकृति शाम्भवी अम्बा, और सदा विकल्प करने वाला मन कौमारीशक्ति तथा शब्दरूपा वाणी वैष्णवीशक्ति में रूपांतरित हो जाते हैं। रूप, रस, गन्ध, स्पर्श आदि की सभी शक्तियां आनन्द भैरव-भैरवी के पूजागृह में आकर सभी सहृदयों के हृदयों में सदा सन्निहित अनुभव के सार रूप-रस को मिलाकर या समरस होकर अभिव्यक्त करने लगती है। आचार्य अभिनवगुप्त की चेतना का रंगमंच रसानुभूति का पूजागृह है, जहां प्रविष्ट होने से शैवी भावना के हिमस्रोत जल से सर्वमलनिवारक स्नान करके श्रद्धानदी के विमलचित्तरूप अभिषेक जल को लेकर और समाधिरूप कुसुमों को अञ्जलि पुट बनाकर रसानुभूतिरूप अपने ही स्वरूप संवित् के साथ ऐक्यानुसन्धान के लिए चलना होगा। क्योंकि आचार्य के मत में रसानुभूति के मधुपात्र में किसी भी प्रकार के ऐन्द्रिय बोध, मानसबोध एवम् अतीन्द्रियबोधों की वर्जना या निषेध का विधान नहीं है।

भारतीय जीवन-साधना में कला-साधना में, इस प्रत्येक पदार्थ में प्रतीयमान होने वाला एक ऐसा सार है जो सदा ही एक नवीन से नवीनतर होती जा रही ऊर्जा को मधुर उत्तेजना या सौष्ठव-सम्पन्न रूप में परिणत कर देता है। आचार्य अभिनवगुप्त कहते हैं कि यह आनन्दानुभूति धनमद, मद्यमद, अंगनासंगमद जैसी नहीं है। यहां जो प्रकाश की भी कल्पना है वह प्रदीप, सूर्य या चन्द्रमा के प्रकाश जैसी नहीं है। अपितु, जन्मजन्मान्तर से चले आ रहे मलिन सुख-भोग की सहस्रों वासनाओं के बोझ के उतर जाने का सुख है। इसके साथ ही अपने ही अज्ञान-तिमिर या मेघों में छिपे हुए अपने ही विस्मृत स्व के शरत् चन्द्र का किसी मौन वनान्तर के निर्मल निशीथ में आविर्भूत हो उठना है।

(दे. *अनुत्तराष्टिका*, श्लोक 4।)

वास्तव में आचार्य अभिनवगुप्त के अभिमत दर्शन के अनुसार शब्द की सम्पूर्ण सृष्टि प्रतिभा का ऐसा खेल है, जो न तो लौकिक या भूत-पदार्थों के संसरण या स्फुरण से निर्मित है, न ही अभौतिक या अतिभौतिक दिव्यता का रहस्यात्मक चमत्कार है, वह तो शब्द के भीतर से होकर स्फुरित होने वाली शब्द-संवित् की लोकालोकमयी सृष्टि है:

माये विद्ये मातृके मानिनि त्वं काये काये स्पन्दसे चित्कलात्मा।
..ध्यायेयं त्वां वाचमन्तर्नदन्तीम्।।

(रहस्यपंचदशिका, श्लोक 8)

वहां शब्दों का अर्थों से जो संबंध है वह भी वाच्य कोटि का भौतिक पद-पदार्थ सम्बन्ध नहीं, अपितु काव्यधर्मिता से स्फुरण होने वाला व्यंजकव्यंग्य सम्बन्ध है। यही सम्बन्ध सहृदय सामाजिक के अनुशीलन का विषय बनकर उसके प्राण और मन को वाक् में प्रतिष्ठित कर देता है और वाक् सहृदय के मन, प्राण को अपने में अभिसूत्रित कर लेती है तो अभिनवगुप्त कहते हैं कि समाधिकाव्य के कवि के मुख से जो भी शब्द उच्चरित होता है वह लोकोत्तर मंत्र हो जाता है। सुख तथा दु:ख के अनुभव से होने वाली संस्थितियां सुख-दु:ख न रहकर मुद्रा का रूप धारण कर लेती हैं। अपनी स्वरसता में से उठता हुआ प्राणों का प्रवाह अद्‌भुत योग में परिणत हो जाता है। इस प्रकार शक्तित्व के परमधाम यानी वर्ण-पद और मंत्र का अनुभव करते हुए ऐसा क्या रह जाता है, जो हमें प्रकाशमयी सृष्टि में नहीं ले जाता।

उस प्रातिभ मंत्र में वर्णक्रम या पदों का क्रम संलक्षित नहीं होता। सम्पूर्ण कायिकी या शरीर की क्रियाएं विगलित होकर आनन्द-मुद्रा का प्रादुर्भाव हो उठता है। योग की वह अवस्था प्रकट हो जाती है जहां प्राण का समग्र प्रवाह ही चुक जाता है। अत: हे भगवति प्रतिभे! तुम्हारे धाम में पहुंच जाने पर सुधी जन को कौन-से वैलक्षण्य का अनुभव नहीं हो जाता। (दे. *अनुभवनिवेदनस्तोत्रम्*, 3, 4)

इस प्रकार, आचार्य अभिनवगुप्त के स्तोत्रकाव्य के अनुशीलन से प्रतीत होता है कि शैव-साधना में क्रमश: बाह्योपाय साधना से आन्तर-उपाय साधना के चरम शिखर पर्यन्त यानी अनुपाय पर्यन्त पूजन-सामग्री एवम् साधन-प्रक्रिया के अंग रूप विभावादिकों में शिवता की भावना एवम् दृढ़ से दृढ़तर होते हुए समावेश के बल से जब अन्त:करण में महासाहसवृत्ति का उदय होता है तो बिना किसी अवरोध के सहसा घटित हुए चमत्कार या उन्मेष से स्वरूपलाभ-रूप-रस उच्छल हो उठता है। अत: शैवों और शाक्तों की दृष्टि से देखें, तो वहां आपको मिलेगा कि साधना-मंडल में जो कुछ भी सामग्री या क्रियाकलाप हैं, वे सभी समावेश अथवा दृढ़तर भावना के बल से शिवदृष्टि का उन्मेष होने पर शिवरूपता में आप्लावित होकर रसदीप्त होने लगते हैं।

इसी महानुभव का एक लघुकाय रूप भारतीय कलाएं अथवा काव्य जब अभिव्यक्त करने लगते हैं, तो बात स्पष्ट हो जाती है कि शैव साधनाक्रम शिव की विभिन्न कलाओं के माध्यम से अखण्डयोग प्राप्त करने की विधि या क्रम है। उसमें योगसाधनारूपों की कठोरता एवम् इन्द्रियनिग्रह आदि अनावश्यक हो उठते हैं। क्योंकि, जब सर्वसाधारण लौकिक सुखों का अनुभव करते हुए भी शिवता के उन्मीलन से आत्मानन्दकला का रस उठता है तो अभिनवगुप्त कहते हैं कि अपनी शिवता में अधिक समादर हो जाने से इन्द्रिय भोगलालसा में तब आदर विगलित होता चला जाता है उसमें विरक्ति स्वाभाविक होती चली जाती है। उलटे बलपूर्वक इन्द्रियों का निग्रह करने से कई बार कई प्रकार की विकृतियां जन्म लेने लगती हैं:

अनादरविरक्त्यैव गलन्तीन्द्रियवृत्तय:
यावत्तु विनियम्यन्ते तावत्तावद्विकुर्वते।।

(*मालिनीविजयवार्तिक, 2.112*)

इस प्रकार, शिवदृष्टि रसदृष्टि के समावेश से तरंगित हृदय वाले सामाजिक की द्वैत अथवा द्वैताद्वैत की सांसारिक वासनाओं को नष्ट करने का कुचक्र नहीं रचती, अपितु 'सर्वं शिवमयम्' की अनुभूति से शेष समस्त अनुभूति-पुंज को समरस कर देती है, जहां अन्य किसी वेद्यान्तर का स्पर्श सम्भव ही नहीं है। इसी एक क्षण को पाकर रूपान्तरित होने के लिए पिछले सहस्राधिक वर्षों से भारतीय कला-साधनाएं यत्नशील रही हैं तथा मूल कृतिकार की रसदृष्टि को उन्मेषित करने के लिए ही नट-नटी आदि पात्र तथा सहृदय सामाजिक अपनी-अपनी सीमा व मर्यादाओं में रहते हुए भी ऐक्य-साधन के लिए प्रयत्न करते हैं।

इस पत्र को प्रस्तुत करते समय मेरी दृष्टि इस ओर रही है कि प्राचीन वैदिक एवम् उपनिषद् सम्बन्धी मन्त्रकाव्य में रस शब्द का बहुधा प्रयोग हुआ है, जिसका सम्बन्ध मूलत: आर्ष बोध से रहा है। भले ही वह कृतिकार में उठा हो या सहृदय में। आचार्य भरतमुनि ने जिस नाट्य अथवा नाटक के सन्दर्भ में प्रस्तुत रस शब्द का प्रयोग किया है वह सन्दर्भ पौराणिक है। पौराणिक सन्दर्भ को भले ही परम्परा की बाध्यता के कारण वैदिक परम्परा से जोड़ने का प्रयास निम्न पद्य में किया हो:

जग्राह पाठ्यं ऋग्वेदात्सामभ्यो गीतिमेव च
यजुर्वेदादभिनयान् रसानाथर्वणादपि।। (*ना.शा., 1.17*)

इस श्लोक से ऐसा प्रतीत होता है कि नाट्यशास्त्र ने जब अभिनवगुप्त अथवा नाट्यकला को 'वागंगसत्त्वोपेत' करके पंचम नाट्यवेद की घोषणा की, तो काव्य और नाट्य को पर्याप्त समीप लाया जा चुका था। वेद और लोक का बन्धन दृढ़तर हो चुका था। किन्तु निश्चय ही वैदिक रस का सन्दर्भ अवश्य ही बदला होगा। क्योंकि जो संहितापाठ ऋषियों की कण्ठ-ध्वनि, सामगान तथा कर और वदन की मुद्राओं के प्रकटन से किया जाता था उसमें वाचिक और आंगिक अभिनय के बीज तो थे ही। किन्तु सामान्य लोक जीवन की कथाप्रियता की भावना, रंगमंच एवम् एक विशिष्ट प्रकार की सुनिश्चित अनुकृति की व्यंजना का भाव वहां कहां रहा होगा। फलत: सभी वर्णों एवम् समानजातीय लोगों के लिए चाक्षुष यज्ञ के प्रतिनिधि पांचवें नाट्यवेद का सर्जन हुआ, जिसमें काव्य के रस से नाट्यरस भिन्न ही रहा होगा। इस सम्बन्ध में प्रो. एस. बारलिंगे का आक्षेप करना उचित भी हो सकता है कि आचार्य अभिनवकृत भरत के *नाट्यशास्त्र* पर लिखी भाष्य-टीका *'अभिनव भारती'* के छठे अध्याय में निरूपित रस-सूत्र की

व्याख्या भरतमुनि के नाट्य-दर्शन के अनुकूल न होकर काव्यात्मक रस-दृष्टि के अनुकूल आरोपित हो गयी है, किन्तु ध्वन्यालोक पर लोचन टीका के रचयिता के रूप में आचार्य अभिनवगुप्त का योगदान सहृदयों के लिए स्वतन्त्र रूप में एक महनीय रचना तो है ही।

13

रसाभास का यथार्थ लक्षण और वास्तविक क्षेत्र

कलानाथ शास्त्री

भारतीय काव्याशास्त्र में सर्वोत्तम काव्य के रूप में जिन भेदों का वर्गीकरण किया गया है (जिसे उत्तम काव्य या ध्वनि काव्य भी कहा गया है) उनमें रस, भाव, रसाभास, भावाभास, भावशान्ति आदि आते हैं। मम्मट ने *काव्यप्रकाश* में काव्य के तीन भेदों में उत्तम काव्य का नाम ध्वनि काव्य[1] बताया हैं, जिसके दो भेद किए हैं: अलक्ष्यक्रम तथा संलक्ष्यक्रम। इनमें प्रथम भेद के अन्तर्गत जिस प्रकार रस और भाव हैं उसी प्रकार रसाभास और भावाभास[2] भी हैं, अर्थात् दोनों उत्तम काव्य के भेद होते हैं। रसाभास और भावाभास को आरम्भ से अनन्त तक सभी आचार्यों ने उत्तम काव्य माना है, किसी ने उसका स्थान थोड़ा भी नीचे नहीं बताया। भरत ने *नाट्यशास्त्र* में रसाभास को अलग से नहीं गिनाया है। आनन्दवर्धन ने इसका अलग से उल्लेख किया है। किन्तु लक्षण नहीं बताया। *ध्वन्यालोक* के टीकाकारों तथा भरत के टीकाकारों द्वारा रसाभास का लक्षण करते समय उसकी परिभाषा जिन शब्दों में दी गई, लगती है उनसे कुछ मत-मतान्तर भी बने जिन पर आज भी कुछ विवेचन की आवश्यकता है। सर्वप्रथम यह ध्यान देने योग्य बात है कि 'आभास' शब्द का एक काल विशेष में जिस प्रकार का अर्थ लगाया जाने लगा था, उसकी प्रतिमा अच्छी नहीं थी। शायद इसका प्रारम्भ न्यायशास्त्र के हेत्वाभास शब्द से हुआ था। वहां किसी कार्य का जो वास्तविक कारण होता था उसे हेतु कहा जाता था, किन्तु जो वास्तविक कारण न होकर कारण जैसा प्रतीत होता था

उसे हेत्वाभास[3] कहा जाता था। यह हेतु नहीं होता था और बिलकुल ग़लत होता था। सम्भवतः इसी साम्य के कारण बाद में आभास शब्द मिथ्या का सूचक भी हो गया और ग़लत तथा हीन का सूचक भी हो गया। शायद इसी कारण प्राचीन हिन्दी में इस प्रकार के वाक्य भी चल पड़े। "उस सभा में तो इस विवाद के कारण बड़ा रसाभास हो गया"। इस प्रकार रसाभास को हीन, गर्हित और निन्दनीय अर्थ मिल गया। यह जगन्नाथ के *रसगंगाधर* से और भी स्पष्ट हो जाता है जहां उन्होंने हेत्वाभास का साम्य बताते हुए रसाभास की परिभाषा में पक्ष-प्रतिपक्ष करने की चेष्टा की है।[4]

विचारणीय बात यह है कि आज रसाभास की जो अर्थच्छाया बनी है उसने क्या काव्यशास्त्र के वास्तविक उद्‌देश्य को धूमिल नहीं कर दिया है ? स्पष्ट है कि यदि रसाभास हीन या गर्हित स्थितियों का सूचक होता, तो उसे रस के समान ही उत्तम काव्य क्यों माना जाता ? पुनः यह दोहराना अनुचित नहीं होगा कि काव्यशास्त्र में रस और रसाभास को उत्तम काव्य की, परिभाषा में एक ही आसन पर रखा गया है, छोटा-बड़ा नहीं माना गया। अब इसकी परिभाषा पर भी ध्यान देना होगा। मम्मट ने रसाभास की जो परिभाषा की, उसमें यह बतला दिया गया कि रस की प्रवृत्ति जहां उचित हो वहां रस और जहां अनुचित हो वहां रसाभास माना जाए। मम्मट ने लिखा, "तदाभासा अनौचित्यप्रवर्तितताः"[5]। यहां अनौचित्य शब्द का अर्थ विचारणीय है। सम्भवतः यह शब्द अभिनवगुप्त ने सर्वप्रथम लिखा है (*नाट्यशास्त्र* की टीका *अभिनवभारती* तथा *ध्वन्यालोक* की टीका *लोचन* में 'अनौचित्येन'[6] तदाभासः) उल्लेखनीय है कि अभिनवगुप्त ने इसकी स्पष्ट परिभाषा नहीं की है कि अनौचित्य यहां किसे माना जाए। सर्वप्रथम मम्मट ने इसकी व्याख्या जिन शब्दों में की उनसे स्पष्ट है कि आभास शब्द का जो तात्पर्य है उसकी कोई भी छाया अनौचित्य शब्द से नहीं मिलती। आभास का तात्पर्य 'अवास्तव' होता है, अनुचित नहीं : जैसे प्रतिबिम्ब। यही परिभाषा *शब्दकल्पद्रुम* आदि शब्दकोषों में दी भी गई है।[7] इससे यह तात्पर्य निकलना चाहिए कि जहां वास्तव में रस हो वहां रस और जहां वास्तव में रस न होकर उसका आभास हो वहां रसाभास माना जाए। अभिनवगुप्त ने रसाभास का जैसा भी निर्वचन किया है और उदाहरण दिए हैं उनसे यही परिभाषा पुष्ट होती है।[8] इसमें उचित अनुचित का कोई झगड़ा खड़ा नहीं होना चाहिए, क्योंकि यह स्पष्ट है कि अनौचित्य ज्यों ही आता है रस समाप्त हो जाता है, काव्यास्वाद सम्भव नहीं रहता और काव्यत्व भी नहीं रहता।[9] फिर अनुचित होते हुए भी उसे उत्तम काव्य मानना कहां तक सम्भव है। कीटानुविद्ध रत्न की तरह कोई शब्दार्थदोष होने पर भी काव्यत्व माना जा सकता है, पर उसके लिए भी रस का होना तो वहां भी ज़रूरी बताया गया है।[10]

इस सबके आधार पर मेरा यह अनुमान है कि रसाभास का सम्बन्ध अनौचित्य की उस परिभाषा से नहीं है जिसे आज हम समझते हैं, जिसके आधार पर सर्वप्रथम

मम्मट जैसे कुछ प्राचीन आचार्यों ने[11] इसकी परिभाषा करने की चेष्टा की है। यह अनुमान इस निष्कर्ष पर आधारित है कि कालिदास आदि महाकवियों के जिन प्रसंगों को लेकर आचार्यों ने रसाभास को रस से अलग माना और उसके बावजूद उसी के समान सिंहासन पर उत्तम काव्य का दर्जा देकर बिठाया, उनके सूक्ष्म विवेचन से यह गुत्थी सुलझ सकती है। अनेक आचार्यों ने रसाभास के उदाहरणस्वरूप इन काव्यों को उद्धृत भी किया है। *कुमारसम्भव* के वसन्त वर्णन में कालिदास ने प्रकृति के सभी पक्षों पर जहां श्रृंगार का प्रभाव बताया वहां इस प्रकार का मार्मिक वर्णन किया कि वसन्त आते ही जिस प्रकार पेड़-पौधों पर यौवन इठलाने लगा, पुष्पों और कलियों जैसे प्रतीक वसन्त (नायक) के साथ स्त्री-पुरुष सुलभ श्रृंगार भावनाओं में डूबे दिखाई देने लगे उसी प्रकार हिरन, हिरनियों को प्रेम से सहलाने लगे, अपनी प्रिया के साथ कलियों के प्यालों से मधु पीने लगा आदि।[12] रस के लक्षण में यह बतलाया गया कि जब स्थायीभाव, विभाव, अनुभाव और संचारीभाव के सहयोग से अभिव्यक्त हो वहां रस होता है। जैसे श्रृंगाररस में दुष्यन्त (आश्रय) विभाव अर्थात् शकुन्तला को देखकर प्रेम चेष्टाएं (अनुभाव) और आवेग आदि (संचारी भाव) अनुभूत[13] करता है उससे उसमें श्रृंगाररस होता है। पाठक के हृदय में जो रति का भाव बीज रूप में विद्यमान होता है वह जब इस प्रकार के काव्य को पढ़कर जागृत हो जाता है तो उसे श्रृंगाररस की निष्पत्ति कहा जाता है।

इसी कथ्य को अनेक आचार्यों ने अनेक रूपों में व्याख्यात किया है। जहां नाटक में नट के अन्दर ऐसा रस दिखाई देता हो वहां श्रृंगार-रस भरत मुनि ने बताया था, किन्तु जहां ऐसा रस अस्तित्व में न हो, उसका आभास मात्र हो, जहां कवि ने अपनी कल्पना से रस बना दिया हो और उससे अलौकिक आनन्द की अनुभूति हो उसे क्या माना जाए, यह प्रश्न भी सामने आया। इसके अतिरिक्त कालिदास के इस वसन्त वर्णन की तरह अन्यत्र भी प्रकृति वर्णन संस्कृत साहित्य में खूब मिलते हैं। यहां पुष्पों और भौरों में वास्तविक रति या श्रृंगार नहीं होता, उसका आभास मात्र होता है, किन्तु उसे कवि इस तरह से निबद्ध करते हैं कि उनमें रति भासित होने लगती है। ठीक वही स्थिति यहां होती है, जिसे पाश्चात्य आलोचकों ने पैथेटिक फैलेसी कहा है। जहां वास्तविक भावनाएं नहीं हो किन्तु हमें भावनाएं लगती हों (आरोप) वहां यह पैथेटिक फैलेसी मानी जाती थी। इसका नाम फैलेसी होते हुए भी किसी निन्दनीय अर्थ में नहीं आता था, यह साहित्य का अच्छा अंग माना जाता था। आज चाहे आधुनिक वैज्ञानिकों ने भौरों और मछलियों तक के सेक्स का विश्लेषण कर दिया हो, पर उस समय पशुओं में रति की असम्भाव्यता उसी प्रकार मानी जाती थी जिस प्रकार पेड़-पौधों में। इसीलिए ऐसे प्रसंगों में जहां वास्तविक रति नहीं है, किन्तु आभासित होती है, श्रृंगार का रसाभास माना गया। सम्भवतः इसी आशय को निबद्ध करने के लिए अभिनवगुप्त ने एक स्थान पर अनौचित्य शब्द इसी दृष्टिकोण से लिख दिया कि जहां रति की सम्भावना न हो वह अनुचित

(असम्भाव्य) और जहां रति सम्भावित हो अर्थात् जहां रति का अस्तित्व उचित पाया जाए वहां उचित। इस अनौचित्य शब्द से ही शायद भ्रम यह हुआ कि जहां गलत या निन्दनीय स्थितियां हो वहां रसाभास माना जाए। इसे लेकर मम्मट ने इसी आधार पर उदाहरण दे दिये और परवर्ती अनेक आचार्यों ने मम्मट का अनुसरण किया।

सम्भवत: यही कारण है कि तब से लेकर अब तक सभी काव्यशास्त्रियों ने हमेशा इस पर संदेह और अस्पष्टता व्यक्त की है कि इसे उत्तम काव्य किस आधार पर माना गया। डॉ. नगेन्द्र ने अपने *रससिद्धान्त* में भी मत-मतान्तर बताते हुए ऐसा ही संदेह[14] व्यक्त किया। वे यद्यपि इस बात का स्पर्श तो कर पाये हैं कि तिर्यक् और अचेतन पदार्थों में रस का आरोप करके रसाभास मानने का कुछ काव्यशास्त्रियों ने मत दिया है और उसे वे पैथेटिक फैलेसी के सिद्धान्त तक भी ले[15] गये हैं, पर लक्षणकारों ने अनौचित्य शब्द का जो लक्षण लिख दिया उसके कारण समाज की परम्पराओं के विरुद्ध शृंगार के वर्णन को भी उन्हें रसाभास मानना पड़ा और इसमें अपने चिन्तन के आधार पर कुछ प्रश्नचिह्न भी उन्होंने लगाए। डॉ. विश्वम्भरनाथ उपाध्याय ने रसाभास को परिवर्तिनी लोकमान्यताओं पर आधृत होने के कारण नये युग में अप्रासंगिक बताया।[16] राजस्थान के कुछ अन्य आलोचकों ने भी जिनमें डॉ. पुष्करदत्त शर्मा और चन्द्रकिशोर गोस्वामी के नाम लिये जा सकते हैं उन्होंने भी ये ही प्रश्नचिह्न उभारकर प्रस्तुत[17] किये और यह अभिमत व्यक्त किया कि लक्षणकारों ने सम्भवत: इस पर उतना विचार नहीं किया जितना होना चाहिए था। इन सब पर उपर्युक्त अभिमत के आधार पर सारे लक्षण और सिद्धांत की व्याख्या की जाये तो कुछ गुत्थियां सुलझ सकती हैं।

जैसाकि ऊपर बताया गया है रसाभास का क्षेत्र वहां माना जाए जहां आश्रय में आलम्बन के प्रति वास्तविक रति आदि स्थायी भावों की सत्ता या अस्तित्व संगत नहीं बैठता (अनुचित या असंगत अथवा असम्भाव्य पाया जाता है), केवल कवि को आरोपित या आभासित होकर प्रतीत होता है, तो कुछ निष्कर्ष सही दिशा में निकल सकेगा। हमारे इस कथन के पीछे अनेक व्याख्याकारों, लक्षणकारों और चिंतकों का समर्थन भी उपलब्ध है। जिन विद्वानों को यह समस्या स्पष्ट प्रतीत हुई उन्होंने भी आभास का यही निर्वचन करने का प्रयत्न किया। इनमें अभिनवगुप्त सर्वप्रथम हैं जिन्होंने शुक्ति में रजत के आभास की उपमा देकर बताया कि जहां रति नहीं केवल 'ऊहित' है अर्थात् रत्याभास है, वहां रसाभास होगा। रावण यह समझता है कि सीता मुझ पर आसक्त है, अत: वह रत्याभास अनुभव करता है। उसकी उस रति में शृंगार तो है, परन्तु परिणति शृंगाराभास की है। भरत के अनुसार नाटक में मंचीय उपयोग के लिए वह बाद में दर्शक के दृष्टिकोण से चाहे हास्यरस की ही सृष्टि[18] करे। *काव्यप्रदीप* टीकाकार गोविन्दठक्कुर[19], *चमत्कारचन्द्रिका* के रचयिता कविचन्द्र, *काव्यानुशासन* के लेखक हेमचन्द्र, *प्रभावृत्ति* के लेखक वैद्यनाथ, *संकेतटीका* के लेखक माणिक्यचन्द्र[20], *काव्यादर्श*[21] के लेखक

सोमेश्वर भट्ट तथा *अलंकार-महोदधि*[22] के लेखक नरेन्द्रप्रभसूरि एवं *काव्य-शिक्षा*[23] के लेखक विनयचन्द्र सूरि ने भी इन्हीं आधारों पर रसाभास उन्हीं क्षेत्रों में मानने पर बल दिया है जहां आश्रय और आलम्बन इस प्रकार के हों जिनमें स्वभावत: रति न होकर आभास या आरोप के कारण कवि द्वारा बतायी गयी हो। ऐसी स्थितियों में रसनिष्पत्ति पूरी होती है, काव्य चमत्कार और आस्वाद भी उतना ही होता है जितना रस में। केवल विवेचन की दृष्टि से सूक्ष्म और अवांतर भेद करने की प्राचीन भारतीय लक्षणकारों की प्रवृत्ति के अंतर्गत दो अलग-अलग क्षेत्र बता दिये गये। कालिदास के वसंत वर्णन में किस सहृदय को उत्तम और उत्कृष्ट रसानुभूति नहीं होगी ? फिर उसे रसाभास किसी अपकृष्टता के कारण थोड़े ही माना गया है।

यहां यह समझ लेना आवश्यक है कि तिर्यक् जातियां अर्थात् पशुओं आदि में रति का अस्तित्व नहीं मानने के कारण उसे ही रसाभास के उदाहरण के रूप में दिया गया है, किन्तु जहां अन्य रसों का प्रश्न है, जैसे भयानक वहां पशु में भी भय की स्थिति मानी जाने के कारण उसे आरोपित या आभास न मानकर रस ही माना गया है। मम्मट ने इसीलिए कालिदास के 'ग्रीवाभंगाभिरामम्' श्लोक को भयानक रस के उदाहरण के रूप में उद्धृत किया[24] है। भयानक रसाभास के रूप में नहीं। यह बात *अलंकारमहोदधि* के लेखक नरेन्द्रप्रभसूरि ने[25] भी स्पष्ट की है। इस तथ्य से भी हमारा यही पक्ष पुष्ट होता है कि सामाजिक लोकमान्यताओं की दृष्टि से उचित-अनुचित का प्रश्न रसाभास के विषय में नहीं उठता, केवल वास्तविक-अवास्तविक का ही उठता है। अनौचित्य शब्द से जो भ्रम पैदा होता है तथा आभास शब्द का अर्थ हेत्वाभास के साम्य के कारण जिस प्रकार अपकृष्ट हो गया है उससे यह सारी विमर्श परंपरा शुरू होना स्वाभाविक ही था, यह अनुमान भी इस विवेचन के बाद स्वभावत: स्पष्ट हो जाता है।

इसी क्रम में यह विचार भी किया जा सकता है कि जिस प्रकार अनौचित्य के कारण भावाभास माना गया, उसी प्रकार उन्हीं स्थितियों में अनौचित्य के रहते हुए यदि भावोदय, भावशान्ति, भावशबलता आदि हों तो उन्हें भावोदयाभास, भावप्रशमनाभास और भावशबलताभास आदि क्यों नहीं माना गया ? इसका भी कोई सुसंगत आधार प्रतीत नहीं होता। अनौचित्य की परिभाषा सामाजिक वर्जना के आधार पर करने के बावजूद भी यह भेद माने जा सकते थे। इसी प्रकार आरोप या आभास के आधार पर निर्वचन करने पर भी क्या यह भेद माने जा सकते हैं? इस पर अधिक विचार अपेक्षित है। ''इस प्रकार भेदों की आवश्यकता नहीं है'', इसके पक्ष में केवल एक ही तर्क दिया जा सकता है, वह यह कि तिर्यक् और अचेतन पदार्थों में रस और भाव का आरोप तो किया जा सकता है, पर इतनी बारीक स्थितियां उनमें कहां पायी जाएंगी कि किस भाव का उदय हुआ या समाप्ति हुई? यह तर्क हमारे इस मत को और पुष्ट करता है, यद्यपि इस तर्क में अधिक वजन नहीं दिखता। हमारा उद्देश्य तो यहां केवल यही है कि रसाभास परिभाषा,

परम्परा, रूढ़ि और लक्षण के विषय के विवेचकों को जो संदेह हुए हैं और अनेक विवेचकों ने इस बात पर बार-बार प्रश्न चिह्न लगाए हैं कि इस जगह रस क्यों नहीं माना गया, रसाभास क्यों माना गया, उन सबका कुछ समाधान उपर्युक्त विवेचन में मिल सकता है। किसी समय विशेष में किसी आचार्य विशेष द्वारा जो परिभाषा लिख दी जाये उसे आधार मानकर चलने से ऐसी स्थितियां पैदा हो जाना असंभव नहीं। स्वयं अंग्रेजी के पैथिटिक फैलेसी शब्द के साथ भी यही हुआ है। दर्शन के क्षेत्र में इसे सम्यक् ज्ञान न मानकर मिथ्या ज्ञान माना गया था, अतः शब्द को देखकर तो यह भ्रम होना ही था कि यह कोई दोष या हीनता की स्थिति है। अतएव रस्किन[26] ने इस पर भी बहुत विवेचन किया है। किन्तु काव्यशास्त्रियों ने इसे काव्य के लिए शोभाजनक और अलंकार स्वरूप ही बताया। हडसन ने इसका स्पष्ट उल्लेख किया कि यह दोष नहीं[27] गुण है। ऐसा ही एक उदाहरण है अर्वाचीन संस्कृत काव्यशास्त्र का सहृदयता शब्द। अधिक सहृदय होना सामान्य स्थिति नहीं है ऐसी विवेचना-सरणि अपनाते हुए रसगंगाधरकार पंडितराज जगन्नाथ ने इसे सहृदयताख्य दोष कहकर उद्धृत किया है।[28] इस शब्द से भी यही लगता है कि यह कोई बुरी चीज है किन्तु स्वयं उन्होंने विवेचन में यह स्पष्ट किया है कि यह काव्य-रसिक के लिए बड़ा गुण माना गया है, जिसके बिना काव्य का आस्वाद ही नहीं हो पायेगा। ऐसी ही कुछ स्थिति रसाभास की भी हुई लगती है। यही कारण है कि डॉ. नगेन्द्र ने *रस सिद्धान्त* में यह बात गले उतरती नहीं पाई कि ऐसे प्रकृतिवर्णनों में (जैसे कालिदास का वसन्तवर्णन) रस क्यों नहीं माना गया? रसाभास क्यों ? डॉ. नगेन्द्र के अन्दर का न्यायप्रिय आलोचक इन वर्णनों की रसवत्ता को अन्य रसविषयों की बजाय किसी भी भांति कम नहीं कर पाता अतएव उसे लगता है कि उसे रसाभास का लांछन देकर नीचा दर्जा दिया जा रहा है। यदि उनके अन्तर्मन में 'रसाभास' शब्द के साथ हेयता का यह एसोसियेशन न होता तो उन्हें इतनी पीड़ा क्यों होती ? रस हो या रसाभास, दोनों उत्तम काव्य हैं। बिलकुल प्रथम श्रेणी के। केवल वर्गीकरण के लिए भेद हैं। प्रथम श्रेणी के ही दोनों डिब्बे हैं, एक उत्तर रेलवे का, दूसरा मध्य रेलवे का, तब क्या कोई छोटा बड़ा हो गया ? फिर यह शोक क्यों ? अन्य सभी आलोचकों के, जिन्होंने इस शब्द की परिभाषा पर प्रश्नचिह्न लगाए हैं, अवचेतन का यह 'हेयता साहचर्य बोध' ही इन सब ऊहापोहों का कारण रहा है। आश्चर्य केवल इतना-सा है कि पंडितराज जगन्नाथ जैसे तत्त्वदर्शी आलोचक भी, नव्यन्याय के इस 'एसोसियेशन' के कारण ही, रसाभास की यही परिभाषा कर गए। उनका मूल आधार तथा अभिगम नव्यन्याय का ही था। अतः ऐसा होना अपरिहार्य था।

संदर्भ

1. "इदमुत्तममतिशयिनि व्यंग्ये वाच्याद् ध्वनिर्बुधैः कथितः।" (*काव्यप्रकाश*, 1-I/4)
2. "रसभावतदाभासभावशान्त्यादिरक्रमः।" (*काव्यप्रकाश*, 4.26)
3. "अनेकान्तो विरुद्धश्चाप्यसिद्धः प्रतिपक्षितः। कालात्ययापदिष्टश्च हेत्वाभासास्तु पंचधा। तल्लक्षणं तु तद्विपर्यकत्वेन ज्ञानस्यानुमितिविरोधित्वं तत्त्वम्।" (*न्यायसिद्धान्तमुक्तावली*, 2.71)
4. "तत्र रसाभासत्वं रसत्वादिना न समानाधिकरणं, निर्मलस्यैव रसादित्वात्, हेत्वाभासत्वमिव हेतुत्वेन इत्येके।" (*रसगंगाधर*, प्रथमानन, पृ. 119)
5. *काव्यप्रकाश* (4.36)
6. *ध्वन्यालोकलोचन*, प्रथम उद्योत
7. प्रतिबिम्बादिवदवास्तवस्वरूपम्। सदृशः प्रतिबिम्बम् इति वेदान्तः। (शब्दकल्पद्रुमः)
8. अनुकृतिरमुख्यता, आभास इति ह्येकोऽर्थः (*ध्वन्यालोकलोचन*, प्रथमोद्योत)
9. सौष्ठवमृतोऽपि नीरसा एव नियमेन भवन्ति, तन्न त्वनौचित्यमेव हेतुः। तदयमेव परमार्थः "अनौचित्यादृते नान्यद्रसभंगस्यकारणम्। प्रसिद्धौचित्यबन्धस्तु रसस्योपनिषत्परा।" (आनन्दवर्धन, *ध्वन्यालोक*, तृतीयोद्योत)
10. "कीटानुविद्धरत्नादिसाधारण्येन काव्यता। दुष्टेष्वपि मता यत्र रसाद्यनुगमः स्फुटः।" (*साहित्यदर्पण*, प्रथम परिच्छेद)
11. "तदाभासा अनौचित्यप्रवर्तिताः।" के बाद भी यद्यपि मम्मट ने कहीं यह स्पष्ट नहीं लिखा है कि अनौचित्य का अर्थ लोक मर्यादा द्वारा निर्धारित उचित-अनुचित विषयों के आधार पर किया जाए किन्तु उन्होंने "स्तुमः कं वामाक्षि" के उदाहरण में जो योजन किया है उससे लगता है कि उन्हीं से इस आशय की परिभाषा प्रारम्भ हुई।
12. देखिए *कुमारसंभव*, तृतीय सर्गः वसन्त वर्णन - "मधु द्विरुः कुसुमैकपात्रे आदि पद्य (3.36)
13. "काव्ये नाट्ये च कविना नटेन च प्रकाशितेषु विभावादिषु, व्यंजनव्यापारेण दुष्यन्तादौ शकुन्तलादिरतौ गृहीतायाम्।" (जगन्नाथ, *रसगंगाधर*, प्रथम आनन-रसलक्षण)
14. *रस-सिद्धांत* के पंचम अध्याय (घ) में उन्होंने इस प्रकार की परिभाषा को नैतिक दृष्टि से तो गले उतरती बताया है, पर प्रश्नचिह्न लगाए हैं कि भक्तिमार्ग की एक शाखा में जहां परकीया भाव तथा बहुवल्लभत्व का प्राचुर्य है वहां क्या होगा। अनुभवनिष्ठ या एकांगी रति फ़ारसी और उर्दू जैसी भाषाओं की शायरी में प्रमुख हैं। अचेतन विषयक और तिर्यक् रति भी कालिदासादि में रसमय लगती है। अतः यह सब "नीतिसम्मत होते हुए भी न्यायसंगत नहीं है और इसीलिए उसे सार्वभौम स्वीकृति प्राप्त नहीं हो सकती।"
15. "यूरोप के काव्य में भी एक ऐसा समय आया था जब विवेकी आलोचकों को प्रकृति के भावनात्मक चित्रों में चैतन्याभास या भावामास (पैथेटिक फैलेसी) नामक दोष की कल्पना करनी पड़ी थी, परन्तु कल्पना के बढ़ते हुए पंखों को छांटने में यह दुर्बल कर्तरी एकदम असमर्थ सिद्ध हुई, कहकर उन्होंने संकेत मात्र किया है।" (घः पंचम अध्याय, *रस-सिद्धांत*)

16. *भारतीय काव्यशास्त्र का अध्ययन*, डॉ. विश्वम्भरनाथ उपाध्याय, सप्तम अध्याय, रसवाद, ''रसाभास और रस की असंगति,'' पृ. 405
17. लेख - ''रसाभास के लक्षण में रूढ़ि सीमा एवं कारण'', श्री चन्द्रकिशोर गोस्वामी *अध्ययन अनुसंधान* पत्रिका जयपुर, अंक 5, मार्च 1977, डॉ. पुष्करदत्त शर्मा, *रससिद्धान्त का चक्रव्यूह और रसाभास* (अध्ययन अनुसंधान पत्रिका, अंक 1 पृ. 22)
18. ''यद्यपि शृंगारानुकृतिर्या तु स हास्य:'' इति मुनिना निरूपितं तथाप्यौत्तरकालिकं तस्य हास्यरसत्वम्। अभिनवगुप्त *ध्वन्यालोकलोचन*, द्वितीयोद्योत।
19. ''तच्चैकाश्रयत्वे तिर्यगादिविषयतायाम्।'' (*काव्यप्रदीप* : काव्यप्रकाश)
20. ''तथा निरिन्द्रियतरुलतातरुनदीशैलादे: सेन्द्रियपश्वादेश्व य: काव्ये कामादिव्यवहारस्तत्र रसभावाभासतैव।'' (संकेतटीका)
21. आभासोनुकृतिरमुख्यतेति एकोऽर्थ:। तेन निरिन्द्रियेषु तिर्यगादिषु चारोपणात् तदाभास:।
22. तिर्यगादिष्विन्द्रियवर्जितेष्वपि च नायकत्वारोपात् रसाभासा, भावाभासा:।
23. निरिन्द्रियेषु तिर्यगादिषु चारोपाद रसभावाभासौ।
24. *काव्यप्रकाश*, चतुर्थ उल्लास: भयानक रस का उदाहरण (नवरस भेद प्रसंग में)
25. इदं च तिर्यगादिमतमाभासत्वं शृंगारविषयमेव, नान्यरसविषयम्। ''ग्रीवाभंगाभिरामम्'' इत्यादावप्याभासत्वप्रसंगात्।
26. *मॉडर्न पेन्टर्स*, खंड 3 भाग 4 ''द पैथेटिक फैलेसी'' अध्याय में उन्होंने इसे विषयिगत दोष माना है।
27. *एन इन्ट्रोडक्शन टु द स्टडी ऑव लिटरेचर*, डब्ल्यू.एच. हडसन, अध्याय 3 ''द स्टडी ऑव पॉयेट्री''।
28. प्रथमानन, रसलक्षण, ''नव्यास्तु'' से प्रारम्भ होने वाला तृतीय मत ''सहृदयतोल्लासितस्य भावनाविषेशषरूपस्य...दोषस्य महिम्ना...।'' स्पष्ट है कि असाधारण स्थिति होने के कारण पंडितराज इसे दार्शनिक या मनस्ताळिवक दृष्टिकोण से सिद्धान्तत: 'दोष' कहते हैं, पर इसे हेय नहीं मानते, श्लाघ्य ही मानते हैं।

14

आनन्दवर्धन की रसदृष्टि के व्याख्याकार आचार्य अभिनवगुप्त

राजेन्द्र मिश्र

महामाहेश्वर आचार्य अभिनवगुप्तपाद प्रत्यभिज्ञादर्शन, काव्यशास्त्र एवं नाट्यशास्त्र की त्रिवेणी में परिस्नात एक युगनिर्माता सिद्धपुरुष थे। आज यदि उनका कर्तृत्व सुरक्षित न होता तो सहस्राब्दियों पुरानी जाने कितनी सारस्वत परंपराएं हमारी परिचयपरिधि में न आ पातीं, क्योंकि उन परंपराओं के प्रवर्तक ग्रन्थ आज उपलब्ध नहीं हैं। आचार्य भट्टतौत, मनोरथ, भट्टनायक एवं उद्भट आदि के प्रस्थानों का प्रामाणिक ज्ञान हमें अभिनवगुप्त की टीकाओं से ही हो पाता है। आचार्य अभिनवगुप्त अपनी टीकाओं में अपने युग के वैदुषीप्रस्थान का अत्यंत विश्वसनीय एवं जीवन्त विवरण प्रस्तुत करते हैं। उनके मन्तव्यों से सहमत होना, न होना एक पृथक् बात है, परन्तु कोई भी विज्ञ अध्येता इस तथ्य को नकार नहीं सकता कि आचार्य अभिनवगुप्त ने व्याख्येय आचार्यों के गूढ़ मर्मों को पूरी निष्ठा एवं क्षमता के साथ समझाने का यत्न किया है।

ध्वनिकार आचार्य आनन्दवर्धन की रसविषयक अवधारणा को भी आमूलचूल विशद बनाने में आचार्य अभिनवगुप्त का योगदान स्तुत्य ही प्रतीत होता है। जहां ध्वनिकार रस का प्रत्यक्षतः उल्लेख नहीं भी करते, आचार्य अभिनवगुप्त उस निगूढ़ रस-सन्दर्भ को उजागर कर देते हैं, अपनी युक्तियों से। इसका रोचक उदाहरण हम *ध्वन्यालोकवृत्ति* के मंगलाचरण 'स्वेच्छाकेसरिणः' आदि में ही पा जाते हैं। इस श्लोक में वीर रस को व्यंग्य बताते हुए आचार्य अभिनवगुप्त कहते हैं: "त्रणं

चाभीष्टलाभं प्रति साहायकाचरणम्। तच्चतत्प्रतिद्वन्द्वि विघ्नापसारणादिना भवतीति। इयदत्र त्रणं विवक्षितम्। नित्योद्योगिनश्च भगवत: सम्मोहाध्यवसाय प्रतियोगित्वेनोत्साहप्रतीतेर्वीररसो ध्वन्यते।''

'सहृदयानामानन्दो मनसि लभतां प्रतिष्ठाम्' अंश की व्याख्या करते हुए आचार्य अभिनवगुप्त जिस प्रकार ध्वनिकार के प्रस्थान को प्रतिष्ठापित करते हैं, वह सचमुच प्रशंसनीय है। अभिनवगुप्त की व्याख्या में 'आनन्द' शब्द का अभिप्राय, रसध्वनि की काव्यात्मता तथा रसध्वनि के सन्दर्भ में हृदयदर्पणकार भट्टनायक का वदतोव्याघातत्व सबकुछ एक ही साथ आ जाता है। निश्चय ही यह विपुल सूचना लोचन के अभाव में न मिल पाती।

अभिनवगुप्त का कहना है कि आनन्द शब्द चर्वणात्मा रस का ही पर्याय है, वही रसध्वनि है और काव्य है, मुख्यभूत आत्मत्व भी उसी का है।[1] वही ध्वन्यर्थ अथवा प्रतीयमानार्थ कहा जाता है। ऐसे काव्यार्थ का, जो कि सचमुच हृदयसंवादी होता है। यह विलक्षण काव्यार्थ पाठक अथवा सहृदय के अंग-प्रत्यंग को उसी प्रकार आप्यायित कर लेता है जैसे अग्नि शुष्क काष्ठ को।[2] परन्तु प्रतीयमानार्थ का यह हृदयसंवाद, यह प्रतीति मात्र सहृदय को ही होनी संगत है। इस प्रकार अभिनवगुप्त की दृष्टि में 'सहृदयता' काव्यार्थानुभव पात्रता की पहली और अन्तिम शर्त है।[3]

व्यंजनात्मक ध्वननव्यापार की इस स्थापना के बाद अभिनवगुप्त ध्वनिविरोधी आचार्य भट्टनायक का खंडन उनकी अपनी ही स्थापनाओं से करते हैं। भट्टनायक स्वयं काव्य में अभिधा, भावना तथा रस चर्वणात्मक (भोजकत्व) व्यापार के समर्थक हैं। भट्टनायक स्वयं मानते हैं कि 'काव्ये रसयिता सर्वो न बोद्धा न नियोगभाक्।' भट्टनायक के इसी मन्तव्य का हवाला देते हुए अभिनवगुप्त कहते हैं कि अभिधा-भावना एवं रसचर्वणात्मक काव्य में आप भी 'रसचर्वणा' को ही काव्यजीवितभूत मानते हैं।[4] तो फिर आप एवं ध्वनिकार की काव्यत्व प्रतिष्ठा में अंतर रहा कहां ? दोनों ही रसचर्वणा को काव्यात्मा मान रहे हैं। बस, शब्दमात्र का भेद है। एक उसे 'ध्वनि' कह रहा है तो दूसरा 'भोजकत्वव्यापार'। अब इस मान्यता के बाद भी यदि हृदयदर्पणकार ध्वनि को 'काव्यात्मा' न मानकर काव्य का अंगमात्र मानें तो क्या कहा जाये ? यह तो 'आत्मस्थापना विरोध' मात्र हुआ।[5]

आचार्य आनन्दवर्धन ने 'योऽर्थ: सहृदयश्लाघ्य:' आदि कारिका द्वारा यह तो संकेत किया कि सहृदयश्लाघ्य: जो अर्थ काव्यात्मा के रूप में व्यवस्थित है, उसके वाच्य एवं प्रतीयमान-दो भेद होते हैं। परन्तु ध्वनिकार की इस कारिका का, वृत्ति के बावजूद, परवर्ती आचार्यों ने सही अर्थ नहीं समझा। फलत: आचार्य विश्वनाथ जैसे ध्वनिसमर्थक आचार्य ने भी इस कारिका को विवादास्पद मानते हुए, भ्रान्तव्याख्या की। सचमुच आत्मभूत प्रतीयमानार्थ का भेद शरीरस्थानीय वाच्यार्थ कैसे बन सकता है ?[6]

परन्तु आश्चर्य है कि *लोचन* का पारायण करने के बाद भी साहित्यदर्पणकार को यह भ्रान्ति क्यों और कैसे हुई ? आचार्य अभिनवगुप्त तो स्पष्टतः कहते हैं कि काव्यार्थ चाहे वाच्य हो अथवा व्यंग्य-होता तो समान ही है ! फिर भी ऐसा क्यों है कि सहृदय किसी (एक) ही अर्थ की श्लाघा करते हैं ? निश्चय ही उस श्लाघ्य अर्थ में कोई वैशिष्ट्य होना चाहिए। वस्तुतः सहृदयों द्वारा प्रशंसित उस अर्थ में जो 'विशेष' है वही प्रतीयमान भाग है और उसी प्रतीयमानार्थ को वैशिष्ट्यहेतु होने के कारण, विवेकशील लोग (काव्य की) आत्मा के रूप में व्यवस्थापित करते हैं। होता यह है कि उस काव्यात्मभूत प्रतीयमानार्थ के साथ वाच्यार्थ की संवलना इतनी प्रगाढ़ होती है कि विमोहित हृदय वाले लोग प्रतीयमानार्थ की (वाच्यार्थ से) पृथकता के विषय में विप्रतिपत्ति (संदेह) कर बैठते हैं, ठीक उन चार्वाकों की तरह जिन्हें शरीर से आत्मा का पृथग्भाव समझ में नहीं आता।

> *स एक एवार्थो द्विशाखतया विवेकिभिर्विभागबुद्ध्याविभज्यते। तथा हि-तुल्येऽर्थरूपत्वे किमिति कस्मैचित् सहृदयाः श्लाघन्ते। तद् भवितव्यं केनचिद् विशेषेण। यो विशेषः स प्रतीयमानभागो विवेकिभिर्विशेषहेतुत्वादात्मेति व्यवस्थाप्यते। वाच्यसंवलनाविमोहितहृदयैस्तु तत्पृथग्भावो विप्रतिपद्यते चार्वाकैरिवात्मपृथग्भावः। ध्वन्यालोकलोचन, टीका,* 2-2

इस प्रकार, आचार्य अभिनवगुप्त 'काष्ठदहनन्याय' द्वारा वाच्यार्थ एवं प्रतीयमानार्थ का भेद स्पष्ट करते हैं। ज्वलनशीलता अग्नि का धर्म है, काष्ठ का नहीं। तथापि काष्ठ और अग्नि का संपर्क होते ही दोनों का पार्थक्य समाप्त-सा दीखता है और अविवेकी व्यक्ति कह बैठता है, 'काष्ठ जल रहा है।' वस्तुतः जलती तो है आग, परन्तु आग के सम्पर्कवश काष्ठ ही जलता प्रतीत होता है। वाच्यार्थ एवं प्रतीयमानार्थ के ऐक्य की भ्रान्ति भी कुछ ऐसी ही है।

ध्वनिकार काव्य को 'ललितोचितसन्निवेशचारु' की संज्ञा देते हैं। इसकी व्याख्या करते हुए लोचनकार एक बार पुनः आनन्दवर्धन की रसदृष्टि को स्पष्ट करते हैं-"ललितशब्देनगुणालङ्कारग्रहणमाह। उचितशब्देन रसविषयमेवौचित्यं भवतीति दर्शनयन् रसध्वनेर्जीवितत्वं सूचयति"।

यह रसध्वनि ही काव्यात्मा है। जो ध्वनिविरोधी ध्वनि को काव्यचारुत्वहेतु गुणालंकार से व्यतिरिक्त नहीं मानते उन्हें करारा उत्तर देते हुए लोचनकार कहते हैं कि (रस) ध्वनि तो काव्य की आत्मा है, न कि काव्य का चारुत्वहेतु। अतएव ध्वनिविरोधियों का हेतु ही असिद्ध है। भला आत्मा शरीर का चारुत्व हेतु होता है। जो अलंकार्य है वह अलंकार कैसे होगा ? जो गुणी है वह गुण कैसे होगा? ठीक उसी प्रकार उपमादि प्रकारों से व्याकृत प्रसिद्ध वाच्यार्थ से काव्यात्मभूत प्रतीयमानार्थ सर्वथा भिन्न ही होता

है। वाच्यार्थ के प्रसिद्ध होने का तात्पर्य है वनितावदन, उद्यान एवं चन्द्रोदयादि के समान लौकिक होना। यह व्याख्या लोचनकार की है।

जैसे काणत्वादि दोषशून्य शरीरावयवों से संवलित तथा अलंकृत रमणी को भी 'यह लावण्यशून्य है', तथा वैसी न होने पर भी (अर्थात् आंगिक दोषयुक्त तथा अनलंकृत होने पर भी) 'यह तो लावण्यामृत चन्द्रिका ही है'-ऐसा व्यवहार सहृदय करते हैं। ठीक उसी प्रकार प्रतीयमानार्थ भी काव्य के प्रसिद्ध अवयवों (गुण, वृत्ति, रीति, अलंकारादि) से सर्वथा व्यतिरिक्त है। आनन्दवर्धन के शब्दों में-

> *यथा ह्यगंनासु लावण्यं पृथङ्निर्वर्ण्यमानं निखिलावयवव्यतिरेकि किमयन्यदेव सहृदयलोचनामृतं तत्त्वान्तरं तदवदेव सोऽर्थः। स हि अर्थो वाच्यसामर्थ्याक्षिप्तं वस्तुमात्रमलंकाररसादयश्चेत्यनेक प्रभेद प्रभिन्नो दर्शयिष्यते।*
>
> *ध्वन्याः,* 2.4 की वृत्ति।

प्रतीयमानार्थ के ध्वनिकार-सम्मत त्रैविध्य को विशद करते हुए आचार्य अभिनवगुप्त अत्यंत युक्तियुक्त विवरण प्रस्तुत करते हैं। उनके विवरण में रसध्वनि की जैसी भव्य प्रतिष्ठा हुई है, वैसी ध्वनिकार के शुष्क वाक्य में नहीं मिलती (तृतीयस्तु रसादिलक्षणः प्रभेदो वाच्यसामर्थ्याक्षिप्तः प्रकाशते)। लोचनकार कहते हैं कि प्रतीयमानार्थ के दो भेद हैं-लौकिक तथा काव्यव्यापारैकगोचर। लौकिक तो वह है, जो शब्दवाच्य भी कदाचित् होता है। वह विधि-निषेधादि अनेक प्रकार वाला 'वस्तुध्वनि' कहा जाता है। वह भी दो प्रकार का है। एक तो वह जो कभी पहले उपमादि संविधानक द्वारा वाच्यालंकारभाव का अनुभव कर चुका है अर्थात् वाच्यार्थरूप में उपमादि अलंकार से अध्यासित रहा है, परन्तु अब अनलंकार रूप ही है। तथापि अपने पूर्व प्रत्यभिज्ञान के बल से, अलंकार्य होते हुए भी ब्राह्मणश्रमण न्याय से 'अलंकारध्वनि' कहा जाता है। दूसरा रूप वह है, जो अनलंकाररूप होने के कारण वस्तुमात्र कहा जाता है।

परन्तु प्रतीयमानार्थ का जो काव्यव्यापारैकगोचर भेद है उसे 'रसध्वनि' कहते हैं। वह तो स्वप्न में भी स्वशब्दवाच्य नहीं होता है, और न ही लौकिकव्यवहार का विषय होता है। तो फिर, वह होता कैसा है ? वह होता है आत्मानुभूत आनन्दचर्वणा व्यापार द्वारा रसनीय (आस्वाद्य) रूप वाला रस। यह रस विभावाऽनुभावादि से संवलित प्राक् निविष्ट रत्यादि स्थायी भाव के संयोग से निष्पन्न होता है। वही काव्यव्यापारगोचर रसध्वनि है। सच पूछिए तो ध्वनि वही है और काव्य की आत्मा भी मुख्यतः वही है। क्योंकि वस्तु एवं अलंकार ध्वनियां भी अन्ततः रसध्वनि में ही पर्यवसित होती हैं। अतएव, आचार्य भट्टनायक ने जो ध्वनि को काव्य का अंग मात्र कहा (आत्मा नहीं) तो उनका यह उपालम्भ शायद वस्तु एवं अलंकारध्वनि के लिये हो। परन्तु रसध्वनि को तो स्वयमेव उन्होंने 'काव्यात्मा' के रूप में अंगीकार किया है।[7]

ध्वनिकार तो रस को साक्षात् शब्दव्यापार का विषय ही नहीं मानते, फलतः वह वाच्य से भिन्न तो होता ही है। यदि रस का वाच्यत्व स्वीकार किया जाये तो वह दो ही प्रकार से संभव है-स्वशब्दनिवेदितत्व द्वारा अथवा विभावादि के प्रतिपादन द्वारा। स्वशब्दनिवेदितत्व का अर्थ है, "शृंगार कहने से शृंगार की तथा करुण कहने से करुण रस की प्रतीति होना।" यदि इस पक्ष को मान भी लिया जाये, तो यह भी मानना होगा कि जहां रसों का स्वशब्दनिवेदितत्व नहीं होगा, वहां उनकी प्रतीति भी नहीं होती। परन्तु काव्य में सर्वत्र तो रसादि स्वशब्दों द्वारा निवेदित होते नहीं। यदि कहीं शृंगार, करुण, हास्यादि शब्द प्रसंगतः प्रयुक्त हो भी जाते हैं वहां भी उन-उन रसों की प्रतीति उन-उन शब्दों से नहीं, प्रत्युत विशिष्ट विभावादि के प्रतिपादन द्वारा ही होती है। आत्मवाचक शब्दों से रस प्रतीति नहीं होती, बल्कि उनका अनुवदन (उल्लेख) मात्र होता है।[8] रसविषयक इस मार्ग को उद्घाटित करते हैं लोचनकार, अपने साहित्यगुरु भट्टेन्दुराज के इस पद्य द्वारा-

यद्विश्रम्य विलोकितेषु बहुशो निःस्थेमनी लोचने
यद्गात्राणि दरिद्रति प्रतिदिनं लूनाब्जिनी नालवत्।
दूर्वाकाण्डविडम्बकश्च निबिडो यत्पाण्डिमा गण्डयो
र्दृष्टे यूनि सयौवनासु वनितास्वेषैव वेषस्थितिः।।

इस पद्य का वैशिष्ट्य बताते हुए आचार्य अभिनवगुप्त कहते हैं – "इत्यत्रनुभावविभावाव बोधनोत्तरमेव तन्मयीभवनयुक्त्यां तद्विभावानुभावोचित चित्तवृत्तिवासनाऽनुरंजितस्व-संविदानन्द चर्वणगोचरोऽर्थो रसात्मा स्फुरत्येव अभिलाष चिन्तौत्सुक्यनिद्राधृति-ग्लान्यालस्यश्रमस्मृति वितर्कादिशब्दाऽभावेऽपि।"

उपर्युक्त पद्य में रसवाचक एक भी शब्द नहीं, तथापि रस की स्फुटप्रतीति में किसी को सन्देह नहीं हो सकता है। आनन्दवर्धन के 'स्वशब्देन सा केवलमनूद्यते' सूत्रवाक्य का भी मनोरम विस्तार लोचनकार ही करते हैं, इस पद्य द्वारा-

याते द्वारवतीं तदामधुरिपौ तद्दत्तझम्पानतां
कालिन्दीतटरूढवञ्जुललतामालिङ्ग्य सोत्कण्ठया।
तद्गीतं गुरुबाष्पगद्गदगलत्तारस्वरं राधया
येनान्तर्जलचारिभिर्जलचरैरप्युत्कमुत्कूजितम्।।

इस पद्य में यद्यपि 'सोत्कण्ठ एवं उत्क' सरीखे रसवाची शब्द प्रयुक्त हुए हैं, परन्तु रसप्रतीति में उनकी कोई विशेष भूमिका नहीं है, जैसा कि लोचनकार मानते हैं । यथा-

अत्र विभावानुभावावम्लानतया प्रतीयेते। उत्कण्ठा च
चर्वणागोचरं प्रतिपद्यते एव सोत्कण्ठशब्दः केवलं सिद्धं

साधयति। उत्कंठमित्यनेन तु उक्तानुभावानुकर्षणं कर्तुं सोत्कण्ठ शब्द: प्रयुक्त इत्यनुवादोऽपि नाऽनर्थक:। पुनरनुभावप्रतिपादने हि पुनरुक्तमतन्मयीभावो वा।

ध्वन्या., 2.4 की लोचनटीका

रसविषयक, अपनी स्थापना के अगले चरण में आनन्दवर्धन पुन: कहते हैं कि केवल शृंगारादि रसवाचक शब्दों से युक्त परन्तु विभावादि के प्रतिपादन से रहित काव्य में रसवत्ता की प्रतीति नहीं होती है। जबकि काव्य में रसवाची शब्द न भी रहें, परन्तु विशिष्ट विभावादि मात्र विद्यमान हों, तो रसादि की निर्बाध प्रतीति होती है। केवल स्वाभिधान से प्रतीति नहीं होती है। इस प्रकार, अन्वयव्यतिरेक दोनों ही दृष्टियों से रसादि का वाच्यार्थ के सामर्थ्य से आक्षिप्त होना ही सिद्ध होता है, न कि उनकी अभिधेयता।

इस प्रकार, वस्तु एवं अलंकार स्वरूप प्रतीयमानार्थ के अनन्तर ध्वनिकार रसध्वनि को सर्वोपरि प्रतिष्ठित करते हुए घोषित करते हैं कि ''काव्यास्यात्मा स एवार्थ:''। लोचनकार इस सूत्र की व्याख्या करते हुए कहते हैं-

स एवेति प्रतीयमानमात्रेऽपि प्रक्रान्ते तृतीय एव रसध्वनिरिति मन्तव्यम्। इतिहासबलात् प्रक्रान्तवृत्तिग्रन्थबलाच्च। तेन रस एव वस्तुत आत्मा वस्त्वलंकारध्वनी तु सर्वथा रसं प्रतिपर्यवस्येते इति वाच्यादुत्कृष्टौ तावित्यभिप्रायेण ध्वनि: काव्यस्यात्मेति सामान्येनोक्तम्।

लोचनम्

रसध्वनि की काव्यात्मता के सन्दर्भ में आचार्य आनन्दवर्धन आदिकवि प्राचेतस वाल्मीकि की चर्चा करते हुए बताते हैं कि क्रौंच-मिथुन के वियोग से उद्भूत (उनका) शोक ही श्लोकत्व को प्राप्त हो उठा था। परन्तु ध्वनिकार के इस सूत्रभूत प्रतिपादन से ही शोक का रसोचित वैभव स्पष्ट नहीं हो जाता। उसे सांगोपांग समझने के लिए आचार्य अभिनवगुप्त का आश्रय लेना अनिवार्य हो जाता है। लोचनकार इस सन्दर्भ की विस्तृत व्याख्या करते हुए बताते हैं कि जो शोक 'श्लोक' बन गया था उसे महामुनि वाल्मीकि का (व्यक्तिगत) शोक नहीं समझना चाहिए। यदि ऐसा होता (अर्थात् यदि वह वाल्मीकि का अपना दु:ख होता) तो उस क्रौंची के दु:ख से वह स्वयं भी दु:खी हो जाते और तब रस की काव्यात्मता के लिए अवकाश ही नहीं रह जाता। जो दु:ख में सन्तप्त हो वह भला श्लोक क्या लिखेगा?[9]

वस्तुत: चर्वणोचित, शोकस्थायिभावात्मक जो करुण रस काव्यात्मा के रूप में प्रतिष्ठित होता है वह लौकिक शोक नहीं होता है, प्रत्युत उससे विलक्षण होता है।

लोक एवं काव्य के स्थायी भावों में यही अन्तर होता है कि क्रान्तदर्शी कवि आत्माराम-स्वभाव होता है। वह रति, शोक, हासादि से निसर्गत: आकण्ठतृप्त होता है।

फलतः इन संवेदनाओं के साथ उसका आत्मीय संस्पर्श नहीं होता है। अपनी इसी साधारणीकृत संवेदना को वह आनन्दमय रस की भूमिका पर प्रतिष्ठित कर पाता है। इसके विपरीत, लौकिक जन रत्यादिभावनाओं के भूखे होते हैं। अतएव, रति, हास, शोक, उत्साहादि के सन्दर्भों में वे तन्मय हो जाते हैं, उन संवेदनाओं को पूर्णतः पचा लेते हैं और फिर, उस आत्मसंस्पर्श के कारण शोक में फूट-फूटकर रोते हैं, हास में अमर्यादित भाव से हंसते हैं तथा रतिसन्दर्भ में सम्भोग एवं विप्रलम्भ की घमछांही का अनुभव करते हैं।

भूखा व्यक्ति वमन क्या करेगा ? वह तो खाली पेट वाला है। परन्तु आत्मारामतया स्थित, आकण्ठ परितुष्ट कवि ही रत्यादि भावों को पचा नहीं पाता, वमित कर देता है। वही है काव्य ! हृदयदर्पणकार आचार्य भट्टनायक का मन्तव्य इसी तथ्य को पुष्ट करता है-'यावत्पूर्णो न चैतेन तावन्नैव वमत्यमुम्।'

अवसर मिलते ही लोचनकार आनन्दवर्धन की रसदृष्टि को प्रकाशित करते हैं। यह दृष्टि ध्वन्यालोक की कारिका अथवा वृत्ति से स्पष्ट नहीं हो पाती। ध्वनिकार कहते हैं कि महाकवियों की वाणी अलोकसामान्य उस 'प्रतिभाविशेष' को अभिव्यक्त करती है।[13] यहां प्रतिभाविशेष का अर्थ क्या हो सकता है ? लोचनकार स्पष्ट करते है-

> *प्रतिपतृन् प्रति सा प्रतिभा नाऽनुमीयमाना, अपितु तदावेशेन भासमानेत्यर्थः। यदुक्तमस्मदुपाध्यायभट्टतौतेन नायकस्य कवेः श्रोतुः समानोऽनुभवस्ततः इति। प्रतिभा अपूर्ववस्तु निर्माणक्षमा प्रज्ञा। तस्या विशेषो रसावेशवैशद्यसौन्दर्य काव्यनिर्माण क्षमत्वम्।*
>
> *लोचनम्*

रस की अलौकिकता तथा अनुमान-स्मरणादि से उसकी व्यतिरिक्तता को लेकर लोचनकार ने सारग्राही विवेचन प्रस्तुत किया है। रस वाच्यार्थ एवं लक्ष्यार्थ से सर्वथा पृथक् है। वस्तुतः रस, भाव, रसाभास, भावाभास, भावोदय, भावसन्धि एवं भावशबलतादि में लक्षणा की उपपत्ति की संभावना ही नहीं है। क्योंकि विभावानुभाव-प्रतिपादक काव्य में मुख्यार्थबाधक तत्त्व के अनुप्रवेश की कोई संभावना ही नहीं। तो फिर रसाद्यर्थ में लक्षणा के लिए अवकाश ही कहां ?[14]

यदि यह कहें कि मुख्यार्थबाधा का क्या प्रश्न ? लक्षणा का तो स्वरूप ही बस इतना है-'अभिधेयाविनाभूतप्रतीतिर्लक्षणोच्यते' अर्थात् वाच्यार्थ से अपृथग्भूत प्रतीति ही लक्षणा है। और इस दृष्टि से, विभावानुभाव आदि से अविनाभूत (अपृथक्) होने के कारण रसादि भी लक्षित ही होते हैं। क्योंकि विभावानुभाव कार्यरूप रस के कारण हैं तथा व्यभिचारी भाव उनके सहकारी।

आचार्य अभिनवगुप्त कहते हैं-मैवम् ! अर्थात् यह नहीं हो सकता। क्योंकि अभिधेय की अविनाभूत प्रतीति को ही लक्षणा मान लेंगे तो 'धूम' शब्द से धुएं का

ज्ञान होने पर (उससे अविनाभूत) अग्नि स्मृति भी लक्ष्यार्थ ही मानी जायेगी। उसके बाद भी, अग्नि से अपृथग्भूत शीतापनोदनस्मृति अग्नि का लक्ष्यार्थ बनेगी। फिर तो लक्ष्यार्थों की परंपरा का पर्यवसान ही नहीं होगा।[10]

यदि यह कहें कि 'धूम' शब्द के स्वार्थ मात्र में विश्रान्त होने के कारण, वहां लक्षणा-व्यापार संगत ही नहीं होगा तो फिर, आचार्य अभिनवगुप्त कहते हैं, बात वही आ गयी कि 'मुख्यार्थ बाध ही लक्षणा का प्राणतत्त्व है।' और इस स्थापना के बाद रसाधर्थ की लक्षणामूलकता सर्वथा असंभव है। क्योंकि विभावादि के प्रतिपादन में बाधक तो कोई है नहीं, और इस प्रकार, धूमज्ञान के अनन्तर अग्निस्मरण की तरह विभावादि की प्रतिपत्ति के अनन्तर रत्यादि चित्तवृत्ति की प्रतिपत्ति जैसा कोई शब्दव्यापार तो रसप्रतीति में होता नहीं।[11]

आचार्य अभिनवगुप्त कहते हैं कि इस प्रसंग में प्रतीति के विशेषज्ञ मीमांसकों से मैं पूछना चाहूंगा कि कैसी रसप्रतिपत्ति आपको अभिमत है ? क्या वह प्रतिपत्ति जो परकीय चित्तवृत्ति मात्र में होती है ? यदि ऐसा ही है, तो निश्चय ही आप भ्रान्त हैं। क्योंकि लोकगत चित्तवृत्ति के अनुमानमात्र में भला क्या 'रसता' है ? अरे, अलौकिक चमत्काररूपी आत्मा वाला तथा काव्यगत विभावादि की चर्वणा से प्राणवान् 'रसास्वाद' स्मरण एवं अनुमानादि द्वारा न्यग्भूत करने योग्य नहीं है। क्योंकि यह रसप्रतीति तो, अनुमान एवं स्मरणादि की सरणि से सर्वथा व्यतिरिक्त तन्मयीभवनोचित चर्वणारूपी प्राण वाली होती है। अब यह चर्वणा किसी अन्य प्रमाण से तो उत्पन्न नहीं हुई कि इस समय उसकी स्मृति आ रही हो। वर्तमान में भी वह किसी प्रमाण से नियंत्रित नहीं है, जो वस्तु ही अलौकिक हो उसमें प्रत्यक्षादि भी प्रमाणभूत कैसे हो सकते हैं ? अतएव, विभावादि का व्यवहार ही अलौकिक है। लोचनकार के शब्दों में-

> *अतएव, रस्यमानताया एषैव निष्पतिर्या प्रबन्धप्रवृत्तबन्धुसमागमादिकारणोदितहर्षादिलौकिकचित्तवृत्तिन्यग्भावेन चर्वणारूपत्वम्। अतश्चर्वणात्राभिव्यंजनमेव। न तु ज्ञापनम्। प्रमाणव्यापारवत्। नाव्युत्पादनम्। हेतुव्यापारवत्। ननु यदि नेयं ज्ञप्तिर्नवा निष्पत्तिः, तर्हि किमेतत् ? न त्वयमसावलौकिको रसः। ननु विभावादिरत्र किं ज्ञापको हेतुः उत कारकः? न ज्ञापको न कारकः अपितु चर्वणोपयोगी। ननु क्वैतद् दृष्टमन्यत्र ? यत एव न दृष्टं तत एवालौकिकमित्युक्तम्। नन्वेवं रसोऽप्रमेयः स्यात्। अस्तु किं ततः ? तच्चर्वणात् एव प्रतीतिव्युत्पत्तिसिद्धेः किमन्यदर्थनीयम् ? नन्वप्रमाणकमेतत्। न। स्वसंवेदनसिद्धत्वात्। ज्ञानविशेषस्यैव चर्वणात्मत्वात्। इत्यलं बहुना। अतश्च रसोऽयमलौकिकः।*

आचार्य अभिनवगुप्त भरत एवं आनन्दवर्धन, दोनों के टीकाकार हैं। ये दोनों मूर्धाभिषिक्त, ग्रन्थ, अनेक प्रतिपाद्य विषयों की समानता के बावजूद भी, प्रस्थानदृष्ट्या पृथक् हैं। एक नाट्यशास्त्रीय परंपरा का पोषक है तो दूसरा काव्यशास्त्रीय परंपरा का।

दोनों ग्रन्थों के बीच प्राय: 1100 वर्षों का अन्तर भी है। इस विशाल अन्तराल में न केवल काव्यशास्त्र अपने सुनिश्चित प्रतिपाद्य के साथ, नाट्यशास्त्र से पृथक् हो चुका था, प्रत्युत नाट्यशास्त्र में व्याख्यात गुण, अलंकार, रस, लक्षण एवं प्रवृत्ति सरीखे वे तत्त्व जो कि अवान्तर काल में काव्यशास्त्र के भी प्रमुख प्रतिपाद्य बने, अंशत: अथवापूर्णत: संशोधित, परिवर्तित अथवा परिवर्तित हो चुके थे।

ऐसी स्थिति में आचार्य अभिनवगुप्त के काव्यशास्त्रीय योगदान का मूल्य और बढ़ जाता है, क्योंकि वह भरत एवं आनन्दवर्धन दोनों की रसदृष्टियों के व्याख्याकार हैं। इन दो दविष्ठ ध्रुवों के बीच उन्हें अपना भी स्वतंत्र मत (रस दृष्टि) प्रस्तुत करना है। आचार्य भरत से लेकर अपने युग तक (दशमशती ई. का उत्तरार्ध) रसविषयक अवधारणा के बदलते मानदण्डों का जैसा प्रामाणिक विवरण लोचनकार ने प्रस्तुत किया है, वह सर्वथा अप्रतिम है। उन्हीं के शब्दों में:

अन्ये पुनर्विभावमनुभावमेव विशिष्टसामग्र्या समर्प्यमाणं तद्विभावनीयानुभावनीय स्थायीरूपवित्तवृत्त्युपचितवासनानुषक्तंस्वनिर्वृत्तिचर्वणाविशिष्टमेव रस:। तन्नाट्यमेव रसा:। अन्ये तु शुद्धं विभावम्, अपरे शुद्धमनुभावम् केचित्तु स्थायिमात्रम्, इतरे व्यभिचारिणम्, अन्ये तत्संयोगम्, एकेऽनुकार्यम्, केचन सकलमेव समुदायं रसमाहुरित्यलं बहुना। काव्येऽपि च लोकनाट्यधर्मिस्थानीये स्वभावोक्तिवक्रोक्ति-प्रकारद्वयेनालौकिकप्रसन्नमधुरौजस्विशब्दसमर्प्यमाणविभावादियोगादियमेव रसवार्ताऽस्तु। अस्तु वा नाट्याद्विचित्ररूपा रसप्रतीति:। उपायवैलक्षण्यादियमेव तावदत्र सरणि:।

ध्वन्यालोकलोचनटीका, 2.4

ध्वन्यालोक द्वितीय उद्योत के लोचन से यह स्पष्ट हो जाता है कि आचार्य अभिनगुप्त भी रस को मूलत: नाट्य का ही विषय मानते हैं। उपर्युक्त लोचनोद्धरण में आये 'काव्येऽपि च' शब्दावली से भी इसी तथ्य की पुष्टि होती है। रस की नाट्यानुगुणता लोचनकार के इस मन्तव्य से पुष्ट हो जाती है:

अत्रोच्यते-रसस्वरूप एव तावद् विप्रतिपत्तय: प्रतिवादिनाम्। तथा हि पूर्वावस्थायां य: स्थायी स एव व्यभिचारिसम्पातादिना प्राप्तपरिपोषोऽनुकार्यगत एव रस:। नाट्ये तु प्रयुज्यमानत्वान्नाट्यरस इति केचित्। प्रवाहधर्मिण्यां चित्तवृतौ चित्तवृत्तेर्वृत्त्यन्तरेण क: परिपोषार्थ:? विस्मयशोकक्रोधादेश्च क्रमेण तावन्न परिपोष इति नानुकार्ये रस:। अनुकर्तरि च तद्भावेन लयाद्यनुकरणं स्यात्। सामाजिकगते वा कश्चमत्कार:? प्रत्युत करुणादौ दु:खप्राप्ति:। तस्मान्नायं पक्ष:। कस्तर्हि ?

इहानन्त्यान्नियतस्यानुकारो न शक्य:, निष्प्रयोजनश्च विशिष्टताप्रतीतौ। ताटस्थ्येन व्युत्पत्त्यभावात्। तस्मादनियतावस्थात्मकं स्थायिनमुद्दिश्य विभावानुभाव-

व्यभिचारिभिः संयुज्यमानैरयं रामः सुखीति स्मृतिविलक्षणा स्थायिनि प्रतीतिगोचरतयाऽऽस्वादरूपा प्रतिपत्तिरनुकर्त्रालम्बना नाट्यैकगामिनी रसः। स च न व्यतिरिक्तमाधारमपेक्षते। किन्त्वनुकार्याभिकाभिमते नर्तके आस्वादयिता सामाजिक इत्येतावन्मात्रमदः।

तेन नाट्य एव रसः, नानुकार्यादिष्विति केचित्। अन्ये तु अनुकर्तरि यः स्थाय्यव भासोऽभिनयादिसामग्रयादिकृतो भित्ताविव हरितालादिना अश्वाभासः स एव लोकातीत तयाऽस्वादापरसंज्ञया प्रतीत्या रस्यमानो रस इति नाट्याद्रसा नाट्यरसाः।

लोचनम्, ध्वन्या., 2.4

वस्तुतः *अभिनवभारती* एवं *लोचन* में उपन्यस्त आचार्य अभिनवगुप्त की गहन काव्यमीमांसाएं किसी स्वतंत्र आकरग्रन्थ से कम नहीं हैं। इन टीकाओं में मूलग्रन्थांश की युक्तियुक्त व्याख्या तो की ही गयी है, परन्तु उससे भी अधिक महत्त्वपूर्ण तथ्य यह है कि यथावसर आचार्य अभिनवगुप्त ने प्रस्थानविरोधी आचार्यों के पक्ष का जबर्दस्त खण्डन भी किया है। कहीं-कहीं तो उन्होंने किसी काव्यतत्त्व विशेष (जैसे रस, ध्वनि आदि) के संदर्भ में, अपने जीवनकाल में विद्वद्गोष्ठियों में प्रचलित 'शास्त्रार्थ' को ही सांगोपांग प्रस्तुत कर दिया है। इस प्रकार, आचार्य अभिनवगुप्त मात्र एक प्रतिभोपदिष्ट टीकाकार ही नहीं प्रत्युत संस्कृत काव्यशास्त्र की सुदीर्घ परम्परा के संवाहक एवं व्याख्याता आचार्य हैं। इन्हीं व्याख्यानों में उनकी मौलिक काव्यमीमांसा के दर्शन भी होते हैं। प्रायः अपने लंबे व्याख्यानों के अनन्तर अभिनव 'तदयमत्र संक्षेपः' कहकर व्याख्यान का निष्कर्ष लिख देते हैं। *नाट्यशास्त्र* के छठे अध्याय में तेन रस एवं नाट्यम् शीर्षक को स्पष्ट करते हुए आचार्य 'नाट्य तथा रस' को संयुक्त रूप से उपन्यस्त करते हैं। यथा-

तत्र नाट्यं नाम नटगताभिनय प्रभाव साक्षात्कारायमाणैकघनमानस-निश्चलाध्यवसेयः समस्तनाटकाद्यन्यतमकाव्यविशेषाच्च द्योतनीयोऽर्थः। स च यद्यप्यनन्तविभावाद्यात्मा तथापि सर्वेषां जडानां संविदि तस्याश्च भोक्तरि भोक्तृवर्गस्य च प्रधाने भोक्तरि पर्यवसानान्नाय काभिधानभोक्तृविशेषस्थायि-चित्तवृत्तिस्वभावः। सा चैकचित्तवृत्तिः स्वरूपमिति प्रतीयमानानन्तचित्तवृत्त्यन्तरशत-विशेषिता, लौकिकगीतगेयपदादिलास्यांगदशकोपजीवनस्वीकृतलक्षणगुणा, अलंकार गीतातोद्यादि सम्यक् सुन्दरीभूतकाव्यमहिमप्रयोगमालाऽभ्यास विशेषाश्रयत्वात् प्रच्याविता, अतएव, साधारणीभूततया सामाजिकानपि स्वात्मसद्भावेन समावेशयन्ती, तादात्म्यादेव चानुमानागमयोगिप्रत्यक्षादि करणकतटस्थप्रमातृप्रमेयलौकिकपरकीयचित्तवृत्तिविलक्षणतया निर्भासमाना, परिमितस्वात्मान्याश्रयता निर्भासनविरहाच्च लौकिकप्रमदादिजनितनिजरति शोकादिवत् तज्जहानादिचित्तवृत्त्यन्तरजननाक्षमा, तत एव निर्विघ्नस्वसंवेदनात्मक हर्षविश्रान्तिलक्षणेन रसनाऽपरपर्यायेण व्यापारेण गृह्यमाणत्वात् रसशब्देनाभिधीयते।

अभिनवभारती, 6.15

आचार्य अभिनवगुप्त की तर्कबुद्धि का क्या कहना ? लक्षणा द्वारा व्यंग्यार्थ प्रतीति की कल्पना करने वाले मीमांसकों को उन्होंने जिस युक्ति से निरस्त किया है, उसे हम पिछले अनुच्छेदों में देख चुके हैं। एक ऐसा ही मार्मिक प्रसंग पुनः उपस्थित होता है, ध्वन्यालोक के द्वितीय उद्योत में-

रसभावतदाभासतत्प्रशान्त्यादिरक्रमः।
ध्वनेरात्मांगिभावेन भासमानो व्यवस्थितः।। 2.3।।

लोचनकार यहां कहते हैं कि क्या सदैव रसादि अर्थ ध्वनि के प्रकार होते है?(ननु किं सर्वदैव रसादिरर्थो ध्वनेः प्रकारः?) इस प्रश्न का निषेधपरक उत्तर देते हुए वे कहते हैं कि वे तभी ध्वनिरूपता को प्राप्त होते हैं जब अंगिभाव से (प्रधानत्वेन) अवभासमान हों। वह रसादि ध्वनि तो व्यवस्थित है ही। उससे शून्य काव्य तो 'नगण्य' ही होता है। यद्यपि काव्य का जीवितभूत तो रस है ही, तथापि उस रस के प्रयोजकभूत किसी अंश (व्यभिचारी भाव) से भी वह रसोचित चमत्कार पुष्कलत्वेन उत्पन्न हो सकता है। तब उसी को 'भावध्वनि' कहा जाता है।[15]

यह 'भावध्वनि' का प्रसंग आचार्य अभिनवगुप्त अपनी ओर से प्रस्तुत कर रहे हैं। ध्वन्यालोक की मूलकारिका अथवा वृत्ति में इसका कोई उल्लेख नहीं है। अब यदि यह प्रसंग प्रारंभ ही हो गया तो, जैसी आचार्य अभिनवगुप्त की प्रकृति है, वह उसे विस्तारपूर्वक समझाकर ही विश्रान्त होंगे।

व्यभिचारी भाव भी उदय, स्थिति एवं अपाय-इन तीन धर्मों वाले होते हैं। यही उनका स्वरूप-लक्षण भी है।[16]

लोचनकार कहते हैं कि व्यभिचारी भाव कहीं उदयावस्था द्वारा, कहीं स्थिति द्वारा, कहीं प्रशमावस्था द्वारा, कहीं (विविध व्यभिचारियों की) सन्धि द्वारा और कहीं अन्तरशबलता द्वारा ही चर्वणास्पद होते हैं। इनके उदाहरण इस प्रकार हैं-

याते गोत्रविपर्यये श्रुतिपथं शय्यामनुप्राप्तया
निर्यातं परिवर्तनं पुनरपि प्रारब्धमंगीकृतम्।
भूयस्तत्प्रकृतं कृतंच शिथिलाक्षिप्तैकदोर्लेखया
तन्वंग्या न तु पारितः स्तनभरः क्रष्टुं प्रियस्योरसः।।

लोचनकार के शब्दों में-अत्र हि प्रणयकोपस्यैवोज्जिगमिषयैव यदवस्थानं 'न तु पारित' इत्युदयावकाश निराकरणात्तदेवास्वादजीवितम्।

तिष्ठेत्कोपवशात्प्रभावपिहिता दीर्घं न सा कुप्यति
स्वर्गायोत्पतिता भवेन्मयि पुनर्भावार्द्रमस्या मनः।
तां हर्तुं विबुधद्विषोऽपि न च मे शक्ताः पुरोवर्तिनीं
सा चात्यन्तमगोचरं नयनयोर्यातेति कोऽयं विधिः।।

प्रस्तुत पद्य में विप्रलम्भ (शृंगार) रस के इतने सद्भाव में भी 'वितर्क' नामक व्यभिचारी भाव, चमत्कार प्रयुक्त होकर आस्वादातिशय उत्पन्न कर रहा है। यह उसकी स्थित्यवस्था है।

प्रशमावस्था के व्यभिचारी भाव द्वारा चमत्कारातिशय उत्पन्न किये जाने का उदाहरण है–

एकस्मिन् शयने पराङ्गमुखतया वीतोत्तरं ताम्यतो–
ऽन्योन्यस्य हृदि स्थितेऽप्यनुनये संरक्षतोर्गौरवम्।
दम्पत्योः शनकैरपाङ्गवलनामिश्रीभवच्चक्षुषो,
भग्नो मानकलिः सहासरभसव्यावृत्तकण्ठग्रहम्।।

यहां ईर्ष्या नामक व्यभिचारी की प्रशमावस्था आस्वादातिशय उत्पन्न कर रही है। इसी प्रकार कोप एवं प्रसाद की सन्धि से उत्पन्न चमत्कारातिशय का उदाहरण देते हैं लोचनकार–

ईससु केसुम्भिआए महचुम्बिउ जेण।
अभिअरसो घोण्टाण पडिजाणिउ तेण।।

त्यक्ते तु कोपे कोपकषायगद्गदमन्दरुदिताया येन मुखं चुम्बितं तेनामृतरसनिगरण विश्रान्तिपरंम्पराणां तृप्तिर्ज्ञातेति कोपप्रसादसन्धिश्चमत्कारस्थानम्। क्वचिद् व्यभिचार्यन्तरशबलतैव विश्रान्तिपदम्। यथा–

क्वाकार्यं शशलक्ष्मणः क्व च कुलं भूयोऽपि दृश्येत सा
दोषाणां प्रशमाय मे श्रुतमहो कोपेऽपि कान्तं मुखम्।
किं वक्ष्यन्त्यपकल्मषाः कृतधियः स्वप्नेऽपि सा दुर्लभा
चेतः स्वास्थ्यमुपैहि कः खलु युवा धन्योऽधरं धास्यति।।

अत्र हि वितर्कौत्सुक्ये मतिस्मरणे शङ्कादैन्ये स्मृतिचिन्तने परस्परं बाध्यबाधक–भावेन द्वन्द्वशो भवन्ती पर्यन्ते तु चिन्ताया एव प्रधानतां ददती परमास्वादस्थानम्। एवमन्यदप्युत्प्रेक्ष्यम्।

इस व्याख्यान के अन्त में लोचनकार एक महत्त्वपूर्ण प्रश्न उठाते हैं। वह यह कि यदि विभावानुभाव भी इसी प्रकार चमत्कारातिशय के हेतु बनें तो क्या उन्हें भी 'विभावध्वनि तथा अनुभावध्वनि' कहा जायेगा ?[17] इसका युक्तियुक्त उत्तर भी स्वयं लोचनकार ही देते हैं यह कहकर कि यदि विभावानुभाव को भी व्यंग्य ही मानना है तो उसे विभावध्वनि या अनुभावध्वनि कहने की क्या आवश्यकता है ? फिर तो उसे वस्तुध्वनि ही क्यों नहीं कहते ?

महामाहेश्वर आचार्य अभिनवगुप्तपाद की काव्यशास्त्रीय प्रतिमा के कुछ उदात्त पक्ष प्रस्तुत आलेख में संकलित किये गये हैं। उनका सारस्वत जीवन अत्यंत महिमामण्डित रहा है। वह वराहगुप्त के पौत्र, चुखल के पुत्र, मनोरथगुप्त के अग्रज, कर्ण एवं क्षेमेन्द्रादि के शिक्षागुरु थे। उन्होंने स्वयं श्री लक्ष्मणगुप्त, भट्टेन्दुराज तथा भट्टतौत से विविध शास्त्रों की शिक्षा प्राप्त की थी। श्रीमदुत्पलभट्ट को अपना 'परमगुरु' मानते हैं। *ध्वन्यालोक* की *चन्द्रिका* नाम की टीका के लेखक को भी आचार्य अभिनवगुप्त अपना सगोत्र एवं पूर्वज बताते हैं (इत्यलं निजपूर्वजसगोत्रैः सह विवादेन। ध्वन्या., 3.2 लोचन, इत्यलं पूर्ववंश्यैः सह विवादेन। लोचन, ध्वन्या, 3.33)

वृहत्प्रत्यभिज्ञाविमर्शिनी की पुष्पिका में आचार्य ने लिखा है – ''इति नवतितमेऽस्मिन् वत्सरेऽन्त्ये युगांशे तिथिशशिजलधिस्थे (4115) मार्गशीर्षावसाने'' आदि। इस कालसंकेत से सिद्ध है कि आचार्य अभिनव दशम शती ई. के उत्तरार्ध एवं ग्यारहवीं शती ई. के प्रारम्भिक भाग में विद्यमान थे। सामान्यतः उनका जीवनकाल इसी के बीच माना जाता है।

आचार्य अभिनवगुप्त की कृतियों में *अनुत्तराष्टिका, क्रमस्तोत्र, तन्त्रसार, तन्त्रालोक, परमार्थचर्चा, परमार्थद्वादशिका, परमार्थसार, परात्रिंशिकाविवरण, प्रकरणस्तोत्र, प्रत्यभिज्ञाविमर्शिनी (बृहती वृत्तिः), प्रत्यभिज्ञाविमर्शिनी (लघुवृत्तिः), बोधपंचदशिका, भैरवस्तोत्र, महोपदेशविंशति* तथा *मालिनीविजयवार्तिक* की परिगणना होती है। इसके अतिरिक्त, उनकी अक्षय्य कीर्ति की आधारभूता चार टीकाएं हैं–

1. *अभिनवभारती* (नाट्यशास्त्र)
2. *लोचन* (ध्वन्यालोक)
3. *विवरण* (काव्यकौतुक)
4. *श्रीमद्भगवद्गीता टीका।*

संदर्भ

1. आनन्द इति। रसस्य चर्वणात्मनः प्राधान्यं दर्शयन् रसध्वनेरेव सर्वत्र मुख्यभूतमात्मत्वमिति दर्शयति। *लोचन टीका*
2. योऽर्थो हृदयसंवादी तस्य भावो रसोद्भवः।
शरीरं व्याप्यते तेन शुष्कं काष्ठमिवग्निना।। *लोचन टीका*
3. येषां काव्यानुशीलनाभ्यासवशाद् विशदीभूते मनोमुकुरे वर्णनीयतन्मयीभवनयोग्यता त एव हृदयसंवादभाजः सहृदयाः। *लोचन टीका*
4. तथा ह्यभिधाभावनारसचर्वणात्मकेऽपि त्र्यंशे काव्ये रसचर्वणा तावज्जीवितभूतेति भवतो ऽप्यविवादो ऽस्ति। यथोक्तं त्वयैव-काव्ये रसयिता सर्वो...। *लोचन टीका*

5. तेन यदुक्तम्-ध्वनिर्नामापरो योऽसौ व्यापारो व्यंजनात्मकः।
तस्य सिद्धेऽपि भेदे स्यात्काव्येऽगंत्वं न रूपिता।। इति तदपिहस्ततं भवति।
6. यच्च ध्वनिकारेणोक्तम्
अर्थः सहृदयश्लाघ्यः काव्यात्मा यो व्यवस्थितः।
वाच्यप्रतीयमानाख्यौ तस्य भेदावुभौ स्मृतौ।। इति।
अत्र वाच्यस्यात्मत्वं काव्यस्यात्मा ध्वनिरिति स्व
वचनविरोधादपास्तम्। - *साहित्यदर्पण:*, प्र.परि.
7. यस्तु स्वप्नेऽपि न स्वशब्दवाच्यो न लौकिकवहारपतितः, किन्तु शब्दसमर्प्यमाणहृदय संवादसुन्दर विभावानुभावसमुदित प्राङ्निविष्टरत्यादिवासनानुराग- सुकुमारस्वसंविदानन्द चर्वणव्यापार रसनीयरूपो रसः। स च काव्यव्यापारैकगोचरो रसध्वनिरिति। स च ध्वनिरेवेति। स एव मुख्यतयात्मेति। यदूचे भट्टनायकेन अंशत्वं न रूपितेति, तद्वस्त्वलङ्कार ध्वन्योरेव यदिनामोपालम्भः, रसध्वनिस्तु तेनैवात्मतयाऽङ्गीकृतः। *लोचन टीका*
8. द्रष्टव्य-*ध्वन्या.* 2.4 की वृत्ति
9. क्रौंचद्वन्द्ववियोगेन सहचरीहननोद्भूतेन साहचर्य ध्वंसनेनोत्थितो यः शोकः स्थायिभावो निरपेक्षयभावत्वाद् विप्रलम्भशृंगारोचितस्थायिभावत्वादन्य एव। स एव तथाभूत विभावतदुत्थाक्रन्दनाद्यनुभावचर्वणया हृदयसंवादतन्मयीभवनक्रमादास्वाद्यमानतां प्रतिपन्नः करुणरसरूपतां लौकिकशोकव्यतिरिक्तां स्वचित्तवृत्तिसमास्वाद्यसारां प्रतिपन्नोरसः परिपूर्णकुम्भोच्छलनवच्चित्तवृत्ति निःस्पन्दस्वभाववाग्विलापादिसमयानपेक्षित्वेऽपि चित्तवृत्तिव्यंजनकत्वादिनयेनाकृतकतयैवावेशवशात्समुचितच्छन्दोवृत्तादि नियंत्रितः श्लोकरूपतां प्राप्तः मा निषादेत्यादि।
10. सविस्तार द्रष्टव्य, *ध्वन्या.*, 1.21, (लोचन.टीका)
11. सविस्तार द्रष्टव्य, वही
12. इदं तावदयं प्रतीतिज्ञो मीमांसक पृष्टव्यः किमत्र परचित्तवमात्रे प्रतिपत्तिरेव रसप्रतीतिरभिमता भवतः नैवं भ्रमितव्यम्। एवं हि लोकगतचित्तवृत्त्यनुमानमात्रमिति का रसता ? यस्त्वलौकिक चमत्कारात्मा रसास्वादः काव्यगतविभावादि चर्वणाप्राणः नासौ स्मरणानुमानादिना खिलीकारपात्रीकर्त्तव्यः। किन्तु लौकिकेन कार्यकारणानुमानादिना संस्कृतहृदयो विभावादिकं प्रतिपद्यमानो न ताटस्थ्येन प्रतिपद्यते। अपितु हृदयसंवादापरपर्यायसहृदयत्व परवशीकृततया पूर्णीभविष्यद्रसास्वादाङ्कुरीभावेनानुमानस्मरणादिसरणिमनाह्यैव तन्ममीभवनोचित- चर्वणाप्राणतया। न चासौ चर्वणा प्रमाणान्तरतो जाता पूर्वं पेनेदानीं समृतिः स्यात्। न चाधुना कुतश्चित्प्रमाणान्तरादुत्पन्ना। अलौकिके प्रत्यक्षाद्यव्यापारात्।' लोचनम्
13. सरस्वती स्वादु तदर्थवस्तु निःष्यन्दमाना महतां कवीनाम्।।
अलोकसामान्यमभिव्यनक्ति परिस्फुरन्तं प्रतिभाविशेषम्।। *ध्वन्या.*, 1.6
14. तद्भेदशब्देन च रसभावतदाभासतत्प्रशमभेदास्तदवान्तरभेदाश्च। न च तेषु लक्षणाया उपपत्तिः। तथाहि विभावानुभावप्रतिपादके शब्दे तत्रार्थे मुख्ये तावद् बाधकाऽनुप्रवेशोऽप्यसम्भाव्य इति को लक्षणावकाशः ? *लोचन टीका*

15. स रसादिध्वनिर्व्यवस्थित एव। नहि तच्छून्यं काव्यं किंचिदस्ति। यद्यपि च रसेनैव सर्वं जीवति काव्यं तथापि तस्य रसस्यैकधनचमत्कारात्मनोऽपि कुतश्चिदंशात्प्रयोजकी भूतादधिकोऽसौ चमत्कारोऽपि भवति। तत्र यदा कश्चिद्दुद्रिक्तावस्थां प्रतिपन्नो व्यभिचारी चमत्कारातिशय प्रयोजको भवति तदा भावध्वनिः।

16. व्यभिचारिण उदयस्थित्यपायत्रिधर्मकाः। यदाह, विविधमाभिमुख्येन चरन्तीति व्यभिचारिणः।

17. नन्वेवं विभावाऽनुभावमुखेनाप्यधिकश्चमत्कारो दृश्यत इति विभावध्वनिरनुभावध्वनिश्च वक्तव्यः। मैवम् विभावानुभावौ तावत्स्वशब्दवाच्यावेव। तच्चर्वणापि चित्तवृत्तिष्वेव पर्यवस्यतीति रसभावेभ्यो नाधिकं चर्वणीयम्। यदि तु विभावानुभावावपि व्यंग्यौ भवतस्तदा वस्तुध्वनिरपि किं न सह्यते? यदा तु विभावानुभावाभासाद्रत्याभासोदयस्तदा विभावानुभावाभासाच्चर्वणाभास इति रसाभासस्य विषयः। यथा रावणकाव्याकर्णने श्रृंगाराभासः। *लोचन टीका, ध्वन्य,* 2.3

15

अभिनवगुप्तपादानां मते रसस्यालौकिकत्वोपपत्तिः

दामोदर राम त्रिपाठी

''रसो वै सः''[1] इति श्रुतेः काव्योपपादितरसानुभवः परब्रह्मानुभव एवेति व्यवतिष्ठते। रसस्यास्वादनाख्योऽनुभवो ब्रह्मानुभवसदृशः। सादृश्यस्यभेदघटितत्वेन सदृशत्वोक्त्या रसास्वादे ब्रह्मास्वादाभिन्नत्वं प्रतीयते। यथा ब्रह्मास्वादे प्रतिकूलवेदनीयं दुःखं नानुभूयते तथैव काव्यास्वादे अखण्डपरमानन्दश्चावभासते। एवं रीत्या द्वयोरपि साम्यक्त्वं समायाति। ब्रह्मास्वादे ब्रह्ममात्रं प्रकाशते, रसे तु विभावाद्यपीति भेदात् सादृश्यम्।[2]

विभावादिभिर्व्यज्यमाना रसप्रतीतिरलौकिकीत्यामनन्त्यभिनवगुप्तपादाचार्याः। प्रत्यक्षादिभिः प्रमाणैर्यज्ज्ञानमुपपद्यते तदेव लौकिकं ज्ञानं भवति। न चात्र लौकिकप्रत्यक्षादि प्रमाणव्यापारः[3] इति कथने चर्वणानिष्पत्तिरलौकिकविभावादि- संयोगबलेनैव सञ्जायते। रसप्रतीतिरियं लौकिकप्रत्यक्षप्रमाणनिरपेक्षा भवति। लौकिकं प्रत्यक्षं निर्विकल्पकं सविकल्पमितिरूपेण द्विविधं भवति। निर्विकल्पकं ज्ञानं नामजात्यादियोजनाविरहितं जायते। रसप्रतीतौ विभावादीनामपि सम्बन्धो जायते अतः निर्विकल्पकज्ञानकोटौ समावेशोऽस्याः कर्तुं न शक्यते। काव्ये नाट्ये च विभावादिरूपस्य काव्यार्थस्य येयं प्रतीतिः सा प्रत्यक्षज्ञानात्मिका इत्यपि कथनं समीचीनं न प्रतिभाति। प्रत्यक्षज्ञानं प्रति इन्द्रियार्थसन्निकर्षस्य कारणतांगीक्रियते। विभावादीनां ज्ञानरूपत्वात् एभिस्सह चक्षुरादीनां सन्निकर्ष एव न सम्भवति। रसमात्रविषयिण्यां चर्वणायां नामरूपाद्युल्लेखासम्भवात् अत्र सविकल्पक ज्ञानस्यास्याप्यवसरो न समायाति। सविकल्पकं ज्ञानं तस्यैव भवति यः खल्वर्थो वाचकलक्षकशब्दैर्व्यवहारयोग्यतामुपैति।[4]

रसस्तु काव्यनाटकदर्शनश्रवणसमन्नतरमेव व्यंजनाख्यव्यापारव्यंग्य एव। अभिलापव्यवहारयोग्यत्वाभावेनैव रसस्य सविकल्पकज्ञानविषयत्वं निराक्रियते।

रसस्य स्वसंवेदनगोचरता प्रमाणीकृता वर्तते। संवेदनं ज्ञानमित्युच्यते। रसस्य स्वात्ममात्रप्रतीतिविषयत्वेनाऽस्य सविकल्पकविषयता स्वीकर्तुं न शक्या। भावनाख्य संस्कारादिवदस्यातीन्द्रियता नांगीक्रियते यतो हि साक्षात्कारविषयो रसोऽस्ति। काव्ये नाट्ये च सहृदयाः रसस्य साक्षात्कारं कुर्वन्तीति कृत्वाऽस्य परोक्षविषयताऽपि खण्डिता भवति।

प्रत्यक्षं ज्ञानं लौकिकालौकिकभेदेन द्विविधम्।[5] अलौकिकं प्रत्यक्षं सामान्यलक्षण ज्ञानलक्षणयोगजभेदात् त्रिविधम्भवति। तत्र सामान्यं लक्षणं स्वरूपं यस्याऽसौ सामान्य लक्षण इति व्युत्पत्त्या सामान्यमिन्द्रियसम्बद्धज्ञानप्रकारीभूतमेव ग्राहयति। तादृशसामान्यस्य सन्निकर्षत्वे चक्षुरिन्द्रियसम्बद्धविशेष्यके धूम इति प्रत्यक्षे प्रकारी भूतेन धूमत्वसामान्यरूपेण समेषां धूमानां प्रत्यक्षं धूम इत्येवंरूपमुत्पद्यते। प्रकृते विभावादिभिः रसप्रतीतौ चक्षुरिन्द्रियसम्बद्धस्य कस्यापि विशेष्यकस्य प्रत्यक्षं न भवति अतोऽत्र सामान्यलक्षणसन्निकर्षस्य नाऽवसरः प्रसरति। ज्ञानलक्षणोऽपि सन्निकर्षः प्रत्यक्षप्रमाहेतुत्वेन स्वीकृतोऽस्ति। सुरभिचन्दनमिति प्रत्यक्षे सौरभांशेऽयं सन्निकर्षः चन्दनांशे चक्षुषस्संयोगसन्निकर्ष इत्युभाभ्यां सन्निकर्षाभ्यामेकं चाक्षुषं ज्ञानमुपलभ्यते। रसचर्वणायां ज्ञानलक्षणप्रत्यासत्तिस्तु पूर्वोक्तसन्निकर्षाभावेन न सम्पद्यते। युक्तयुंजानभेदतो योगजप्रत्यक्षस्य द्वैविध्यं समायाति। तत्र युक्तयोगिनामीश्वरानुग्रहेण विशिष्टज्ञानप्रसादेन च मनसा निखिलपदार्थानामलौकिकप्रत्यक्षात्मकं ज्ञानं सर्वदैव भवति। युंजानयोगिनान्तु चिन्तासहकृतेन मनसा यद्विषयकः संयमस्तद्विषयकमलौकिकसाक्षात्कारात्मकं ज्ञानं जायते। अत्रेदं विचारणीयं यत् योगिनामपि प्रत्यक्षात्मकमलौकिकं ज्ञानं तत्तदिन्द्रियजन्यमेव भवति न त्वन्येन्द्रियविषयस्यान्येन्द्रियसाक्षात्कारविषयत्वम्। रसप्रतीतौ विभावादिपरामर्शस्य प्राधान्येन स्वस्वरूपात्ममात्रविषयकात् मितियोगिज्ञानाद्वैलक्षण्यं समायाति। रसप्रतीतिरियं विलक्षणा तथा चास्यां प्रतीतौ विभावादिभिः आनन्दांशरूपस्य अभिव्यक्तया ज्ञाप्यत्वव्यवहारोऽप्युपद्यते।

केचन विद्वांसोऽस्य अलौकिकत्वसिद्धत्वे रसस्य प्रतीतिमलौकिकप्रत्यक्षेणोप-पादयन्ति।[7] सामान्यलक्षणप्रत्यासत्या न मनागपि विभावादीनां प्रतीतिः कर्तुं शक्या। विभावादिषु अलौकिकत्वन्तु सम्बन्धविशेषस्वीकारपरिहारनियमानध्यवसायेनैव सम्भवति। रसस्य प्रत्यक्षादिप्रमाणाऽगोचरत्वेनैव वैशिष्ट्यं प्रतिपाद्यते अभिनवाचार्येण।

रसस्यालौकिकत्वसिद्धयेऽस्य कार्यज्ञाप्यरूपाभ्यां व्यतिरेकोऽपि वर्ण्यते। विभावानुभावव्यभिचारिसंयोगाद्रसनिष्पत्तिरिति सूत्रे संयोगादिति पंचम्या विभावादीनां हेतुत्वं कल्प्यते। लोकव्यवहारे कारकज्ञापकरूपा द्विविधा हेतुता दृश्यते। तत्र विभावादीनां रसं प्रति कारकरूपा हेतुता भवितुं नार्हति। न्यायदर्शने समवाय्यसमवायिनिमित्तभेदात् त्रिविधा कारणता स्वीक्रियते। तत्र समवायिकारणं द्रव्यस्यैवेति विज्ञेयमिति रीत्या विभावादीनां ज्ञानरूपत्वेन समवायिकारणता न सम्भवति। विभावादीनां रसं प्रति निमित्तकारणताऽपि न स्वीकर्तुं

शक्या यतो हि लोके निमित्तकारणनाशेऽपि कार्यदर्शनात् विभावादिविनाशेऽपि रससिद्धिप्रसंगस्स्यात् रसस्तु विभावादिजीवितावधिरेव अतोऽत्र निमित्तकारणता मनागपि न सम्भवा। एवमेव विभावादीनां रसं प्रति ज्ञापकत्वरूपा कारणताऽपि निराक्रियते। सिद्धस्यैव वस्तुनः ज्ञाप्यता भवति। धूमादित्यादाविव संयोगादिति पंचम्या न ज्ञापकत्वमर्थः।

रसस्य निष्पत्तिरिति विग्रहे स्थायिन उत्पत्तिर्न प्रतीयते किन्तु विशेषणभूतचर्वणाया एव उत्पत्तिः। चर्वणागतोत्पत्तेस्सम्भवादेव उत्पन्नो रस इति व्यवहारस्सम्भवति।[8]

समेषामपि रसानां सुखरूपतयाऽलौकिकत्वं सिद्धयति। अभिननवगुप्तपादाचार्याणां सर्वेऽपि सुखप्रधानाः स्वसंविच्चर्वणारूपस्य एकघनस्य प्रकाशस्य आनन्दकरत्वात्। रसास्वादे लौकिकहर्षदुःखादीनां अनुभूतिर्न जायते अत्र स्वसंवेदनाया एव आस्वादो भवति। विभावादय आत्मनि यदज्ञानावरणं तन्निरस्य आनन्दस्यैव उद्‌बोधका भवन्ति। रसिकः आनन्दरूपायाः संवेदनाया एव आस्वादं करोति। लोके 'उपादेयाऽपि ये हेयास्तानुपायान् प्रचक्षते' इति नयेन व्यवहारे कार्यसिद्धौ जातायां लौकिका उपायास्तु हेया भवन्ति किन्तु रसप्रतीतौ हेतुत्वेन प्रकल्पिता विभावादयो न खलुस्वकीयमस्तित्वं तिरोदधति। विभावादिजीवितावधिरेव रस इति सिद्धान्तेन विभावादीनामसत्त्वे रस चर्वणाऽपि न सम्भाव्यते। अतोऽत्र लौकिकोपायापेक्षया विभावादीनां वैलक्षण्येन एतेषामलौकिकत्वं सिध्यति। ''तथाभूतविभावानुभावचर्वणतया हृदयसंवादतन्मयीभवनक्रमात् आस्वाद्यतां प्रतिपन्नः स्थायी'' इत्यभिनवगुप्तमतानुसारेण विभावादिभिरेव स्थायी आस्वाद्यतामुपैति। काव्ये नाट्ये चालौकिकविभावादीनां वर्णनात् एतेषामलौकिकत्वं समायाति।

लोकोत्तरवर्णनानिपुणकविकर्म एव काव्यमिति रीत्या कविः स्ववर्णनानैपुण्येन लौकिकमपि वर्णनं स्वानुभूत्या अलौकिकत्वेनैवोपस्थापयति। मुखस्य कमलत्वादिरूपेणो-पस्थापनमेव लोकोत्तरवर्णनमिति कृत्वा काव्यास्यालौकिकत्वं सेद्धुमर्हति।

पण्डितराजजगन्नाथेनाऽपि काव्यस्य लोकोत्तरत्वसिद्धये ''रमणीयार्थप्रतिपादकः शब्दः काव्यमिति'' काव्यलक्षणमुदाहृतम्। अनुभवसाक्षिकत्वेनैव काव्यस्य लोकोत्तरत्वं सिद्धयति। अत्र सहृदयहृदयैकमात्रस्य प्रामाण्यमन्येषां प्रत्यक्षादीनां प्रमाणानां काव्यार्थप्रतिपत्तये नावसर इति लोकोत्तरपदोपन्यासेन प्रतिपादिम्भवति।

लौकिकप्रत्यक्षादिप्रमाणनैरपेक्ष्येणकाव्यस्य जीवानुभूततत्त्वस्य सहृदयमात्र संवेद्यत्वेनाऽस्यालौकिकत्वं सर्वथा समीचीनमिति प्रतिपादयितुं शक्यते। मानाधीना हि मेयसिद्धिरिति नयेन लौकिकप्रमेयप्रतिपत्तावेव प्रत्यक्षादीन्यनुग्राहकत्वेन प्रकल्पितानि भवन्ति। रसस्य सहृदयसंवेदनगोचरत्वेनऽस्य प्रतिपत्तये पूर्वोक्तानि प्रमाणानि किलानि भवन्ति।

संदर्भ

1. *तैत्तिरीयोपनषिद्*, 2.7.1
2. *काव्यप्रकाश*, बालबोधिनी टीका, पृ. सं. 93

3. *अभिनवभारती*, षष्ठ अध्याय, पृ. सं. 485
4. *साहित्य दर्पण*, कुसुम प्रतिमा टीका, पृ. सं. 84
5. *काव्यप्रकाश,* चतुर्थ उल्लास रस प्रकरण
6. *न्यायसिद्धान्तमुक्तावली*, प्रत्यक्षखण्ड
7. *भारतीय साहित्यशास्त्र,* गणेशत्र्यम्बक देशपांडे
8. *काव्यप्रकाश*, विवरण टीका

16

रससिद्धान्त की प्रेरणा: शब्दब्रह्मवाद

हरिराम मिश्र

काव्यों एवं नाटकों में अन्त:सार के रूप में विद्यमान रसतत्त्व का विश्लेषण भरत से लेकर आज तक काव्यशास्त्र का मुख्य प्रतिपाद्य विषय रहा है। मन्त्रद्रष्टा ऋषियों ने सम्पूर्ण ज्ञान के आदिस्रोत वेदों में रस शब्द का आनन्द अर्थ में बहुश: प्रयोग किया है। *ऋग्वेद* के दशम मण्डल में 'यो व: शिवतमो रस:'[1] कहा गया है। वहीं पर दो अन्य मन्त्र प्राप्त होते हैं, जिनमें रस शब्द का प्रयोग काव्यात्मतत्त्व के अर्थ में किया गया प्रतीत होता है। वे मन्त्र हैं-

1. *पावमानीयो अध्येतृषिभि: सम्भृतम् रसम्।*
   सरस्वती तस्मै दुहे क्षीरं सर्पिर्मधूदकम्।।
2. *य: पावमानीरध्येत्यृषिभि: सम्भृतं रसम्।*
   सर्वं स पूतमश्नाति स्वदितं मातरिश्वना।। [2]

उपनिषदों में स्थूल तत्त्वों की अपेक्षा सूक्ष्म तथा व्यापक की व्याख्या में अधिक ध्यान दिया गया है। *तैत्तिरीयोपनिषद्* में स्पष्ट रूप से कहा गया है कि वह अर्थात् मूलतत्त्व रस ही है तथा रसस्वरूप इस तत्त्व की प्राप्ति से मानवमात्र को आनन्द की अनुभूति होने लगती है-'*रसो वै स:। रसं ह्येवायं लब्ध्वानन्दी भवति।*'[3] यहां इसे स्पष्ट रूप से आनन्दानुभूति का स्रोत माना गया है। वस्तुत: सम्पूर्ण भारतीय चिन्तन का मूल उद्देश्य प्राणिमात्र के दु:ख की आत्यन्तिक निवृत्ति करते हुए उसे आनन्दानुभूति के स्तर तक पहुंचाना ही रहा है। आचार्यों ने अपने सम्प्रदायों का आश्रय लेते हुए इसी मूल धारणा

को प्रधान मानकर अपने-अपने सिद्धांतों की प्रतिष्ठा की है। प्रतिपाद्य सबका वही था, केवल मार्ग भिन्न-भिन्न थे। किसी आचार्य ने ज्ञान को ही इसका सर्वोत्तम साधन माना है, किसी ने तपस्या को तो किसी ने कर्मकाण्ड आदि को।

वैयाकरण आचार्य इन मोक्षसाधक साधनों से संतुष्ट नहीं हुए। इन्हें प्रतीत हुआ कि ये साधन अपूर्ण हैं, कठिन हैं। फलत: इन्होंने यह माना कि शब्दतत्त्व के स्वरूप को जान लेने से समस्त अभीष्टों की सिद्धि हो जाती है। इनकी दृष्टि में मोक्ष को प्राप्त करने की इच्छा रखने वाले व्यक्तियों के लिए व्याकरणरूप यह मार्ग अत्यन्त सीधा एवं आसान है। किन्तु काव्यों का निर्माण और सरल साधन के रूप में किया गया है। काव्यों के निर्माण में मूल धारणा ही यह थी कि सरलमति वाले व्यक्ति भी इस साधन से आनन्द की अनुभूति कर सकें। काव्यशास्त्रियों ने एक तथ्य यह भी स्पष्ट किया है कि काव्य से मानव को सद्य: परनिर्वृत्ति होती है। काव्य के श्रवणादि के समानान्तर ही रसास्वादन से समुद्भूत उस आनन्द की प्राप्ति होती है जिसमें आनन्दातिरिक्त अन्य समस्त वेद्य तिरोहित हो जाते हैं। यह आनन्दानुभूति ही काव्य का पारमार्थिक प्रयोजन है। इसी गवेषणा में साहित्यशास्त्रियों को रस तत्त्व की प्राप्ति हुई। इनके अनुसार रस ही काव्य में प्रधान तत्त्व है। इसके बिना किसी अर्थ की अभिव्यक्ति सम्भव नहीं है। आचार्य भरत की *नाट्यशास्त्र* में उक्ति है : *'नहि रसादृते कश्चिदर्थ: प्रवर्तते।'*[4]

आचार्य भरत के अभिप्राय को स्पष्ट करते हुए अभिनवगुप्त ने माना है कि काव्य का फल है आनन्द की प्राप्ति, वह रस के बिना सम्भव नहीं है। रस की स्थिति में ही विभावादि पदार्थों के व्याख्यान के लिए बुद्धि में उपस्थित होते हैं। सामाजिक, व्याख्याता एवं नट आदि को होने वाली आनन्द की अनुभूति रस के कारण होती है। अतएव, इनकी अपेक्षा से रस को काव्य में प्रधान तत्त्व के रूप में स्वीकार किया गया है।[5]

रस का एक सिद्धांत के रूप में सर्वप्रथम आचार्य भरत के *नाट्यशास्त्र* में उल्लेख प्राप्त होता है। उनका रस के स्वरूप की मूल धारणा को प्रतिपादित करने वाला- *'विभावानुभावव्यभिचारिसंयोगाद्रसनिष्पत्ति:'* यह सूत्र ही परवर्ती काव्य-शास्त्रियों द्वारा अनेक प्रकार से व्याख्यायित होता रहा। सामान्यत: इसका अर्थ है- 'विभाव, अनुभाव एवं व्यभिचारी भावों के संयोग से रसनिष्पत्ति होती है। भरत ने यहाँ पर रस को आस्वाद्य माना है। सूत्र की व्याख्या में इन्होंने स्वयं स्पष्ट किया है कि जिस प्रकार अनेक व्यञ्जनों, औषधियों एवं द्रव्यों के संयोग से पेय रस की निष्पत्ति होती है, उसी प्रकार नाना भावों के उपयोग से रस की निष्पत्ति होती है। जिस प्रकार गुड़ आदि द्रव्यों, व्यञ्जनों तथा औषधियों के संयोग से षाडवादि रसों की निर्वृत्ति होती है उसी प्रकार नाना भावों से उपगत स्थायी भाव भी रसरूपता को प्राप्त हो जाते हैं। भरत ने यहां पर स्वयं भी यह कहा है कि रससंज्ञा आस्वाद्यत्वप्रयुक्त है, अर्थात् रस आस्वाद्य होता है। सामाजिक आस्वाद्य रूप में रस का अनुभव करते हैं।[6]

आचार्य भरत ने भावों की व्याख्या के अनन्तर प्रतिपादित किया है कि जिस प्रकार नाना प्रकार के द्रव्यों से व्यञ्जन की भावना की जाती है, उसी प्रकार भाव अभिनयों के साथ होकर रसों की भावना कराते हैं। न भाव से हीन रस की कल्पना की जा सकती है और न रस से हीन भाव की। इस प्रसंग में भरत ने एक महत्त्वपूर्ण बात यह भी कही है कि जिस प्रकार वृक्ष के मूल बीज हैं तथा वृक्ष, पुष्प, फल आदि के मूल हैं, उसी प्रकार भावों के मूल कारण रस हैं। रसों के कारण ही भाव व्यवस्थित होते हैं-

न भावहीनोऽस्ति रसो न भावो रसवर्जितः।
परस्परकृता सिद्धिस्तयोरभिनये भवेत्।।
यथा बीजाद् भवेद् वृक्षो वृक्षात्पुष्पं फलं यथा।
तथा मूलं रसाः सर्वे तेभ्यो भावा व्यवस्थिताः।। [7]

यह आचार्य भरत की केन्द्राभिमुखी प्रवृत्ति का निदर्शन है। आचार्य भरत के इसी विवेचन को आधार बनाकर अन्य आचार्यों ने रस के स्वरूप को निर्धारित करने का प्रयास किया है। आचार्यों के द्वारा इस रसस्वरूप के निर्धारण में विभिन्न दर्शनों का प्रभाव पड़ना स्वाभाविक था, क्योंकि जिन आचार्यों ने इस विषय का विचार किया है, वे विभिन्न दर्शनों से स्वतः सम्बद्ध थे। वस्तुतः किसी भी भारतीय शास्त्र को समझने के लिए उससे सम्बद्ध विभिन्न शास्त्रों का परिशीलन आवश्यक होता है। भर्तृहरि ने स्वीकार किया है कि विभिन्न आगमों के सिद्धान्तों का पर्यालोचन करने से मानवीय प्रज्ञा विवेक को प्राप्त करती है। अन्य सम्बद्ध शास्त्रों के सिद्धांतों की व्याख्या के बिना मात्र अपने सम्प्रदाय के तर्कों से प्रतिपाद्यमान शास्त्रों के सिद्धान्त पूर्णता को नहीं प्राप्त करते-

प्रज्ञा विवेकं लभते भिन्नैरागमदर्शनैः।
कियद्वा शक्यमुन्नेतुं स्वतर्कमनुधावता।। [8]

साहित्यशास्त्रियों ने इस बात को अक्षरशः स्वीकार किया है। इन्हें अपने सिद्धान्तों की व्याख्या के लिए जहां से भी जो कुछ प्राप्त हुआ, उसका उपयोग करने में इन्होंने तनिक भी संकोच नहीं किया। रस सिद्धान्त की व्याख्या के प्रसंग में आचार्य अभिनवगुप्त ने स्पष्ट रूप से स्वीकार किया है कि रससिद्धान्त को स्पष्ट करने के लिए विज्ञानवाद, द्विधा अभिधान, स्फोटतत्त्व, सत्कार्यवाद एवं एकत्व दर्शन अर्थात् अद्वैतवाद का आश्रय लिया गया है।[9] यहाँ पर अन्य दार्शनिक वादों के साथ वैयाकरणों को अभिमत स्फोट तत्त्व का उल्लेख किया गया है। इस लेख में काव्यशास्त्रियों को रस की व्याख्या में व्याकरणतन्त्र ने कहाँ तक प्रभावित किया है इस तथ्य को स्पष्ट करने का प्रयास किया जा रहा है। वैयाकरणों का शब्द-सम्बन्धी अन्वाख्यान काव्यशास्त्रियों को महत्त्वपूर्ण आधार प्रदान करता है। वैयाकरणों ने शब्दतत्त्व का जो पारमार्थिक विवेचन प्रस्तुत किया है रस की व्याख्या में काव्यशास्त्रियों ने उसका पूर्ण उपयोग किया है।

शब्दब्रह्म की अवधारणा वेदों तथा उपनिषदों में ही प्राप्त होने लगती है। वेदों में शब्दतत्त्व के व्यापक स्वरूप को अभिव्यक्त करते हुए कहा गया है–

अहं सुवे पितरमस्य मूर्धन् मम योनिरप्स्वन्तः समुद्रे।
ततो वितिष्ठे भुवनानु विश्वोतामूं द्यां वर्ष्मणोपस्पृशामि।।[10]

यहाँ पर शब्दतत्त्व को व्यापक, सर्वातीत, समस्त विश्व का उत्पादक, प्रशस्य तथा गतिशील बताया गया है। *कैवल्योपनिषद्* में भी समस्त संसार प्रपञ्च को शब्दतत्त्व में प्रतिष्ठित एवं उसी में लीन बताया गया है यथा–

मय्येव सकलं जातं मयि सर्वं प्रतिष्ठितम्।
मयि सर्वं लयं याति तद् ब्रह्माद्वयमस्म्यहम्।।[11]

वैयाकरणों ने वेदों एवं उपनिषदों में प्रतिपादित शब्दब्रह्मविषयक इस धारणा को और अधिक स्पष्ट किया है। इन्होंने समस्त दार्शनिक वादों को विवेचित करते हुए उस परमतत्त्व को शब्दब्रह्म, अक्षरतत्त्व, शब्दतत्त्व आदि नामों से अभिहित किया है। इसी परमतत्त्व को जगत् का मूल कारण, नित्य, सर्वव्यापक एवं सर्वातीत माना है। महाभाष्यकार पतञ्जलि ने परमतत्त्व शब्दब्रह्म की गंभीर व्याख्या कर यह प्रतिपादित किया है कि परमतत्त्व सर्वत्र व्याप्त है। जो कुछ दिखाई पड़ रहा है वह उसी के कारण है–

चत्वारि शृङ्गा त्रयोऽस्य पादा द्वे शीर्षे सप्त हस्तासोऽस्य।
त्रिधा बद्धो वृषभो रोरवीति महो देवो मर्त्यां आविवेश।।[12]

इस वेदमन्त्र की व्याख्या करते हुए पतञ्जलि ने शब्दब्रह्म की तात्त्विक व्याख्या प्रस्तुत की है। यहाँ पर इन्होंने उस महान् देव शब्दब्रह्म के नित्य तथा अनित्य दो स्वरूपों को मान्यता दी है। अर्थतत्व का वर्षण करने के कारण इसे वृषभ कहा जाता है। यह महादेव शब्दतत्त्व ही है। यह सभी मनुष्यों में समाविष्ट है। भर्तृहरि ने इस स्थल पर अपना अभिमत प्रस्तुत करते हुए माना है कि शब्दतत्त्व के दो स्वरूप हैं– नित्य तथा अनित्य। स्थान करण आदि के द्वारा अविवृत शब्द नित्य है तथा इनके द्वारा विवृत अनित्य। अनित्य शब्द वैखरी रूप है। व्यावहारिक है। इससे सम्पूर्ण लोक व्यवहार प्रवृत्त होता है। यह परावाणी रूप पुरुष के प्रतिबिम्ब अर्थात् सादृश्य को गृहीत करता है तथा समस्त व्यवहार का निमित्त कारण है। नित्य शब्द तो समस्त साध्यसाधन व्यवहार तथा पदपदार्थ भेद व्यवहार का उपादान कारण है। यह क्रमरहित है। यह सभी प्राणियों के अन्तःकरण में आत्मरूप से सन्निविष्ट है। विकृतियों का यह प्रभवस्थान है। कर्मजन्य पुण्य-पाप रूपी वासनाओं का आश्रय तथा सुख-दुःख का अधिष्ठान है। प्रलय के समय परावाक् रूप

उसी पुरुष में सभी भावों का विलय हो जाता है तथा सृष्टि के आदि में उसी से सभी भावों का जन्म होता है। यह प्रसव एवं उच्छेद शक्ति से युक्त है। इस प्रकार यह महान् शब्द वृषभ, सर्वेश्वर तथा सर्वशक्तिसम्पन्न है। वाक्तत्त्व के ज्ञान से युक्त वैयाकरण अहंकाराश्रित सम्पूर्ण संशयरूप तथा वासनारूप ग्रन्थियों को तोड़कर, भेद का नितान्त परित्याग कर इस शब्दब्रह्म में संसृष्ट हो जाता है अर्थात् ब्रह्म का साक्षात्कार करता है।[13]

भर्तृहरि समस्त अर्थतत्त्व को शब्दतत्त्व का विवर्त मानते हैं। सम्पूर्ण विकारों की प्रलयावस्था में वर्ण, मात्र, पद आदि आनुपूर्वी रहित अतएव संवर्तरूप तथा पदार्थों में परस्पर भेद का अवधारण न होने से अव्याकृत शब्दाख्य ब्रह्म से जगदादि समस्त प्रपंच समुद्भूत होते हैं।

वैयाकरणों का शब्दब्रह्म विषयक यह विवेचन भरत के द्वारा प्रस्तुत वाक् तत्त्व के स्वरूप की पूर्ण व्याख्या प्रस्तुत करता है। भरत ने वाणी के महत्त्व को स्वीकार करते हुए कहा है–

वाङ्मयानीह शास्त्रणि वाङ्निष्ठानि तथैव च।
तस्माद् वाचः परं नास्ति वाग्घि सर्वस्य कारणम्।।[14]

यहां पर भरत ने वाणी को समस्त संसार का कारण माना है। भरत की इस कारिका की व्याख्या में आचार्य अभिनवगुप्त स्पष्ट रूप से स्वीकार करते हैं कि भरत की मान्यता का आधार 'वागेव विश्वा भुवनानि जज्ञे' यह श्रुति है तथा भर्तृहरि आदि वैयाकरण आचार्यों ने प्रमाणोपन्यास पुरःसर जगत् के शब्द विवर्तादिरूपत्व का जो व्याख्यान प्रस्तुत किया है, उसका यहां अनुसन्धान कर लेना चाहिए–

'वागेव विश्वा भुवनीति श्रुतेः' शब्दविवर्तादिरूपत्वं च प्रसाधितं तत्रभवद्भिर्भर्तृहरिप्रभृतिभिरिति तदिहानुसरणीयम्।[15]

वस्तुतः महाभाष्यकार के शब्दतत्त्व के विवेचन से भरत मुनि अवश्य परिचित रहे होंगे। भरत द्वारा प्रतिपादित वाक्तत्त्व की व्यापकता को और अधिक स्पष्ट करते हुए अभिनवगुप्त ने माना है कि भगवती भारती मोक्षरूप पुरुषार्थ के लिए उपाय है। वाणी सम्पूर्ण तत्त्वों की अवभासिका तथा समस्त व्यवहार की निर्वाहिका है। अवभासना अर्थात् तत्त्वों का प्रत्यायन ही निर्वाण है–

चतुर्थगोपायभूता परमपुरुषार्थस्वभावा विश्वकारणभूता भगवती भारती। एवं वागेवावभासिका सैव निर्वाहिकी अवभासनैव हि परमार्थतो निर्वाणम्।।[16]

अभिनवगुप्त के इस विवेचन में पतञ्जलि एवं भर्तृहरि द्वारा प्रस्तुत शब्दतत्त्व के व्याख्यान का स्पष्ट प्रभाव है। इस शब्दतत्त्व के व्याख्यान से ही काव्यशास्त्रियों ने रससिद्धान्त के पल्लवन में प्रेरणा प्राप्त की है।

रस का स्वरूप

भरत के रस सूत्र की व्याख्या में अभिनवगुप्त के द्वारा रस का स्वरूप निर्धारित करते हुए कहा गया है कि लोक में जो कारण, कार्य और सहकारी रत्यादि के द्योतक तथा पोषक माने गये हैं वे यदि काव्य तथा नाट्य में उपयुक्त किये जाते हैं तो विभाव, अनुभाव तथा संचारीभाव कहलाते हैं। काव्य में उपनिबद्ध विभावादि अलौकिक होते हैं। इन विभावादिकों से अभिव्यक्त चर्व्यमाणतैकप्राण रस की सहज अनुभूति होती है। रस विभावादि के रहने पर ही रहता है। पानक के चर्वण में एला, मरिच आदि वस्तुओं के समुदाय से सम्पादित विलक्षण आस्वाद्यता जिस प्रकार रहती है, उसी प्रकार विभावादि वैलक्षण्येन रस की चर्व्यमाणता मानी गयी है। चर्वणा के अतिरिक्त काल में इसकी सम्भावना नहीं की जा सकती इसको आस्वादरूप ही मानना पड़ता है, क्योंकि रस चर्वणा के अतिरिक्त कुछ भी नहीं है। यह अलौकिक, चमत्काररूप, स्मृत्यादि से विलक्षण तथा ब्रह्मास्वादसहोदर है।

1. साहित्यशास्त्री रस को आस्वादरूप मानते हैं। यह स्वाकारवदभिन्नत्वेन आस्वाद्य होता है। जिस प्रकार कोई विशिष्ट योगी ही ब्रह्म का साक्षात्कार करता है, उसी प्रकार विशिष्ट पुण्यों वाले, वासनाख्य संस्कार से युक्त कोई ही सहृदय मनुष्य रस की आस्वाद्यता में समर्थ होता है। काव्यार्थ की भावना का आस्वाद आत्मानन्द समुद्भव होता है। वास्तविक दृष्टि से रस आस्वाद रूप होता है। आस्वाद्य आदि उसमें आरोपित मात्र होते हैं, वास्तविक नहीं। रस एकरूप होता है। भेद आदि की कल्पना व्यवहार निर्वाह के लिए की जाती है।[17]

काव्यशास्त्रियों के इस विवेचन में अद्वैत दर्शन के साथ-साथ वैयाकरणों का भी स्पष्ट प्रभाव परिलक्षित होता है। भर्तृहरि ने स्वीकार किया है कि शब्दतत्त्व समस्त संसार का मूल कारण है। वह एकरूप है। फिर भी उस एक परमतत्त्व की भोक्ता, भोक्तव्य तथा भोगरूप में कल्पना कर लोकव्यवहार का निर्वाह किया जाता है। ये सब भेद अवास्तविक हैं। परमार्थतः वही एक तत्त्व है। संसार में भोक्ता, भोक्तव्य तथा सुखदुःखाद्यनुभवरूप भोग जो कुछ भी आभासित रहते हैं वे सब शब्दब्रह्म के अतिरिक्त कुछ भी नहीं है। इस परमतत्त्व से भिन्न किसी अतिरिक्त तत्त्व की कल्पना नहीं की जा सकती-

एकस्य सर्वबीजस्य यस्य चेयमनेकधा।
भोक्तृभोक्तव्यरूपेण भोगरूपेण च स्थितिः॥[18]

इस प्रकार, भर्तृहरि काव्यशास्त्रियों के लिए रस को स्वाकारवदभिन्न मानने के लिए पर्याप्त आधार प्रस्तुत कर देते हैं।

2. भट्टनायक आदि काव्यशास्त्री रस का आविर्भाव सत्त्व के उद्रेक से स्वीकार करते हैं।[19] रजस् एवं तमस् के अप्राधान्य में अन्तःकरण में सत्त्व का उद्रेक होता है। इस स्थिति में अन्तःकरण सांसारिक रागद्वेष से मुक्त हो जाता है तभी सहृदय सामाजिक को रस की अनुभूति होती है। आचार्य भर्तृहरि व्याकरण का महत्त्व प्रतिपादित करने के साथ-साथ इस तथ्य का भी उद्घाटन करते हैं कि व्याकरण द्वारा वाणी के दोषों का परिहार हो जाने के कारण कत्व, खत्व आदि, पदत्व, वाक्यत्व आदि तथा तारत्व, मन्द्रत्व आदि धर्मों से असंकीर्ण, समस्त वाग्विकारों की प्रकृति शब्दतत्त्व का वैयाकरण अर्थात् वाणी के साधक को निर्भ्रान्त अनुभव होने लगता है। दोषों का परिहार या अभाव सत्त्व की ही अवस्था है। शब्दतत्त्व का निर्भ्रान्त साक्षात्कार तभी हो सकता है जब शब्दसंस्कार का सम्यग् ज्ञान हो गया रहता है-

तस्माद्यः शब्दसंस्कारः सा सिद्धिः परमात्मनः। [20]

काव्यशास्त्री भी सत्त्व के उद्रेक में अलौकिक काव्यार्थ के परिशीलन को हेतु मानते हैं-

तत्र हेतुस्तथाविधालौकिककाव्यार्थपरिशीलनम्।[21]

3. काव्यशास्त्री रस को अखण्ड मानते हैं। रस की अनुभूति विभाव, अनुभाव एवं व्यभिचारी भावों के समुदाय से ही होती है, पृथक्-पृथक् नहीं। अतः रस अखण्ड है। रस की अखण्डता का एक हेतु यह भी है कि सहृदय को रसानुभूति तभी होती है जब आत्मा तन्मय हो जाता है। उस स्थिति में मात्र भेद की भी कल्पना नहीं की जा सकती-

(क) *अखण्ड इत्येक एवायं विभादिरत्यादिप्रकाशसुखचमत्कारात्मकः।*
(ख) *तादात्म्यादेवास्याखण्डत्वम्। रत्यादयो हि प्रथममेकैकशः प्रतीयमाना सर्वेऽप्येकीभूताः स्फुरन्त एव रसतामापद्यन्ते।*[22]

वैयाकरणों ने तो महान् संरम्भ के साथ शब्दतत्त्व की अखण्डता का प्रतिपादन किया है। इनके मत में वाक्यस्फोट ही पारमार्थिक है। वह अखण्ड है। जिस प्रकार पदों में वर्णों की कल्पना तथा वर्णों में तदवयवों की कल्पना मात्र व्यावहारिक है, उसी प्रकार व्यवहार के निर्वाह के लिए पदों की कल्पना भले ही कर ली जाय, वस्तुतः वाक्य में किसी प्रकार का भेद सम्भव नहीं है-

पदे न वर्णा विद्यन्ते वर्णेष्ववयवा न च।
वाक्यात्पदानामत्यन्तं प्रविवेको न कश्चन।।[23]

अद्वैत वेदान्त में ब्रह्मतत्त्व को अखण्ड माना गया है। इस प्रकार, रस को अखण्ड मानने में काव्यशास्त्री व्याकरण तथा वेदान्त दोनों से प्रभावित हैं।

4. काव्यशास्त्रियों के मत में रस स्वप्रकाशरूप है। भट्टनायक को भी रस की स्वप्रकाशरूपता स्वीकृत थी–'प्रकाशानन्दमयसंविद्विश्रान्तिसतत्त्वेन भोगेन भुज्यते।'[24]

मम्मट के अनुसार रस प्रकाशस्वरूप होने के कारण सम्मुख परिस्फुरणशील रहता है। आचार्य विश्वनाथ ने भी रस को स्वप्रकाशरूप मानते हुए कहा है कि रस्यमानता के ही साररूप होने के कारण रस प्रकाशशरीररूप है। विश्वनाथ ने स्वत: इस प्रसंग में एक प्रश्न उपस्थित किया है कि यदि रत्यादि मिलकर रसरूप होते हैं, तो रस की स्वप्रकाशता तथा अखण्डता अनुपपन्न है ? किन्तु इस समस्या का निराकरण करते हुए इन्होंने माना है कि रस रत्यादिज्ञानस्वरूप है। ज्ञान की स्वप्रकाशता तो निर्विवाद है। अत: रस की स्वप्रकाशता एवं अखण्डता दोनों की उपपत्ति हो जाती है–

1. *तदुक्तं रस्यमानतासारत्वात् प्रकाशशरीरादनन्य एव रस:।*
2. *रत्यादिज्ञानतादात्म्यादेव यस्माद्रसो भवेत्।*
   ततोऽस्य स्वप्रकाशत्वमखण्डत्वं च सिद्ध्यति।।[25]

शब्दतत्त्व की स्वप्रकाशशीलता का वैयाकरणों ने बड़े आग्रह के साथ प्रतिपादन किया है। भर्तृहरि तो शब्दतत्त्व की प्रकाशरूपता के विवेचन में यहाँ तक कह जाते हैं कि प्रकाशस्वरूप नित्यत: व्यवस्थित वाक्शक्ति यदि न हो तो ज्ञान की प्रकाशकता ही समाप्त हो जाये। इसी के प्रकाश से सब प्रकाशित होते हैं। यह प्रकाशों का भी प्रकाशक है। शब्दतत्त्व की प्रकाशशीलता को स्पष्ट करते हुए यह वाक्य भी कहा गया है कि जो प्रकाश एवं अप्रकाश दोनों का प्रकाशक है उसी शब्दतत्त्व में समस्त स्थावर जंगमात्मक लोक उपनिबद्ध है–

1. *वाग्रूपता चेन्निष्क्रामेदवबोधस्य शाश्वती।*
   न प्रकाश: प्रकाशेत सा हि प्रत्यवमर्शिनी।।[26]
2. *यश्च प्रकाशाप्रकाशयो: प्रकाशयिता शब्दाख्य: प्रकाश:। तत्रैतत् सर्वमुपनिबद्धं यावत् स्थास्नु चरिष्णु च।*[27]

अत: रस की स्वप्रकाशरूपता के विवेचन में साहित्यशास्त्री वैयाकरणों से प्रभावित प्रतीत होते हैं।

5. काव्यशास्त्री रस की चैतन्यरूपता का भी प्रतिपादन करते हैं– *रजस्तमोवैचित्र्यानुविद्धसत्त्वमयनिजचित्स्वभावनिवृत्तिविश्रान्तिलक्षण:।*[28]

भर्तृहरि ने शब्दतत्त्व की चैतन्यरूपता को अभिव्यक्त करते हुए माना है कि शब्दतत्त्व के कारण ही समस्त प्राणियों में चैतन्य की स्थिति रहती है। यह चैतन्य सर्वत्र व्याप्त रहता है। समस्त कार्यों में प्रवृत्ति इसी शब्दतत्त्वरूपी चेतना के कारण होती है–

सैषा संसारिणां संज्ञा बहिरन्तश्च वर्तते।
तन्मात्रामनतिक्रान्तं चैतन्यं सर्वजन्तुषु।।[29]

अतः रस की चैतन्यरूपता की अवधारणा में भी काव्यशास्त्रियों को भर्तृहरि से सहयोग मिला होगा।

काव्यशास्त्री रस की चर्वणा को चिदानन्दमय तथा परब्रह्मास्वादसहोदर मानते हैं- *सत्त्वमयनिजचित्स्वभावनिर्वर्तितविश्रान्तिलक्षणः परब्रह्मास्वादसविधः। स एव च प्रधानभूतोंऽशः सिद्धरूप इति।*[30]

साहित्यशास्त्रियों ने यद्यपि रसास्वाद को आत्मानन्द का ही आस्वाद स्वीकार किया है, किन्तु वह आस्वाद ब्रह्मास्वाद से कुछ अवर कोटि का है। प्रकृतितः दोनों अभिन्न है। दोनों की आस्वादरूपता समान है। किन्तु दोनों में गुण मात्र का अन्तर होता है। रसास्वाद सावधि होता है। जब तक विभावादि की स्थिति रहती है तभी तक विगलित वेद्यान्तर चिन्मय आनन्द की रसचर्वणा में अनुभूति होती है, अन्यथा नहीं। इस प्रसंग में वैयाकरणों का मत भिन्न है। वे मानते हैं कि शब्दतत्त्व के प्रवृत्तितत्त्व अर्थात् शब्दब्रह्म के स्वरूप को जिसने जान लिया है, वह ब्रह्मामृत अर्थात् ब्रह्मानन्द की अनुभूति करता है। जिस प्रकार वेदान्तियों का ब्रह्मतत्त्व नित्य, चिन्मय तथा अखण्ड है उसी तरह वैयाकरणों का शब्दतत्त्व नित्य, चिन्मय तथा अखण्ड है-

अनादिनिधनं ब्रह्म शब्दतत्त्वं यदक्षरम्।
विवर्ततेऽर्थभावेन प्रक्रिया जगतो यतः।[31]

अतएव, भर्तृहरि ने शब्दतत्त्व एवं ब्रह्मतत्त्व में अभेद माना है। वस्तुतः भर्तृहरि ने शब्दतत्त्व को परब्रह्म की कोटि तक पहुँचाकर व्याकरण से भी चरम-लक्ष्य मोक्ष का प्रतिपादन कर व्याकरण को दर्शन कहलाने का अधिकारी बना दिया है।

6. रसनिष्पत्ति के विवेचन में भी काव्यशास्त्री वैयाकरणों से प्रभावित हैं। अभिनवगुप्त ने आनन्दवर्धन का अनुसरण करते हुए अपने पूर्वाचार्यों के मतों में विप्रतिपत्तियों का निर्देश कर रस की अभिव्यक्ति को स्वीकार किया है। इनके मत में अलौकिक विभावादि के द्वारा रस की अभिव्यक्ति होती है। साधारणीकृत विभावादि के साथ स्थायीभावों के व्यङ्ग्यव्यञ्जक भाव सम्बन्ध की उपपत्ति होती है इससे रस अभिव्यक्त होता है। यही रत्यादिभाव अभिव्यक्त होकर अलौकिक चमत्कार की अनुभूति कराते हैं। अभिव्यक्तिवाद का आचार्य आनन्दवर्धन ने ही विधिवत् विवेचन किया था। उन्होंने ध्वनि सिद्धान्त की व्याख्या में स्पष्ट किया है कि मुख्य ध्वनि रसध्वनि ही है। रसध्वनि सर्वदा व्यंग्य ही हुआ करती है। उसमें वाच्यता की शंका लेशमात्र भी नहीं रहती। परवर्ती मम्मट, विश्वनाथ आदि आचार्य भी रस की अभिव्यक्ति को ही स्वीकार करते हैं। वस्तुतः ध्वनिवादियों को व्यङ्ग्यव्यञ्जकभाव सम्बन्ध तथा अभिव्यक्ति

का सिद्धान्त वैयाकरणों से ही प्राप्त हुआ था। अभिव्यक्ति का शास्त्रीय विवेचन सर्वप्रथम वैयाकरणों ने ही किया था।

वैयाकरणों ने शब्द से अर्थप्राप्ति के प्रसंग में स्फोट सिद्धान्त का प्रतिपादन किया है। ध्वनियां व्यञ्जक होती हैं तथा स्फोट रूप शब्द व्यंग्य। ध्वनियों के द्वारा अभिव्यक्त स्फोट रूप शब्द से अर्थ की प्रतीति हो जाती है। ध्वनिसिद्धान्त की प्रतिष्ठा में आनन्दवर्धन ने वैयाकरणों के इन्हीं विचारों का भरपूर लाभ उठाया है। ध्वनि का लक्षण करते हुए आनन्दवर्धन ने स्पष्ट रूप से कहा है कि जब अर्थ अपने आपको तथा शब्द अपने अर्थ को गौण बनाकर उस प्रतीयमानार्थ को अभिव्यक्त करते हैं तब वह काव्यविशेष विद्वानों द्वारा ध्वनि कहा जाता है। ध्वनिशब्द का यह व्यवहार आनन्दवर्धन के अनुसार निर्मूल नहीं है। समस्त विद्याओं का मूल होने के कारण वैयाकरणों को ही प्रधान विद्वान् माना जाता है। इन्होंने स्पष्ट रूप से श्रूयमाण वर्णों के लिए ध्वनि शब्द का प्रयोग किया है। अत: इन्हीं विद्वानों को आधार बनाकर इस ध्वनि सिद्धान्त का प्रवर्तन किया जा रहा है:

यत्रार्थ: शब्दो वा तमर्थमुपसर्जनीकृतस्वार्थौ।
व्यङ्क्त:काव्यविशेष: स ध्वनिरितिसूरिभि:कथित:।।

सूरिभि: कथित इति विद्वदुपज्ञेयमुक्ति: न तु कथञ्चित् प्रवृत्तेति प्रतिपाद्यते। प्रथमे हि विद्वांसो वैयाकरणा:, व्याकरणमूलत्वात् सर्वविद्यानाम्। ते च श्रूयमाणेषु वर्णेषु ध्वनिरिति व्यवहरन्ति।[32] विरोधियों के आक्षेपों को शान्त करने के लिए वैयाकरणों के मत का आश्रय लेते हुए आनन्दवर्धन ने अन्यत्र भी कहा है कि परिनिश्चित, निरपभ्रंश, शब्दब्रह्म को स्वीकार करने वाले वैयाकरण विद्वानों के मत का आश्रय लेकर ही यह ध्वनिव्यवहार प्रयुक्त हुआ है– *परिनिश्चितनिरपभ्रंशशब्दब्रह्मवादिनां विपश्चितां मतमाश्रित्यैव प्रवृत्तोऽयं ध्वनिव्यवहार:।*[33]

इससे यह स्पष्ट है कि काव्यशास्त्रियों को अपने अभिमत की पुष्टि के लिए वैयाकरणों से पर्याप्त प्रेरणा प्राप्त हुई है। वैयाकरणों का सम्पूर्ण विवेचन एकात्मता का है। यद्यपि लोकव्यवहार के लिए वे अनित्य स्फोट अथवा भाषा, वर्ण, पद, पदावयव के रूप में भेदों को स्वीकार करते हैं, किन्तु परमार्थत: शब्दतत्त्व नित्य अखण्ड तथा चैतन्य रूप है। सब कुछ इसी में समाहित है। इतना अवश्य है कि वैयाकरणों तथा अन्य दार्शनिकों के सिद्धान्तों का उपयोग करते हुए काव्य शास्त्रियों ने काव्यात्मभूत रस की विवेचना में अपनी मौलिकता का परिचय दिया है तथा रसभावना से सहृदय सामाजिकों को कैसे आनन्दानुभूति होती है इसकी स्पष्ट एवं मौलिक व्याख्या प्रस्तुत की है। रस की अलौकिकता आदि के विवेचनों में काव्यशास्त्रियों की अद्भुत प्रतिभा के निदर्शन होते हैं।

संदर्भ

1. *ऋग्वेद संहिता*, 10.9.2
2. *ऋग्वेद संहिता*, 10.67.31 एवं 32
3. *तैत्तिरीयोपनिषद् ब्रह्मानन्दवल्ली*, सप्तम अनुवाक्
4. *नाट्यशास्त्र*, *अभिनवभारती* सहित, पृ. 272
5. *अभिनवभारती*, *नाट्यशास्त्र*, 6.31
6. *नाट्यशास्त्र का भाष्य*, 6.31
7. *नाट्यशास्त्र*, 6.34 एवं 35
8. *वाक्यपदीय*, 2.492
9. अत्र च विज्ञानवादो द्विधाभिधानं स्फोटतत्त्वम्।
   सत्कार्यवाद एकत्वदर्शनमित्यादि द्रष्टव्यम्।। *अभिनवभारती*, *ना.शा.* 1, पृ. 294
10. *ऋक्संहिता*, 10.125.7
11. *कैवल्योपनिषद्* 1.19
12. *ऋक्संहिता*, 57.3
13. *महाभाष्य पस्पशाह्निक*, पृ. 24 एवं वाक्यपदीय स्वोपज्ञवृत्ति, 1.130
14. *नाट्यशास्त्र*, 14.3
15. *नाट्यशास्त्र*, *अभिनवभारती*, 14.3
16. *नाट्यशास्त्र*, *अभिनवभारती*, 14.3
17. *नाट्यशास्त्र*, *अभिनवभारती*, 6.31
18. *वाक्यपदीय*, 1.4
19. *काव्यप्रकाश*, चतुर्थ उल्लास, पृ. 90
20. *वाक्यपदीय*, 1.132
21. *साहित्यदर्पण*, विमला टीकासहित, पृ. 49
22. *साहित्यदर्पण*, विमला टीका सहित, पृ. 63
23. *वाक्यपदीय*, 1.73
24. *काव्यप्रकाश*, चतुर्थ उल्लास, पृ. 90
25. *साहित्यदर्पण*, विमला टीका सहित, पृ. 50 तथा *साहित्यदर्पण*, 3.28
26. *वाक्यपदीय*, 1.124
27. *ध्वन्यालोकलोचन*, द्वितीय उद्योत में उद्धृत वृत्ति, पृ. 42,43
28. *ध्वन्यालोक*, द्वितीय उद्योत, पृ. 42, 43
29. *वाक्यपदीय*, 1.126
30. *ध्वन्यालोक*, द्वितीय उद्योत, पृ. 42,43
31. *वाक्यपदीय*, 1.1
32. *ध्वन्यालोक*, 1.13 तथा उसी की वृत्ति
33. *ध्वन्यालोक*, पृ. 481

17

रसास्वादः

रहसविहारी द्विवेदी

रसोयं कुत आगतो यो हि आस्वाद्यते अत्राह भरतः–'विभावानुभावव्यभिचारिसंयोगाद्रसनिष्पत्ति' रिति। भरतेन कुतोऽयं गृहीतः? स्वयं स वक्ति *जग्राह पाठ्यमृग्वेदात् सामभ्यो गीतमेव च यजुर्वेदादभिनयान् रसानाथर्वणादपि।* (ना.1.16) कथनमिदं वेदान् प्रति भरतस्य श्रद्धामात्र मुताहो वस्तुस्थितिरप्ये तादृशी? आस्वादो नाम चित्तवृत्तेः सविकल्पानन्दास्वादनम्। आनन्द प्राप्तिकामना 'अथर्ववेदारम्भ एव व्यक्तीकृता विराजते

> *'पुनरेहि' वाचस्पते देवेन मनसा सह।*
> *वसोस्पते नि रमय मय्येवास्तु मयि श्रुतम्।।* (*1.1.2*)
>
> (हे वाचस्पते! देवेन मनसा सह पुनः एहि। हे वसोस्पते! निरमय श्रुतं मयि मयि-एव-अस्तु।)

वस्तुतोऽस्मिन् मन्त्रे गुरोः साक्षात्कृतं तत्त्वं (ज्ञानं) तदाकारत एव शिष्ये निहितं स्यादिति भावना स्फुटी भवति या कविसहृदययोः स्थितिमिव व्यनक्ति। अथर्ववेदेऽन्ततश्च

> *'मधुमतीरोषधीर्द्याव आपो मधुमन्नो भवत्वन्तरिक्षम्।*
> *क्षेत्रस्य पतिर्मधुमान्नो अस्त्वरिष्यन्तो अन्वेनं चरेम।।'* (20/143/8)
>
> (ओषधीः द्यावः आपः मधुमतीः, नः अन्तरिक्षं मधुमत् भवतु, क्षेत्रस्य पतिः नः मधुमान् अस्तु, अः रिष्यन्तः एनम् अनु चरेम।)

ऋग्वेदे मधुमद्वचः कविवाग्वैशिष्ट्ये समाम्नातम्। यथा-

'वत्सो वां मधुमद्वचो शंसीता काव्यः कविः।' (ऋ. 8.8.11)

प्रसंगेऽस्मिन् दण्डिनः कारिका स्मृतिपथमायाति-

मधुरं रसवद्वाचि वस्तुन्यपि रसस्थितिः
येन माद्यन्ति धीमन्तो मधुनेव मधुव्रताः।। (*काव्यादर्शे 1.51*)

एतेन स्फुटमिदं यत् काव्ये नाट्ये च मधुरत्वं रसवत्त्वञ्च वैदिकपरम्परातोऽपि प्राप्तम्। संयोगश्रृंगाराद्युहारणान्यपि वेदेषु प्राप्यन्ते। तद्यथा-

अभ्रातेव पुंस एति प्रतीचो गर्तारुगिव सनये धनानाम्।
जायेव पत्य उशती सुवासा उषा हस्रेव निरिणीते अप्सः।। (ऋ. 1/124/7)

वीररसपरिपाक प्रसंगा ऋग्वेदे यजुर्वेदे चानेकधा प्राप्यन्ते। तद् यथा-ऋग्वेदस्य (1/32) इन्द्रसूक्तं यजुर्वेदस्य च सप्तदशाध्यायस्य कण्डिका 40-42 इत्यादि। उदाहरणार्थम्

'अहन् वृत्रं वृत्रतरं व्यंसमिन्द्रो वज्रेण महता बधेन।
स्कन्धांसीव कुलिनशेना विकृक्णऽहिःशयत उपपृक् पृथिव्याः।।'
(ऋ. 1/32/5)

'अभिगोत्राणि सहसा गाहमानो उदयो वीरः शतमन्युरिन्द्रः।
दुश्च्यवनः पृतनाषाडयुध्योऽस्माकं सेना अवतु प्रयुत्सु।।' (*यजु.* 17/39)

एवं वेदेषु सिद्धान्तदिशा प्रयोगदिशा चोभयथा रसस्यावस्थितिर्निमाल्यते। नाट्यशास्त्रस्य षष्ठेऽध्याये रसास्वादविषये भरतमुनिः प्रश्नं समुत्थाप्य समादधाति। तदेवम्

अत्राह-रस इति कः पदार्थः?
उच्यते आस्वाद्यत्वात्।
कथमास्वाद्यते रसः?

रसनेन्द्रियेण रसप्रत्यक्षं लोके प्रसिद्धं किन्तु काव्यरसः न तादृशः प्रसिद्धोऽतोऽयं प्रश्नः कृतः। अस्यां स्थितौ काव्यरसमौपचारिकं गौणलाक्षणिकं वा मत्वाऽस्याख्या सम्भाव्यते। अत उत्तरयन् वक्ति नाट्यशास्त्रकारः

> यथा हि नाना संस्कृतमन्नं भुञ्जाना रसानास्वादयन्ति सुमनसः पुरुषा हर्षादींश्चाधिगच्छन्ति तथा नानाभावाभिनयव्यञ्जितान् वागङ्गसत्त्वोपेतान् स्थायिभावानास्वादयन्ति सुमनसः प्रेक्षकाः हर्षादींश्चाधिगच्छन्ति। तस्मान्नाट्यरसा इत्यभिव्याख्याताः।

एताभिरुक्तिभिर्नाट्यरसानां विशिष्टं व्याख्यानं विद्यते अत्रानुवंश्यौ श्लोकौ भवतः

'यथा बहुद्रव्ययुतैर्व्यञ्जनैर्बहुभिर्युतम्।
आस्वादयन्ति भुञ्जाना भक्तं भक्तविदो जनाः।
भावाभिनयसंबद्धान् स्थायिभावांस्तथा बुधाः।
आस्वादयन्ति मनसा तस्मान्नाट्यरसाः स्मृताः।।' (*ना.शा.* 6/33, 34)

आस्वादसादृश्यवशाल्लौकिकरसवन् नाट्यसोऽत्र प्रतिष्ठापितः।

रसशब्दस्य प्रयोगोऽनेकेष्वर्थेषु भवति। लोकव्यवहारे मधुरादिषड्रसाः (मधुराम्ल लवणकटुकषायतिक्तभेदात्) सन्ति। पारद-विषय-सार-जल-संस्कार-क्वाथाभिनिवेश-देहधातुप्रभृतिष्वर्थेषु रसशब्दप्रयोगो दृश्यते किन्तु प्रकृते सन्दर्भे शृंगाराद्यर्थे प्रयुक्तस्य रसशब्दस्य कोऽभिप्रायः? किं नाम तत्प्रवृत्तिनिमित्तम्? स स्वविशिष्टस्यार्थस्य नियमनं कथं करोति?

प्रयोक्ता ज्ञानग्राहकश्चास्य विशिष्टार्थग्रहणे कथं प्रवृतौ भवतः? एतादृशानां प्रश्नानां समाधानार्थं भरतो रसास्वादनस्य विधानं विदधाति। एवं रस आस्वाद्योऽस्ति तदास्वादयिता च सामाजिकः। अत्र भरतो लौकिकेनोदाहरणेन तथ्यमिदं स्फुटी करोति। यथा नानाव्यञ्जनैः सुसंस्कृत स्यादन्नस्योपभोक्ता सहृदयः (सुमना) भवति। तथैव विभावैरनुभावैः वाचिकसात्त्विकाभिनयैश्चाभिभूतः सहृदयः प्रेक्षकः (सामाजिक) स्थायिभावरूपस्य रसस्यास्वादनं करोति प्राप्नोति च हर्षादीनि।

अत्र प्रश्नः समुदेति यल्लोके रसास्वादनं रसनेन्द्रियेण भवति, शृंगारादयो रसास्तु काव्यगता नाट्यगता वा भवन्ति येषामास्वादनं न रसनेन्द्रियेण भवति, अपितु मनसा सम्पद्यते। अयं तावन्मानसो व्यापारः। रसविषये द्वे परम्परे प्राप्येते एका द्रुहिणस्य अपरा च वासुकेः। यद्यपि *नाट्यशास्त्रे* बहुधा द्रुहिणस्य परम्परा स्पष्टतो निर्दिष्टा तथापि भावेभ्यो रसः सम्भाव्यते, तथ्यमिदं यथासम्भवं वासुकिमतमुद्धरहन् भरतः पुष्णाति। यथा

'नाना द्रव्यैर्बहुविधैर्व्यञ्जनं भाव्यते यथा।
एवं भावा भावयन्ति रसाभिनयैः सह।।' (*ना. शा.* 6/36)

शारदातनयेन भावप्रकाशे 'इति वासुकिनाप्युक्तो भावेभ्यो रसंभव' इत्युक्तं श्लोकमुद्धरता व्यलेखि।

वस्तुतो भरतकृतरसविवेचनं नाट्यरसस्य विवेचनमस्ति तथापि तत्सिद्धये चान्यान्यपि तत्त्वानि समीहितानि सन्ति येषां संग्रहो भरतेनैवमकारि -

'रसा भावा ह्यभिनया धर्मीवृत्तिप्रवृत्तयः।
सिद्धिः स्वरास्तथातोद्यं गानं रंगश्च संग्रहः।।' (*ना.शा.* 6/10)

नाट्यशास्त्रे एतान्येव तत्त्वानि विमर्शितानि सन्ति। एतेषु तत्त्वेषु परस्परं कः सम्बन्धः? अस्योत्तरमभिनवगुप्तपादाचार्यैरेवं प्रत्यपादि:

समग्रेषु प्रयोगेषु द्योतमान एक एवार्थो नाट्यमस्ति यश्च नटस्याभिनयात् स्फुटीभवति दर्शकेन च निष्कम्पेन मनसाऽखण्डरूपेण गृह्यते। नाट्यगता विभावादयस्तत्र मूलरूपा भवन्ति किन्त्वेतेषां मूलरूपाणां पर्यवसानं संवेदनासु भवति। एताः संवेदनाः तेन पात्रेण भोग्यभोक्तृभावेन सम्बद्धा भवन्ति। नाट्येऽनेकसंवेदनानामनेके भोक्तारो भवन्ति, तेषु सत्सु समेषां पर्यवसानं प्रधाने भोक्तरि भवति। अयं प्रधानो भोक्ता नाट्यनेता भवति समग्रे नाट्यव्यापारे सूत्रसदृशी तस्य स्थायिनी चित्तवृत्तिरेव तस्य नाट्यस्यैकार्थो भवति।

लोकव्यवहारे इयं चित्रवृत्तिर्व्यक्तिसम्बद्धा भवति। अत एव तस्यां स्वकीयत्वस्य परकीयत्वस्य सीमा भवति किन्तु सैव चित्तवृत्तिर्यदा नाट्यप्रयोगेण द्योतते तदा लौकिकव्यक्तिबन्धनान्मुक्ता भवति, आश्रयति च गायन–वादन–नर्तनालंकारादिभिर्विधीयमानं सुन्दरं प्रयोगम्। चेल्लौकिकचित्तवृत्तेराश्रयः कश्चिद्विशिष्टो जनस्तर्हि नाट्ये नोदीयमानायाश्चित्तवृत्तेराश्रयः स प्रयोग एव भवति न तु जनः व्यक्ति बन्धनान्मुक्ता सती सा चित्तवृत्तिः साधारणीभूता भवति। दर्शको यदा नाट्यप्रयोगं पश्यति तदा प्रयोगतोऽभिव्यक्ता साधारणीभूता सती दर्शके व्याप्ता भवति दर्शकं च प्रयोगे सम्मेलयति प्रयोगे सम्मिलिते सति दर्शकस्य प्रयोगेण तादात्म्यं भवति। एवं दर्शको नाट्याद्बहिर्न भवति, अत एव नाट्यसिद्धौ दर्शनदिशा भरतो वक्ति :

> '*एवं भावानुकरणे यो यस्मिन् प्रविशेन्नरः*
> *स तत्र प्रेक्षको ज्ञेयो गुणैरेतैरलंकृतः॥*'' (ना. 27/59)

नाट्यप्रयोगावलोकनसमये दर्शकस्य यो भावानुप्रवेशो नाट्ये भवति स एव प्रमाणति यत्प्रयोगतोऽभिव्यक्ताचित्तवृत्तिः लौकिकाया व्याक्तिसम्बद्धायाश्चित्तवृत्तेर्भिन्ना भवति। लोकव्यवहारेऽपि अनुमानादिभिः प्रमाणैः परकीयाश्चित्तवृत्तेर्ज्ञानं भवति किन्तु तत्रानुमातुस्तादात्म्यं न भवति। नाट्येऽभिव्यञ्जितायाश्चित्तवृत्तेः प्रतीतिर्दशके व्यक्तिसीम्नि न भवति तस्मिन् क्षणे प्रभातुर्व्यक्तिगतसीमा नष्टप्राया भवति। अत एव लौकिकैः कारणैः समुत्पन्नानां प्रेमशोकादीनां सदृशीयं चित्तवृत्तिर्न भवति यतो हि अस्या आसक्तिस्तिरस्कारो वा दर्शके न भवति। अतोऽत्रदर्शकस्य चित्तवृत्तिर्निर्विघ्ना प्रतीयते यया मनोऽत्र विश्रान्तिमनुभवति। इयं निर्विघ्ना चित्तवृतिः दर्शकगतनाट्यप्रयोगतादात्म्याभिव्यञ्जिता स्वसंवेदनैव अस्ति यल्लक्षणं मनो विश्रान्तिर्विद्यते नायं रसनाव्यापार आस्वादो वा। अत्राह–*अभिनवभारत्यां श्रीमदभिनवगुप्तपादाचार्यः*

> *तत एवं निर्विघ्नस्वसंवेदनात्मकविश्रान्तिलक्षणेन रसनापरपर्यायेण व्यापारेण गृह्यमाणत्वाद् रसशब्देनाभिधीयते। तेन रस एव नाट्यम्।*

अयं रसनाव्यापाररूपोऽर्थादास्वादरूपो रस एक एव, इमं रसमभिनवगुप्तो महारसं वदति। अयं महारसो विभावादिवैचित्र्याद् यद्वैचित्र्यं प्राप्नोति तद्वैचित्र्यंमाश्रित्य शृंगारादिरसविभागा: प्रभवन्ति। अभिनवगुप्तमतमेवम् :

> *ततश्च मुख्यभूतान्महारसात् स्फोटसदृशीव असत्यानि वा, अन्विताभिधानदृशीव उभयात्मकानि सत्यानि वा अभितान्वयदृशीव सत्समुदायरूपाणि वा रसान्तराणि भागाभिनिवेशदृष्टानि रूप्यन्ते।'*
>
> *आस्वादरूपो रस एक एव तथापि विभावादिभेदाद् रसभेदो दृश्यते-'विभावादिभेदो रसभेदे हेतु:'*
>
> *नाट्यगतं सर्वमप्युपादानं रसानुवर्ति वरीवर्ति अत एव भरतो वक्ति 'नहि रसादृते कश्चिदर्थ: प्रवर्तते।'*

रसनिपरपेक्षदशायां विभावादीनां न किमपि महत्त्वम्। नाट्यवस्तुनो रसनिरपेक्षो न कश्चिद्धेतु:। अत एव प्रख्यातकथावस्तुनि मूल इतिहासेऽपि कवि: परिवर्तनं करोति। लौकिकदृष्ट्या यानि कारणकार्याणि अन्ये वा व्यापारा भवन्ति तेषां समेषां काव्ये नाट्ये वा रसनिरपेक्षं स्थानं न भवति। एवं कवि-नट-दर्शक-शास्त्रकारादीनां दृष्ट्या काव्ये नाट्ये च रसस्यैव प्राधान्यं भवति। अत एव भरत: पूर्वं रसविवेचनं विधाय ततो रसानुगामित्वान्नाट्यांगानां विवेचनमकरोत्। अनया दृष्ट्या भरतस्य प्रसिद्धस्य रसनिष्पत्तिसूत्रस्य विभावानुभावव्यभिचारिसंयोगाद् रसनिष्पति: इत्यस्य पर्यालोचनं कर्तव्यमिति साधु।

भावानां सङ्ख्या भरतमुनिना एकोनपञ्चाशत् प्रतिपादिता। येषु स्थायिभावाऽष्टौ विद्यन्ते अष्टौ च सात्त्विकभावा: त्रयस्त्रिशत् च संचारिभावा: सन्ति। काव्यश्रवणानन्तरं सहृदये भावजगत: सूक्ष्ममूर्तीनां भावानां च निर्मितिर्भवति। एतेषामेव भावनात्मकानामालम्बनोद्दीपनानां भावान् सहृदयोऽनुभवति। कवौ एतादृशी क्षमता भवति यद् येन पात्रेण सह स यादृशं भावं सहृदये समुत्पादयितुं वाञ्छति तादृशं तन्मानसलोके रचयति। एवं नानाभावमूर्तीनां भावभावनानांच यदा-एतादृश: परिपाको भवति यन्न किमपि पृथग् ज्ञानं तिष्ठति सर्वा भावमूर्तयो सम्मिल्य एकस्यां विशेषभावनक्रियायामेकाकारा भवन्ति तदा सहृदयो रसास्वादस्थितौ भवति। स्फुटतया लौकिकस्थूलरूपादिमयास्वादस्थितिर्भिन्ना, अत एवात्र लोकोत्तरत्वं भवति। काव्यस्य श्रोता स्वस्यैव चित्तेन स्वकीययैवानुभूत्या भावजगत् सृजति। अत एवोच्यते यत्सहृदयो यावान् तन्मयीभवनयोग्यस्तावानेव रसास्वादनार्हो भविष्यति।

काव्ये केवलौ शब्दार्थौ भवतो न कश्चिदन्य आधार: शब्दतो गृहीतो लौकिक: स्थूलार्थ: सहृदयहृदये भावरूपेण परिणतो भवति। चित्रकलादिषु शब्दा न भवन्ति तत्र वर्णरेखादिभिरर्थावबोधो भवति। चित्रकारो यथा वाञ्छति तथा भावा सहृदये समुत्पद्यन्ते, नाट्यं जटिलं भवति, तस्मिन् कविसहृदययो: सम्बन्ध: अभिनेत्र स्थापितो भवति। अत्रैकस्य माध्यमस्य वृद्धिर्भवति। अत्र कविनिबद्धोऽर्थ: प्रथमतोऽभिनेतुर्भावरूपमुद्बुद्बुद्धं करोति

ततः स तस्मै भावरूपाय स्थूलं मूर्तमाकारं ददाति। अयञ्च स्थूलमूर्ताकारस्ततः पुनः सहृदयचित्तवृतौ नूतनतया भावरूपाणि रचयति। एवं नाट्ये वस्तुतो द्वयोः कलाकारयोः (कविनटयोः) चेतनमनसः पावनीभूय सहृदयस्य भावजगन्निर्मितं भवति, अतः तदधिकमास्वाद्यं भवति। अत एवाभिनवभारत्यां (1/10) उक्तम् गुणालंकाराभ्यां काव्यशरीरं मनोहरं भवति तत्र च रसः प्राणरूपो भवति। श्रव्यकाव्येऽपि तन्मयीभवनत्वाच्चित्त-वृत्तिर्निमग्नाकारा भवति किन्तु तस्मिन् अभिनीयमाननाट्यप्रत्यक्षवत् साक्षात्कारात्मको बोधो न भवति किन्तु नाट्ये एतादृशी प्रतीतिर्भवति।

ध्वनिवादिनो रसं व्यङ्ग्यार्थं स्वीकुर्वन्ति। रसो विभावानुभावादिभिर्व्यज्यते। न तु विभावा (शकुन्तलादुष्यन्तादयः) नानुभावा (आलिङ्गनादिचेष्टाः) न च व्यभिचारिणः (ग्लानिशंकासूयादयः) स्वयमेव रसाः सन्ति। मीमांसका अभिधालक्षणे द्वे वृत्ती विहाय तृतीयां व्यञ्जनां वृत्तिं न मन्वते। तेषां मते वाक्ये तात्पर्यार्थो भवति। अयं तात्पर्यरूपो वाक्यार्थो रसबोधं यावद् गत्वा विश्रान्तो भवति। मीमांसकानां मतस्य मूलं यत्परः शब्दः स शब्दार्थः, इतीदं सूत्रं वर्तते। एतेषां मतमस्ति यमर्थं बोधयितुं शब्दः प्रयुक्तः स एव तस्यार्थः। अत्र द्वितीयार्थस्तावदेवं संभाव्यते यच्छब्दः सम्बन्धमर्यादया सीमितो भूत्वा यमर्थं सूचयति स एव तस्यार्थः। मीमांसकाः सम्बन्धमर्यादां स्वीकुर्वन्ति अतस्ते तात्पर्यार्थं मन्वते। अत्र व्यञ्जनावृत्तिर्न भवति यतोहि व्यञ्जना संसर्गमर्यादया बद्धा न भवति। दशरूपककारदिशा तात्पर्यस्य न कापि सीमा, स तात्पर्ये तादर्थ्ये च भेदं न मनुते, अतो व्यञ्जनावृत्त्या योऽर्थो ध्वन्यते तस्य पृथङ्नामकरणमनिवार्यं भवति। अतो व्यञ्जनावृत्तेरस्वीकृतिर्नोचिता। तथापि रसस्य व्यङ्ग्यार्थमात्रस्वीकृतौ काठिन्यं प्रतीयते। यतो हि रसः, अनुभूतिरस्ति न तु अनुभूतिविषयः, भावास्तु विभावे भवन्ति दर्शकमनसि तेषामेकं मानसं सूक्ष्ममुत्पद्यते येन स स्वानुभूतिभिरेवाह्लादितो भवति। प्रायशः समेप्याचार्या रसं कार्यं ज्ञाप्यं वा न मन्वते। रसः पूर्वत उपस्थितोऽपि न भवति यद्वस्तु न पूर्वत उपस्थितं तत्तु व्यञ्जनावृत्तिविषयोऽपि न भवति, रसो दर्शकचित्तेऽनुभूयते न तु नटचित्ते। अतो व्यञ्जनावृत्तिः केवलं श्रोतुर्दर्शकस्य वा चित्ते विभावानुभावसंचारिभावानुत्पादयति, यत्कथ्यमानं तस्मादि्भन्नं यन्नोक्तं तमर्थमुपस्थापयति। भरतमुनेः रसनिष्पत्तिसूत्रस्य तात्पर्यमेवंभवितुमर्हति यत्सहृदयचित्तेषु वासनारूपेण स्थिताः स्थायिनो भावा विभावादिभिर्व्यञ्जिताः सन्तः रसरूपं गृह्णन्ति। रूपकेषु व्यञ्जनायाः साधनानि न केवलं शब्दा अपितु नटस्य चेष्टा अपि भवन्ति। एवं रूपकेष्वेकतः कविनिबद्धशब्देभ्योऽपरतश्चाभिनयेभ्यो रसाभिव्यञ्जनं भवति। चेद् व्यञ्जनाशब्दशक्तिरभिनयश्च शक्मिात्रं तर्हि सा प्रस्तुतभावान् व्यञ्जितमात्रं करोति किन्तु तामनुभूतिं न व्यनक्ति या शब्दाभिनयाभ्यां बहिरस्ति। अत आह आचार्यरामचन्द्रशुक्लः 'भाव की अवस्थिति नायक नायिका में होती है और रस की अनुभूति श्रोता या दर्शक में होती है। पात्र के मन में रस नहीं होता जो व्यक्त किया जा सके।' सन्दर्भेऽस्मिन् प्रायशः काव्यशास्त्रिणो भट्टनायकनिर्दिष्टौ भावकत्वभोजकत्वव्यापारौ येन केनापि रूपेण

स्वीकुर्वते। तात्पर्यमेतद् यद् कविनिबद्धशब्देषु नटाभिनयेषु चैतादृक् सामर्थ्यं भवति येन श्रोतुर्दर्शकस्य भावनायास्तादात्म्यं भवति। अस्यां स्थितौ पात्रणां विशेषरूपं तिरोभूतं भवति तत्र केवलं साधारणीकृतं रूपं भवति ततो भोजकत्वव्यापार आविर्भवति, एतेन साधारणीकृतैर्विभावादिभिस्तद्भावनास्वादने सहृदयः समर्थो भवति। सहृदयस्तावत्कीदृशो भवतीति लोचनकृता प्रतिपादितमेव *'येषां काव्यानुशीलनाभ्यासवशाद् विशदीभूते मनोमुकुरे वर्णनीयतन्मयीभवनयोग्यता ते स्वहृदयसंवादभाजः सहृदयाः।'*

कवेर्वर्णनचातुर्येण पात्रेषु वैशिष्ट्यमायाति किन्त्वेतानि विशेषीकृतपात्रणि लौकिकानि भवन्ति सहृदयस्य चित्तेषु श्रवणेन दर्शनेन वा यानि पात्रणि निर्मितानि भवन्ति तानि सहृदयानुभूतिगतानि भवन्ति अतस्तानि अलौकिकानि भवन्ति। सहृदयः स्वानुभूत्या स्वभावजगतः शकुन्तलादुष्यन्तयोर्निर्माणं करोति, तत्सूक्ष्मभावमिश्रणेन स रसानुभवं करोति। अर्थो यदालौकिको भवति तदा सामान्यभावानुभूत्या निर्मितत्वाल्लौकिकवैशिष्ट्यानामेव्यं रूपं भवति यत् साधारणीकरणं वक्तुं शक्यते। इदमपि ध्यातव्यं यत् सर्वत्र पात्रेण सह तादात्म्यं न भवति केषुचिद्रसेषु श्रोतुरालम्बनः स एव भवति य आश्रयस्य, एवं रूपेणाश्रयेण तादात्म्यं संभवति क्वचिदाश्रयएव श्रोतुरालम्बनो भवति। यत्राश्रयेण सह सहृदयस्य तादात्म्यं भवति तत्र रसः पूर्णाङ्गो भवति। अन्यविधे रसेऽपूर्णता भवति। प्रथमा स्थितिः प्रायशः शृंगारे वीरे वा भवति एतौ समधिकौ भावात्कौ भवतः अन्ये च प्रायःकल्पनात्मका भवन्ति।

सत्कवयोऽपि रसास्वादस्थितिं वर्णयन्तो दृश्यन्ते, यथा *वाल्मीकिरामायणे* बालकाण्डे उत्तराकाण्डे च काव्यश्रवणप्रसंगः प्राप्यते। स चैवम् :

विचित्रार्थपदं सम्यक् गायकौ समचोदयत्।।
तौ चापि मधुरं रक्तं स्वचित्तायतनिःस्वनम्।।
तन्त्रीलयवदत्यर्थं विश्रुतार्थमताम्।
आह्लादयत् सर्वगात्राणि मनांसि हृदयानि च।
श्रोत्राशयसुखं गेयं तद्बभौजनसंसदि। (*बाल* 4/3435)
अहो गीतस्य माधुर्यं लोकानां च विशेषतः।
चिरनिवृत्तमप्येतत् प्रत्यक्षमिव दर्शितम्। (*बाल.* 4/17)
आह्लादयत् सर्वगात्राणि मनांसि हृदयानि च।। (*बाल.* 4/34)
(उत्तर. 94/13)

कवेर्वर्णनचातुर्यं, काव्यप्रस्तुतीकरणे पाठनपाटवं, रूपके चाभिनयकौशलं सहृदयहृदयाह्लादे कारणं भवति। कालिदासेन तथ्यमिदं मुहुर्मुहुः स्फुटीकृतम् :

स्थालीपुलाकन्यायेन कानिचित् स्थलानि द्रष्टव्यानि
पाठक उदारवाक् स्यादित्यावश्यकम्
'सूतात्मजा सवयसः प्रथितप्रबोधं

प्राबोधयन्नुषसि वाग्भिरुदारवाचः' (रघु. 5/165)
पुराणस्य कवेस्तस्य वर्णस्थानसमीरिता।
बभूव कृतसंस्काराचरितार्थैव भारती।। (तत्रैव 10/35)
इति तेभ्यः स्तुतीः श्रुत्वा यथार्था हृदयंगमाः।
प्रसादाभिमुखो वेधाः प्रत्युवाच दिवौकसः।।
पुराणस्यकवेस्तस्य चतुर्मुखसमीरिता।
प्रवृत्तिरासीच्छब्दानां चरितार्थाचतुष्टयी। (कुमार. 2/15,16)
काव्यगायनप्रसंगस्तावदेवं वरीवर्ति
'वृत्तं रामस्य वाल्मीकेः कृतिस्तौ किन्नरस्वनौ।
किं तद्येन मनो हर्तुमलं स्यातां न शृण्वताम्।।
रूपे गीते च माधुर्यंतयोस्तज्ज्ञैर्निवेदितम्।
ददर्श सानुजो रामः सुश्राव च कुतूहली।।
तद्गीतश्रवणैकाग्रा संसदश्रुमुखी बभौ।
हिमनिष्यन्दिनी प्रातर्निर्वातेव वनस्थली।।

अन्यत्रपि रसानुभूति विषये कालिदासेन व्यङ्ग्यभङ्ग्या निर्देशो व्यधायि :

दृष्टे वस्तुन्युपचितरसाः प्रेमराशी भवन्ति। (उ. मे. 49) प्रियवचन कृतोऽपि योषितां दयितजनानुनयो रसादृते। प्रविशति हृदयं न तद्विदां मणिखि कृत्रिमरागयोजितः।। (*विक्रमो.* 2/21)

अंगैरन्तर्निहितवचनैः सूचितः सम्यगर्थः
पादन्यासो लयमनुगतस्तन्मयत्वं रसेषु।
शाखयोनिर्मृदुरभिनयस्तद्विकल्पानुवृत्तौ
भावो भावं नुदति विषयाद् रागबन्धः स एव।।

(*माल.* 2/8)

रम्याणि वीक्ष्य मधुरांश्च निशम्य शब्दान्
पर्युत्सुकी भवति यत्सुखितोऽपि जन्तुः।
तच्चेतसा स्मरति नूनमवबोधपूर्वं
भावस्थिराणि जननान्तरसौहृदानि।।

(*शाकु.* 5/2)

कालिदासदिशा काव्यास्वादनवेलायां तत्त्वान्वेषणराहित्यमपेक्षितं भवति– 'वयं तत्त्वान्वेषान्मधुकर! हतास्त्वं खलु कृती।' (*शाकु.* 1/21)

महाकविर्भवभूतिरपि रसानुभूतिविषये व्यङ्ग्यभङ्ग्या संकेतयति तद्यथा :

'सुमन्त्रः– भूयसांजीविना धर्म एषः, यत्र स्वरसमयी कस्यचित्काचित्प्रीतिः यत्र लौकिकानामुपचारस्तारामैत्रकं चक्षूराग इति, तदप्रतिङ्रव्येयनिबन्धनं प्रेमाणमामनन्ति।

अहेतुः पक्षपातोयस्तस्य नास्ति प्रतिक्रिया।
स हि स्नेहात्मकस्तन्तुरन्तर्भूतानि सीव्यति।।' (उ. रा. च. 5/17)
तथाच '*यदृच्छासंवादः किमु गुणगणानामतिशयः*
पुराणो वा जन्मान्तरविविडबद्धः परिचयः।
निजो वा सम्बन्धः किमु विधिवशात्कोऽप्यविदितो
ममैतस्मिन् दृष्टे हृदयमवधानं रचयति।।' (तत्रैव 5/16)
अन्यच्च- स एष ते बल्लभबन्धुवर्गः
प्रासंगिकीनां विषयः कथानाम्।
त्वां नामशेषामपि दृश्यमानः
प्रत्यक्षदृष्टामिव नः करोति।।" (तत्रैव 2/6)

वस्तुतः कविसदृशी भावना भवति तदैव सहृदयः काव्यास्वादे समर्थो भवति। यथा भक्तिभावपूर्णकाव्यास्वादे कश्चिदभक्त एवं तत्पूर्णानन्दं गृह्णति

'प्राचेतसो मुनिवृषा प्रथमः कवीनां
यत्पावनं रघुपतेः प्रणिनाय वृत्तम्।
भक्तस्य तस्य समरंसत मेऽपि वाचः
तत्सुप्रसन्नमनसःकृतिनो भजन्ताम्।।' (म. च. 1/7)

एवं कवयोऽपि स्पष्टरूपेण रसास्वादस्थितिं निरूपयन्ति। काव्यशास्त्रिभिः पण्डितराजप्रभृतिभिः रसनिष्पत्तिस्तदास्वादप्रक्रिया च साधु प्रत्यपादि। तत्पुनरालेख्येन न कश्चिल्लाभः रूपकास्वादे रसास्वादः प्रामुख्यं भजते। 'रसादिश्चात्मा' वाक्यं रसात्मकं काव्यमित्यादिना रसस्य, काव्ये नाट्ये वात्मत्वं प्रसिद्धं किन्तु 'काव्यस्यात्मा ध्वनिः' *'रीतिरात्मा काव्यस्य' 'वक्रोक्तिः काव्यजीवितम्'*

'औचित्यं रससिद्धस्य स्थिरं काव्यस्य जीवितम्'
'काव्येऽलंकार एवात्मा स एवास्मिन् स्थितो यतः'

(आचार्य रेवाप्रसाद द्विवेदिमतेन) प्रभृतिकथनेष्वपि काव्यस्य आत्मतत्त्वं संकेतितं विद्यते। आत्मनो नाम यद् रसः तर्हि ध्वनिरीतिवक्रोक्ति-औचित्य-अलंकारादि तन्नाम कियदुचितमिति विचारणीयं विद्यते। अत्रोक्तसंकेतितानां काव्याह्लादतत्त्वानां सम्प्रतिकैः रसप्रस्थानम् ध्वनिप्रस्थानं, रीतिप्रस्थानं, वक्रोक्तिप्रस्थानं, रसप्रस्थानम् अलंकार-औचित्यप्रस्थान मिति नामानि ह्यकारिष। तत्तदाचार्या एतानि तत्त्वानि सर्वाधिकेन महत्त्वेनोपस्थापयन्ति स्वस्थापितं तत्त्वं च परमं मन्वते। आधुनिकतमाश्च बिम्बविधानसौन्दर्यविधानमित्यादिनाम्ना नूतनं काव्यतत्त्वं स्वीकुर्वन्ति। रसेतरप्रस्थानेषु विधानेषु वा यद्वैशिष्ट्यं तत्सर्वविधकाव्येषु रूपकेषु च संगच्छते। अतः सर्वाणि तत्त्वानि आश्रित्य सम्प्रति शोधपत्रेषु शोधप्रबन्धेषु

काव्यमूल्यांकनं क्रियते तेषु च तत्तत्तत्त्वानि सोदाहणं समीक्ष्यन्ते। अस्यां दिशि विचारणायां लोकोत्तराह्लाद एव समानरूपेण सर्वत्र प्राप्यते। मम विनम्रे मते तु :

'अलंकारो रसोरीतिर्ध्वनिर्वक्रोक्तिरौचिती।
यान्ति लोकोत्तराह्लादमर्णवं सरितो यथा।।
सौन्दर्यस्य प्रतीकस्य बिम्बस्यापि गतिस्तथा।
प्राप्यते तद्विदाह्लादे शब्दाह्लादस्य काव्यता।।''

मम काव्यतत्त्वमीमांसानाम्नि काव्यशास्त्रीप्रकाशनाधीने कारिकावृत्तिमये ग्रन्थे काव्यलक्षणं :

तावदतएव एवं कृतं वरीवर्ति–
'लोकोत्तरे हृदाह्लादे लोकोद्‌बोधे च संगता।
प्रज्ञावतः कवेः सद्वाक् काव्यमित्यभिधीयते।।' ग्रन्थेऽस्मिन्नभिनवकाव्यतत्त्वानां स्वरूपमेव स्थिरीकर्तुं विनम्रप्रयासो विहितस्तद् यथा :

बिम्बविधानम्
'काव्यसृष्टिक्षणे कर्तुश्चित्ते नानानुभूतयः।
कल्पनामधिरोहन्त्यो वैखरी व्यक्तिबिम्बिताः।
भावकेन्द्रियसंस्काराત્તા भावावेष्टितास्तथा।
प्रत्यक्षमिव दृश्यन्ते काव्यबिम्बः स कथ्यते।।
स बाह्याभ्यन्तराभ्याञ्च करणाभ्यां द्विधा मतः।
वाह्ये दृश्यं ध्वनिः स्पर्शो गन्धास्वादौ च पञ्चधा।।
आभ्यन्तरे स्थितो भावः प्रज्ञा चेति द्विधाकृतः।
प्रत्येकं बहवो भेदाः संकरैकत्वभेदतः।। (का. त. मी. 12)

सौन्दर्यविधानाम् :
'रम्याकृतेः स्वरूपाद्‌यत् तत्त्वमास्वाद्यमस्ति तत्।
तद्विदाह्लादने युक्तं सौन्दर्यमभिधीयते।।'
कालिदासदिशा विश्वसृजो निर्मतेः सौन्दर्यदिदृक्षायाः

स्थितिस्तावदेवम्–

'सर्वोपमाद्रव्यसमुच्चयेन यथाप्रदेशं विनिवेशितेन।
सा निर्मिता विश्वसृजा प्रयत्नादेकस्थसौन्दर्यदिदृक्षयैव।।' (कुमारसंभवे)

डॉ. गोविन्द चन्द्र पाण्डेयदिशा-

आस्वाद्यो ज्ञानमात्रेण विमृश्यश्च स्वरूपतः।
आकारगतोत्कर्षः तत् सौन्दर्यमभिधीयते।। (*सौन्दर्यदर्शनविमर्शे* 1/87)

प्रतीकविधानाम्

सम्बन्धात्साहचर्याद्वाऽपाततो या समानता।
प्रतीयते वा प्रत्येति भिन्नयोर्हि पदार्थयोः।।
व्यनक्त्यप्रस्तुतं यत्र पदार्थः प्रस्तुतो यदा।
प्रस्तुतोऽयं च संकेतः प्रतीकः काव्यगो भवेत्।।

सम्प्रति रसास्वादे नूतनरसा अपि दृश्यन्ते। द्वयोः स्वरूपमत्र प्रस्तूयते :

प्रक्षोभरसः

स्थायी भावोऽस्य संवेगः स च संवेदनात्मकः।
आलम्बनं सन्तापो दलितानां च पीडनम्।।
उद्दीपनं परौद्धत्यं दीनानां शोषणं छलम्।
अनुभावोऽस्य सङ्घर्षचेष्टाक्लेशसमुद्भवः।।
व्यभिचारिण एतस्यामर्षावेगदयादयः।
'सुखिनः सन्तु सर्वेऽपीति हेतुः पुष्टिकारकः।। (*का.त.मी.* 98)

राष्ट्रभक्तिरसः

'स्थायी भावोऽस्य राष्ट्रस्यानुरागस्तद्धितावहः।
आलम्बनं राष्ट्राय जीवनाहुतिभावनम्।
अनुभावाऽस्य राष्ट्रस्य संरक्षणाविचेष्टितम्।
व्यभिचारिण एतस्य हुतात्मत्वादिभावनाः।
'राष्ट्रं सुरक्षितं भातु' हेतुनाऽनेन पुष्यते।।'

(*का. त. मी.* 15)

सम्प्रति काव्यस्य नव्यप्रकारा अपि दृश्यन्ते यत्र सहृदय आनन्दमनुभवति यथा प्रगतिशीलकाव्यम्, उपन्यासः, नभोनाट्यम (रेडियोरूपकम्) हास्यं व्यङ्ग्यञ्चेत्यादयः। केषाञ्चन स्वरूपमेवं मयाऽकलितम्

प्रगतिशीलकाव्यम्-

समस्या नूतना व्याप्ता जनतायाश्च चेतना।
राष्ट्रस्य चेतनाभक्तिर्नारीजागरणं नवम्।।

जातिधर्मादिसङ्घर्षो जननेतुः प्रवृत्तयः
संस्कृतिः सर्वहाराणां श्रमिकाणां च शोषणम्।।
इत्यादीनि वर्ण्यन्ते काव्येऽस्मिन् प्रगतिश्रिते।

उपन्यासः

गद्यकाव्यं बृहद्बन्ध उपन्यासोऽभिधीयते।
अस्मिन् युगोचितं वस्तु पात्रं कविसमीहितम्।
देशकालोचितं चित्रं गद्यशिल्पं मनोहरम्।
कल्पितं चापि तत्सर्वं यथार्थं सत् प्रतीयते।।

नभोनाट्यम् (रेडियोरूपकम्)

अवस्थानुकृतिर्नाट्यं नेदं दृश्यतयोच्यते।
वस्तुतः श्रव्यमेवैतद् यतो न प्रेक्ष्यते जनैः।।
प्रसारणेऽस्य चोच्चारेऽभिनेतुः केवलो ध्वनिः
श्रोतृभिर्व्योमवाणीतः श्रूयतेऽभिनयात्मकः।।
प्रयोगश्चास्य मञ्चेऽपि क्वचित्सम्भाव्यते ह्यतः।
दृश्यश्रव्यमयं चैतन् नभोनाट्यं प्रकीर्तितम्।।

हास्यं व्यङ्ग्यञ्च

नेदं हास्यरसः पूर्वो न व्यङ्ग्यं व्यञ्जनाश्रितम्।
हास्यं चाद्य विनोदार्थं व्यङ्ग्यं विकृतिसूचकम्।।
एतदर्थं प्रयुज्यन्ते सर्वाः शब्दस्य शक्तयः।
प्रायशोऽभिधयैवैतद् गद्यं पद्यं च लिख्यते।।
स्वार्थिनां धूर्तनेतॄणां धार्मिकानां च वृत्तयः।
हास्यव्यङ्ग्यविधानेऽस्मिन् वर्ण्यन्ते प्रेरणात्मिकाः।।

शोधपत्रेऽस्मिन् वैदिककालतोऽद्यावधि काव्यास्वादस्य रसास्वादस्य वाऽवस्थिति-निरूपिता। साम्प्रतिके युगे प्राचीनदृशा नव्यदृशा चाध्ययनस्य, समीक्षणस्य शोधस्य च प्रवृत्तिर्दरीदृश्यते। अतः पत्रस्य परिसमाप्तौ स्वोपज्ञकाव्यविधालक्षणानि मयात्र संयोजितानि।

18

अभिनवगुप्त का स्वातन्त्र्यवाद एवं साधारणीकरण की उनकी अवधारणा

प्रकाश पाण्डेय

स्थायी प्रबुद्धहृदये व्यभिचारिभूत: कामाकुलासु जनतासु महानुभाव:।
अन्तर्विभावविषयो रसमात्रमूर्ति: श्रीमान् प्रसन्नहृदयोऽस्तु मम त्रिणेत्र:।।
(*अभिनवभारती, अध्याय, 7*)

रसबोध प्रक्रिया के अपरिहार्य तत्त्व 'साधारणीकरण' की सङ्कल्पना से सम्बद्ध तीन व्याख्याएँ संस्कृतसाहित्यसमालोचना के इतिहास में पूर्णत: मौलिक एवं परस्पर भिन्न अवधारणाओं से युक्त हैं। प्रथमव्याख्या मीमांसक भट्टनायक की है। इस व्याख्या में साधारणीकरण रसानुभूति तक पहुंचाने वाली क्रिया अथवा व्यापार[1] है। इनकी व्याख्या को *अभिनवभारती* एवं अन्य ग्रन्थों में प्राप्त उद्धरणों के आधार पर ही समझ सकते हैं क्योंकि इनका मूलग्रन्थ '*हृदयदर्पण*' अभी तक उपलब्ध नहीं हो पाया है। द्वितीय व्याख्या स्वातन्त्र्यवादी आचार्य अभिनवगुप्त की है। इस व्याख्या में साधारणीकरण भावविशेष या प्रतीतिविशेष है। प्रतीति की इसी अवस्था में रसास्वाद सम्भव होता है।[2] तृतीय व्याख्या अद्वैतवेदान्ती पण्डितराज जगन्नाथ ने दी है। वे साधारणीकरण को अविद्याजन्य भ्रान्ति के समतुल्य अवस्था समझते हैं, जहाँ एक अनिर्वचनीय प्रतीति उत्पन्न होती है।[3]

तीनों व्याख्याएँ व्याख्याताओं की अपनी-अपनी दार्शनिक आधारभूमि पर प्रतिष्ठित हैं। वस्तुत: रस अन्तर्मुख बोधरूप या अलौकिकचित्तवृत्तिग्राह्य किंवा मानससाक्षात्कारात्मक

है। अतः स्वाभाविकरूप से रसबोधप्रक्रिया का विवेचन दार्शनिक आधारभूमि पर ही सम्भव है। किन्तु यदि किसी व्याख्याता के व्याख्यान का अनुवदन करते समय उसकी व्याख्या का दार्शनिक आधार उपेक्षित कर दिया जाए, अथवा उसे भिन्नरीति से व्यक्त किया जाए, तब यह अपरिहार्य हो जाता है कि उस सैद्धान्तिकव्याख्या के मर्म पर पुनर्दृष्टिपात किया जाए। यद्यपि अभिनवगुप्तपादाचार्य (आगे से आचार्य पदाभिधेय) के रसाभिव्यक्ति के सिद्धान्त को अधिकतर साहित्यसमालोचक स्वीकार करते हैं, किन्तु साधारणीकरण की आचार्यसम्मत अवधारणा को अनुचितरूप में अनूदित करने की एक लम्बी परम्परा शताब्दियों से चली आ रही है। विशेष रूप से *काव्यप्रकाश* के टीकाकारों ने इस मिथ्यानुवाद की परम्परा का पोषण किया है। सोमेश्वर (13वीं शती ई.) के *काव्यादर्श* से लेकर, *दीपिका*, *दर्पण*, *साहित्यचूडामणि*, *सम्प्रदायप्रकाशिनी*, *मधुमती*, *सारबोधिनी*, *सुधासागर* आदि प्रतिष्ठित टीकाओं ने साधारणीकरण की आचार्यसम्मत अवधारणा की स्पष्टता को अस्पष्टता में परिवर्तित कर दिया है। ये सभी साधारणीकरण को नायक-नायिका का सामान्यीकरण समझते हैं।[4] गोविन्द ठक्कुर थोड़ी सावधानी से सम्बन्धिविशेष का अभाव रूप समझते हुए सर्वसम्बन्धित का निषेध भी कर देते हैं।[5] टीकाकारों की व्याख्याओं का प्रभाव मूलग्रन्थकर्ताओं पर तो हुआ ही रामचन्द्रशुक्ल, गुलाबराय, केशवप्रसादमिश्र आदि आधुनिक युग के समालोचक भी इन उलझी हुई एवं अस्वाभाविक प्रतीत होने वाली व्याख्याओं से प्रभावित दिखाई देते हैं।[6]

ऐसा भी नहीं था कि *काव्यप्रकाश* के सभी टीकाकारों ने आचार्य के मत का मिथ्यानुवाद ही किया हो। माणिक्यचन्द्र (1160 ई.) एवं रुचक या रुय्यक की '*संकेत*' टीकाएँ, परमानन्दभट्टाचार्य कृत *विस्तरिका* या *विस्तारिका*, सुबुद्धिमिश्रकृत *तत्त्वपरीक्षा* आदि प्राचीन टीकाएँ आचार्य सम्मत अवधारणा को समुचित रीति से प्रकाशित करती हैं,[7] किन्तु इनका प्रभाव आधुनिक निबन्धों एवं व्याख्याओं में कम दिखाई देता है।

अतः यह निबन्ध आचार्य सम्मत साधारणीकरण की अवधारणा को उनके स्वातन्त्र्यवाद के सिद्धान्तों के आलोक में स्पष्टतर करने एवं उसका सम्यक् अनुवदन करने की दिशा में एक विनम्र प्रयास है।

कश्मीरीय शैवदर्शन के अद्वैतप्रस्थान के आचार्यों ने काव्य को एक अलौकिक सृष्टि मानकर सम्पूर्ण समालोचना प्रत्यभिज्ञादर्शन के आलोक में की है। उनके प्रत्येक काव्यशास्त्रीय सिद्धान्त में स्वातन्त्र्यवाद की मान्यताएँ अनुस्यूत हैं। यहाँ तक कि राजानक आनन्द (*काव्यप्रकाश* के एक टीकाकार) ने *काव्यप्रकाश* को '*शिवतत्त्वप्रकाश*' का पर्याय कह दिया है।[8] साधारणीकरण के सम्बन्ध में आचार्य के समक्ष भट्टनायक पूर्वपक्ष के रूप में उपस्थित थे। उनका कथन था कि साधारणीकरण विभावादि के ज्ञान को नियतसम्बन्धविहीन अवस्था तक पहुंचाने वाली भावनात्मिका क्रिया है। यह क्रिया काव्य में दोषाभाव एवं गुणालंकारयुक्तता के कारण एवं रूपक में

वाचिक-कायिक-सात्त्विक आहार्य के अभिनयन के कारण होती है।[9] वस्तुतः भावना संस्काररूपा एवं आत्मगुण है। भावना ही दृष्ट, श्रुत एवं अनुभूत विषयों की स्मृति एवं प्रत्यभिज्ञान का कारण है। देश, काल, जाति का व्यवधान होने पर भी स्मृति एवं प्रत्यभिज्ञा के समय वह व्यवधान तिरोहित रहता है। इस दृष्टि से स्मृति तथा संस्कार या वासना स्वरूपतः अभिन्न हैं। अतः नाट्यदर्शन या काव्यश्रवण के समय पूर्वदृष्ट, श्रुत या अनुभूत तत्सदृश विषयों की वासना सामाजिक में अभिव्यक्त होती है, तब उनकी स्मृति स्फुरित होती है। स्मृति से पुनः संस्कार एवं संस्कार से साक्षात्कार होता है। यही प्रक्रिया है भावकत्व व्यापार की, एवं सामाजिक इसी आत्मगुण से विभाव आदि को भावना का विषय बनाता है। स्पष्ट है कि भट्टनायक विभाव के विभावनत्व को उसका स्वरूपधर्म नहीं स्वीकार करते, अपितु भावना की प्रक्रिया से उपपन्न करते हैं।

आचार्य को अनुभवसिद्ध साधारणीकरण पर किसी प्रकार की विप्रतिपत्ति नहीं थी। वे स्वयं कहते हैं कि दृश्य-श्रव्य विषयों में साधारणभाव सम्यक्तया उपपन्न होता है।[10] उन्हें साधारणीकरण के स्वरूप का विवेचन मात्र असंगत प्रतीत होता है। साधारण्य से सम्बद्ध व्याख्यान के समय आचार्य के मन में कुछ प्रश्न अवश्य रहे होंगे, जैसे :

1. साधारणीकरण अवस्था विशेष है अथवा प्रक्रिया विशेष?
2. यदि अवस्था विशेष है तो वह किसकी अवस्था है? विभावादि की अथवा सामाजिक की?
3. इस अवस्था के लिए योग्य भावभूमि क्या है?
4. उस भावभूमि के लिए बाधकतत्त्व क्या हैं? उन्हें कौन दूर कर सकता है और कैसे?

उपपत्ति के अतिरिक्त इसके स्वरूप के सम्बन्ध में भी सम्भावित आशंकाएँ मन में रही होंगी। जैसे :

1. साधारण्य का स्वरूप क्या है ? उसकी उपपत्ति किस प्रकार सम्भव होती है?
2. साधारणभाव अनुपपन्न होने पर रसबोध में क्या हानि है? विशेषतः यदि सहृदयसाधारणीकरण न हो तो भी विभावादि तो तद्वत् ही होंगे, उन्हीं के कारण रसनिष्पत्ति होती है तो फिर सहृदय साधारणीकरण की क्या आवश्यकता?
3. क्या साधारणावस्था भ्रान्तिज्ञानावस्था है।[11]

साधारणीकरण का आचार्य सम्मत अर्थ है, 'निर्विघ्नता की अवस्था में जायमान प्रतीति। विभाव आदि विषय निर्विघ्न प्रतीत होने पर ही रसनीय होते हैं।[12] विभावादि में

विभावनत्व व्यञ्जना द्वारा सिद्ध है। उन्हें सामाजिक की भावना से उपपन्न करना उचित नहीं है। यदि भावक या कवि पर विभावनत्व आदि निर्भर होगा तो काव्य तथा शब्द एवं अर्थ का कोई वैशिष्ट्य नहीं होगा। 'काव्येन भाव्यन्ते रसा:' इस उक्ति के आधार पर काव्य के स्वरूप अर्थात् दोषाभाव एवं गुणालंकारमयता से ही विभावादि की आस्वादयोग्यता व्यञ्जना द्वारा उपपन्न हो जाती है। साथ ही साधारणभाव रसाभिव्यक्ति की सामग्री है। उसे प्रक्रियारूप मानना संगत नहीं है। साधारण्य, रस दशा के अव्यवहित पूर्वक्षण की अवस्था है[13]। यह अवस्था सहज नहीं अपितु अनेक लौकिक नियमों के समापन के पश्चात् उद्‌बुद्ध होती है। साधारण प्रतीति के बाधक विघ्नों को *अभिनवभारती* में आचार्य ने इस प्रकार विश्लेषित किया है :

1. सम्भावना विरह[14]

साधारणीकरण तन्मयीभवन की योग्यता उत्पन्न करने वाली अवस्था है। किन्तु यदि ज्ञान के विषय को ज्ञाता असम्भव मान ले तो उस विषय के प्रति उसकी संवित् उन्मुख नहीं होगी। फिर तन्मयता के लिए तो कोई अवकाश ही नहीं रहेगा। इस बाधा को काव्य का अधिकारी[15] सहृदयप्रमाता[16] अपनी दो प्रकार की क्षमताओं से दूर करता है,

(क) सामान्यत: प्रसिद्ध वस्तु-वर्णन के प्रसंग में स्वहृदय संवाद[17] की क्षमता से सम्भावना उद्‌भावित करता है।

(ख) कृष्ण के दावाग्नि-पान एवं हनुमान् के समुद्रलङ्घन आदि दृश्यों के सन्दर्भ में नायकों के इतिवृत्त की निर्विवाद प्रसिद्धि के कारण उनकी क्रियाओं में दृढ विश्वास से औचित्य देखता है। इस प्रकार कौतुकपूर्ण वर्णनों की असम्भाव्यता सहृदय के व्यापक अध्ययन के संस्कारों से दूर होती है।

2. विषयावेशविवशता[18]

यद्यपि यह बाधा सहृदय से सम्बद्ध है, तथापि इसे दूर करने का दायित्व कवि पर होता है। यदि वर्णनीय विषय प्रमाता से किसी प्रकार से सम्बद्ध प्रतीत होगा तो वह लौकिक विषयों की भाँति उसे सुख, दु:ख, राग, ईर्ष्या आदि वैषयिक भावों से आविष्ट करेगा। इस अवस्था में प्रतीति साधारणावस्था में नहीं होगी। इस बाधा को कवि अपनी प्रतिभा से समाप्त करता है। वह अपने वर्णनों, प्रयोगों की सज्जा इतनी कुशलता से करता है कि किसी प्रकार के वैषयिक सम्बन्ध का भान नहीं होता। इसके लिए अनेक उपाय भरतमुनि ने नाट्यशास्त्र में सुझाए हैं।[19] यदि कवि अपनी कलाचातुरी से भावक को वैषयिक आवेश से सुरक्षित कर पाता है तभी उसके वर्णनों में प्रतीतिसाधारण्य हो पाता है।

3. निजसुखादिविवशता[20]

अपने सुख–दु:ख से विह्वल व्यक्ति सहृदय होने पर भी किसी अन्य भाव के प्रति अपनी संवित् का अभिनिवेश नहीं कर पाता। वैवश्य की अवस्था में प्रतीति असहज होगी एवं साधारणावस्था नहीं होगी। इस वैवश्य को प्रयोक्ता या कवि अपनी प्रतिभा से दूर करता है। उसमें सौन्दर्यबोध एवं अभिव्यक्ति का अतिशय सामर्थ्य अपेक्षित है। अपनी प्रस्तुति से सर्वसाधारण को लालित्य से रञ्जित करने की क्षमता कवि में होनी चाहिए। सर्जन ऐसा चमत्कारपूर्ण हो कि 'अहृदय' या नीरस व्यक्ति भी निर्मलहृदय वाला रसिक बन जाए। तब सहृदय का वैवश्य सहज ही समाप्त हो जाएगा। इस बाधा का सीधा सम्बन्ध साधारणीकरण से है। सौन्दर्यबोध के मार्ग में वर्णनीय की हृदयावर्जकता ही साधारणभाव का बीज बनता है।

निजसुखादि विवशता का यह तिरस्करण सकलवैषयिकोपरागशून्य योगी की मानसिक अवस्था से भिन्न होता है। योगी के एकघन आनन्दानुभव में लक्ष्य प्राप्ति की इच्छा सम्मिलित होने से विषयावेशविवशता का विघ्न वर्तमान होता है। किन्तु काव्यबोध के क्षण में विषयान्तर का लेश भी नहीं होता।

4. प्रतीत्युपायवैकल्य एवं अस्फुटता[21]

वर्णनीय विषय की प्रस्तुति की रीति में यदि विशृंखलता हो अथवा प्रतीयमान वस्तु अस्वाभाविक प्रतीत हो रही हो तो भी प्रतीति साधारणभावापन्ना नहीं होती। इस बाधा को भी सर्जक या कवि दूर करता है। सभी प्रमितियाँ प्रत्यक्ष पर आधारित होती हैं।[22] यदि प्रत्यक्षलिंग प्रतीतिरूप होगा तो प्रमिति अनुमानात्मिका होगी। अत: काव्यसृष्टि अथवा अभिनय का लिंगव्यापार से भिन्न प्रत्यक्षायमाण होना आवश्यक है।[23]

5. अप्रधानता[24]

विभावादि का विभावनत्व आदि व्यापार स्थायी के लिए होता है, अत: विभावादि अप्रधान हैं। अप्रधान में किसी की संवित् विश्रान्ति नहीं होती उसमें सापेक्षता नियमत: बनी रहेगी। अत: काव्यप्रयोग में स्थायी की अभिव्यक्ति के प्रति सर्जक को सावधान रहना चाहिए तभी प्रमिति साधारणीकृत होगी।

6. संशययोग[25]

विभाव, अनुभाव, व्यभिचारीभाव के रूप में जिन तत्त्वों, चेष्टाओं, वस्तुओं का वर्णन किया जाता है, वे व्याप्यव्यापकसम्बन्ध से स्थायी के साथ सम्बद्ध नहीं होते। आंसू निकलने के लिए आनन्द या शोक ही आवश्यक नहीं हैं आंखों के विकार से भी आंसू

आ सकते हैं। अतः वर्णनीय विभावादि को स्थायी से संयुक्त-भासित होना आवश्यक है तभी वह आभास सहृदयप्रतीति में सम्यक् स्थित होगा। यह संयोग कवि की कला पर निर्भर होता है।

ये सभी विघ्न प्रतीति की साधारणावस्था के लिए बाधक हैं एवं इन्हें प्रतीति उत्पन्न करने वाला प्रयोक्ता कवि एवं प्रतीति ग्रहण करने वाला सहृदय दोनों अपनी योग्यता से दूर करते हैं। इन बाधाओं के न होने पर साधारण्यावस्था उल्लसित होती है। इस प्रकार निर्विघ्नता साधारणीकरण के लिए समुचित भाव भूमि बनती है, तब साधारण भाव उल्लसित हो जाने पर पुनः विघ्नों के लिए अवकाश नहीं रहता।[26] विषय निर्विघ्न प्रतीत होकर रसनीय होते हैं एवं विषयी सहृदय स्वसंवित् विश्रान्तिरूप रसना से आस्वाद की अवस्था प्राप्त करता है। अतः साधारणीकरण का क्षेत्र विस्तृत है तथा विषय एवं विषयी दोनों से सम्बद्ध है।[27]

विषयसाधारण्य

स्वातन्त्र्यवाद में सामग्रीकारणता का सिद्धान्त स्वीकार किया जाता है।[28] किसी भी कार्य के समग्र हेतुओं की समुदित (एकसाथ) हेतुता होती है। घट निर्माण में मिट्टी, दण्ड, चक्र, कुलाल, सूत्र आदि व्यस्त रूप में फलनिष्पत्ति करने में समर्थ नहीं होते, अन्यथा प्रत्येक हेतु पृथक्-पृथक् घट निर्माण करने में सक्षम होता। क्योंकि कारण भेद से कार्य भेद का नियम अकाट्य है। अतः स्वीकार करना होगा कि दण्डादि समग्र पदार्थ समुदित रूप से एकवपु होकर ही कारणसामग्री बनते हैं तथा वे ही एक हेतु के रूप में प्रमाता की संवित् में विश्रान्त होते हैं। कोई भी प्रमाता व्यस्त दण्ड आदि को घट के हेतु के रूप में ग्रहण नहीं करता, अपितु सामग्री को ही ग्रहण करता है :

अत एव घटोद्भूतौ सामग्रीहेतुरुच्यते।
सामग्री च समग्राणां यद्येकं नेष्यते वपुः।।
हेतुभेदान्न भेदः स्यात्फले तच्चासमंञ्जसम्।

(*तन्त्रालोक*, 9.30, 31)

इसी प्रकार विभाव, अनुभाव, व्यभिचारीभाव इन सभी का स्थायी के साथ संयोग, तथा स्थायीभाव स्वयं समुदित होकर एक सामग्री के रूप में रसास्वाद के हेतु बनते हैं।[29] समुदयता इन सभी में समवेत होकर भिन्न नाम से व्यवहृत होती है। यह विभावादि का सह-आधारणीकरण या साधारणीकरण है।

प्रत्येक वेद्य भाव, वह लौकिक हो या अलौकिक स्वातन्त्र्यवाद में स्व-प्रकाश होता है। किसी प्रकाशान्तर से प्रकाशित न होना उसका स्वभाव है।[30] वह अपने स्वप्रकाश नामक धर्म से ही भासित होता है।[31] अतः कोई भी विषय जब जिस रूप में भासमान होता है, तब वही उसका स्व-रूप बन जाता है।

अत एक यदा येन वपुषा भाति यद्यथा।
तदा तथा तत्तद्रूपमित्येषोपनिषत् परा।। (*तन्त्रालोक*, 10.82)

विभावादि यदि किसी अन्य प्रयोजन से पृथक् व्यक्त हों तब उनका स्वरूप विभावत्वादि रूप होगा। किन्तु मात्र विभावत्वेन निर्विघ्न प्रतीति से रस का कोई उपकार नहीं होता। साधारणावस्थावपन्न सामग्री शरीर से व्यक्त होने पर उसके आभास में सर्वसञ्चेत्यता (सर्वग्राह्यता) नामक गुण अतिशायी हो जाता है।[32] यही साधारण्य उसका अपना स्वरूप, वेद्यता या प्रकाश है। अतः साधारण्यावस्था में सर्वप्रमातृवेद्यता स्वरूपधर्म के रूप में स्वीकार करना चाहिए।

आचार्य ने विषय साधारण्य के तीन उत्तम उदाहरण दिए हैं :

अत एवोच्यते मल्लनटप्रेक्षोपदेशने
सर्वप्रमातृतादात्म्यं पूर्णरूपानुभावकम्।।

तन्त्रालोक, 10.86

कौतुकपूर्ण मल्लयुद्ध, नटप्रेक्षा, नृत्तगीतकाव्यादि, तथा गुरूपदेश इन तीनों स्थलों में भासमान भावों में सर्वग्राह्यता होती है। सम्पूर्ण दृश्य स्वयं को सामग्रीरूप में प्रकाशित करता है, जैसे शिखरस्थ व्यक्ति के लिए सम्पूर्ण नगर समग्रतया भासित होता है। इतना ही नहीं इस प्रकरण में जयरथ *श्रीप्रत्यभिज्ञा* को उद्धृत करते हैं,[33] कि कोई भी विषय जब समग्रतया अपने पूर्णरूप का अनुभावक बनता है, तब उसमें सर्वप्रमातृवेद्यता होती है। पूर्णता का अर्थ है, विगलितवेद्यान्तरतया उसी देशकाल में अन्याकाङ्क्षारहित परामर्श या निर्विघ्नप्रतीति। सामग्रीप्रतीति का समर्थन आचार्य ने लोचन में भी किया है।[34]

प्रत्येक भाव में नियत प्रमातृवेद्यता एवं अनियतप्रमातृवेद्यता का स्वातन्त्र्य है, जो उसके स्वरूप या भासमानता पर निर्भर है।[35] नियत प्रमातृवेद्यता अपूर्ण रूपा होती है, अतः चमत्कार शून्य होती है। किन्तु जहाँ सामूहिक वेद्यता होती है वहीं चमत्कार है, क्योंकि वह पूर्णरूपानुभाविका या साधारणभावापन्ना होती है।[36] विषय साधारण्य के चमत्काररूपता पर आचार्य का विशेषबल है। यद्यपि नृत्तकाव्यादि संवित्ति प्रत्येक संवेत्ता को अलग-अलग भी चमत्कृत करती है तथा यदि एक भाव से अनेकवेद्यता का अवभास हो तो वह अवभास स्वात्मविश्रान्तिमय परामर्श कराते हुए क्रमशः प्रमाताओं के पारस्परिक भेद को शिथिल करके उनमें आभास के स्तर पर ऐक्य स्थापित कर देता है। उस ऐक्य की अवस्था में एकैक प्रमातृसंवेद्यता की अवस्था की भाँति शुष्कता नहीं होती, अपितु सरसता होती है। उस वेद्यता में अतिशय चमत्कारकारिता का आवेश रहता है।[37] स्पष्ट है कि विषयविभावादि सामग्री के स्वात्मशक्ति के कारण अतिशयचमत्काररूपता, सकलसहृदयवेद्यता रूपमें साधारण्य उपपन्न है। काव्यशास्त्र में आचार्य ने इसी स्वात्मशक्ति या स्वातन्त्रय को व्यञ्जन, प्रकाशन, प्रत्यायन आदि शब्दों से समझाया है।

विषयीसाधारणीकरण

यद्यपि सभी भावों का संवित् में संवित् का भोक्ता में पर्यवसान होने का नियम है। अत: विषयी सहृदय का विषयाभास के साथ आधाराधेय भाव-रूप सह. आधारणीकरण स्वत: सिद्ध है। क्योंकि सामग्रीसाधारण्य रूप में बहुवेद्यता का पर्यवसान सकलसहृदयसंवाद या आभासैक्य में होता है। तथापि तन्मयीभवन की योग्यता एवं स्वात्मानुप्रवेश की उपपत्ति के बिना सहृदय साधारणीकरण अस्फुट प्रतीत होता है।

शैवमत में सामान्य सामाजिक पूर्ण चेतना से भिन्न न होते हुए भी चेतना के स्वातन्त्रयशक्ति के कारण अपूर्ण होता है।[38] वह मायाजनित[39] कलानियतिरागविद्या एवं काल नामक कञ्चुकों से आवृत्त होता है। अत: उसमें सीमितकर्तृता, कर्त्तव्याकर्त्तव्यनियमबद्धता, विषयावेश, सीमितज्ञान कालक्रम का बोध अत्यन्त दृढ़ अवस्था में रहते हैं।[40] साधारणीकरण में बाधक विघ्नों में प्रथम विघ्न प्रमाता के इसी सामान्यस्वभाव का परिणाम होता है। किन्तु चेतना के भेद में अभेदानुसंधान-रूपा स्वातन्त्र्य शक्ति के कारण[41] सर्ववेद्य काव्य आदि भावों के अनवरत अध्ययन, मनन आदि के द्वारा सर्ववेद्य को एकीकृतचित्तवृत्ति से ग्रहण करने की योग्यता उत्पन्न हो जाती है। विशेषत: सौन्दर्य या कला-परामर्श के सन्दर्भ में सकलसमवेत के चित्त में एकतानता अनुभव सिद्ध है।

तत्रापि,
क्वचिदाभासे प्रमातृनेकीकरोति नितम्बिनीनृत्त इव प्रेक्षकान्।
तावति तेषामाभासे ऐक्यम्।।

(*ईश्वरप्रत्यभिज्ञाविवृति*, भाग 1, पृ. 194)

नृत्तगीत आदि कलाएँ स्वरूपत: ऐसी हैं, जहाँ सभी रसिक समान रूप से एक ही वेद्य को पूर्णतया ग्रहण करते हैं यथा-

तथा ह्येकाग्रसकलसामाजिकजन:।
नृत्तं गीतं सुधासारसागरत्वेन मन्यते।।

(*तन्त्रालोक* , 10.85)

सहृदय साधारण्य के सामान्य दशा के विवेचन से ही आचार्य सन्तुष्ट नहीं होते अपितु परमानन्द की दशा में संविद्विश्रान्ति के साथ-साथ प्रमातृता-विश्रान्ति के भाव तक ले जाते हैं। उनका कथन है कि वैषयिक आनन्द से विलक्षण शृंगार आदि रस, नाट्य, काव्य, संगीत इत्यादि सन्दर्भों में विषयावेश आदि किसी भी प्रकार के विघ्न नहीं होते। इसी कारण तद्भिन्न सभी प्रकार के भावों का आत्यन्तिक तिरस्कार हो चुका होता है। अत: वह रसना, चर्वणा, निर्वृत्ति प्रतीति ही प्रमातृताविश्रान्ति का रूप धारण कर लेती

है। प्रमातृ भाव प्रतीति में विलीन हो जाता है। यह अलौकिक परामर्श प्रधानरूप से हृदय का लक्षण है। ऐसा हृदय विभावादि के प्रकाशभाग अर्थात् व्यञ्जन के वेद्य विभावादि में विश्रान्त या तद्रूप होने पर भी उसमें स्वयं को विलीन कर देता है। यह समर्पण हृदय की निर्मलता है तथा इस प्रमिति एवं प्रमातृ के ऐक्य में हृदय के इसी वैशिष्ट्य को ही तो सहृदयता कहते हैं :

यत्रापि अत्यन्तमन्यथाभावमतिक्रम्य सुखमास्वाद्यते अर्जनादिसम्भाव्यमान-विघ्नान्तरनिरासात् वैषयिकानन्दविलक्षणशृंङ्गारादौ नाट्यकाव्यादिविषये तत्र वीतविघ्नत्वादेव असौ रसना चर्वणा निर्वृतिः प्रतीतिः प्रमातृताविश्रान्तिरेव। तत एव हृदयेन परामर्शलक्षणेन प्राधान्यात् व्यपदेश्या व्यवस्थितस्य अपि प्रकाशभागस्य वेद्यविश्रान्तस्य अनादरणात् सहृदयता उच्यते।

(*ईश्वरप्रत्यभिज्ञाविवृत्तिविमर्शिनी*, भाग 2, पृ. 179)

क्योंकि इस स्थल पर भी देह प्राण सुख इत्यादि आभासांश का भेद पूर्णतः विगलित नहीं होता, अतः पूर्ण ऐक्य न होकर आभास मात्र का हृदय के साथ सहअसाधारणीकरण रूप ऐक्य होता है।[42]

आचार्य ने बोध के तीन स्वरूपों का विवेचन किया है। 1. बोधमूल 2. बोधमध्य 3. बोधाग्र। समस्त सृष्टि के भेदात्मक स्वरूप एवं स्मृति के ज्ञान को बोध मूल कहा गया है। इस बोध का स्वरूप 'इदं अहं जानामि' इस रूप में होता है। यह सामान्य अनुभूति है। बोध की स्थूलावस्था है। इदन्ता का प्राधान्य होने से भेदज्ञान अत्यन्त स्पष्ट होता है[43]।

जब परिदृश्यमान वस्तु इदं अहं इस रूप में स्वात्मविश्रान्त हो, इदन्ता एवं अहन्ता का भेद समाप्त हो गया हो, आधाराधेय-सा प्रतीत हो तो वह बोधमध्य है :

समस्ततत्त्वभावोऽयं स्वात्मन्येवाविभागकः।
बोधमध्यं भवेत्किञ्चिदाधाराधेयलक्षणम्।।

(*तन्त्रालोक*, 13.14)

यही बोधमध्य का स्वरूप विषय विभावादि एवं विषयी प्रमाता की प्रमिति के साधारणीकरण में दिखाई देता है। जहाँ दोनों उपस्थित हैं किन्तु भेदाभास नहीं है। बोधाग्र इससे आगे की दशा है जहाँ इदन्ता चिद्बोध में विलीन होती है। निस्तरङ्ग चिद्बोध रूप में परम आनन्द की अनुभूति मात्र होती है।[44] इसका साम्य रसास्वाद से है। इसीलिए रसास्वाद ब्रह्मानन्दसहोदर है। ब्रह्मानन्द इसलिए नहीं है, क्योंकि वह वास्तविकसृष्टि के साथ तादात्म्यापन्न न होकर काव्य सृष्टि से तादात्म्य स्थापित करना है। आचार्य इस तथ्य को भी स्पष्ट करते हैं :

मधुरादिरसास्वादे तु विषयस्पर्शव्यवधानम्। ततोऽपि काव्यनाट्यादौ तद्वदवधानशून्यता तद्वदवधानसंस्कारानुवेधस्तु तत्रापि तु। तथोदितव्यवधानांश- तिरस्क्रियासावधानहृदया लभन्त एव परमानन्दम्।

(*ईश्वरप्रत्यभिज्ञाविवृत्तिविमर्शिनी* भाग 2, पृ. 179)

इस परम साधारण्य भाव के लिए सहृदयता का स्तर भी परमावस्था का होना चाहिए। प्रमाता परशक्तिपात से पवित्रीकृत हृदय वाला एवं बहुश्रुत होना चाहिए जो बिरले ही होते हैं, ''नरशक्तिशिव इति तु सर्वंसह: प्रतिपत्तिक्रम: परमेश्वरेच्छा-स्वातन्त्र्यसृष्ट: इत्यलं परशक्तिपातपवित्रितबहुश्रुतसहृदयसोपदेशकतिपयजनहृदयहारिण्या प्रसक्तानुप्रसक्त्या।'' (*त्रिंशिकातत्त्वविवेक*, पृ. 81)

चमत्कार एवं साधारणीकरण

साधारणीकरण के सर्ववेद्यभाव रूप स्थिर होने पर चमत्कार के साथ उसका अविनाभावसम्बन्ध भी स्थिर होता है। जिस प्रकार साधारणभाव समुदितविभावादि एवं उसके कारण सहृदयों की प्रमिति के ऐक्य का स्वरूप धर्म है, उसी प्रकार यह एकीकृतप्रमिति स्वयं चमत्काररूपा होती है।[45] चमत्कार शब्द को आचार्य ने विषयविषयी उभयगत एवं एकघनवृत्ति रूपों में तीन प्रकार से परिभाषित किया है।

प्रथम अर्थ में चमत्कार शब्द स्वात्मविश्रान्ति एवं आस्वादरूप है। जब चित्त किसी संवित् के प्रति निरपेक्ष होकर स्वात्मविश्रान्ति की अवस्था में होता है, उस अवस्था को चमत्त्व या आस्वादावस्था कहते हैं। उस काल की समग्र ज्ञानात्मिका क्रिया चमत्कार है:

चमत्कारो हि 'इति स्वात्मनि अनन्यापेक्षे विश्रमणम् एवं भुञ्जानतारूपं तदेव संरम्भे विमृशति न अन्यत्र अनुधावति। चमदिति क्रियाविशेषणम्।

(*ईश्वरप्रत्यभिज्ञाविवृत्तिविमर्शिनी*, भाग 3, पृ. 251)

चित्त की इस आनन्दात्मक एकघनता को आचार्य और भी स्पष्ट करते हैं। यथा–

तस्मादनुपचरितस्य संवेदनरूपतानान्तरीयत्वेन अवस्थितस्य स्वातन्त्र्यस्यैव रसैकघनतया परामर्श: परमानन्दो निर्वृत्तिश्चमत्कार उच्यते।

(*ईश्वरप्रत्यभिज्ञाविवृत्तिविमर्शिनी*, भाग 2, पृ. 179)

यह साधारणीकरण की पूर्णावस्था है।

द्वितीय व्याख्या में चमत्कार शब्द साधारणीकृतभावाभिव्यञ्जक काव्य का पर्याय है:

अखंड एव वा शब्दो निर्विघ्नास्वादवृत्ति:

तत्रैव, भाग 3, पृ. 251

तृतीय व्याख्या में विषय एवं विषयी के साधारण्य या एक प्रकाशमात्रता की दशा में पूर्वोक्त बोधमध्यरूप निर्विघ्नावस्था की रसनरूपता को चमत्कार कहा गया है। जब किसी विषय का वेद्यान्तरसंस्पर्शशून्यदशा में परामर्श हो रहा हो तथा उस अवस्था में हृदयस्पन्द के समुच्छलन में उस परामर्शमयकाव्य के द्वारा अव्यक्त अनुकरण हो रहा हो तो उसे चमत् शब्द से व्यक्त किया जाता है। यही तो है कलासृष्टि एवं सहृदय-हृदय के प्रकाश का समान अधिकरण पर प्रतिष्ठित होना या साधारणावस्था में होना :

> *चमदिति वा आन्तरस्पन्दान्दोलनोदितपरामर्शमयशब्देनाव्यक्तानुकरणम्। काव्यनाट्यरसादावपि भाविचित्तवृत्त्यन्तरोदयनियमात्मकविघ्नविरत एव आस्वादो रसनात्मा चमत्कारः।* (*तत्रैव*)।

चमत्कृति में चित्त की एकघनता निस्तरङ्गता अथवा आनन्दात्मकता है, विस्मय का भाव नहीं है जैसा कि साहित्यदर्पणकार समझते हैं।[46] यहाँ चित्तविस्तार के स्थान पर हृदय का समर्पण प्रधान है।

अभिनवभारती में भी आचार्य ने साधारणभावरूपा निर्विघ्नप्रतीति को चमत्कार का पर्याय बताया है।[47] काव्य में वस्तु, अलंकार एवं रसध्वनियों में से प्रत्येक चमत्कार रूप है उन सभी की प्रतीति बहुप्रमातृवेद्य होती है। अतः बहुप्रमातृवेद्यत्वरूप साधारणीकरण उन सभी स्थलों पर होता है। यह अवश्य है कि रसबोध में साधारणभाव अतिशायी होता है तथा वस्त्वलङ्कारध्वनियों का पर्यवसान रस में स्वीकृत है। अतः रसबोध प्रक्रिया के व्याख्यान में ही इसे अधिक महत्त्व दिया है। *तन्त्रालोक* के पूर्वोक्त उदाहरण में उल्लिखित मल्ल, नटप्रेक्षा या नृत्तगीतकाव्य आदि तथा उपदेश को क्रमशः वस्तुध्वनि, अलङ्कारध्वनि एवं रसध्वनि के समतुल्य माना जा सकता है। क्योंकि मल्लयुद्धादि कौतुकपूर्णवस्तुपरक दृश्य हैं, नटप्रेक्षा, रमणीनृत्य, सुमधुरगीत आदि वस्तुसज्जा एवं स्वरसज्जा प्रधान दृश्य-श्रव्य है, गुरु का उपदेश, गीता आदि स्वात्मविश्रान्ति एवं परमानन्दानुभावक हैं, जैसे रस होता है। इनकी समतुल्यता से स्पष्ट है कि जिस भी स्थल पर चमत्कारातिशय है वहाँ वह चमत्कार विषय एवं प्रमाता के आभास में ऐक्य के कारण ही है। ऐक्य में एक शब्द संख्या वाचक न होकर प्रकाश या ज्ञान के अभेद मात्र का वाचक है।[48]

अतिशय चमत्कारात्मक सर्वसञ्चेत्यता साधारणीकृत भाव का स्वरूप धर्म है, यह सिद्धान्त निष्कलंक है। इस सिद्धान्त का आधार स्वान्त्र्यवाद का यह सिद्धान्त बनता है कि द्रव्यगुणकर्म का सत्त्व उनके स्वातन्त्र्य अर्थात् सत्तासमवाय के कारण है। इस प्रकरण में *तन्त्रालोक* 10/73.74 पर जयरथ का व्याख्यान प्रासंगिक एवं महत्त्वपूर्ण है :

काव्यप्रकाश के द्वितीय उल्लास में उद्धृत वाक्यपदीय के *'न गौः स्वरूपेण गौः नाप्यगौः गोत्वाभिसम्बन्धात्तु गौः'* वाक्य में गोत्व स्वतः सिद्ध है। उसे अपने लिए जात्यन्तर

की आवश्यकता नहीं है। जिस प्रकार कार्य, कारण में या सामान्य (जाति) विशेष (व्यक्ति) में स्वयं अप्रकटरूप में समवायवृत्ति से स्थित होता है। तथा समवाय अपने आश्रय में अपने स्वातन्त्र्य से स्थित है, वह अपने लिए किसी समवायान्तर की अपेक्षा नहीं रखता। जिस प्रकार गमन-क्रियावान् व्यक्ति न तो स्वरूपतः गमनक्रियावान् है न तद्भिन्न है, अपितु गमनक्रिया के कारण गन्ता है। उसी प्रकार कोई भी भाव सकलधर्मयुत होने पर भी न तो स्वरूपतः वेद्य है न अवेद्य है, अपितु वेद्यता नामक धर्म के कारण वेद्य है। किञ्च यह वेद्यता स्वसामर्थ्य से वेद्य है उसके लिए अन्य वेद्यता की आवश्यकता नहीं है। यही भावों की स्वयंप्रकाशता या स्वातन्त्र्य है। वह वेद्यता जिस प्रकार की होगी वेद्य उसी रूप में प्रकाशित होंगे। कलासृष्टि में विभावादि की वेद्यता स्वतः ही परस्पर समुदित सामग्रीरूपा साधारणावस्था में होती है उसे अपने स्वरूप प्रकाशन के लिए किसी व्यापारान्तर की अपेक्षा नहीं होती। इसलिए चमत्कार निर्वेश एवं समापत्ति का भी पर्याय है।[49]

साधारणीकरण एवं भ्रान्ति

रसबोधप्रक्रिया के अन्तिम मौलिकविचारक पण्डितराज जगन्नाथ ने साधारणीकरण के भाव को वेदान्त की भ्रान्ति के समान माना है। काव्यप्रकाश के कुछ प्राचीन टीकाकार भी इसी सिद्धान्त के पोषक प्रतीत होते हैं, जो प्रभाकर मीमांसा के भ्रान्तिज्ञान के समान विषय-विषयी साधारण्य के भेदाग्रह-निबन्धन को स्वीकार करते हैं।[50] किन्तु आचार्य साधारणीकरण को निर्भ्रान्त एवं पूर्णप्रतीति रूप में स्वीकार करते हैं। पण्डितराज को रस की आनन्दरूपता सिद्ध करने के लिए इसी कारण पर्याप्त परिश्रम करना पड़ा। तथापि आचार्य का पण्डितराज के द्वारा प्रतिपादित आस्वाद के स्वरूप के विषय में विशेष मत भेद नहीं दिखाई देता। आचार्य उसे साक्षिरूप मानते हैं तो पण्डितराज साक्षिभास्य! बस इतना ही भेद है।

वेदान्तमत में शुक्ति में अविद्यावशात् अनिर्वचनीय रजत उत्पन्न होता है। अतः विषयगत भ्रान्ति अभिमत है। किन्तु आचार्य भ्रान्ति के इस स्वरूप एवं अविद्या की अनिर्वचनीयता को स्वीकार नहीं करते हैं; साधारणीभाव यदि अविद्याकल्पित भ्रान्तिरूप होगा तो उसे उत्तरकालिक किसी ज्ञानान्तर से बाधित भी होना चाहिए। किन्तु रसदशा में ज्ञानान्तर का अवकाश नहीं होता तथा दशा की समाप्ति के पश्चात् आस्वाद भी नहीं होता, फिर बाध किसका होगा ? स्वातन्त्र्यवादी आचार्य के मत में भ्रान्ति की व्याख्या कुछ इस प्रकार है :

"इदं रजतं स्थिरं सर्वप्रमातृसाधारणमर्थक्रियायोग्यम्" यह मानस भ्रान्ति का उदाहरण है। आभास काल में रजतज्ञान सत्य है। अन्यथा आदानवृत्ति नहीं होगी। रजतांश एवं इदमंश में पृथक्-पृथक् भ्रान्ति नहीं होती, क्योंकि रजत की भासमानता ही अबाधित

रहती है। बाधकाल में भी 'रजतं न भातम्' यह प्रतीति किसी की नहीं होती। क्योंकि मानसज्ञान में रजताभास उपस्थित है। इदमंश में भ्रान्ति नहीं होती, क्योंकि इदन्ता बाधकाल में भी यथावत् रहती है। अत: रजतांश एवं इदमंश के मेलनांश में ही भ्रान्ति सिद्ध होती है। मेलानांश में जो इदं है वही रजत है। यही सामानाधिकरण्य विमर्श भ्रान्ति है। इस प्रकार भ्रान्ति सम्बन्धनिष्ठा है, विषयनिष्ठा नहीं है।

भ्रान्ति के सम्बन्धनिष्ठ होने से प्रभाकरसम्मत भेदाग्रहनिबन्धन अख्याति भी विचारणीय है। भ्रान्ति बाधक ज्ञान का स्वरूप है, 'नेदं रजतं स्थिरं प्रमात्रन्तरागम्यमर्थक्रियाकारि'। भ्रान्ति ज्ञान नियत प्रमाता को ही सम्भव है अन्य या सर्वप्रमाता के लिए नहीं, क्योंकि भ्रान्तिस्थल के रजत में शून्यता नामक धर्म होता है। तद्विशिष्ट रजत अन्य प्रमाता के लिए अगम्य होता है। आभास काल में भेद का लेश भी प्रतीत नहीं होता अत: भेदाग्रह कहना समुचित नहीं, किन्तु प्रमात्रन्तरसा-धारणत्वाभाव के कारण भ्रान्ति स्थल में रजत की असत्ता सिद्ध होती है। अत: सर्वप्रमातृगम्यता व्यापक एवं रजताभास व्याप्य है। व्यापक के अभाव के कारण व्याप्य का भी अभाव सिद्ध होता है। इसे अपूर्णताख्याति नामक अख्याति कहते हैं। भेदाग्रह एक को हो सकता है सभी को नहीं। साधारणीकरण का स्वरूप ही सर्वप्रमातृगम्यतारूप होता है। अत: वह निर्भ्रान्त अवस्था है। इस प्रकरण में विस्तरिकाकार परमानन्दचक्रवर्ती की पंक्तियाँ प्रासंगिक हैं:

> *आत्मविशेषरत्यादिविशेषसाक्षात्कारविशेषसम्बन्धविशेषरूपासाधारणग्रहे परस्पर वैधर्म्यावगतौ विषयनानात्वेनैकत्वरूप्यविरहाद् विसंवाद: स्यात् संवादेनैव प्रामाण्यग्रहणात् अनेकस्याभ्रान्तत्वात्॥*
>
> (*काव्यप्रकाश*, उल्लास, 4, *विस्तरिका*)

अनिर्वचनीयता तो शैवमत में सर्वथा अस्वीकृत है। इसका निराकरण आचार्य ने अत्यन्त मनोरम शैली में किया है। भासमान वस्तु अनिर्वचनीय नहीं हो सकती। किसी भी प्रकार की युक्ति आभास का अपलाप नहीं कर सकती। अत: किसी प्रतीति को अनिर्वचनीय कहना दुस्साहस मात्र है :

> *अनिर्वचनीया सेति चेत्। कस्येति न विद्म: भाति च अनिर्वाच्येति यक्षभाषा। युक्त्या नोपपद्यते इति चेत्। भासनातिक्रमणे का युक्ति .... तदिदं शशशृंङ्ग-गगनकुसुमच्छेदकमुक्तम्।*
>
> (*ईश्वरप्रत्यभिज्ञाविवृत्तिविमर्शिनी*, भाग, 3, पृ. 248)

इस प्रकार साधारणीकरण को दोषविशेष का परिणाम, भ्रान्ति का एक रूप या अनिर्वचनीय प्रतीति नहीं, अपितु निर्भ्रान्त आभास की एक अवस्था मानना आचार्य को अभीष्ट है। जहाँ प्रमेय प्रमाण एवं प्रमिति प्रकाशमात्र स्वरूप होते हैं।

अभिनवमतस्वारस्य

प्रत्यभिज्ञादर्शन किसी भी भासमानवस्तु का निषेध नहीं करता, अपितु भात एवं भासमान के स्वरूपों में ऐक्य का अनुसन्धान करता है।[51] जिस प्रकार शिव की चिद्भूमि में विश्व दर्पण में प्रतिबिम्बित नगर की भाँति उन्मीलित है एवं प्रमाण प्रमेय तथा प्रमाता सभी चेतना के धरातल पर एक हैं, उनका व्यस्तरूप स्वयं में अपूर्ण एवं सापेक्ष है, उसी प्रकार काव्य कवि की चिद्भूमि में उन्मीलित है। उसके बहिर्मुख स्वरूप को कवि की इच्छा से निर्मित कलात्मिका सृष्टि समझते हुए उसका विवेचन करना चाहिए, तथा साधारणीकरण के स्वरूप-व्याख्यान के अवसर पर लौकिक वैषयिकता की अवधारणा को पृथक् रखना चाहिए। कवि किसी ऐतिहासिक पात्र को अपनी कलात्मिका सृष्टि का नायक बनाता है। उस पात्र के वास्तविक इतिवृत्त के कारण निर्मित सामाजिकों में प्रसिद्ध छवि एवं उदात्तता के प्रतिमानों को अपनी कलात्मिका रचना में अनुस्यूत करता है। कुछ इस प्रकार से उपरञ्जित करता है कि उसका चित्रण केवल आनन्द या लोकरञ्जन में पर्यवसित हो। इसके लिए वह इतस्ततः बिखरी हुई लौकिक कारणसामग्री को एकत्र कर, उन्हें सभी प्रकार के नियमों से मुक्त करता हुआ उसके आभासांश को प्रमुखतया ग्रहण करके अपनी अलौकिक रचना तैयार करता है, एक ऐसी रचना जहाँ एक ही स्थल पर अनेक देश-काल की वस्तुएँ अलंकरण का साधन बनी होती हैं, शब्दों का, वर्णों का चुना हुआ क्रम गुण का रूप धारण किए रहता है। इस प्रकार की प्रकाशमयी सृष्टि होती है, कला जगत् की। वहाँ रामादि पात्रों की अवधारणा स्फुट होती है, घटनाक्रम की शुष्क ऐतिहासिकता का महत्त्व प्रतीत्युपाय वैकल्य एवं अस्फुटता नामक दोषों को दूर करने मात्र तक होता है। अपनी इस अलौकिक सृष्टि रचना में कवि अपनी योग्यता एवं सहृदयता के बल पर जितनी कुशलता व्यक्त कर पाता है, प्रतीति साधारण्य में उतनी तीव्रता होती है। आनन्दराजानक ने उचित ही कहा:

वस्तुतो विभावनानुभावनसञ्चारणात्मकव्यापारत्रयवत्त्वमेव विभावादित्वं येषां व्यापाराणां रत्यादेरीषत्प्रकाशः, स्फुटतरः प्रकाशः, स्फुटतमः प्रकाशः।।

(*काव्यप्रकाश टीका*, चतुर्थ उल्लास, रस प्रकरण)

साधारणीकरण में 'च्वि' प्रत्यय इस तथ्य का व्यंजक है कि लोक में जो वस्तुएँ समान अधिकरण पर ज्ञान मात्र रूप में अधिष्ठित नहीं हैं, उनमें व्याप्यव्यापक सम्बन्ध भी नहीं है। उन्हें व्याप्यव्यापक बनाकर किसी स्थायी भाव के अनुकूल सज्जित करके आभास मात्र के रूप में एक अधिकरण में स्थापित कर दिया जाता है। इस कलात्मिका अभिव्यक्ति में स्वरूपतः इतना आकर्षण उत्पन्न हो जाता है कि सहृदय के हृदय को बलात् आकर्षित कर संवित् के स्तर पर उसका भी सामानाधिकरण्य कर लेता है, या आभास के एक स्वरूप में परिवर्तित कर देता है। यहां पुनः आनन्दराजानक की पक्तियाँ प्रासंगिक प्रतीत होती हैं:

परकीयायाश्चित्तवृतेरात्मीयचित्तवृत्त्यभेदेन परामर्शो हृदयसंवाद: तस्य च स्वपर, विभागाभावाद्देशकालविभागाभावाच्च व्यापकत्वेन प्रतीते: साधारण्यम्। अतएव परमाद्वयज्ञानतुल्यं तस्य हि अहमित्येव परामर्शात् तद्व्यतिरिक्त- स्यान्यस्याभावात्।।

(वही)

इस प्रकार सामूहिक प्रतीति का सह-आधारण कलासौन्दर्य की शक्ति है।

अत: साधारणीकरण शब्द से सामान्यीकरण अर्थ करना, सीता आदि का कामिनीमात्र रूप में स्फुरण बताया जाना, अथवा वैयक्तिकता का विगलन मात्र बताया जाना मात्र अभीष्ट नहीं है। साधारणीकरण को Generalisation या Depersonalisation आदि शब्दों से नहीं व्यक्त किया जा सकता। सुबुद्धिमिश्र ने *तत्त्वपरीक्षा* में स्पष्ट कहा है :

वस्तुत: स्त्रीत्वादिकमपि न स्फुरति। लौकिक एव तदपेक्षणात्।।

सर्वबोध्यता का तात्पर्य भी सर्वसम्बद्धता से नहीं है, अपितु अनियतनिष्ठता से है। काव्यवर्णित शकुन्तला न तो परमार्थत: ऐतिहासिक है, न लौकिक कान्ता, अपितु स्वरूपमात्र है, उसमें ऐतिहासिक शकुन्तला के सभी धर्म विद्यमान होते हुए कवि की भावप्रौढिनिबद्ध अलौकिकता भी है। नियतता का यही भाव सामाजिक के हृदय को व्याप्त करने वाली साधारण प्रतीति का कारण बनता है। आचार्य स्पष्टत: कहते हैं :

तथापि नटस्य निर्गुणत्वात् रामादेरपरमार्थसत्त्वात् च नियततां विजहत: साधारणीभावमनुप्राप्ता: सामाजिकजनमपि मृगामोददिशा व्याप्नुवन्ति।।

(*अभिनवभारती*, अध्याय, 6, पृ.489)

आचार्य ने अनियत विभावादि के साधारणरूप एवं सहृदय के आभास के साथ ऐक्य को दर्शाने के लिए दो उदाहरण दिए हैं :

व्याप्तिग्रह इव धूमाग्न्योर्भयकम्पयोरिव (*तत्रैव*, पृष्ठ 473)

अर्थात् विभावादि के स्वरूपाभास के बल से सहृदय के तदनुकूलभाव, व्याप्त एवं न्निद्रूप होते हुए भी भासमान हो जाते हैं। यहाँ यह कथन भी अभीष्ट नहीं है कि सामाजिक की स्वकान्ता-विषयक रति का साधारणीकरण होता है। जहाँ निजता ही नहीं है वहाँ स्वकान्ताविषयिणी रति कहाँ होगी ? साथ ही 'न हि देवदत्त: एकस्यां स्त्रियां रक्त: अन्यासु विरक्त:' इस न्याय से स्वकान्ता विषयिणी रति मात्र का सामाजिक में होना आवश्यक भी नहीं है। यदि सर्वसाधारण या सर्वसम्बद्ध रति का विभावन स्वीकार करें तो तटस्थता का भाव होगा, रसनीयता नहीं होगी। यदि आवेग की उद्दामता के कारण रसनीयता होगी तो भी नियतिनिष्ठ सुख की भाँति लौकिक कामित्व निश्चित है। इसलिए

आचार्य ने प्रमिति में ऐक्य की पुष्टि की है। प्रमिति के ऐक्य में अनियत निष्ठता होती है, क्योंकि उस ऐक्य की कारणसामग्री विभावादि में अनियतनिष्ठता है। अनियतनिष्ठ स्थायी सर्वसहृदय, संवित् रूप हो सकता है। स्पष्ट है कि जिस प्रमेय (स्थायीरति) की प्रमिति का साधारणीकरण होता है वह स्वयं रति की ऐसी अवस्था है, जो ज्ञान मात्र होती है, एकघनवृत्तिरूप होती है। यहां संकेतकार की पंक्तियाँ स्मरणीय हैं :

> *सर्वसाधारणप्रतीतौ ताटस्थ्यमेव न रसनीयत्वम्। रसनीयतायामपि सुखवत् नियतनिष्ठत्वे कामित्वमेव स्यात्। तस्मात् अनियतनिष्ठत्वेन सर्वप्रमातृणां यो रसनीयः स सर्वप्रमातृतावलम्बनेनैव रस्यते। अत एव रङ्गमण्डपान्तःप्रविष्टानां सकलानामपि हृदयसंवादभाक्त्वम् उच्यते।।* (*काव्यप्रकाश उल्लास* 4, *संकेत*)

इस प्रकार की अनियतता केवल व्यंग्य-व्यञ्जक शब्दार्थ ही प्रकाशित कर सकते हैं। मात्र व्यञ्जन या प्रकाशन का ही सामर्थ्य है कि वह ज्ञान रूप होने के कारण नियतता का परित्याग कर अभिव्यक्ति को देश-काल, सम्बन्ध-सम्बन्धि आदि से मुक्त, प्रतीतिरूप में सहृदय-संवाद या प्रमिति के ऐक्य में पर्यवसित करा सकता है, तथा वही पूर्ण एवं निर्भ्रान्त साधारणीकरण होगा।

आचार्य के इस काव्यदर्शन के आलोक में साधारणीकरण के विषय में उठाई गई वे सभी विप्रतिपत्तियाँ समाहित हो जाती हैं, जिन्हें गत कई दशकों से विभिन्न विद्वानों ने उठाया है तथा उनका विश्लेषण लौकिक कार्यकारण सिद्धान्तों या लौकिक मनोरचना एवं व्यापार के आधार पर किया है।

संदर्भ

1. *अभिनवभारती*, भाग एक, पृष्ठ 277, बड़ौदा संस्करण, 1956
2. वही, पृष्ठ 278 एवं आगे। काव्यमाला संस्करण
3. *रसगंगाधर*, प्रथम आनन
4. *काव्यप्रकाश*, सोलह टीकाओं के साथ, भाग दो, दिल्ली संस्करण, 1999
5. वही
6. इनके विचारों को विस्तृत रूप से, *चिन्तामणि*, भाग एक, 'साधारणीकरण एवं उक्तिवैचित्र्यवाद' *रस-सिद्धान्त*-नगेन्द्र, *सहृदय एवं साधारणीकरण*-डा. राममूर्ति त्रिपाठी, आदि में देखें।
7. *काव्यप्रकाश निदर्शन*, आनन्दराजानक, डॉ. गयाचरण त्रिपाठी द्वारा सम्पादित (प्रकाशकाधीन) में उद्धृत 'तत्त्वपरीक्षा'
8. वही, प्रथम उल्लास, उपोद्घात।
9. *अभिनवभारती*, भाग एक, पृष्ठ 277
10. दृश्यश्रव्योस्तु बहुतरसाधारण्योपपत्तिः, वही, अध्याय 1, पृष्ठ 11

11. *अभिनवभारती*, भाग एक, पृष्ठ 299
12. वही, पृष्ठ 341
13. वही, पृष्ठ 288
14. वही, पृष्ठ 280
15. वही, पृष्ठ 279
16. वही, पृष्ठ 284
17. वही,
18. वही, पृष्ठ 281
19. *नाट्यशास्त्र*, अध्याय 5
20. *अभिनवभारती*, भाग एक, पृष्ठ 281
21. वही, पृष्ठ 281
22. सर्वा चेयं प्रतिमयः प्रत्यक्षपरा 'न्यायसूत्र भाग 1-3, *अभिनवभारती*, पृष्ठ 281 में उद्धृत
23. वही
24. वही
25. वही, पृष्ठ 282
26. वही, पृष्ठ 285
27. वही पृष्ठ 280
28. *तन्त्रालोक*, 9.30, 31 जयरथकृत टीका
29. *अभिनवभारती*, पृष्ठ 285
30. *तन्त्रालोक*, 10.75
31. वही, 10.76
32. वही, 10,85 जयरथकृत टीका
33. वही, 10.86 टीका
34. *ध्वन्यालोक* लोचन, पृष्ठ 190, चौखम्बा संस्करण
35. *तन्त्रालोक*, 10.79-81
36. वही, 10.86 टीका
37. वही, 10.87 टीका
38. चास्य स्वातन्त्रया शक्तिः संकोचशलिनी सैव। प्रत्यभिज्ञाहृदयकारिका
39. *पराप्रावेशिका*, पृष्ठ 9
40. वही
41. स्वातन्त्र्यं चास्य भेदनं भेदिते च अन्तरनुसन्धानेन अभेदनम्।।
    ईश्वरप्रत्यभिज्ञाविमर्शिनी, भाग 1, पृष्ठ 31
    प्रकाशस्य परदशायां चमत्कारात्मयोर्विमर्शस्तदेव स्वातन्त्र्यम्।
    ईश्वर प्रत्यभिज्ञाविवृत्तिविमर्शिनी भाग 3, पृष्ठ 25
42. *अभिनवभारती* भाग एक, पृष्ठ 287, *ईश्वरप्रत्यभिज्ञाविवृत्ति* भाग 1, पृष्ठ 194
43. *तन्त्रालोक*, 8.12 विवेक

44. वही, 8.14 विवेक
45. *ईश्वरप्रत्यभिज्ञाविवृत्तिविमर्शिनी*, भाग 3, पृष्ठ 25
46. चमत्कारश्चित्तवृत्तिविस्ताररूपो विस्मयापरपर्यायः।/साहित्यदर्पण, 3.2
47. *अभिनवभारती*, भाग एक, पृष्ठ 280
48. *तन्त्रालोक*, 2.23
49. *अभिनवभारती*, भाग एक, पृष्ठ 280
50. द्रष्टव्य-*काव्यप्रकाश विस्तारिका* एवं *काव्यप्रदीप*
51. विस्तृत विवेचन देखें-*ईश्वरप्रत्यभिज्ञाकारिका*, 2.3.13 पर विमर्शिनी एवं तिष्ठतिविमर्शिनी
52. *तन्त्रालोक*, 1.27, सम्बन्धसिद्ध, पृष्ठ 5

19

रसानुभूति प्रतिभान के रूप में

नवजीवन रस्तोगी

रसानुभूति की अपनी अवधारणा को समझाने के लिए अभिनवगुप्त अनेक पारिभाषिक शब्दों का प्रयोग करते हैं, जैसे, आस्वाद, संविद्विश्रान्ति, रसना, चमत्कार, भोग, चर्वणा इत्यादि।[1] इतने शब्दों का प्रयोग करने के पीछे दो कारण जान पड़ते हैं। एक तो ऐतिहासिक अपने से पूर्व से चली आ रही समग्र सौन्दर्यशास्त्रीय परम्परा को उसकी विविधता में समेट लेना चाहते हैं। दूसरे कारण का संबंध रस की, प्रक्रिया और स्वरूप दोनों ही पक्षों को लेकर, बहुआयामी और अत्यन्त व्यापक प्रकृति से है जिसको एक निश्चित पारिभाषिक अभिधान से बांधना कठिन है। अभिनवगुप्त की समग्रतावादी दृष्टि के अनुसार इस प्रकार का, प्रक्रिया और स्वरूप में विभाजन आरोपित है। सम्भवतः यही कारण है कि भरत के प्रसिद्ध रस-सूत्र, जो कि आपाततः सभी दृष्टियों से एक प्रक्रिया सूत्र है, को अपनी विश्रुत टीका *अभिनवभारती* की अवतरणिका में लक्षणसूत्र[2] के नाम से प्रस्तुत करते हैं और रसना तथा रस को रस के समग्रतामूलक प्रत्यय के अविच्छेद्य घटक मानते हैं। इस लेख में हमारा प्रयोजन बहुत सीमित है। रस के सर्वांगीण स्वरूप पर विचार न कर रसानुभूति के लिए प्रयुक्त पारिभाषिकपर्यायों में से एक 'प्रतिभान' का हम अध्ययन करेंगे और यह देखने की चेष्टा करेंगे कि प्रतिभानात्मकता से रसानुभूति का कौन-सा पक्ष उजागर होता है।

अभिनवगुप्त के प्रतिभानपरक प्रकृत विवेचन को संदर्भ मिला है कालिदास के प्रसिद्ध श्लोक "रम्याणि वीक्ष्य" (*अभि. शा.* 5. 2) पर उनकी टिप्पणियों में। रानी हंसपदिका के गीत को सुनकर जनमी दुष्यन्त की मानसिक आकुलता का कलात्मक

स्वरूप क्या है, उसके विचारार्थ अभिनवगुप्त कालिदास की इन पंक्तियों को उद्धृत करते है। अत: सर्वप्रथम हम अभिनवगुप्त की प्रतिभान सम्बन्धी अवधारणा का अनुशीलन करेंगे। तदनन्तर ये देखने का प्रयास करेंगे कि इन पंक्तियों में कालिदास की वस्तुनिष्ठ स्थिति क्या है, साथ ही इन पंक्तियों का दोहन करने में अभिनवगुप्त के तर्क और निहितार्थ क्या हैं ? हम यह भी देखेंगे कि कालिदास के श्लोक से रस-सन्दर्भ के अन्य बिन्दुओं पर, अभिनवगुप्त के अन्य ग्रन्थों के आलोक में, क्या प्रकाश प्रड़ता है?

अभिनवभारती में अभिनवगुप्त ने प्रतिभान शब्द का प्रयोग साक्षात्कारात्मक प्रतीति के अर्थ में किया है।[3] यद्यपि संदृब्ध स्थल पर साक्षात्कारात्मक स्मृति के पर्याय रूप में इसका विनियोग हुआ है, पर आवश्यक नहीं है कि यह प्रतीति स्मृतिरूप ही हो। यह प्रत्यक्षात्मक, मानस अध्यवसायरूप या स्मृतिरूप कोई भी प्रतीति हो सकती है। स्मृति, संकल्प, अध्यवसाय आदि तार्किक विधाओं का नाम धारण करती हुई भी अपनी साक्षात्कारात्मकता के कारण यह उनसे भिन्न हो सकती है।[4] कलानुभूति के अधिकारी अर्थात् सहृदय की विशेषता को बताने के लिए अभिनवगुप्त फिर से इस शब्द का प्रयोग करते हैं।[5] निर्मल प्रतिभान से सम्पन्न सहृदय नाट्य का अधिकारी है। इसी अर्थ में नाट्याचार्यो की विशेषता के रूप में प्रतिभान शब्द का प्रयोग किया गया है। कवि-हृदय को तत्क्षण समझ लेना नाट्याचार्य की पहचान है।[6] आपातत: एक जैसे लगने पर भी ऊपर के दोनों प्रयोगों में अंतर है। पहला प्रतिभान विशुद्ध साक्षात्कारात्मक अनुभूति के अर्थ में है जबकि शेष दोनों प्रयोग प्रतिभा के उस रूप को द्योतित करते हैं, जिसे परम्परा में भावयित्री प्रतिभा कहा गया है।

अभिनवगुप्त ने भावक के साहाय्य को द्योतन अर्थात् व्यञ्जना का प्राण कहा है।[7] इस बात को प्रकारान्तर से पुष्ट करते हुए अभिनवगुप्त का मानना है कि भावक की प्रतिभा जब तक नट द्वारा अभिनीयमान चरित्र के स्वरूप में विश्रान्त नहीं होती तब तक साधारणीकरण संभव नहीं होता।[8] स्वगत और परगत देश-काल आदि की उपाधियों के अपाकरण के लिए ही भरत पूर्वरंग आदि का विधान करते हैं। रसनात्मक विघ्नविनिर्मुक्त प्रतीति के ग्राह्य विषय को रस माना गया है और अभिनवगुप्त द्वारा इस प्रसंग में प्रतिपादित विघ्नों में से यह दूसरा विघ्न है, जिसका सीधा सम्बन्ध भावक से बताया गया है। रस-व्यञ्जना, काव्य-सर्जना या अपूर्व अर्थ के निर्माण की शक्ति के रूप में अभिनवगुप्त ने प्रतिभा का उल्लेख शतश: किया है।[9] प्रतिभा का यह वह पक्ष है जो परम्परा में कारयित्री के नाम से जाना जाता है पर महत्त्वपूर्ण होते हुए भी रसानुभूति के स्वरूपानुशीलन में यह हमारे लिए बहुत साम्प्रतिक नहीं है।

रस-सूत्र के व्याख्या-प्रसंग से अभिनवगुप्त ने प्रतिभान का अनेक संदर्भो में प्रयोग किया है और सन्दर्भ परिवर्तन से प्रतिभान के अर्थ बदलते गए हैं। यहां तक कि अनेक अर्थ आपातत: विरोधी लगते हैं। अत: एक पारिभाषिक तौर पर रसानुभूति की

पारिभाषिक अवधारणा के रूप में उसका स्वरूप स्थिर करना आवश्यक होगा। भट्टनायक के मत की आलोचना करते हुए अभिनवगुप्त ने रसना और प्रतिभान को दो भिन्न प्रतीतियों के रूप में लिया है। प्रतीति की दृष्टि से एकरूपता होने पर भी उपायभेद प्रतीतिवैलक्षण्य का कारण बनता है।[10] *लोचन* में अभिनवगुप्त इसी बात को सन्दर्भ-भेद से लगभग इन्हीं शब्दों में दुहराते हैं और काव्यार्थ या काव्यानुभूति का नियामक चर्वणा या भोग को मानते हैं और प्रतिभानकृत प्रतीति को उपायभेद के आधार पर इससे भिन्न बताते हैं।[11] यहाँ भेद का कारण है हृदयसंवाद से उपकृत विभावादि सामग्री की उपायता का लोकोत्तर होना। इस सन्दर्भ को आगे बढ़ाते हुए अभिनवगुप्त दर्शन-भेद से शब्द-वृत्ति के रूप में व्यञ्जना और प्रतिभा या अर्थ रूप में व्यंग्य और प्रतिभा में अन्तर करते हैं। रस-सूत्र पर अपनी टीका में अपने मत के उपोद्घात में ही रस को काव्यार्थ रूप से प्रस्तुत करते हुए अभिनवगुप्त काव्यार्थ को शब्दार्थ से विलक्षण या शब्दशरीरोत्तीर्ण मानते हैं। जीवन के सामान्य प्रसंगों में शब्द से होने वाले अर्थ-बोध और काव्य से होने वाले अर्थ-बोध अर्थात् रस-बोध में प्रक्रियागत साम्य है। इस प्रक्रिया के तीन चरण हैं (1) श्रोता का व्यक्तिगत शाब्दिक अर्थ-बोध, (2) देश और काल के तिरस्कार द्वारा सामान्यीकृत बोध और (3) तत्पश्चात् आत्म-संक्रमण रूप-बोध। प्रक्रिया की एकरूपता के बावजूद काव्यार्थ और अन्यत्र शब्दार्थ का भेद अधिकारी की पात्रता के कारण होता है और शाब्दी होने पर भी काव्य-प्रतीति अनुभूतिरूप या दूसरे शब्दों में शब्द या वाक्य के शाब्दिक अर्थ-ग्रहण के उपरान्त मानस साक्षात्कार का रूप लेती है। इस सन्दर्भ में इस शब्दशरीरोत्तीर्णा साधारणी करणात्मिका संक्रान्तिस्वभावा प्रतीति को दर्शन-भेद से प्रतिभा, भावना, विधि, नियोग आदि भिन्न-भिन्न आख्याओं से पुकारा गया है।[12]

ऐसा लगता है कि ठीक ऊपर जिस प्रतिभा का उल्लेख किया गया है उसका सम्बन्ध व्याकरणदर्शन से है। इस सम्भावना को बल मिलता है अभिनवगुप्त के प्रौढ़ दार्शनिक ग्रन्थ *ईश्वरप्रत्याभिज्ञाविवृतिविमर्शिनी* से जहाँ तीन विभिन्न सन्दर्भों में प्रतिभा या प्रतिभा प्रमाण का सम्बन्ध अन्यों से जोड़ा गया है। एक प्रसंग है स्वभावहेतु और कार्यहेतु में विशेषण के ग्रहण का।[13] दूसरा है कार्यकारणभाव की सिद्धि में सार्वत्रिकता के निश्चय का[14] और तीसरा है युक्ति की परिभाषा का।[15] पहले मत को उन्होंने ''गरै:'' से जोड़ा है। दूसरे में अन्य मतों से अपना अन्तर बताते हुए प्रत्यक्षानुलम्भपंचक की स्वतन्त्र आत्मतत्त्व में विश्रान्ति को ही अपने यहां प्रभविष्णु माना है और तीसरे में भर्तृहरि की ''समाधाननैर्मल्यात्मिका प्रतिभा'' की अपेक्षा प्रत्यभिज्ञा दर्शन में प्रमाणयोजनात्मक प्रमातृस्वातन्त्र्य को ही युक्ति माना है।

प्रतिभा और प्रतिभान के लोकादृत प्रयोगों से अलग करते हुए रसप्रतीति को प्रतिभान संज्ञा से निरूपित करने में अभिनवगुप्त का मन्तव्य क्या है, इसका अध्ययन साम्प्रतिक होगा।

रसानुभूति को प्रतिभान से समीकृत कर अभिनवगुप्त हमें अपने दर्शन के केन्द्र में उसकी सारी ऐतिहासिक परिणतियों के साथ प्रतिष्ठित कर देते हैं और इसका दूरगामी प्रभाव उनके कलाचिन्तन के विभिन्न पक्षों पर दिखाई पड़ता है। रस की अवधारणा के दो आयाम हैं, वह अनुभूति भी है और अनुभूति का विषय भी। अनुभूति के रूप में वह अव्यवहित मानस प्रतीति है और विषय के रूप में वह निर्विघ्न प्रतीति का ग्राह्य है। प्रतीति की निर्विघ्नता का आशय है सुख व दु:ख से जन्म लेने वाली ग्रहण और त्याग की इच्छा से मुक्त होना। दूसरे शब्दों में, रसानुभूति विघ्नरहित साक्षात्कारकल्प अनुभूति है और उस प्रतीति से ग्राह्य चित्तवृत्ति भी रस है। अभिनवगुप्त के ये निष्कर्ष प्रतिभान की उनकी अपनी अवधारणा की देन हैं। प्रतिभान केवल अनुभूति और अनुभाव्य की ही व्याख्या नहीं करता, वह अनुभाविता के स्वरूप को भी परिभाषित करता है। इसीलिए सामाजिक को विमल प्रतिभान से संपन्न कहा गया है। इसका अर्थ यह है कि सामाजिक का हृदय स्वच्छ दर्पण जैसा है और इस स्वच्छता के कारण उसका मनोदर्पण वर्णनीय को प्रतिबिम्बित करता हुआ उससे एक रूप होने की क्षमता रखता है। सामाजिक या अधिकारी को सहृदय इसीलिए कहा जाता है कि वह कविहृदय के साथ सहज संवाद की स्थिति में निरन्तर रहता है।[16]

अभिनव के दार्शनिक ग्रन्थों, विशेषत: *तंत्रालोक*, *ईश्वरप्रत्यभिज्ञाविमर्शिनी* और *ईश्वरप्रत्यभिज्ञाविवृत्तिविमर्शिनी*, में प्रतिभान की धारणा के साथ अन्य अवधारणाओं के अनेक समीकरण मिलते हैं, जिनमें चार महत्त्वपूर्ण हैं– पहला है वाक् के साथ, दूसरा है प्रकाश के साथ, तीसरा है महेश्वर या माहेश्वर के साथ और चौथा है प्रत्यभिज्ञा के साथ।

पहले समीकरण में हम देखते हैं कि परा वाक् को प्रतिभा कहा गया है और कवि को अपूर्व काव्यार्थ-सृष्टि में समर्थ[17] इसलिए माना गया है कि वाक् का अर्थ ही है समस्त विश्व को[18] और स्वरूप को अभिव्यक्त कर सकने की सामर्थ्य।[19] यहाँ अनजाने ही हम एक अवान्तर समीकरण में प्रवेश कर जाते हैं और वह है प्रतिभान और विमर्श का। कवि की सृष्टि प्रत्यय-सृष्टि है और सामाजिक की अनुभूति है शब्द-सृष्टि का आत्म-विमर्शन, अपने में अपरिच्छिन्नतया प्रकाशन।[20] अत: कारयित्री और भावयित्री का जो भेद हमने ऊपर देखा है वह सिर्फ आरोपित सिद्ध होता है क्योंकि दोनों के वाग्रूप होने का निहितार्थ है दोनों में मूल तत्त्व की अन्विति का होना। *मालिनीविजयोत्तरतंत्र* में रुद्रशक्ति के समावेश के अनेक चिह्नों में एक चिह्न कवित्व शक्ति का उदय भी है। यहां महत्त्वपूर्ण बात यह है कि यह कवित्व मध्य तीव्र शक्तिपात के फलस्वरूप उदित माना गया है और शक्तिपात का कारण प्रतिभा का उदय बताया गया है। परमेश्वर के शक्तिपात से जब यह संकोच समाप्त हो जाता है तो प्रमाता का अपना सहज स्वभाव प्रकट हो उठता है।[21] कलात्मक संदर्भ की भाषा में कहा जा सकता

है कि कवित्व अर्थात् काव्य-कर्तृत्व असंकुचित प्रमाता की पहचान है। जिनकी बुद्धि या प्रतिभा बन्धनों से मुक्त हो चुकी है, उनकी सहज अभिव्यक्ति काव्य है। प्रतिभा के उदय का अर्थ है सारे पदार्थों के वास्तविक तत्त्व का ज्ञान, जिसके फलस्वरूप साधक शिव की सत्ता में अर्थात् अपने में ही विश्रान्त हो जाता है और दर्पण में पड़ने वाली छाया की भाँति बिम्ब और प्रतिबिम्ब दोनों ही रूपों में अन्दर और बाहर शिव को ही देखता है अर्थात् विश्व को शिवैकघन रूप से देखता है। हेय ओर उपादेय दोनों के रहस्य से परिचित होने के कारण वह केवल अपने आत्मसंवेदन में निमग्न रहता है।[22]

सामान्यत: वाचक शब्द या संकेत मायीय वर्णो से बनते हैं, इसलिए उनका सामर्थ्य एक-एक विषय के लिए नियत होता है। पर संकेत-निरपेक्ष होने के कारण सारे वर्ण वस्तुत: प्रमारूप हैं। उच्छलित होती हुई प्रमारूप परा संवित्ति में विश्रान्ति का स्वाद लेने वाले वर्णों में सारे पदार्थों के आमर्शन और अभिधान का सामर्थ्य है। संकेत निरपेक्ष होने के कारण ही ये प्रमा कहलाते हैं।[23] वर्णों की प्रमारूपता के समान रूप से उपलब्ध होने पर भी कोई तो महाकाव्य की रचना कर डालता है और कोई एक वाक्य भी नहीं लिख सकता। प्रमाताओं के इस भेद का कारण है निज प्रमा पर पड़ा हुआ अनवधान का आवरण। जैसे-जैसे स्वाभाविक प्रमाबोध का उन्मेष बढ़ता जाता है वैसे ही वैसे व्यक्ति की सर्जनात्मकता में उत्तरोत्तर चमत्कार दिखाई पड़ने लगता है।[24]

वाक् (या विमर्श) के बाद प्रतिभान का दूसरा समीकरण है प्रकाश की धारणा के साथ। काश्मीर शैव दर्शन की आधारभूत प्रवृत्ति है सत् को प्रकाश और विमर्श को एक समग्र के रूप में परिभाषित करने की ओर। दूसरे को प्रतिबिम्बित कर सकना और प्रतिबिम्बित भावराशि के साथ अपने को एकाकार कर सकना प्रकाश का पारिभाषिक स्वभाव है।[25]

यही स्वभाव सहृदय का बताया गया है, श्रवणीय या वर्णनीय के साथ तन्मयीभवन योग्यता से युक्त होना।[26] इस प्रतिबिम्बन-सामर्थ्य के मूल में है प्रकाश की सीमातीत निर्मलता। स्वच्छता का अर्थ है अपने स्वरूप को भासित किए बिना विश्व को अपने से एकात्मतया भासित कर सकना।[27] या, अपने स्वरूप को छोड़े बगैर भिन्न वस्तु को अपने से अभिन्नतया दिखा सकना।[28]

परन्तु यह प्रकाश का मुख्य स्वभाव नहीं है। मुख्य स्वभाव है विमर्शन कर सकना।[29] प्रतिभा का स्वरूप है प्रतिभान-भान को प्रतिभासित कर सकना।[30] जैसा हम देख चुके हैं केवल भासित कर सकने की क्षमता ही नहीं, भासित का भावन कर सकने की क्षमता भी प्रतिभा है। ''घड़ा दिखाई पड़ता है'' इसका संबंध विषय से है, पर यह वाक्य तब तक सार्थकतया बोधगम्य नहीं होता जब तक कि ''घड़ा मुझे दीखता है या मुझे भासित होता है'' इस रूप में प्रमातृविश्रान्त होकर भासित नहीं होता।

त्रिक दर्शन की परमार्थ-मीमांसा में परमशिव और विश्व का सम्बन्ध ठीक वैसा ही है, जैसे दर्पण और उसमें प्रतिबिम्बित बाह्य जगत् का।[31]

एक सूक्ष्म अन्तर यह है कि दर्पण में जहां बिम्ब बाह्य होता है, परमशिव और कला में आत्मस्वातन्त्र्य से घनीभूत चेतना ही बिम्बवत् भासित होती है और संविद्दर्पण में होती है।[32] कला चिन्तन के सन्दर्भ में हम इसके निहितार्थ तक पहुंचते हैं प्रकाश और प्रतिभान के समीकरण द्वारा। सहृदय का चित्त एक निर्मल दर्पण की भांति है, जो अनुभव विषय को स्फुट और तात्कालिक रूप से भासित करने में समर्थ है। सहृदयता का अर्थ है अनुभव के केन्द्र तक पहुँचना और मनोमुकुर में अर्पित विषय-सामग्री से तादात्म्य कर सकना। इसका परिणाम है रसानुभूति में एक प्रकार की साक्षात्कारात्मकता या अव्यवहितता का उदय।

इस बिम्ब-प्रतिबिम्बभाव का एक आयाम और भी है। प्रेक्षागार या अन्यत्र जहां अनेक सामाजिक नाट्य या वृत्त का आनन्द लेते हैं वहाँ विकस्वर संवित् के कारण आनंद की मात्रा बहुत बढ़ जाती है। एक की बुद्धि दूसरे में प्रतिबिम्बित होकर वैसे ही विकसित होती है, जैसे एक स्थल पर अनेक दर्पण होने से पारस्परिक प्रतिबिम्बन से दीप्त होकर प्रकाश अनायास बढ़ जाता है।[33] यद्यपि आनन्दमग्न हर एक की अपनी संवित्ति अलग है फिर भी सर्वतन्मयता का फल यह होता है कि नृत्तादि की प्रेक्षा के अवसर पर वह पूर्णानन्द का आस्वादन करती है।[34] विकस्वर सौन्दर्यानुभूति में बिम्ब-प्रतिबिम्बभाव की प्रवृत्ति दो प्रकार से होती है। सामान्य प्रकार तो है जो विषय और विषयी अर्थात् प्रमाता और कलावस्तु के बीच घटित होता है। विशेष प्रकार है जो विषयी और विषयी के मध्य परस्पर संक्रमण से घटित होता है। दूसरा कारण है आनन्दात्मक संवित् का निष्प्रतिघ (अर्थात् अबाधित या निर्विघ्न) होना। यह संभव होता है उपयोगितामूलक और स्वार्थमूलक दृष्टि के परिहार द्वारा। जब स्वार्थ नहीं रहा तो हानादान बुद्धि भी नहीं रहती, फलतः जलन, निन्दा आदि संकोच के कारणों के हट जाने पर चेतना में केवल आनन्द का ही योग रहता है।[35] निष्प्रतिघत्व का दूसरा आधार है विजातीयता का परिहार। जैसे ऊंचे-नीचे धरातल में हाथ फेरने पर वस्तु का समरस प्रत्यक्ष नहीं होता, वैसे ही ईर्ष्यादि विजातीय अंशों के रहने पर संवित् में तन्मयता नहीं आती।[36] निष्प्रतिघ की यह परिभाषा अभिनवगुप्तकृत नैर्गल्य, जो कि प्रकाश का प्राण है, की परिभाषा की याद दिलाती है, विजातीय का अभाव और अत्यन्त निविड सजातीय के साथ एक मात्र संगति[37] अर्थात् समतल भाव से निरन्तर अवस्थित रहने के कारण ऊंच-नीच के परिहारपूर्वक आत्मसंहति ही निर्मलता है।[38] दूसरे शब्दों में, प्रकाशात्मक निर्मल संवित् ही विकस्वर होती है।

इसका दूसरा फलितार्थ यह होता है कि कलानुभूति, जिसका *अभिनवभारती* में वीतविघ्नरसानुभूति के रूप में पल्लवन किया गया है, के बीज प्रकाश की धारणा में अन्तर्गर्भित हैं। इस प्रतीति में, जैसा कि हमने विस्तार में देखा है, विजातीय कलाविघ्नों का अभाव और आनन्द की एकघनता ही रसचर्वणा है।

शब्दश: उद्घोष के साथ प्रतिभान के जिस समीकरण का आश्रय लिया गया है वह है महेश्वर या प्रत्यभिज्ञा-प्रतिपादित चरम सत् और परम प्रमाता के साथ।[39] आपातत: एक विरोधाभासी शब्दावली का आश्रय लेते हुए सार्वजनीन अनुभव में उपलभ्यमान विभिन्न विषयों के क्रम से रूपित प्रतिभा और अक्रम, अनन्त, चिद्रूप महेश्वर दोनों में आन्तरिक और पारमार्थिक एकता का घोर अनुसन्धान किया गया है। बाह्य अनुभव जगत् में हमारे सारे अनुभव क्रमिक होते हैं और इसकी क्रमरूपता की व्याख्या कल्पित प्रमाता की अपेक्षा से की जा सकती है, परन्तु प्रश्न है कि विशुद्ध ज्ञानात्मक स्थिति में अनुभूयमान क्रम की व्याख्या कैसे की जाए? ज्ञान के विभिन्न प्रकारों में ज्ञान के अंदर देश और काल न होने के कारण, प्रत्यक्ष और स्मृति या अनादिवासनाओं में अभिव्यक्ति को लेकर पाए जाने वाले क्रम की व्याख्या के लिए उत्पल और अभिनव प्रतिभान का आश्रय लेते है। उनके अनुसार यद्यपि ''प्रतिभाति घट:'' आदि ज्ञान आपातत: विषयोपश्लिष्ट मालूम पड़ते हैं तथापि वस्तुत: यह विषय का अपना रूप न होकर ज्ञान का ही एक भासन प्रकार है जो प्रमातृविश्रान्त होकर ही अर्थ ग्रहण करता है। प्रतिभा का स्वभाव है कि दैशिक और कालिक क्रमों के प्रतिबिम्बतया उपरक्त होकर भी स्वरूपत: अक्रम है और परम प्रमाता से एक वपु है। प्रतिभा को पुल्लिग में महेश्वर कहा जाने का कारण है बोधों के अधिष्ठान रूप माहेश्वर्य और प्रमातृत्व से प्रतिभा का उपचित या पुष्ट होना।[40]

काव्यानुभूति के क्षेत्र में इसका अर्थ है कि बिना बाह्य उपादान के काव्य-सर्जना का और रस-संवेदना का भावन-सामर्थ्य। माहेश्वर्य और प्रमातृत्व की शाब्दिक व्यंजना यही है। कवि सृष्टि देश-काल आदि के परिच्छेद से रहित संवित्स्वभाव है और उसके अंदर भासित होने वाला समस्त देश, काल गत वैचित्र्य कवि/सहृदय के स्वातन्त्र्य से संविद्रूप में उद्गत होता है। आंतरिक क्रम से रूपित संवित्-स्वभावा यह प्रतिभा ही समग्र रस व्यापार का आश्रय है और तद्रूप में वही प्रमाता है। यह हमारे आत्मसंवेदन से प्रमाणित है।[41]

चौथा महत्त्वपूर्ण समीकरण है प्रतिभान और प्रत्यभिज्ञान का। अभिनवगुप्त की दृष्टि में हमारा सारा ज्ञान प्रत्यभिज्ञानात्मक है। शक्ति के आविष्करण द्वारा शक्तिमान् की प्राप्ति सारे प्रत्यभिज्ञा व्यापार का लक्ष्य है। लोक जीवन में अतीत का ज्ञान जब पलटकर भासमान बनता है तब उस ज्ञान को हम प्रत्यभिज्ञानात्मक कहते हैं। वैसे ही, परमार्थ जीवन में महेश्वर की प्रत्यभिज्ञा का अर्थ है, ''प्रतीपम् आत्माभिमुख्येन ज्ञानं प्रकाश:''। अर्थात् स्वात्मरूप महेश्वर का अविच्छिन्न भासन जब उसी की शक्ति से विच्छिन्न-सा लगता है उस समय उस शक्ति के आविष्करण द्वारा शक्तिमान् के अनुसन्धान की यात्र प्रत्यभिज्ञानमयी यात्र का आकार ग्रहण करता है। इसे भी प्रतिभान की शब्दावली में व्यक्त किया गया है।[42] दार्शनिक दृष्टि से यह सारा विषयोल्लेखन

वस्तुधर्म की भांति हमारे अनुभव का विषय बनता है और फिर प्रमाता की ओर उन्मुख होकर प्रमातृ-विश्रान्त या प्रमात्रश्रित होकर प्रमातृधर्मतया उन्मेवित होता है। प्रतिभा और महेश्वर के उपरि प्रतिपादित एकात्मतानुसंधान के द्वारा इसी तथ्य को हृदयंगम कराने की चेष्टा की जाती है। इसके अतिरिक्त प्रतिभान कहकर इस प्रत्यभिज्ञानात्मक बोध की साक्षात्कार स्वभावता को भी उजागर किया गया है।[43] कला-संदर्भ में नाट्यवस्तु, काव्यवस्तु या कलावस्तु जो विभावादि विषय-सामग्री के रूप में हमारे समक्ष आती है वह सहृदय के समक्ष अभिमुखा होती हुई प्रमाता की संवित् में विश्रान्त होती हुई रसानुभूति कहलाती है। प्रत्यभिज्ञान का दूसरा स्तर तब दिखाई देता है जब अनादि वासना के बल से सहृदय सारी व्यक्तिगत उपाधियों का तिरस्कार करता है, विघ्नों के अपसारण द्वारा मल का अपसारण करता हुआ साधारणीकरण के माध्यम से विभावादि से उपस्कृत अपनी ही चित्तवृत्ति का आस्वादन करता है। इस प्रकार साधारणीकरण की पूरी प्रक्रिया आत्मजातीय स्वरूपानुसन्धान तथा सांस्कृतिक अवचेतन के आत्म-लाभ की ही प्रक्रिया है। इस सन्दर्भ में रसानुभूति के लिए ''संविद्विश्रान्ति'' का प्रयोग व्यष्टि और समष्टि दोनों स्तरों पर, बड़ा अन्वर्थ है।

अब हम अपने लेख के दूसरे अंश की ओर आते हैं। यहां स्मरण दिलाना अनवसर न होगा कि अभिनवगुप्त ने कालिदास के प्रसिद्ध श्लोक ''रम्याणि वीक्ष्य मधुरांश्च निशम्य शब्दान्''[44] की व्याख्या के व्याज से रस प्रतीति की प्रतिभारूपता को प्रतिष्ठित करने का सुविचारित और मौलिक उद्यम किया है। कलाशास्त्रियों को यह श्लोक अत्यन्त प्रिय रहा है और भारतीय कला सिद्धान्त के स्वरूपोन्मेष में उन्होंने इसका प्रभूत उपयोग किया है।[45] स्वयं कालिदास को भी इस श्लोक की सौन्दर्य शास्त्रीय सम्भावनाओं का भरपूर आभास है। *अभिनवभारती* में दो स्थलों पर और *ईश्वरप्रत्यभिज्ञाविवृत्तिविमर्शिनी* में एक स्थल पर अभिनवगुप्त इसे उद्धृत करते हैं।[46] कहना न होगा कि ये तीनों सन्दर्भ या तो रसानुभूति से संबद्ध है या रसाभिव्यक्ति से।

अभिनवगुप्त की व्याख्याओं के आलोक में हम इस श्लोक की प्रासंगिकता और अर्थवत्ता का विश्लेषण करेंगे।

श्लोक के संदर्भ से लगभग हम सभी परिचित हैं। रानी हंसपदिका संगीतशाला में वीणा गीत गा रही हैं। ताल और लय से शुद्ध गीत की ओर विदूषक राजा का ध्यान खींचता है।[47] राजा ध्यान से सुनता है।[48] रानी स्वविस्मृति के लिए दुष्यन्त को उलाहना दे रही है। गीत प्रीति, संगीत और भावना में पगा हुआ है। प्रशंसा में राजा के उद्गार निकल पड़ते हैं ''अहो रागपरिवाहिणी गीतिः''। विदूषक चिढ़ाता है कि क्या इसका अभिप्राय समझ रहे हो। राजा कहता है कि हाँ हमने एक बार प्रेम किया था। रानी वसुमती उसी को लेकर मुझे उपालम्भ दे रही है। लज्जित राजा रानी को मनाने के लिए माधव्य को उसके पास भेजता है। माधव्य के जाते ही राजा अत्यन्त उत्कण्ठित हो उठता

है। राजा अपने से पूछता है कि ऐसी क्या बात है कि गीत का अर्थ सुनकर मैं अकारण उन्मत्त हो उठा हूं जबकि मेरा कोई भी प्रिय जन मुझसे बिछड़ा नहीं है। क्योंकि मीठे शब्द और सुन्दर दृश्यों से प्रसन्नता के स्थान पर आकुलता जन्म ले रही है। और फिर अपने को समझाता है कि सुन्दर पदार्थों को देखकर और मीठे बोल सुनकर सुखी मनुष्य भी जो बेचैन हो उठता है पहले से अनजानी बात को मन से याद करता है। इसका कारण यह जान पड़ता है कि दूसरे जन्म की मैत्री हृदय में वासना रूप से आकर स्थिर हो गयी है।[49]

कालिदास के इस श्लोक में काव्यार्थ बोध में हम निम्नलिखित अवस्थाएं या चरण पाते हैं-

1. औन्मुख्य	माधव्य दुष्यन्त का हंसपदिका के गीत की ओर ध्यान खींचता है।		
2. निर्विकल्पक ऐन्द्रिय प्रत्यक्ष	माधव्य को चुप कराकर राजा ध्यान से गीत सुनता है।		
3. सविकल्पक प्रत्यक्ष			
विषयगत	1.	सौन्दर्यग्राहिणी इन्द्रियों में से श्रवण का प्रयोग : शब्द श्रवण	
	2.	शब्दों की लय-ताल-बद्ध गानरूपता का निश्चय	इन्द्रिय प्रत्यक्ष
	3.	गान की भावतरलता का अभिज्ञान (अहो रागपरिवाहिणी गीतिः)	माध्यस्थ्य विगमन
विषयिगत	1.	गीत के अर्थ का बोध- (शब्दार्थ)	
	2.	प्रणयवंचिता का उपालम्भ (व्यंग्यार्थ)	
4. प्रमाता की व्यक्तिगत प्रतिक्रिया	हंसपदिका को मनाने के लिए माधव्य को भेजना		

5. प्रमाता की रागात्मक प्रतिक्रिया (''राग'' आत्मक चमत्कृति)	ज्ञात कारण के अभाव में दुष्यन्त की उन्मनस्कता	हार्दिक स्पन्दमानता या आनन्दशक्ति
6. पर्युत्सुकता की मन:स्थिति (''अभिलाष''-आत्मक चमत्कृति)	मधुर शब्दों के लौकिक श्रवण का साधारणीकरण	साधारणीकरण
7. काव्यार्थ विमर्श	सुन्दर रूपों के दर्शन और मधुर गीत का श्रवण मन को उत्कंठित करता है	तन्मयीभाव या सहृदयता
8. मूल्य बोध (पूर्वजन्म के सौहृद की स्मरण रूप चर्वणा/प्रत्यक्ष कल्प संवेदन ''औत्सुक्य'' आत्मक चमत्कारिता)	पर्युत्सुकता का चर्वण	आस्वाद या रसानुभूति

अभिनवगुप्त की दृष्टि से जब हम इस उद्धरण पर विचार करते हैं तो हम देखते हैं कि कालिदास के इस श्लोक का उपयोग उन्होंने रसानुभूति की अपनी धारणा को स्पष्ट करने के लिए किया है। रसानुभूति, न उत्पत्ति है, न अनुकृति और न भुक्ति। इन सब मतों को तिरस्कृत कर देने के बाद रस के स्वरूप को बताना उनका दायित्व बन जाता है। *अभिज्ञानशाकुन्तल* के ही एक श्लोक ''ग्रीवाभङ्गाभिरामम्'' का विश्लेषण करते हुए वह रस को काव्यार्थ की शब्दावली में प्रस्तुत करते हैं, जो निर्विघ्न साक्षात् हृदयानुप्रवेशात्मक प्रतीति का विषय है। उस प्रतीति की साक्षात्कारकल्पता के लिए नटादि सामग्री का आश्रय लिया जाता है। सामाजिक की इस निर्विघ्न एकघन प्रतीति को अभिनवगुप्त 'चमत्कार' संज्ञा से अभिहित करते हैं और इससे जन्य शारीरिक विकारों को भी चमत्कार कहते हैं।[50] इस बात को समझाने के लिए अभिनवगुप्त एक प्राकृत गाथा का आश्रय लेते हैं, जिसका तात्पर्य है कि हरि आज भी यह सोच-सोचकर आश्चर्यचकित है कि लक्ष्मी के चन्द्रकला के कंद जैसे सुन्दर अंग समुद्रमन्थन के समय मन्दराचल से पिस क्यों न गये।[51] यहां यह ध्यान देने योग्य बात है कि विष्णु का सोचना या याद करना एक ही बात है। अभिनवगुप्त की दृष्टि में कभी न तृप्त होने वाले भोग

के द्वारा सामाजिक आवेश चमत्कार है। इस दृष्टि से भोग करने वाले सामाजिक, जिसकी बुद्धि पर अद्भुत भोग का स्पन्द पूरी तरह से छा गया है, की अनुभूति चमत्कार है।[52] भले ही वह साक्षात्कारात्मक प्रतीति के रूप में स्फुरित हुई हो या मानस अध्यवसाय, संकल्प या स्मृति के रूप में स्फुरित हुई हो। अपनी इस स्थापना को पुष्ट करने के लिए अभिनवगुप्त ''रम्याणि वीक्ष्य'' को उदाहृत करते हैं। यहाँ ''स्मरति'' पद से जिस स्मृति का संधान किया गया है वह तार्किकों द्वारा प्रतिपादित स्मृति नहीं है। क्योंकि उस स्मृति के लिए तो अतीत में उसका अनुभव आवश्यक है।[53] अत: ''स्मरति'' का प्रयोग यहाँ अनुभूति के लिए औपचारिक है क्योंकि उस अनुभव की प्रकृति साक्षात्कारात्मक है। रसप्रतीति का महत्त्वपूर्ण घटक उसका बाह्य संदर्भ या रूप-विधा न होकर सामाजिक की भावगत प्रतिक्रिया और उसकी आस्वादरूपता में है।[54]

''रम्याणि वीक्ष्य'' की एक महिमा यह भी है कि जहां ''ग्रीवाभङ्गाभिरामम्'' इत्यादि कवि के दृश्य-विधान के अंग हैं और उनके विश्लेषण से हम किसी निष्कर्ष पर पहुँचते हैं, वहाँ यह श्लोक हमें कवि या नाटकार के अपने दृष्टिकोण से परिचित कराता है। ऊपर के विवेचन से एक बात और स्पष्ट है कि वह यह कि रस की अवधारणा को समझने के लिए प्रतिभान और चमत्कार दो आधारभूत अवधारणाएँ हैं। प्रतिभान की अवधारणा का उपयोग रसानुभूति की साक्षात्कारकल्पता को पुष्ट करने के लिए किया गया है, वहीं चमत्कार की अवधारणा का उसकी लोकोत्तर आस्वादमयता, रसनारूपता, चर्वणास्वभावता को निष्पन्न करने के लिए। ''रम्याणि वीक्ष्य'' इन दोनों प्रत्ययों के बीच सेतु बनता हुआ दोनों को समीकृत करता है।

ईश्वरप्रत्यभिज्ञाविवृत्तिविमर्शिनी में चमत्कारिता के संदर्भ में अभिनवगुप्त ''रम्याणि वीक्ष्य'' को उद्धृत करते हैं और ''चमत्कार'' को ''इच्छा'' से समीकृत करते हैं। चमत्कारिता है भुञ्जानरूपता अर्थात् आत्मास्वादयितृत्व। यही सहृदयता है। आत्मास्वादयितृत्व रूप चमत्कार का स्वरूप है स्वात्मविश्रान्ति। यह स्वात्मविश्रान्ति इच्छा के स्वरूप को भी परिभाषित करती है, क्योंकि इच्छा में वेद्यजगत् और ज्ञान-प्रक्रियाएं अभिन्न रूप से विश्रान्त रहती हैं। स्वात्मविश्रान्तिरूपा इच्छा कई रूपों में प्रकट होती है। जहाँ स्वात्मविश्रान्ति का संबंध ऐसे विषय से है जिसकी विशेषता का कथन नहीं किया गया है अर्थात् जहाँ विषय सामान्यकार हैं, वही इच्छा के लिए ''राग'' शब्द का प्रयोग करते हैं। जहाँ स्वात्मविश्रान्ति का सम्बन्ध ऐसे विषय से है जिसकी विशेषताएं ज्ञात हैं-अर्थात् जिसका विषय विशिष्ट है वहां इच्छा को ''काम'' शब्द से पुकारा जाता है।[55] सामान्याकार विषय वासनारूप से ही इच्छा में स्वात्मविश्रान्त रहते हैं।[56] यहाँ पूर्वजन्म से समागत मैत्री भाव वासना रूप से स्वात्म-विश्रान्त रहता है। इसकी पुष्टि में ''रम्याणि वीक्ष्य'' को अभिनवगुप्त उद्धृत करते हैं।[57] इसी प्रकार औत्सुक्य भी सामान्याकार है और इच्छा का वह रूप है जो ऐसी शंका से अनुविद्ध है जो अभिलषणीय के नित्य

पास रहने से ही दूर हो सकती है। इस प्रकार दुष्यन्त के मन में पनपने वाली आत्मविश्रान्ति की तीन अवस्थाएं हैं-मधुर शब्दों के श्रवण मात्र से जागृत ''राग'', जननान्तरीयवासना के रूप में अवस्थित ''अभिलाष'' और अनजानी प्रियता को पाने की ललक रूप औत्सुक्य चमत्कारिता रूप इच्छा के ही आत्मारोहण सोपान है। इसी प्रकार इच्छा के अन्य रूपों का अनुसंधान किया जा सकता है।

अभिनवभारती के 14वें अध्याय में, जिसका सम्बन्ध वाचिक अभिनय से है, अभिनवगुप्त फिर से इस श्लोक को उद्धृत करते हैं।[58]

यह श्लोक छह श्लोकों के समूह का अंग है जहाँ पाँच अपने आरम्भिक प्रतीकों से और यह पूरा उद्धृत किया गया है। भरत का कहना है नट को प्रयोगकाल में और कवि को काव्यनिर्माण के समय वाणी में प्रयास करना चाहिए। क्योंकि वाणी सकल प्रयोगों का आधार है। अभिनवगुप्त इन पद्यों को सरस काव्य का निदर्शन मानते हैं। पर, यदि कोई शंका करे कि इन सभी पद्यों में एक प्रकार से स्वशब्दवाच्यत्व दोष आ गया है, क्योंकि यदि केवल विभावादि होते और ''औत्सुक्य'' (पर्युत्सुकी भवति) आदि को उसके नाम से न कहा जाता तो इसमें उत्तम काव्य की संभावनाएं थीं। इस शंका का निराकरण करते हुए अभिनवगुप्त का कहना है औत्सुक्य आदि के प्रयोगमात्र से इस प्रतीति में कोई बाधा नहीं होनी चाहिए क्योंकि स्मृति, औत्सुक्य आदि शब्दों का प्रयोग यदि संकेतग्रहण की याद नहीं कराता तो रसप्रतीति में कठिनाई नहीं होनी चाहिए। दूसरे इससे भी महत्त्वपूर्ण बात यह है कि स्वशब्दवाच्यता के न होने पर विभावादि से भी जहाँ रस की प्रतिति होती है वहाँ पर भी जब काव्य की पूर्ण प्रक्रिया को नहीं जानेंगे तब तक विभावादि से रस की प्रतीति नहीं होगी।

निहितार्थ यह है कि इस श्लोक में 'पर्युत्सुकी भवति', 'स्मरति' आदि शब्दों का प्रयोग हुआ है, पर उससे रसबोध खण्डित नहीं होता और न उसकी उत्तम काव्यता को चोट पहुंचती है, क्योंकि इन शब्दों का प्रयोग संकेत या वाचक के रूप में नहीं हुआ है। यहां रसबोध होता है काव्य निर्माण की पूर्ण प्रक्रिया में कवि की अंतर्दृष्टि द्वारा। क्योंकि कवित्व का अर्थ है काव्यरचना-सामर्थ्य न कि चित्तवृत्तिप्रतिपादकत्व।[59]

इस बिन्दु पर पहुंचकर प्रो. गोविन्द चन्द्र पांडे को उद्धृत करने का लोभ संवरण नहीं कर पा रहा हूं जो कि अभिनवगुप्त के विचारों को ही प्रतिध्वनित करते लगते हैं-''साहित्यिक आलोचना की दृष्टि से रस एक व्यंग्य अर्थ है जो कि भावसम्बद्ध होते हुए भी भाव के साथ सर्वथा एकात्मक नहीं है, जिसका पता विभावादि से चलता है। ... साहित्यिक मूल्य के रूप में एक विशिष्ट आधुनिक आलोचक ने रस को कृति का संपूर्ण कहा है। उसे कृति का असंलक्ष्यक्रम व्यंग्य अर्थ कहा जा सकता है जिसमें उसके सभी अंशों की सांकेतिकता उपस्थित होकर एक संपिंडित भाव सम्प्रेषित करती है।... किन्तु यह स्मरणीय है कि वस्तुतः उद्बुद्ध या उत्पन्न न होकर केवल व्यंग्य होता हुआ

भाव स्वयं मनोवैज्ञानिक यथार्थ न होकर तदाकारक सम्प्रेषणीय अर्थ ही ठहरता है।''[60] भाव की यह संपिंडितता जहाँ भी, जैसे भी सम्भव हो रसानुभव निर्बाध रहेगा। अलोकसामान्य सहृदयता से संपन्न जन केवल एक श्लोकमात्र से या प्रस्तुत के अंशमात्र से भी इस संपिंडित प्रभाव को ग्रहण कर सकता है। मुक्तक काव्य परंपरा की सार्थकता इस दृष्टि से प्रमाणित होती है। यहाँ दुष्यन्त की काव्यानुभूति हंसपदिका को केवल एक गीति से संभव हुई है। अभिनवगुप्त इसमें बहुत स्पष्ट है।[61]

लगता है कालिदास की इन पंक्तियों का अभिनवगुप्त ने बहुत गंभीरता से आकलन किया था। *अभिनवभारती* और *लोचन* का संबंध मुख्यत: नाट्यार्थ/काव्यार्थ से है। *ईश्वरप्रत्यभिज्ञाविमर्शिनी* और *विवृतिविमर्शिनी* में उन्हीं से संबद्ध विचारों को दार्शनिक आधार दिया गया है। परन्तु जहाँ तक *तंत्रालोक* और *परालत्रशिका* विवरण का संबंध है उनका कलाशास्त्रीय अभिनिवेश नृत्त और गीत में अपेक्षाकृत अधिक दिखाई देता है और उसमें भी खास तौर पर गीत और वादन में कालिदास की ''रम्याणि वीक्ष्य'' कहने पर भी इस सारे विभाव-परिवेश का आग्रह ''मधुरांश्च निशम्य'' पर है। इस श्लोक द्वारा प्रक्षिप्त नाटकीय व्यापार में हम नाटक में एक लघुनाटक को देखते हैं जहां दुष्यन्त सामाजिक बन जाता है और हंसपदिका का आतोद्यपूर्वक गान विभाव। यद्यपि अभिनव *तंत्रालोक* में कालिदास के इस श्लोक का जिक्र नहीं करते पर इसके मूलभाव का दोहन अपने सैद्धान्तिक प्रतिष्ठापन में करते हैं, इसमें संदेह नहीं है। अभिनवगुप्त मधुर गीत में कलात्मक हृदयता की अधिक संभावना करते हैं।

अभिनवगुप्त का मन्तव्य है कि मधुर गीत आदि को सुनकर तटस्थता के परित्याग हो जाने के कारण श्रोता उस गीत के साथ एक तान हो जाता है। उस समय श्रोता के हृदय में जो स्पन्दमानता है, उस गीत के साथ तन्मय होकर स्पन्दित होना है, वही आनन्द शक्ति है। इस आनन्द शक्ति का ही प्रसाद है कि वह श्रोता को सहृदय, रसिक बना देती है।[62] यद्यपि इस श्लोक में कालिदास दो सौन्दर्यग्राहिणी ज्ञानेन्द्रियों का ही उपयोग करते हैं और दृश्य-श्रव्य काव्य परम्परा इन्हीं की उपजीविनी है। *तंत्रालोक* में अभिनवगुप्त इनका विस्तार करते हैं। मधुर गीत जो कि श्रवणेन्द्रिय का विषय है के साथ अभिनवगुप्त त्वगिन्द्रिय के विषय चन्दनादि के शीतल स्पर्श में भी आनन्द के उसी उद्रेक की संभावना करते हैं। वस्तुत: अभिनवगुप्त के टीकाकार जयरथ इसे पाँचों ज्ञानेन्द्रिय-विषयों का उपलक्षण मानते हैं। फिर भी जहाँ तक सिद्धान्त के उपबृंहण का प्रश्न है अभिनवगुप्त गीत और संगीत पर ही विचार करते हैं, क्योंकि गीत और संगीत नाद रूप होने के कारण परा संवित् के अधिक निकट हैं और इस साजात्य के कारण उनके श्रवण से सद्य: तन्मयीभाव होता है। यह तन्मयीभाव ही रसिकत्व का स्रोत है।[63]

बाह्य पदार्थ की सुखात्मकता और दु:खात्मकता तभी तक रहती है जब तक यह प्रमाता की व्यक्तिगत सत्ता से जुड़ा रहता है। पर जब उपयोगितामूलक सम्बन्ध का स्थान कलात्मक सम्बन्ध ले लेता है और विषय का ग्रहण किसी प्रयोजन की तुष्टि के लिए

नहीं होता उस क्षण द्रष्टा का ताटस्थ्य गल जाता है और निर्वैयक्तिकीकृत प्रमाता में विषय प्रतिबिम्बित होने लगता है, उस समय विषय का अनुभव न सुखकारी रूप में होता है, न दुःखकारी रूप में, द्रष्टा के साधारणीकृत चित्त में केवल एक स्फुरण उत्पन्न होता है, जिससे आत्मा का आनन्द पक्ष उद्रिक्त हो उठता है। मधुर गीत सुनने पर रसिक की ठीक ऐसी ही स्थिति होती है। अभिनवगुप्त के मत में संगीत से होने वाली कलानुभूति वस्तुतः पारमार्थिक आनन्द की अनुभूति है। अतः अभिनवगुप्त का सुचिन्तित निष्कर्ष है कि जो शरीर आदि की सीमा को लांघकर गीतादि विषय के साथ इस अतिशय तन्मयता से वंचित रह जाता है वह वस्तुतः सहृदय नहीं, अहृदय है।[64]

अभिज्ञानशाकुन्तल के इस श्लोक और अभिनवगुप्त द्वारा इसके कलाशास्त्रीय दोहन के प्रसंग से हमने देखा कि कला-सर्जना और कलानुभूति में क्रमशः सर्जन और संवेदन की पूरी अंतःप्रक्रिया का संकेतन भी अभिनवगुप्त ने किया है। मधुर गीत के श्रवण से लेकर आस्वादपर्यन्त कलाजन्य अनुभव की जिन स्थितियों से सामाजिक गुजरता है उनका आकलन इस प्रकार किया जा सकता है–[65]

इन्द्रिय प्रत्यक्ष	(मधुर गीत का श्रवण)
माध्यस्थ्यविगमन	या (हानादानबुद्धि त्याग)
तटस्थता परित्याग	
हार्दिक स्पन्दमानता	(आनन्द शक्ति)
तन्मयता	(सहृदयता)
आस्वाद	(मूल्य बोध)

इस निबन्ध में हमारी आत्मारोपित सीमाएं रही हैं। कथ्य की भी और पद्धति की भी। ''प्रतिभान'' शब्द से रसानुभूति को अपने दार्शनिक और कलाशास्त्रीय सन्दर्भ में पुष्ट करने में अभिनवगुप्त ने कालिदास की उक्ति की समर्थ सांकेतिकता का उन्मीलन करते हुए जिस पद्धति का आश्रय लिया है, उसी का आंशिक अनुवाद करते हुए कतिपय निष्कर्षों पर पहुँचने की चेष्टा की गयी है। आंशिक इसलिए कि श्लोक की व्याख्या के उपसंहार में उन्होंने रस की अवधारणा को व्यापकतम विस्तार देते हुए रस के अपने से पूर्व के सारे इतिहास का समन्वयन करते हुए उसका यौक्तिकीकरण (rationalization) किया है-

> *सर्वथा तावदेषास्ति प्रतीतिरास्वादात्मा यस्यां रतिरेव भाति। तत एव विशेषान्तरानुपहितत्वात् सा रसनीया सती न लौकिकी न मिथ्या नानिर्वाच्या न लौकिकतुल्या न तदारोपादिरूपा। तथैव चोपचयावस्थाऽस्तु देशाद्यनियन्त्रणात्। अनुकारोऽप्यस्तु भावानुगामितया करणात्। विषयसामग्र्यपि भवतु विज्ञानवादावलम्बनात्। सर्वथैव रसनात्मकवीतविघ्नप्रतीतिग्राह्यो भाव एव रसः।*[66]

पर वह किसी आगामी अध्ययन का ही विषय हो सकता है। यहाँ केवल इतना ही कहना पर्याप्त होगा कि रसध्वनि के जिस सिद्धान्त का विकास प्रत्यभिज्ञादर्शन की पृष्ठभूमि में हुआ, विशेषकर "चमत्कार" की जिस अवधारणा के आसूत्रण द्वारा ज्ञान की आस्वादात्मकता की खोज हुई वह शब्द की आत्मशरीरोत्तीर्णता के सिद्धान्त को बड़ी समर्थता के साथ स्थापित करता है। शब्द की अपने से परे जाने की और अपनी सार्थकता को तलाशने की प्यास सारी कला और ध्वनि सिद्धान्त का बीज है। "इस सिद्धान्त के अनुसार", प्रो. गोविन्दचन्द्र पांडे के शब्दों में,[67] "सभी रूपों में शैवी चेतना का प्रकाश होता है और उसके विमर्श या घनीभूत प्रत्यक्ष से मन में एक अंत: स्पन्द उदित होता है जो उनके अर्थ की पहचान एवं रस के सारभूत चमत्कार से अभिन्न है। इस रमणीयता को देखने, सुनने से जो भाव और आकुलता मन में उद्बुद्ध होती है वह मानो किसी की याद दिलाती है। यह आन्तरिक भाव का उदय ही बाह्य विषय को रूपान्तरित कर उनके प्रत्यक्ष को सघन अनुभूति बना देता है।" यही प्रतिभान है, यही चमत्कार है।[68]

संदर्भ

1. तथा हि लोके सकलविघ्नविनिर्मुक्ता संवित्तिरेव चमत्कारनिर्वेशरसनास्वादनभोगसमापत्तिलयविश्रान्त्यादिशब्दैरभिधीयते। –*नाट्यशास्त्र* पर *अभिनवभारती* (*अ. भा.*), *Natyasastra of Bharatamuni* के नाम से प्रकाशित, बड़ौदा, 1926, पृ. 272
2. एवं क्रमहेतुमभिधाय रसविषयं लक्षणसूत्रमाह। वही
3. प्रतिभानापरपर्याया साक्षात्कारस्वभावेयम् इति। *अभिनवभारती*, पृ. 280
4. अत्र हि स्मरतीति या स्मृतिरुपदर्शिता सा न तार्किकप्रसिद्धा। पूर्वमेतस्यार्थस्य अननुभूतत्वात्। अपितु प्रतिभानापरपर्यायसाक्षात्कारस्वभावेयमिति। वही, पृ. 279
5. अधिकारी चात्र विमलप्रतिभानशालिहृदय:। वही, पृ.
6. चकारेण प्रत्युत्पन्नप्रतिभानत्वं दर्शयति। अनेन झटिति कविहृदयग्रहणयोग्यत्वं नाट्याचार्यगुण इति सूचयति। वही, पृ. 21
7. प्रतिपत्तुर्प्रतिभासहकारित्वं ह्यस्याभिद्योतनस्य प्राणत्वेन उक्तम्। *लोचन*, पृ. 68 अभिनव का रस-विवेचन, नगीनदास पारेख, मूल गुजराती से हिन्दी अनुवाद, वाराणसी, 1974, पृ. 44 पर उद्धृत
8. स्वरूपस्य निह्नवात् रूपान्तरस्य चारोपितस्य प्रतिभा संविद्विश्रान्तिवैकल्येन स्वरूपे विश्रान्त्यभावात्। इति स एव सर्वो मुनिना साधारणीभावसिद्ध्या रसचर्वणोपयोगित्वेन परिकरबन्ध: समाश्रित:। *अभिनवभारती*, पृ. 291
9. कतिपय उद्धरण इस प्रकार हैं :
   (क) कवेरपि स्वहृदयायतनसततोदितप्रतिभाभिधानपरवाग्देवतानुग्रहोत्थितविचित्रऽपूर्वार्थ निर्माणशक्तिशालिन: प्रजापतेरिव कामजनितजगत:। वही, पृ. 4

(ख) कवेर्य: प्रतिभात्मा प्रथमपरिस्पन्द: तद्व्यापारबलोपनता: गुणा: प्रतिभावत एव हि रसभिव्यञ्जनसामर्थ्यं माधुर्यादेरुपनिबन्धनसामर्थ्यं, न सामान्यकवे: -वही *अ.भा.* 2, बड़ौदा, 1934, पृ. 296

(ग) तेन स्वभावप्रतिभादर्शनानुविद्धा भगवती वाणी स्वरसोपनिपतिता स्वरसंभार प्रभावानुरोधेनैव आरोहावरोहक्रमं भजते। प्रतिभादृष्टिशून्यत्वात् अन्धपदवदारोहादि न भजेत्। वही, पृ. 339

10. प्रतीत्यादिव्यतिरिक्तश्च संसारे को भोग इति न विद्म:। रसनेति चेत् सापि प्रतिपत्तिरेव। केवलमुपायवैलक्षण्यान्नामान्तरं प्रतिपद्यतां दर्शनानुमितिश्रुत्युपमितिप्रतिभानादिनामान्तरवत्। -*अभिनवभारती*, पृ॰ 277

11. सर्वपक्षेषु प्रतीतिरपरिहार्या रसस्य।...यथा प्रतीतिमात्रत्वेन अविशिष्टत्वेऽपि प्रात्यक्षिकी आनुमानिकी आगमोत्था प्रतिभानकृता योगिप्रत्यक्षजा च प्रतीतिरूपायवैलक्षण्यादन्यैव तद्वदियमपि प्रतीतिश्चर्वणा भोगापरनामा भवतु।... तन्निदानभूताया हृदयसंवादाद्युपकृताया विभावादिसामग्रया लोकोत्तररूपत्वात् (*ध्व. लो.*, पृ. 187)

12. यथा दर्शनं प्रतिभाभावना विध्युद्योगादिभाषाभिर्व्यवहृता प्रतिपत्तिस्तथैव काव्यात्मकादपि शब्दादधिकारिणोऽधिकास्ति प्रतिपत्ति:। -*अभिनवभारती*, पृ. 278

13. ननु विशेषणग्राहि किं तत्र प्रमाणम्। उक्तमेव परै: ''यौक्तिकं मानसं वा प्रत्यक्षं लोकप्रसिद्धिरागम: प्रतिभाविशेषोऽनन्तजन्माभ्यासमूलस्तत्कालघटितो वार्थापत्तिर्वा।'' *ईश्वरप्रत्यभिज्ञाविवृत्तिविमर्शिनी*, अभिनवगुप्त, (खंड तीन), *काश्मीर ग्रन्थावलि*, 1938-43, *अ. भा.* 2, पृ. 197

14. इति प्रत्यक्षानुपलम्भपञ्चकादेव अस्मद्दर्शनोचितान्तर्मुखसंवेदलक्षणस्वतन्त्रत्मतत्त्वविश्रमादेव कार्यकारणभावसिद्धि:। तत्रपि च सार्वत्रिकतानिश्चये व्यवहारतो व्युत्पत्तितो वा आगमाद्वा स्वप्रतिभाया वा जन्मान्तराभ्यासोदिताया: समवधारिता भगवन्नियतिशक्तिरेव प्रभवन्ती निरूपणीया स्वपर्यायेण अभिमतं साधयन्तौऽनुमानरूपतां नातिवर्तन्ते। वही पृ. 205

15. तस्माद् युक्तिरिति...''समाधाननैर्मल्यात्मिका प्रतिभा'' इति तु तत्रभवद्भर्तृहरिप्रभृतय:। तदनुसारमेव च अयम् ''अमन्दत्वं प्रज्ञाया'' इति अर्थापत्तिरिति मीमांसका:। ... प्रमाणयोजनात्मकं प्रमातृस्वातन्त्र्यमेव युक्तिरिति प्रत्यभिज्ञातत्त्ववित्। यत्किञ्चिदपि अङ्गीकुर्वता अवश्यमेव पर्यन्ते प्रमातृस्वातन्त्र्यमेव ज्ञानक्रियाशक्तियोजनात्मकमङ्गीकर्तव्यम् इति असकृदुक्तम्।-वही, पृ. 208

16. (क) अधिकारी चात्र विमलप्रतिभानशालिहृदय:। -*अभिनवभारती*, पृ. 279

(ख) तत्र ये स्वभावतो निर्मलमुकुरहृदया:...वही, पृ. 291

(ग) सहृदयत्वं हृदयस्य हि कविहृदयतादात्म्यापत्तियोग्यतैव। -वही, *अ. भा.* 2, पृ. 339

(घ) विगतरागद्वेषा: मध्यस्थवृत्तय: निर्मलहृदयमुकुरे सति तन्मयीभवनयोग्यतोपेता आहितरसास्वादा: सामाजिका:। -वही, *अ. भा.* 2, पृ. 16

(ङ) येषां विशदीभूते मनोमुकुरे वर्णनीयतन्मयीभवनयोग्यता ते स्वहृदयसंवादभाज: सहृदया:। *ध्व. लो.* पृ. 39,40

17. कवेरपि सहृदयायतनसततोदितप्रतिभाभिधानपरवाग्देवतानुग्रहोत्थितविचित्रऽपूर्वनिर्माणशक्ति-शालिनः प्रजापतेरिव कामजनितजगतः। - *अ. भा.* पृ. 4
18. वक्ति विश्वमभिलपति प्रत्यवमर्शेन इति च वाक्। -*ईश्वरप्रत्यभिज्ञाविमर्शिनी*, सं. पांडेय तथा अय्यर (दो खण्ड), इलाहाबाद 1938, भा. 1 पृ. 253
19. वक्ति स्वरूपं विमृशतीति च वाक् तस्यां च एतत् परिदृश्यमानं
वाङ्मयं प्रमितिलक्षणपरामर्शरूपसंवेदनानुविद्धतया शब्दैकशरीरं विश्वं यथाक्रमेण विकसिता। -*ई. प्र. वि. वि.*, भा.1, पृ. 15
20. स्वात्मा परामृश्यते, स्वात्मत्वेन प्रकाश्यते...ततः चैत्रेण चेत्यते इति उच्यते।
ई. प्र. वि., भा. 1, पृ. 251
21. अज्ञानरूपता पुंसि बोध्यसंकोचिते हृदि।
संकोचे विनिवृत्ते तु स्वस्वभावः प्रकाशते।।
-*तंत्रलोक* (तं), *विवेक* (तं. वि.) के साथ (8 खण्ड)
सं. रामचन्द्र द्विवेदी तथा नवजीवन रस्तोगी, दिल्ली, 1987, 13.213
22. सर्वभावविवेकात्तु सर्वभावपराङ्मुखः।।
क्रीडासु सुविरक्तात्मा शिवभावैकभावितः।
माहात्म्यमेतत्सुश्रोणि प्रातिभस्य विधीयते।।
स्वच्छायादर्शवत्पश्येद्बहिरन्तर्गतं शिवम्।
हेयोपादेयतत्त्वज्ञस्तदा ध्यायेन्निजां चितिम्। तं. 13. 180-182
23. उच्छलत्संविदामात्रविश्रान्त्यास्वादयोगिनः।।
सर्वाभिधानसामर्थ्यादनियन्त्रितशक्तयः।
सृष्टाः स्वात्मसहोत्थेऽर्थे धरापर्यन्तभागिनि।।
आमृशन्तः स्वचिद्भूमौ तावतोऽर्थानभेदतः।
वर्णौघास्ते प्रमारूपां सत्यां विभ्रति संविदम्।। वही, 11.63.65
24. यथा यथा चामृतं तद्रूपमतिरिच्यते।।
तथा तथा चमत्कारतारतम्यं विभाव्यते। 11ए, 76,77
25. प्रकाशस्य असंसृष्टस्य-परसारूप्यं प्रतिबिम्बायमानपरतादात्म्यक्षमत्वमस्ति स्वभावान्तरम् ...। *ई. प्र. वि. वि.*, 2, पृ. 177
26. तं. 3.240, 41; *अभि. भा.*, 2, पृ. 339; *ध्व. लो. लो.* पृ. 39, 40
27. तेन संवित्तिमुकुरे विश्वमात्मानमर्पयत्।
नाथस्य वदनेऽमुष्य विमलां विश्वरूपताम्।।
अत्यन्तस्वच्छता सा सत्स्वाकृत्यनवभासनम्।।
अतः स्वच्छतमो बोधो रत्नं त्वाकृतिग्रहात् तं. 3.44-48
28. स्वस्मिन्नभेदाद् भिन्नस्य दर्शनक्षमतैव या।
अव्यक्तस्वप्रकाशस्य नैर्मल्यं तद्गुरूदितम्।। तं. 3, 8
29. तथापि न तत् मुख्यं जडेऽपि मणिमुकुरप्रभृतौ तस्य संभवात्, विमर्शस्तु जडे न संभवति इति अनन्यविषयत्वात् स मुख्य आत्मेति युक्तम्। *ई. वि. वि. वि.*, 2, पृ. 177

30. प्रतिभाति घट इति यद्यपि विषयमुपश्लिष्यन्ती इयं क्रिया लक्ष्यते, तथापि न अस्य तत् स्वज्योतिः किन्तु संवेदनमेव तत् तथा भाति मां प्रतिभातीति प्रमातृनिष्ठतयैव स्फुरणात्। वही, पृ. 339
31. तत एव आर्द्राशयः सरसविमलहृदयः अतएव विश्वरूपपरमेश्वरसमावेशोचितहृदयः। वही, पृ. 29
32. इसी प्रकार नट-प्रक्रिया की तुलना ध्यानादि की प्रक्रिया से की जा सकती है, जो एक प्रकार से परमशिव और विश्व के समीकरण का अनुवदन है। ध्यान, भावना एवं समाधि में भी बिम्ब के अभाव में भावना, स्मरण एवं ध्यान की घनता से भी प्रतिबिम्ब की उत्पत्ति सम्भव है।
33. उच्छलननिजरश्म्योघः संवित्सु प्रतिबिम्बितः।।
बहुदर्पणवद्दीप्तिः सर्वायेताप्ययत्नतः।। *तं.* 28.374,75
34. आनन्दनिर्भरा संवित्प्रत्येकं सा तथैकताम्।।
नृत्तादौ विषये प्राप्तपूर्णानन्दत्वमश्नुते। वही, 28.377
35. ईर्ष्यादिसंकोचकारणाभावतोऽत्र सा।।
विकस्वरा निष्प्रतिघं संविदानन्दयोगिनी।। -*तं.* 28.377,78
36. अतन्मये तु कस्मिंश्चित्रस्थे प्रतिहन्यते।।
स्थपुटस्पर्शवत्संविद्विजातीयतया स्थिते।। वही, 28.378,79
37. नैर्मल्यं चातिनिविडजातीयैकसंगतिः।। वही, 3.7
38. नैरन्तर्येण अवस्थानात् स्थपुटत्वादिपरिहारेण श्लक्ष्णत्वात् आत्मसंहतत्वम् नैर्मल्यम्। *तं. वि.* 2, पृ. 360
39. या चैषा प्रतिभा तत्तत्पदार्थक्रमरूषिता।
अक्रमानन्तचिद्रूपः प्रमाता स महेश्वर :।।- *ई. प्र. का.* 1. 7. 1
40. चित्तत्त्वस्य या अन्तरक्रमाभासता प्रमाता महेश्वरः सा प्रतिभा
इति प्रमातृत्वमाहेश्वर्याभ्यामुपचिता लब्धपरिपोषा।-*ई. प्र. वि. वि.*।। पृ. 340,41
41. "या प्रतिभा एषा" इति सर्वस्य सर्वदैव स्वप्रकाशा वस्तुतश्च अंतर्मुखेन वपुषा देशकालकलनावैकल्यात्...स एव...यो महेश्वरः प्रमाता। सा च प्रतिभा अनपह्नवनीया। *ई. प्र. वि. वि.*, 2, पृ. 339, 40
42. तत एव भट्टचन्द्रानन्देन-
"पश्यतो रूपमालेखाद्भातो भानानुषङ्गि यत्।
प्रतीयमानं प्रतिभा भावानाम्....। वही, पृ. 339
43. भट्टशंकरनन्दनेन अपि
"साक्षात्कारः स्वतःसिद्धः सा स्फुरद्रूपतास्य हि" घटः स्फुरति इति हि कोऽर्थः।
अहं तावत् प्रकाशात्मा घटरूपेण स्फुरामि...तथा...तदेकरूपतारूढोऽपि घट एवमिति।
अत उक्तं भट्टचन्द्रानन्देन-
"पश्यतो रूपमालेखाद् भातो भानानुषङ्गि यत्।
स्वरूपभानं प्रतिभा भावनां...।।" इत्युक्त्वा "...सात्मसंश्रया।।" इति वही, पृ. 199, 200

44. रम्याणि वीक्ष्य मधुराँश्च निशम्य शब्दान् पर्युत्सुकीभवति यत्सुखितोऽपि जन्तुः।
तच्चेतसा स्मरति नूनमबोधपूर्वं भावस्थिराणि जननान्तरसौहृदानि।।

अभि. शा. 5.2

45. देखिए, भारतीय परम्परा के मूल स्वर, गोविन्दचन्द्र पाण्डे, दिल्ली, 1981, पृ. 94-118; *Rasa Theory*, G.K. Bhat, Baroda, 1994, pp. 44-46; 'Pratibhana', G.K. Bhat, Abori, 1978, pp. 499-509.

46. *नाट्यशास्त्र* (*अभि. भा.*) भा. 1, पृ. 281; भा. 2, पृ. 222; *ई. प्र. वि. वि.*, भा. 2, पृ. 251-52

47. भो वअस्स। संगीद-सालवभन्तरे अवहाणं देहि। ताल-लय विसुद्धाए वीणाए सर-संजोओ सुणीअदि। जाणे तत्तहोदी हंसबदिआ वणपरिअअं करेदित्ति।
Kalidasa : *Abhijnana-sakuntalam – A Synthetic Study*, R.M. Bose, Calcutta, 1931, 5th Anka, p. 1.

48. तूष्णीं भव यावदाकर्णयामि। वही

49. केवल कालिदास के शाकुन्तल में ही नहीं, अन्यत्र भी इस अबूझ उत्कण्ठा के दर्शन होते हैं। रघुवंश में विश्वामित्र के आश्रम को देखकर राम के मन में ऐसी ही बेचैनी घिर आती है :
वामनमाश्रमपदं ततः पावनं श्रुतमृषेरुपेयिवान्।
उन्मनाः प्रथमजन्मचेष्टितानि अस्मरन्नपि बभूव राघवः।।' -रघु. ।।. 22
Charles Dickens के Oliver Twist को रमेन्द्र मोहन बोस उद्धृत करते हैं-
"Thus a strain of gentle music, or the rippling of water in a silent place, or the odour of a flower, or the mention of a familiar word will sometimes call up sudden remembrances of scenes that never were in this life...which some brief memory of a happier existence long gone by would seem to have awakened; which no voluntary exertion of mind can recall." -वही, पृ. 10,11

50. सा चाविघ्ना संवित् चमत्कारः। तज्जोऽपि पुलकोल्लुकसनादिर्विकारश्च चमत्कारः। *अभि. भा*, भा.1, पृ. 281

51. अज्ज वि हरी चमक्कई कह कह वि ण मंदरेण दलिआइ।
चन्दकलाकंदलसच्छाइं लच्छीइं अंगाई। *ना. शा.* (*अभि. भा.*) भा. 1, पृ. 28

52. तथाहि स च तृप्तिव्यतिरेकेणाच्छिन्नो भोगावेश इत्युच्यते।
भुञ्जानस्य अद्भुतभोगस्पन्दाविष्टस्य चमतः करणं चमत्कार इति।
स च साक्षात्कारस्वभावो मानसोऽध्यवसायो वा सङ्कल्पो स्मृतिर्वा तथात्वेन अस्तु।
यदाह 'रम्याणि वीक्ष्य...। वही

53. अत्र हि स्मरतीति या स्मृतिरुपदलशता सा न तालृककप्रसिद्धा।
पूर्वमेतस्यार्थस्य अनुभूतत्वात्। अपितु प्रतिभानापरपर्यायसाक्षात्कारस्वभावेयमिति। *ना. शा.* (*अभि. भा*), पृ. 281

54. सर्वथा तावदेषास्ति प्रतीतिरास्वादात्मा यस्यां रतिरेव भाति। -वही, पृ. 280

55. सर्वत्र हि चमत्कार एव इच्छा, स च परमभूमावपि अस्ति।...सैव हि इति। चमत्कारिता हि भुञ्जानरूपता स्वात्मविश्रान्तिलक्षणा सर्वत्र इच्छा। *ई. प्र. वि. वि.* 3, पृ. 252
56. क्वचित्तु स्वात्मविश्रान्तिर्भावान्तरमनागूरितविशेषमपेक्ष्य उत्थाप्यते तत्र सा इच्छा राग इत्युच्यते आगूरितविशेषतायां तु काम इति। वही
57. आदिग्रहणाद् अभिलाषमूलो भावान्तरं सामान्याकारमपि वासनावशेषमात्रेण आस्ते यथाह ... "भावस्थिराणि जननान्तरसौहृदानि" इति औत्सुक्यं च नित्यतत्संनिधान व्यपगतशंकानुविद्धा इच्छैवेति। एवमन्यदनुसर्तव्यम्। वही
58. "तथा सहासरभसव्यावृत्तकण्ठग्रहं" "वपुर्लसलसद्बाहुलक्ष्म्या:",
"कतिचिदहानि वपुरभूत्केवलमलसेक्षण तस्या:"
रम्याणि वीक्ष्य मधुराँश्च निशम्य शब्दान्
पर्युत्सुको भवति यत्सुखितोऽपि जन्तु:।
तच्चेतसा स्मरति नूनमबोधपूर्वं
भावस्थिराणि जननान्तरसौहृदानि।। *शाकुं.* 5.2
"निद्रानिमीलितदृशो मदमन्थराया" विवृण्वती शैलसुतापि भावमङ्गै": इत्यादिकाव्येषु सहृदयहृदयसागरसमुच्च्लद्राकामृगाङ्कप्रतिबिम्बेषु जीवितभूतानां हासालस्यौत्सुक्य निद्रामदागमाभिलाषागमादिनां शब्दस्पृष्टत्वेन विभावानुत्साध्यस्वभावत्वे वीतरागतेव बककाकक्रीडाकल्पनैव स्यात् -*अ. भा.*, 2, पृ. 221, 222
59. न तु सर्वो वक्ता कविरित्यतिप्रसङ्गलक्ष्यमाणप्रबन्धबन्धुरं काव्यनिर्मातृत्वं हि कवित्वं, न चित्तवृत्तिप्रतिपादकत्वम्।...विभावादिभ्योऽपि पूर्णकाव्यप्रक्रियापरिगतमन्तरेण न रसादय:। -*अ. भा.*, भा. 2, पृ. 223
60. *भारतीय परम्परा के मूल स्वर*, पृ. 105
61. तेन ये काव्याभ्यासप्राक्तनपुण्यादिबलादतिसहृदयास्तेषां परिमित-विभावाद्युन्मीलनेन परिस्फुट एव साक्षात्कारकल्प: काव्यार्थ: स्फुरति, अतएव तेषां काव्यमेव प्रतीत्युत्पत्तिकृत्, अनपेक्षितनाट्यमपि। - *अभि. भा.*, भा.1, पृ. 288; *Comparative Aesthetics*, K.C. Pandey, Vol. 1, pp. 186.87 पर उद्धृत
62. तथा हि मधुरे गीते स्पर्शे वा चन्दनादिके।।
माध्यस्थ्यविगमे यासौ हृदये स्पन्दमानता।
आनन्दशक्ति: सैवोक्ता यत: सहृदयो जन:।। *तं.* 3. 209, 210
63. तदस्यां नादरूपायां संवित्सविधवृत्तित:।।
साजात्यात्तन्मयीभूतिर्झगित्येवोपलभ्यते। -वही 3. 239,240
64. येषां न तन्मयीभूतिस्ते देहादिनिमज्जनम्।
अविदन्तो मग्नसंविन्मानास्त्वहृदया इति। -*तं.* 3.240,241
65. पीछे "रम्याणि वीक्ष्य" की विश्लेषण तालिका (पृ. 16) में हमने इन सोपानों का अनुसंधान और संकेतन करने का प्रयास किया है।
66. *अ. भा.*, 1, पृ. 280; यहां पाठ संशोधित है। मुद्रित पाठ अत्यन्त भ्रामक है।
67. *भारतीय परंपरा के मूल स्वर*, पृ. 117-118

68. अभिनवगुप्त से मिलाइए : ''अत्र तु दर्शने विषयस्यापि विमर्शमयत्वात् अभिलापमयत्वमेव वस्तुतः। ...भवतु वा क्षणमात्रस्वभावः साक्षात्कारः तत्रापि अस्ति विमर्शः।'' *ई. प्र. वि.*, पृ. 288-291

20

करुणविप्रलम्भ एवं कामदशाएं: अभिनवगुप्त के विशेष सन्दर्भ में

सुषमा कुलश्रेष्ठ

रसराज शृंगार के दो अधिष्ठान हैं-सम्भोग एवं विप्रलम्भ। विप्रलम्भ को आचार्यों ने चतुर्विध माना है-(1) पूर्वराग-विप्रलम्भ, (2) मान-विप्रलम्भ, (3) प्रवास-विप्रलम्भ और (4) करुण-विप्रलम्भ। भोजराज ने *शृंगारप्रकाश* में विप्रलम्भ शब्द की व्युत्पत्ति करते हुए कहा है कि यह शब्द 'लभ्' धातु में वि और प्र उपसर्ग जोड़ने से बना है। 'लभ्' धातु का अर्थ है प्राप्ति, प्र का अर्थ है प्रकर्ष तथा वि का अर्थ है वञ्चना। जहाँ प्राप्ति (अभीष्ट प्राप्ति) की इच्छा प्रकर्षरूपेण होती है फिर भी वञ्चना होती है, वहाँ विप्रलम्भ होता है।[1] हेमचन्द्र के अनुसार विप्रलम्भ की निरुक्ति है-

सम्भोगसुखास्वादलोभेन विशेषेण प्रलभ्यते आत्माऽत्रेति विप्रलम्भ:[2]

करुण एवं शृंगार स्पष्टरूपेण पृथक् रस हैं किन्तु शृंगार के अधिष्ठानों विशेषत: विप्रलम्भ की करुण से अतिशय निकटता परिलक्षित होती है। शृंगार के अन्तर्गत दस कामदशाएं आती हैं। इन दशाओं अथवा अवस्थाओं में अन्तिम अवस्था मरण है। अत: मृत्यु भी शृंगार की परिधि में आ जाती है, किन्तु मृत्युजनित शोक करुण रस का स्थायिभाव होता है। विप्रलम्भ तथा करुण के बीच अन्तर केवल स्थायिभाव का है। विप्रलम्भ शृंगार का स्थायिभाव रति है, जबकि करुण का स्थायिभाव शोक है। रति और शोक में परस्पर भेद यह है कि रतिभावसंयुक्त व्यक्ति अपने प्रिय को पाने की आशा

रखता है और उसकी यह आशा देश-काल के बन्धन से मुक्त होती है। विप्रयोग में आशा का बन्धन ही सद्यःपाति प्रणयिहृदय को रोके रहता है।[3] शोक में इसी आशा का अभीष्ट का विनाश है। उस विनाश के कारण का कोई निवारण सम्भव नहीं है, जिससे पुनर्मिलन की सम्भावना समाप्त हो जाती है। अतः हम कह सकते हैं कि विप्रलम्भ शृंगार की अभिव्यक्ति में मृत्यु व्यभिचारिभाव के रूप में ग्रहण की जाती है एवं जैसे ही वह मृत्यु स्थायिभाव का रूप ग्रहण कर लेती है, तो वह विप्रलम्भ की परिधि पार कर करुण बन जाता है।

यहाँ करुण तथा विप्रलम्भ के विषय में आचार्यों की मान्यताएँ प्रस्तुत हैं।

करुण और विप्रलम्भ के नैकट्य को स्पष्ट करते हुए भरतमुनि कहते हैं-

यद्ययं रतिप्रभवः शृंगारः कथमस्य करुणाश्रयिणो भावा भवन्ति। अत्रोच्यते पूर्वमेवाभिहितं सम्भोगविप्रलम्भकृतः शृंगार इति। वैशिकशास्त्रकारैश्च दशावस्थोऽभिहितः।[4]

अर्थात् यदि यह प्रश्न हो कि शृंगार रस जो रति से उत्पन्न होता है तो उसमें करुण रस में रहने वाले भाव कैसे होते हैं? इसका समाधान यह है कि शृंगार सम्भोग और विप्रलम्भ दो प्रकार का होता है। इसमें जो विप्रलम्भ शृंगार है उसमें करुण रस के समान निर्वेदादि व्यभिचारिभाव भी होते हैं। यह केवल हमारा मत नहीं है, अपितु कामशास्त्र के आचार्यों ने भी काम की दस अवस्थाओं का निर्देश किया है और उनमें करुणसम्बन्धी अवस्थाओं का भी उल्लेख शृंगार में पाया जाता है। करुण और विप्रलम्भ के भेद को और अधिक स्पष्ट करते हुए भरतमुनि कहते हैं-

करुणस्तु शापक्लेशविनिपतितेष्टजनविभवनाशवधबन्धसमुत्थो निरपेक्षभावः। औत्सुक्यचिन्तासमुत्थः सापेक्षभावो विप्रलम्भकृतः।[5]

अर्थात् शाप के कारण अथवा इष्टजन से वियोग, विभव के नाश, मृत्यु अथवा बन्धन के कारण करुण रस होता है। इसमें निरपेक्षभाव प्रधान होता है अर्थात् करुण में पूर्ण नैराश्य की अवस्था विद्यमान रहती है, किन्तु विप्रलम्भ में सापेक्षभाव रहता है अर्थात् विप्रलम्भ में अभिलाषा निरन्तर विद्यमान रहती है। इस प्रकार करुण और विप्रलम्भ दोनों में अन्तर है। भरतमुनि के विवेचन से यह प्रकट है कि विप्रलम्भ की निराशा में आशा का अस्तित्व सतत वर्तमान रहता है और क्षणमात्र के लिए भी यह आशा वियोगीजन से अलग नहीं होती। इस प्रकार विप्रलंभ करुण के अतिशय निकट होते हुए भी उससे पूर्णतः पृथक् है।

रुद्रट के अनुसार वियुक्त पुरुष और नारी के रति व्यवहार को विप्रलम्भ शृंगार कहते हैं-

व्यवहारः पुंनार्योरन्योन्यं रक्तयो रतिप्रकृतिः।
शृंगारः स द्वेधा सम्भोगो विप्रलम्भश्च॥
सम्भोगसंगत्योर्वियुक्तयोर्यश्च विप्रलम्भोऽसौ॥[6]

रुद्रट के मतानुसार पुरुष और नारी की पारस्परिक रति जब उनके एक-दूसरे से पृथक् रहने पर भी विद्यमान रहती है, तो उसे विप्रलम्भ शृंगार कहते हैं। भोजराज ने विप्रलम्भ की चर्चा करते हुए *सरस्वतीकण्ठाभरण* में स्पष्टतः कहा है कि रति नामक भाव जब प्रकर्ष को प्राप्त होकर भी अपने अभीष्ट तक नहीं पहुंचता है, तब विप्रलम्भ शृंगार होता है-

भावो यदा रतिर्नाम प्रकर्षमधिगच्छति।
नाधिगच्छति चाभीष्टं विप्रलम्भस्तदोच्यते॥[7]

भोजराज के मत में अभीष्ट का अर्थ केवल प्रिय व्यक्ति ही नहीं प्रत्युत अभीष्ट भाव भी है। शारदातनय ने *भावप्रकाशन* में विप्रलम्भ का लक्षण न देकर उसके दो भेदों अयोग और वियोग का कथन किया है। उनके मतानुसार अयोग का लक्षण इस प्रकार है-

परस्परं विभावाद्यैर्यूनोरद्‌भुतरागयोः।
असङ्गतिरयोगोऽस्मिन्दशावस्था द्वयोरपि॥[8]

जो कभी मिले नहीं हों, ऐसे अद्‌भुत राग वाले युवक और युवती की परस्पर विभावादि से उत्पन्न असङ्गति अयोग है अर्थात् विभावादि के रहने पर भी उनका मिलन नहीं होता। इस अयोग में काम की दस अवस्थाएं होती हैं।

वियोग में सम्भोगमग्न युवक और युवती का विप्रकर्ष होता है:

वियोगो विप्रकर्षः स्याद्यूनोः सम्भोगमग्नयोः।
वियोगोऽपि द्विधा मानप्रवासकृतभेदत ः॥[9]

इन दोनों भेदों से करुण का साम्य देखते हुए वे कहते हैं कि अयोग एवं वियोग में सामान्य विभावादि करुण के अनुरूप ही होते हैं, तथापि रति स्थायिभाव की अनुवृत्ति होने से ये शृंगार के ही भेद हैं-

साधारण्याद्विभावादेरत्रायोगवियोगयोः
करुणस्यानुरूप्येऽपि रतिस्थाय्यनुवृत्तितः॥[10]

*साहित्यदर्पण*कार विश्वनाथ महापात्र भोजराज का अनुकरण करते हुए विप्रलम्भ को इस प्रकार प्रस्तुत करते हैं-

यत्र तु रतिः प्रकृष्टा नाभीष्टमुपैति विप्रलम्भोऽसौ।।[11]

अर्थात् रति के प्रगाढ़ होने पर भी जब प्रिय-समागम नहीं हो पाता तो उसे विप्रलम्भ कहते हैं। प्रिय-समागम के लिए उन्होंने 'अभीष्ट' पद का प्रयोग किया है, जिससे नायक अथवा नायिका अभिप्रेत हैं।

रसगंगाधरकार पण्डितराज जगन्नाथ ने विप्रलम्भ का सूक्ष्म विवेचन करते हुए उसके मौलिक अर्थ की उद्‌भावना की है। उनका अभिमत है-

तत्र श्रृंगारो द्विविधः संयोगो विप्रलम्भश्च रतेः संयोगकालावच्छिन्नत्वे प्रथमः वियोगकालावच्छिन्नत्वे द्वितीयः। संयोगो न दम्पत्योः सामानाधिकरण्यम्। एकशयनेऽपीर्ष्यासद्‌भावो विप्रलम्भस्यैव वर्णनात्। एवं वियोगोऽपि न वैयधिकरण्यं दोषस्योक्तत्वात्। तस्माद् द्वाविमौ संयोगवियोगाख्यावन्तः करणवृत्तिविशेषौ यत् संयुक्तवियुक्तश्चास्मीति धीः[12]

पण्डितराज जगन्नाथ के अनुसार श्रृंगार दो प्रकार का है-संयोग एवं विप्रलम्भ। यदि स्त्री-पुरुष के संयोग के समय प्रेम हो तो संयोग श्रृंगार तथा वियोग के समय हो तो विप्रलम्भ श्रृंगार परन्तु संयोग का अर्थ 'एक स्थान पर रहना' नहीं है, क्योंकि एक शय्या पर शयन करते हुए युगल में भी यदि ईर्ष्यादि हों तो विप्रलम्भ रस का ही निरूपण किया जाता है। इसी प्रकार वियोग का अर्थ भी अलग रहना नहीं है क्योंकि वही दोष वहाँ भी कहा जा सकता है। अतः यह मानना चाहिए कि संयोग ओर वियोग एक प्रकार की चित्तवृत्तियाँ हैं और वह है-संयुक्त हूं (मिला हुआ हूँ) और वियुक्त हूं (बिछड़ा हुआ हूं)-यह ज्ञान। 'संयुक्त हूं' इस प्रकार का मनोभाव ही संयोग है और 'वियुक्त हूँ इस प्रकार का मनोभाव ही वियोग है।

आचार्यों के पूर्वोद्धृत अभिमतों से यह पूर्णतः स्पष्ट है कि करुण और विप्रलम्भ दोनों की सम्भावना इष्ट-वियोग की स्थिति में होती है। अतः उसके पश्चात् दोनों के सीमा-निर्धारण की आवश्यकता अनुभूत हुई।

भरतमुनि ने दोनों के अन्तर को बहुत स्पष्टरूप से निर्दिष्ट किया है। उनके अनुसार करुण निरपेक्षभाव है, जबकि विप्रलम्भ सापेक्षभाव। भरत के द्वारा प्रयुक्त निरपेक्ष और सापेक्ष शब्द निराशा और आशा को अभिव्यक्त करते हैं। निरपेक्ष निराशामय (Pessimistic) भाव है, जबकि सापेक्ष आशामय (Optimistic) भाव है। विप्रलम्भ में अस्थायी वियोग होता है और मिलन की प्रत्याशा भी बनी रहती है। आशा की ज्योति जैसे ही बुझी कि करुण का क्षेत्र आ जाता है। संसार का शाश्वत सत्य मृत्यु एक ऐसी सीमा-रेखा है, जिसके एक ओर आशा की क्षीण ज्योति जगमगाती दिखाई देती है और दूसरी ओर बुझी हुई। अतएव, मृत्यु को करुण एवं विप्रलम्भ का सीमा-निर्धारक बनाया गया।

विप्रलम्भ एवं करुण के मध्य एक विशिष्ट सोपान है और वह है करुणविप्रलम्भ। विप्रलम्भ शृंगार के चतुर्विध भेदों में करुणविप्रलम्भ भी परिगणित है। यद्यपि करुण विप्रलम्भ की चर्चा रुद्रट, भोजराज, शिङ्गभूपाल एवं विश्वनाथ महापात्र प्रभृति आचार्यों ने की है, किन्तु हमारी विनम्र सम्मति में इस विप्रलम्भ-भेद का संकेत प्रकारान्तर से *अभिनवभारती* में अभिनवगुप्तपादाचार्य द्वारा भी किया गया है, जिसकी चर्चा हम अन्य आचार्यों के मतों को प्रस्तुत करने के अनन्तर करेंगे।

रुद्रट के अनुसार करुणविप्रलम्भ का लक्षण इस प्रकार है-

करुणः स विप्रलम्भो यत्रान्यतरो म्रियेत नायकयोः।
यदि वा मृतकल्पः स्यात्तत्रान्यस्तद्गतं प्रलपेत्।।[13]

अर्थात् नायक या नायिका दोनों में से किसी एक की मृत्यु हो जाये अथवा कोई एक मृतकल्प हो और दूसरा तद्गत प्रलाप करे तो उसे करुणविप्रलम्भ कहते हैं।

भोजराज ने तो विश्वनाथ कविराज से पूर्व ही विप्रलम्भ को चतुर्विध माना है-

भावो यदा रतिर्नाम प्रकर्षमधिगच्छति।
नाधिगच्छति चाभीष्टं विप्रलम्भस्तदोच्यते।।
पूर्वानुरागो मानश्च प्रवासः करुणश्च सः।
पुरुषस्त्रीप्रकाण्डेषु चतुःकाण्डः प्रकाशते।।[14]

करुण विप्रलम्भ के सम्बन्ध में भोजराज की उक्ति है -

लोकान्तरगते यूनि वल्लभे वल्लभा यदा।
भृशं दुःखायते दीना करुणः स तदोच्यते।।[15]

अर्थात् प्रिय युवक के दूसरे लोक में चले जाने पर जब उसकी प्रियतमा अतिशय दुःखी होती है, तब वहाँ करुणविप्रलम्भ होता है। इनके अभिमतानुसार दो प्रेमियों में किसी एक की मृत्यु हो जाती है और कालान्तर में उनका पुनर्मिलन सम्पन्न हो जाता है या फिर वस्तुतः मृत्यु होती नहीं, समझ ली जाती है तथा बाद में पुनर्मिलन हो जाता है तो वहाँ करुण-विप्रलम्भ शृंगार होता है।

ऐसा प्रतीत होता है कि इन आचार्यों ने करुणविप्रलम्भ को करुण की सीमारेखा में रखकर देखा है। प्रश्न यह है कि प्रेमी के लोकान्तरगमन पर प्रेमिका विलाप करे तो यदि इसे करुण विप्रलम्भ माना जाये तो फिर करुण कहाँ होगा? यहाँ रति स्थायी है अथवा शोक स्थायी है? जहाँ पूर्ण निराशा होगी, वहाँ करुण ही होगा, करुणविप्रलम्भ नहीं। भरतमुनि ने इस भेद को करुण एवं विप्रलम्भ के प्रसंग में बड़ी चातुरी से स्पष्ट किया है-

करुणस्तु शापक्लेशविनिपतितेष्टजनविप्रयोगविभवनाशवधबन्धनसमुत्थो निरपेक्षभावः। औत्सुक्यचिन्तासमुत्थः सापेक्षभावो विप्रलम्भकृतः। एवमन्यः करुणो अन्यश्च विप्रलम्भ इति।[16]

करुण में पूर्ण निरपेक्षभाव अर्थात् निराशा की अवस्था होती है, जबकि विप्रलम्भ में सापेक्षभाव अर्थात् अभिलाषा सतत विद्यमान रहती है। इस प्रकार रति प्रवृत्तिमूलक है एवं शोक निवृत्तिमूलक।

करुणविप्रलम्भ वह श्रृंगार-प्रकार है जिसे प्रेमी और प्रेमिका में से किसी एक के दिवंगत हो जाने किन्तु पुनरुज्जीवित हो सकने की अवस्था में, जीवित बचे दूसरे के हृदय के शोकसंवलित रतिभाव का अभिव्यञ्जन कहा गया है। करुणविप्रलम्भ वस्तुतः करुण का भ्रमोत्पादक वियोग-श्रृंगार-प्रकार है, जैसा 'रसार्णवसुधाकर' में शिङ्गभूपाल के कथन से स्पष्ट है-

द्वयोरेकस्य मरणे पुनरुज्जीवनावधौ।।
विरहः करुणोऽन्यस्य सङ्गमाशानुवर्तनात्।
करुणभ्रमकारित्वात् सोऽयं करुण उच्यते।।
संचारिणोऽनुभावाश्च करुणेऽपि प्रवासवत्।।[17]

विश्वनाथ महापात्र ने भी विप्रलम्भ को चतुर्विध माना है। करुणविप्रलम्भ को व्याख्यायित करते हुए वे कहते हैं-

यूनोरेकतरस्मिन्गातवति लोकान्तरं पुनर्लभ्ये।
विमनायते यदैकस्ततो भवेत् करुणविप्रलम्भाख्यः।।[18]

अर्थात् नायक-नायिका में से एक की मृत्यु हो जाने पर दूसरा जो दुःखी होता है, उस अवस्था को करुणविप्रलम्भ कहते हैं, परन्तु यह तभी होता है जब लोकान्तरगत व्यक्ति से मिलन की आशा हो। यहाँ यह ध्यातव्य है कि प्रिय और प्रिया में से किसी एक की आत्यन्तिक मृत्यु से मिलन की अत्यन्त निराशा अथवा लोकान्तर में मिलन की अवस्था में करुण रस ही होगा (क्योंकि मिलन की आशा के अभाव में रति सम्भव नहीं है, वहां तो शोक ही सम्भव है) करुणविप्रलम्भ नहीं-

पुनरलभ्ये शरीरान्तरेण वा लभ्ये तु करुणाख्य एव रसः।[19]

विश्वनाथ महापात्र जन्मान्तर में मिलन की आशा को करुण रस मान रहे हैं, किन्तु जन्मान्तर में मिलन की आशा से तो रति की सत्ता विद्यमान ही रहेगी। अतः वहाँ भी करुणविप्रलम्भ ही स्वीकार करना चाहिए।

करुणविप्रलम्भ शृंगार एवं करुण के भेद को अतिशय चातुरी के साथ भोजराज ने *शृंगारप्रकाश* में स्पष्ट किया है। इन दोनों में हेतु, फल, विषय तथा स्वरूप के आधार पर भेद प्रस्तुत करते हुए वे कहते हैं–

रत्यैकहेतुः करुणः प्रीतिदयाद्यनेकहेतुः शोकः
पुनः सङ्गमफलः करुणोऽपि पुनः सङ्गमफलः शोकः।
स्त्रीपुंसविषयः करुणोऽस्त्रीपुंसविषयः शोकः
सप्रत्याशारूपः करुणः निष्प्रत्याशारूपः शोकः।।[20]

अर्थात् करुणविप्रलम्भ का एकमात्र हेतु रति है, जबकि करुण के प्रति दया आदि अनेक हेतु होते हैं। करुणविप्रलम्भ का फल पुनः संगम है, किन्तु करुण में पुनः समागम कदापि सम्भव नहीं है। करुणविप्रलम्भ स्त्री और पुरुष मात्र का विषय है, जबकि करुण में ऐसा नहीं है। करुणविप्रलम्भ में मिलन की प्रत्याशा सदा बनी रहती है, जबकि करुण में प्रत्याशा का नितान्त अभाव रहता है।

निष्कर्षतः विप्रलम्भ के विषय में कहा जा सकता है कि शोक की प्रकृति से युक्त होने पर भी करुणविप्रलम्भ का विरह में अन्तर्भाव हो जाता है, क्योंकि उसके मूल में रति स्थायिभाव के रूप में सतत विद्यमान रहती है। विश्वनाथ प्रभृति आचार्य कादम्बरी के पुण्डरीक–महाश्वेता–वृत्तान्त में, पुनरुज्जीवित होने वाले पुण्डरीक की मृत्यु पर महाश्वेता के शोकसंविग्न रतिभाव के अभिव्यञ्जन को करुणविप्रलम्भ के अन्तर्गत स्वीकार करते हैं। *कादम्बरी* में पुण्डरीक की मृत्यु के पश्चात् महाश्वेता एवं कपिञ्जल के विलाप से करुण की अभिव्यक्ति होती है, किन्तु नभोवाणी से जैसे ही महाश्वेता के हृदय में पुण्डरीक के पुनर्मिलन की आशा का सञ्चार होता है, तत्काल ही रतिभाव उद्बुद्ध हो जाता है और वहाँ करुण से करुणविप्रलम्भ की सत्ता आ जाती है–

किञ्चाकाशसरस्वतीभाषानन्तरमेव शृंगारः, सङ्गमप्रत्याशया रतेरुद्भवात्।
प्रथमं तु करुण एव, इत्यभियुक्ता मन्यन्ते।[21]

आचार्य विश्वेश्वर के मतानुसार पुण्डरीक–महाश्वेता का आकस्मिक पुनर्मिलन अद्भुत रस की सृष्टि करता है। उनकी सम्मति में मृत्यु के अनन्तर पुण्डरीक का पुनर्जीवित होना कवि–कल्पनामात्र है। यहां घटना के परिप्रेक्ष्य में अन्त तक करुण की सत्ता होनी चाहिए, क्योंकि मृत्यु के अनन्तर पुनर्जीवन की कोई सम्भावना नहीं होती। पुनर्जीवन जैसी अवस्था की सम्भावना तब हो सकती है जब मृत्यु हुई ही न हो, किन्तु समझ ली गयी हो। इसलिए इस अप्रत्याशित मिलन को अद्भुत रस की परिधि में माना जा सकता है।

तरुण समीक्षक श्री शैलेश कुमार मिश्र की सम्मति में "आचार्य विश्वेश्वर का मत असङ्गत प्रतीत होता है, क्योंकि अद्‌भुत की सत्ता केवल उसी क्षेत्र तक है जब दिव्यपुरुष नभोमण्डल से अवतरित होकर दोनों के पुनर्मिलन की भविष्यवाणी करता है। अतः विस्मय की सत्ता अल्पकालीन है और वह व्यभिचारिमात्र होकर रह गया है।"[22]

धनञ्जय, शारदातनय प्रभृति आचार्य इस प्रसंग में प्रवासविप्रलम्भ मानते हैं। यहाँ प्रवासविप्रलम्भ मानना समीचीन नहीं है, क्योंकि प्रवास में सशरीर देशान्तरगमन होता है जबकि करुण में केवल प्राणों का लोकान्तरगमन होता है। यहाँ *रसार्णवसुधाकरप्रणेता* शिंगभूपाल का मत द्रष्टव्य है–

नन्वेवं प्रवासकरुणयोः को भेद इति चेत् उच्यते।
शरीरेण देशान्तरगमने प्रवासः प्राणैर्देशान्तरगमने करुण इति।।[23]

व्याख्येय दृष्टान्त में पुण्डरीक का अशरीर लोकान्तरगमन करुण की परिधि में आता है, क्योंकि एक की मृत्यु पर दूसरे के विलाप से करुण का अभिव्यञ्जन होता है, प्रवासविप्रलम्भ का नहीं। मृत्यु के अनन्तर दैवी प्रभाव से पुनर्जीवित होने पर वहाँ मिलन की आशा होने से करुणविप्रलम्भ मानना समीचीन है। इस सन्दर्भ में विविध आचार्यों के मतों का विवेचन करने के अनन्तर हम कह सकते हैं कि उपरि प्रस्तुत रसात्मक अनुभूति का अन्तर्भाव न करुण में हो सकता है और न ही विप्रलम्भ में। अतएव करुणविप्रलम्भ की सत्ता स्वीकार करना ही सर्वाधिक समीचीन है।

विश्वनाथ प्रभृति आचार्य कादम्बरी के पुण्डरीक–महाश्वेता–वृत्तान्त में, पुनरुज्जीवित होने वाले पुण्डरीक की मृत्यु पर महाश्वेता के शोकसंविग्न रतिभाव के अभिव्यञ्जन को करुणविप्रलम्भ के अन्तर्गत स्वीकार करते हैं। इसी प्रकार कुमारसम्भव के रतिविलाप में सर्वप्रथम अभिव्यंग्य रस करुण प्रतीत होता है किन्तु आकाशवाणी द्वारा रति के हृदय में कामदेव से पुनर्मिलन की आशा जग उठने के बाद सहृदय–हृदय करुणविप्रलम्भ का आस्वाद ले सकता है। हमारी सम्मति में कुमारसम्भव का रतिविलाप करुणविप्रलम्भ का श्रेष्ठ निदर्शन है। अपने मत की पुष्टि में हम शिंगभूपाल द्वारा प्रस्तुत करुणविप्रलम्भ का रतिविलापस्थ उदाहरण तथा वृत्ति प्रस्तुत करते हैं :

अथ मदनवधूरुपप्लवान्तं व्यसनकृशा प्रतिपालयांबभूव।
शशिन इव दिवातनस्य रेखा किरणपरिक्षयधूसरा प्रदोषम्।।

कुमारसम्भवे, 4.46

अत्र आकाशसरस्वतीप्रत्ययेन रतेर्विप्रलम्भः कृशत्वाद्यनुमितैर्ग्लान्यादिभिः व्यभिचारिभावैः पोषितः समयपरिपालनादिभिरनुभावैर्व्यज्यते।

अत्र केचिदाहु:-करुणो नाम विप्रलम्भशृङ्गारो नास्ति। उभयालम्बनस्य तस्य एकत्रैवासम्भवात्। यत्र त्वेकस्यापाये सति तदितरगता: प्रलापादयो भवन्ति स शोकान्न भिद्यते इति। तदयुक्तम्। यत्र पुनरुज्जीवनेन संभोगो नास्ति तत्र सत्यं शोक एव। यत्र सोऽस्ति तत्र विप्रलम्भ एव।[24]

शृंगारतिलक एवं *रसकलिका* में भी विप्रलम्भ के चार भेद उल्लिखित हैं-

विप्रलम्भाभिधानोऽयं शृंगार स्याच्चतुर्विधः।
पूर्वानुरागो मानाख्यः प्रवासः करुणात्मकः।।[25]
तत्रा विरहश्चतुर्विधः पूर्वानुरागमानाख्यप्रवासकरुणात्मकः[26]

आचार्य विश्वनाथ ने पूर्वराग विप्रलम्भ में दस कामदशाएँ-अभिलाष, चिन्ता, स्मृति, गुणकथन, उद्वेग, संप्रलाप, उन्माद, व्याधि, जड़ता एवं मृति बताई हैं।[27] अन्य आचार्यों के अनुसार उन्होंने कामदशाओं की एक भिन्न सूची भी दी है-नयनप्रीति, चित्तासंग, संकल्प, निद्राच्छेद, तनुता, विषयनिवृत्ति, त्रपानाश, उन्माद, मूर्च्छा एवं मृति।[28] विश्वनाथ ने प्रवास विप्रलम्भ की दस कामदशाएं अलग से निर्दिष्ट की हैं जो इस प्रकार हैं :

अंगेष्वसौष्ठवं तापः पाण्डुता कृशतारुचिः।।
अधृतिः स्यादनालम्बस्तन्मयोन्मादमूर्च्छनाः।
मृतिश्चेति क्रमाज्ज्ञेया दश स्मरदशा इह।।[29]

आचार्य विश्वनाथ ने यद्यपि करुणविप्रलम्भ की कामदशाओं का पृथक् निर्देश नहीं किया है, किन्तु सभी आचार्यों द्वारा निर्दिष्ट कामदशाएं वहां भी दृष्टिगत होंगी, ऐसा माना जा सकता है। इसी तथ्य को ध्यान में रखकर जब हम रतिविलाप को पढ़ते हैं तो वहाँ विलाप कामदशा की बहुलता के साथ अन्य कामदशाओं को भी पाते हैं।

महाकवि भवभूति ने प्रस्तुत पद्य में सीता के द्विविध वियोग को प्रदर्शित कर विप्रलम्भ एवं करुण के अन्तर को प्रकट करने का प्रयास किया है-

उपायानां भावादविरतविनोदव्यतिकरै-
र्विमर्दैर्वीराणां जगति जनितादद्भुतरसः।
वियोगो मुग्धाक्ष्याः स खलु रिपुघातावधिरभूत्
कथं तूष्णीं सह्यो निरविधरयं त्वप्रतिविधः।।[30]

अभिप्राय यह है कि सीताहरणजनित सीता का वह प्रथम वियोग रावणप्रभृति शत्रुओं के विनाशपर्यन्त रहने वाला सावधिक वियोग था। वहाँ पुनर्मिलन की आशा विद्यमान थी, अतः वहाँ विप्रलम्भ था। सीता का यह उपायाभावजन्य निरवधि वियोग जीवनपर्यन्त रहने वाला है, अतः करुण रस की परिधि में आता है।

इस प्रकार रुद्रट, रसकलिकाकार, शिंगभूपाल एवं विश्वनाथ महापात्र ने स्पष्टत: करुणविप्रलम्भ की सत्ता को स्वीकार किया है। कुछ आचार्यों यथा मम्मट को करुणविप्रलम्भ मान्य नहीं। उन्होंने करुणविप्रलम्भ के पाँच भेदों-अभिलाष, विरह, ईर्ष्या, प्रवास तथा शापज को स्वीकार किया है। करुण तथा करुणविप्रलम्भ के अतिसूक्ष्म अन्तर के कारण हेमचन्द्र, मम्मट, जगन्नाथादि आचार्यों ने इसका करुण में ही अन्तर्भाव कर लिया है।

पण्डितराज जगन्नाथ करुणविप्रलम्भ के पृथक् अस्तित्व को स्वीकार नहीं करते हैं। इसलिए उन्होंने उसका अंशत: करुण में तथा अंशत: विप्रलम्भ में अन्तर्भाव किया है। उनके मतानुसार स्त्री-पुरुष के परस्पर वियोग से जो विकलता उत्पन्न होती है, वह निश्चित रूप से शोक है, किन्तु वह शोक करुण का स्थायिभाव तब बन सकता है जब वह प्रेमपात्र के मरणज्ञान के साथ हो, क्योंकि प्रेमपात्र के मरणज्ञान के रहने पर ही स्त्रीपुरुष के वियोग से उत्पन्न विकलता प्रधान हो जाती है। प्रेमपात्र कहीं जीवित है, ऐसा ज्ञान रहने पर वह शोक स्थायिभाव न होकर व्यभिचारिभाव मात्र होता है, क्योंकि उस अवस्था में शोक से पुष्ट की गयी रति की ही प्रधानता होने से वहाँ विप्रलम्भ होता है-

स्त्रीपुंसयोस्तु वियोगे जीवितत्वज्ञानदशायां वैक्लव्यपोषिताया रतेरेव प्राधान्याच्छृंगारो विप्रलम्भाख्यो रस: वैक्लव्यं तु सञ्चारिमात्रम्।[31]

प्रेमपात्र के मरणज्ञान के रहने पर स्त्री-पुरुष के वियोग से उत्पन्न व्याकुलता ही प्रधान होती है और रति उसे पुष्ट करने वाली होती है। अत: वैसी स्थिति में करुण रस की ही अवस्थिति होगी-

मृतत्वज्ञानदशायां तु रतिपोषितस्य वैक्लव्यस्येति करुण एव।[32]

दैवी कृपा से पुनर्जीवनप्राप्ति होने पर पण्डितराज को विप्रलम्भ ही स्वीकार्य है-

यदि तु सत्यपि मृतत्वज्ञाने, देवताप्रसादादिना पुनरुज्जीवनज्ञानं कथञ्चित् स्यात्, तदालम्बनस्यात्यन्तिकनिरासाभावाच्चिरप्रवास इव विप्रलम्भ एव न स करुण:[33]

तात्पर्य यह है कि प्रेमपात्र के मरणज्ञान के रहने पर भी जब दैवी कृपा से किसी तरह उनके पुनर्जीवित होने का ज्ञान होगा तब प्रेमपात्र के सर्वदा के लिए विनष्ट न होने के कारण चिरकालिक प्रवास की भाँति विप्रलम्भ ही होगा, करुण नहीं। आचार्य जगन्नाथ इस प्रसंग को विप्रलम्भ में परिगणित करते हैं, किन्तु उन्होंने अन्य आचार्यों को स्वीकार्य करुणविप्रलम्भ का भी निर्देश किया है तथा अपनी सहमति अथवा असहमति का भी कोई उल्लेख नहीं किया है-

केचित्तु रसान्तरमेवात्र करुणविप्रलम्भाख्यमिच्छन्ति।[34]

भरतमुनि के निर्देशानुसार रसराज श्रृंगार के दोनों अधिष्ठानों-सम्भोग एवं विप्रलम्भ में आलस्य, उग्रता और जुगुप्सा को छोड़कर शेष तीस व्यभिचारिभाव होते हैं जिनमें मरण भी सम्मिलित है-

व्यभिचारिणश्चास्यालस्यौग्र्यजुगुप्सावर्ज्याः।[35]

अभिनवगुप्त ने *अभिनवभारती* में विप्रलम्भ श्रृंगार में अभिलाष से लेकर मरण पर्यन्त दस कामदशाओं का उल्लेख किया है। इसी मरण (व्यभिचारिभावरूप अथवा कामदशारूप) का वर्णन तो इष्टनाशजनित करुण में भी होता है। फिर करुणविप्रलम्भ में दृश्यमान मृत्यु और करुण में सम्पद्यमान मृत्यु में क्या अन्तर है? विप्रलम्भ में मृत्यु का वर्णन किया जाना चाहिए अथवा नहीं? मृत्यु के वर्णन से रसविच्छेद होगा कि नहीं ? आदि अनेक प्रश्नों का समाधान अभिनवगुप्त, विश्वनाथ और आनन्दवर्धन ने अलग-अलग प्रसंगों में अपने-अपने ढंग से किया है, जिससे अनेक नूतन तथ्य उद्घाटित होते हैं।

अभिनवगुप्त के मतानुसार श्रृंगाररस में मृत्यु का वर्णन नहीं करना चाहिए क्योंकि वैसी स्थिति में रतिरूप अवस्था का सम्बन्ध ही विच्छिन्न हो जाता है। यदि मरण का वर्णन किया भी जाये तो शीघ्र प्रत्यापत्ति अर्थात् पुनर्मिलन जहाँ सम्भव हो, ऐसे मरण का उल्लेख किया जा सकता है। इसका फल यह होगा कि शोक इस पुनर्मिलन के कारण स्थान नहीं प्राप्त कर सकेगा और इस प्रकार रतिविच्छेद नहीं होगा। यहाँ ध्यातव्य है कि अभिनवगुप्त ने यद्यपि श्रृंगार में मरण के उल्लेख तथा रसप्रवाह को लक्ष्य कर अपना अभिमत प्रकट किया है, किन्तु प्रकारान्तर से उन्होंने करुणविप्रलम्भ भेद का बीजन्यास कर दिया है। विप्रलम्भ में जब मरण का उल्लेख इस ढंग से किया जाये कि अल्पकाल में ही प्रत्यापत्ति अर्थात् पुनर्जीवन का भी उल्लेख कर दिया जाये और रसप्रवाह भी विच्छिन्न न होने पाये तो वहाँ करुणविप्रलम्भ तो स्थापित हो ही जायेगा। इसलिए मेरी विनम्र सम्मति में करुणविप्रलम्भ का प्रकारान्तर से निर्देश अभिनवगुप्तपादाचार्य ने निम्नलिखित रूप से किया है तथा अपने अभिमत की सम्पुष्टि में रघुवंश के अष्टम सर्ग के अन्तिम पद्य को प्रस्तुत किया है जो इस तथ्य का स्पष्ट परिचायक है कि अजविलाप करुणविप्रलम्भ का श्रेष्ठ निदर्शन है-

तादृश्यां दशायां स्वजीवितनिन्दात्मिकायां तद्देहोपभोगसाररत्यात्मकावस्थाबन्धोऽपि विच्छिद्यत एवेति असम्भव एव। मरणमचिरकालप्रत्यापत्तिमयमत्र मन्तव्यम्। येन शोकोऽवस्थानमेव न लभते। यथा-

तीर्थे तोयव्यतिकरभवे जह्नुकन्यासरय्वो-
र्देहत्यागादमरगणनालेख्यमामाद्य सद्यः
पूर्वावस्थाधिकचतुरया संगतः कान्तयासौ
लीलागारेष्वरमत पुनर्नन्दनाभ्यन्तरेषु।। रघुवंशे, 8.94

अत एव सुकविना वाक्यभेदेनापि मरणं नाख्यातम्। प्रतीतिविश्रान्तिस्थानत्वपरिहाराय तृतीयपादेन विभावानुसन्धानकं दर्शनम्। पुनर्ग्रहणेन स एवार्थः सुतरां द्योतितः।[36]

जाह्नवी और सरयू के संगम से निर्मित तीर्थ पर शरीरत्याग करने के कारण तुरन्त देवताओं की गणना में आ जाने से वे अज पहली अवस्था से अधिक चतुर अर्थात् पूर्व अवस्था से भी अधिक सुन्दर कान्ता इन्दुमती के साथ नन्दनवन के भीतर स्थित क्रीडाभवन में पुनः विहार करने लगे। यहाँ पर तत्काल होने वाले पुनर्मिलन के कारण मरणजनित शोक को अज के हृदय में स्थान नहीं मिला। इसलिए सुकवि कालिदास ने वाक्यभेद करके भी 'मरण' शब्द का प्रयोग नहीं किया, अपितु प्रतीति के विश्रान्ति-स्थान के परिहार के लिए पद्य के तृतीय पाद में कान्ता इन्दुमती रूप विभाव का अनुसन्धान दिखलाया है और चतुर्थ पाद में 'पुनः' पद के ग्रहण से वही सम्भोगरूप अर्थ प्रकाशित कर दिया है।

'रघुवंश' के अष्टम सर्ग में इन्दुमती के दिवंगत हो जाने पर जो अजविलाप उपन्यस्त है, वस्तुतः उसमें अनुस्मृति, विलाप तथा अन्य अनेक कामदशाएं विद्यमान हैं। यहां प्रश्न सम्भाव्य है कि आलम्बन के नष्ट हो जाने पर कामदशा कैसी? यह विषय अतिगम्भीर है कि वहाँ करुण रस की अवस्थिति मानी जाय या फिर करुणविप्रलम्भ श्रृंगार की। हमारी सम्मति में अजविलाप में करुणविप्रलम्भ श्रृंगार की अवस्थिति मानना अधिक उपयुक्त होगा, तभी वहाँ कामदशाओं की अवस्थिति मानी जा सकती है। इन्दुमती दिवंगत हो जाती हैं, किन्तु महाराज अज भी गंगा एवं सरयू के जल के मिश्रण से बने तीर्थ में देहत्याग कर पुनः अपनी प्रिया के साथ समागम-सुख प्राप्त करते हैं।[37]

पूर्वाचार्यों ने करुणविप्रलम्भ का जो विवेचन प्रस्तुत किया है, उसमें तथा अजविलाप की स्थिति में अन्तर केवल इतना है कि वहाँ आलम्बन के नष्ट हो जाने पर तथा पुनरुज्जीवित होने पर आश्रय के साथ उसका मिलन होता है और यहाँ आश्रयरूप अज अपने नष्ट हुए आलम्बन (कान्ता इन्दुमती वस्तुतः हरिणी नामक देवांगना) के साथ स्वकीयदेहत्यागानान्तर स्वर्ग में समागम-सुख प्राप्त कर रहे हैं। अजविलाप को भी यदि हम करुणविप्रलम्भ श्रृंगार के अन्तर्गत स्वीकार करें तो वहाँ अज की दशाएँ कामदशाओं के अन्तर्गत परिगणित की जा सकेंगी। वस्तुतः यह विषय विद्वानों द्वारा अवधानप्रदान तथा विवेचन की अपेक्षा रखता है। हमारी सम्मति में अजविलाप को करुणविप्रलम्भ श्रृंगार के अन्तर्गत माना जा सकता है। हम अपने मत की पुष्टि में रघुवंश के अष्टम सर्ग के अन्तिम पद्य तथा श्रीमदरुणगिरिनाथ की टीका को प्रस्तुत करते हैं-

तीर्थे तोयव्यतिकरभवे जह्नुकन्यासरय्वो-
र्देहत्यागादमरगणनालेख्यमासाद्य सद्यः।

पूर्वाकाराधिकचतुरया संगतः कान्तयासौ
लीलागारेष्वरमत पुनर्नन्दनाभ्यन्तरेषु।।[38]

प्रकाशिका–उपसंहरति। तीर्थ इति। तीर्थविशेषस्त्विष्टसाधनतया निर्दिष्टः, तस्य तथा प्रसिद्धेः। अमरगणनायां लेख्यं न्यस्ताक्षरं, पत्रमित्यर्थः। तस्यासादनन्नाम तत्र न्यस्तत्वम्। तेन पदप्राप्तेः स्थैर्यमुक्तम्। सद्यः अविलम्बितम्। पूर्वाकारा अधिकचतुरा च। पूर्वाकारत्वं सैवेयमिति प्रतीत्यर्थम्। अनेन हरिणीरूपेणैवेन्दुमती जातेति गम्यते। अधिकचतुरत्वं दिव्यानुभावत्वात्। नन्दनाभ्यन्तरेषु नन्दनस्याभ्यन्तरवर्तिषु। अत्राश्रयविच्छेदे रसात्यन्तविच्छेदो माभूदिति कविकुलचक्रवर्तिना मरणस्यानुवाद्यत्वेनोपनिबन्धः कृतः, न तु विश्रान्तिधामतया विधेयत्वेनेत्यवसेयम्।[39]

हमारी सम्मति में *रघुवंश* के अष्टम सर्ग का यह अन्तिम पद्य यहां आश्रयरूप अज तथा आलम्बनरूप इन्दुमती जो अब अपने वास्तविक स्वरूप अर्थात् हरिणी नामक देवांगना के रूप में हैं, का सुखद संगम निरूपित है, इस तथ्य का स्पष्ट परिचायक माना जा सकता है कि अजविलाप को करुणविप्रलम्भ के अन्तर्गत स्वीकार कर लिया जाये। वस्तुतः यह विषय विद्वानों द्वारा अन्वेषणीय एवं विवेचनीय है।

श्रृंगार में मरण का उल्लेख किस प्रकार किया जाय–इस सम्बन्ध में ध्वन्यालोककार आनन्दवर्धन का मत इस प्रकार है–

श्रृंगारे वा मरणस्यादीर्घकालप्रत्यापत्तिसम्भवे कदाचिदुपनिबन्धो नात्यन्तविरोधी। दीर्घकालप्रत्यापत्तौ तु तस्यान्तरा प्रवाहविच्छेद एवेत्येवंविधेति वृत्तोपनिबन्धनं रसबन्धप्रधानेन कविना परिहर्तव्यम्।[40]

श्रृंगार में शीघ्र मिलन की सम्भावना होने पर मरण का कदाचित् उपनिबन्धन अत्यन्त विरोधी नहीं है, किन्तु दीर्घ काल पर मिलन होने पर रस का बीच में ही प्रवाहविच्छेद हो जायेगा। अतः मरण के अनन्तर पुनः प्रत्यापत्ति का वर्णन इतने कम समय में होना चाहिए, जिससे सहृदयों के श्रृंगाररसास्वादन में कोई विच्छेद न हो और उन्हें रसराजामृत का सम्पूर्ण रसास्वाद सुलभ हो।

आचार्यों द्वारा निर्दिष्ट कामदशाओं में अन्तिम है मरण कामदशा जिसके विषय में उनके मत इस प्रकार हैं :

मरण

नाट्यशास्त्र	सर्वैः कृतैः प्रतीकारैर्यदि नास्ति समागमः कामाग्निना प्रदीप्ताया जायते मरणन्ततः।।
श्रृंगारतिलक	उपायैर्विविधैर्नार्या यदि न स्यात्समागमः। कन्दर्पशरभिन्नाया मरणं जायते ततः।।

नाटकलक्षणरत्नकोश-	मरणं प्राणच्छेद: यथोक्तम् यत्नैरलभमानेष्टसंगमेऽन्त: प्रदीपित:। कामाग्निर्ज्वलयत्यंगान्यदोष इस लंङ्घनम्।।
भावप्रकाशन-	आस्ववस्थासु विहितै: प्रतीकारै: समागम:। न भवेद्यदि कामाग्निदग्धयोर्मरणं भवेत्।।
उज्जवलनीलमणि-	तैस्तै: कृतै: प्रतीकारैर्यदि न स्यात्समागम:। कन्दर्पबाणकदनात्तत्र स्यान्मरणोद्यम:।।[41]

जब नायक अथवा नायिका एक-दूसरे को प्राप्त करने के लिए सभी प्रकार के उपाय कर लें, किन्तु उन्हें प्रिय की प्राप्ति न हो सके तो ऐसी स्थिति में मरण नामक कामदशा आती है। ऐसी स्थिति में प्रेम की ज्वाला शरीर को भी दग्ध कर देती है। रूपगोस्वामी के अनुसार ऐसी दशा में नायक अथवा नायिका अपनी सारी प्रिय वस्तुएं अपने वयस्यों को समर्पित कर देते हैं। भ्रमर, मन्द पवन, ज्योत्स्ना और कदम्ब आदि इसके अनुभाव होते हैं-

तत्र स्वप्रियवस्तूनां वयस्यासु समर्पणम्।
भृंगमन्दानिलज्योत्स्नाकदम्बानुभवादय:।।[42]

इस मरण दशा को काव्यों अथवा नाटकों में निबद्ध किया जाय अथवा नहीं इस सम्बन्ध में शास्त्रकारों में मतभेद है। पुन: यदि इसे निबद्ध किया जाय भी तो उसका स्वरूप क्या हो, इस सम्बन्ध में भी विवाद बना हुआ है। भरत मुनि मात्र इतना कहकर ही मौन हो जाते हैं कि अन्तिम दशा का प्रदर्शन नहीं करना चाहिए। आचार्य रुद्रट इसे अशोभन मानते हैं और इसीलिए उसे काव्योचित नहीं मानते हैं। आचार्य सागरनन्दी तो स्पष्ट शब्दों में कहते हैं कि यह दशा नाटकीय घटना का अंग नहीं हो सकती है। आचार्य शारदातनय मरण को अमंगलसूचक मानते हुए उसे युवक-युवती के बीच वर्ण्य नहीं मानते हैं। विश्वनाथ महापात्र के अनुसार मरण का वर्णन करने से रस विच्छिन्न हो जाता है, अत: उसका वर्णन नहीं किया जाना चाहिए-

नाट्यशास्त्र-	एवं स्थानानि कार्याणि कामतन्त्रं समीक्ष्य तु। अप्राप्तौ यानि काम्यस्य वर्जयित्वा तु नैधनम्।।
शृंगारतिलक-	गरणं किं त्वरौन्दर्यात्तयो: कैश्चिन्न गिबध्यते।।
नाटकलक्षणरत्नकोश-	तस्यैवंविधस्य मरणस्य लक्षणमनंगवृत्तित्वादाचार्येण नोपवलृणतमलमस्योपन्यासेन।
भावप्रकाशन-	अमंगलं स्यान्मरणमिति यूनोर्न कल्प्यते।
साहित्यदर्पण-	रसविच्छेदहेतुत्वान्मरणं नैव वर्ण्यते।।[43]

आचार्य रुद्रट मरण का काव्य-निबन्धन स्वीकार नहीं करते हुए कहते हैं कि कुछ लोग नायक अथवा नायिका के प्रत्युज्जीवन की इच्छा से मरण का वर्णन करते हैं। ऐसा प्रख्यात कथा में तो चल सकता है, किन्तु उत्पाद्य कथा के लिए यह उचित नहीं है, क्योंकि यदि एक के मरने पर किसी प्रकार दूसरा जीवित भी रह जाये तो वहाँ प्रेम कहाँ रह जाएगा-

अन्ये तदपि बध्नन्ति प्रत्युज्जीवनवाञ्छया।
वृत्तानुवादे तच्छस्तमुत्पाद्ये प्रायशो न हि।।
एकस्मिंस्तु मृतेऽप्यन्यो यदि जीवेत्कथंचन।
का स्नेहगणना तत्र म्रियते चेन्न संगमः।।[44]

आचार्य धनिक भी इसी तथ्य के पोषक हैं। वे कहते हैं कि श्रृंगार के आलम्बन में कभी भी मरण का वर्णन नहीं करना चाहिए। मरण की तैयारी का संकेत-मात्र किया जा सकता है- श्रृंगाराश्रयालम्बनत्वेन मरणे व्यवसायमात्रमुपनिबन्धनीयम्। अन्यत्र कामाचार।[45]

विश्वनाथ महापात्र श्रृंगार में मरण दशा के चित्रण को वर्जित मानते हुए आगे कहते हैं कि यदि इस दशा का चित्रण किया भी जाय तो वह दो रूप में हो सकता है-मरणासन्न दशा के रूप में अथवा मरण की हार्दिक अभिलाषा के रूप में, जहां मरण के बाद पुनः जीवन का निर्देश किया जाय। यथा-

जातप्रायं तु तद्वाच्यं चेतसाकांक्षितं तथा।
वर्ण्यतेऽपि यदि प्रत्युज्जीवनं स्याददूरतः।।[46]

आचार्य विश्वनाथ ने स्वयं ही इन दोनों प्रकार की मरण दशाओं का वर्णन निम्नलिखित श्लोकों के माध्यम से किया है-

शेफालिकां विदलितामवलोक्य तन्वी
प्राणान् कथंचिदपि धारयितुं प्रभूता।
आकर्ण्य सम्प्रति रुतं चरणायुधानां
किं वा भविष्यति न वेद्मि तपस्विनी सा।।[47]

अरे मित्र! तुम्हारी तन्वी प्रेमिका का हाल क्या कहूँ? जब उसने खिले हुए शेफालिका फूलों को देखा, तब बड़ी कठिनता से प्राण धारण किया, किन्तु इस समय मुर्गे की ध्वनि को सुनकर, कहा नहीं जा सकता है, उसकी क्या स्थिति होगी।

विश्वनाथ महापात्र के उपर्युक्त श्लोक में नायिका की मरणासन्न दशा का चित्रण हुआ है। इसमें कहा गया है कि रात्रि में तो नायिका प्रिय से मिलन की आशा में किसी

तरह जीवन धारण किए रही, लेकिन जब उसने मुर्गे की आवाज़ सुनकर यह जान लिया होगा कि अब प्रातःकाल हो गया है तो पता नहीं अब उसकी क्या स्थिति हो गयी होगी, अर्थात् सम्भवतः वह अब जीवित नहीं होगी। तथा-

रोलम्बाः परिपूरयन्तु हरितो झकांरकोलाहलै-
र्मन्दं मन्दमुपैतु चन्दनवनीजातो नभस्वानपि।
माद्यन्तः कलयन्तु चूतशिखरे केलीपिका: पञ्चमं
प्राणाः सत्वरमश्मसारकठिना गच्छन्तु गच्छन्त्वमी।।[48]

भौंरे अपने मधुर कूजन से दिशाओं को भर दें, मलयानिल के मन्द झोंके चारों ओर विद्यमान हो जाएं, आम्र-मंजरी की सुगन्धि से मतवाले कोयल पञ्चम स्वर में कूक उठें और पत्थर से भी कठोर मेरे प्राण, जितनी जल्दी हो, मुझे छोड़कर चले जायें।

उपर्युक्त श्लोक में आचार्य विश्वनाथ ने ऐसे प्रेमी का वर्णन किया है, जिसका प्रिय जब उसको मिल नहीं पाता है तो वह प्रेमी अन्ततः अपनी मृत्यु को वरण करने की अभिलाषा प्रकट करता है। प्रत्युज्जीवन रूप जिस तीसरे प्रकार की मरणदशा का संकेत शास्त्रकारों ने किया है उस पर विचार करते हुए आचार्य विश्वनाथ ने कहा है कि कादम्बरी के महाश्वेता और पुण्डरीक के वृतान्त में यह प्रकार परिलक्षित होता है, किन्तु इसे करुणविप्रलम्भ के अन्तर्गत ही रखा जा सकता है-कादम्बर्या महाश्वेतापुण्डरीकवृत्तान्ते। एष च प्रकारः करुणविप्रलम्भविषय इति।[49]

आचार्य रुद्रट ने भी प्रत्युज्जीवन-रूप मरणदशा को स्वीकार किया है, किन्तु उन्होंने इसके लिए प्रख्यात कथा को आधार माना है। ऐसी स्थिति में कादम्बरी में आने वाली कथा में इसका वर्णन उचित नहीं माना जायेगा, क्योंकि कादम्बरी की कथा प्रख्यात नहीं है, अपितु वह उत्पाद्य है।

यहाँ भरतमुनि, रुद्रट, आनन्दवर्धन, अभिनवगुप्त, धनञ्जय, भोजराज, मम्मट, हेमचन्द्र, विश्वनाथ कविराज, शिंगभूपाल एवं पण्डितराज जगन्नाथ के श्रृंगार एवं करुण रस से सम्बद्ध मतों का विश्लेषण प्रस्तुत किया गया।

निष्कर्षतः कहा जा सकता है कि करुणविप्रलम्भ श्रृंगार रस का भेद है। अतः यह रतिस्थायिमूलक है तथा करुण रस शोकस्थायिमूलक है। करुणविप्रलम्भ प्रवृत्तिमूलक सापेक्षभाव है और करुण निवृत्तिमूलक निरपेक्षभाव है।

अभिनवगुप्त का स्पष्ट अभिमत है कि श्रृंगार के अनन्तर नियमतः करुण होता है। वे कहते हैं-

श्रृंगारानन्तरं नियमेन करुणः।
रतिप्रलापेषु च श्रृंगार एव करुणस्य जीवितम्-

'हृदये वससीति मत्प्रियं यदवोचस्तदवैमि कैतवम्।
उपचारपदं न चेदिदं त्वमनंग कथमक्षता रतिः।।'
इत्याद्युक्तिषु।[50]

कुमारसम्भव, 49

अर्थात् कुमारसम्भव में रति के प्रलाप में शृंगार ही करुण रस का जीवित है, प्राण है। यथा– ''हे दयित! 'तुम मेरे हृदय में रहती हो', इस प्रकार का प्रियवचन तो तुमने कहा था, उसे मैं कपट (छल) समझती हूं। यदि उपचारमात्र न होता तो तुम तो जलकर अंगहीन (अनंग) हो गये और तुम्हारे हृदय में वास करने वाली रति अक्षत कैसे रहती?'' यहां पर शृंगार रस के आधार पर ही करुण रस की उत्पत्ति हो रही है।

यहाँ हमने अभिनवगुप्त का मत प्रस्तुत किया, किन्तु हमारी विनम्र सम्मति में यहाँ भी करुणविप्रलम्भ का संकेत स्वीकार किया जा सकता है।

अब तक प्रस्तुत विवेचन के आधार पर कुमारसम्भव का रतिविलाप तथा रघुवंश का अजविलाप करुणविप्रलम्भ के श्रेष्ठ निदर्शन हैं। रतिविलाप तथा अजविलाप में अनेक कामदशाओं का सुष्ठु निरूपण हुआ है, जिसका विस्तरेण उल्लेख यहाँ प्रसंगप्राप्त है।

रतिविलाप

प्रलाप कामदशा

1. अथ सा पुनरेव विह्वला वसुधालिंगनधूसरस्तनी।
   विललाप विकीर्णमूर्धजा समदुःखामिव कुर्वती स्थलीम्।।
2. उपमानमभूद्विलासिनां कारणं यत्तव कान्तिमत्तया।
   तदिदं गतमीदृशीं दशां न विदीर्ये कठिनाः खलु स्त्रियः।।
3. क्व नु मां त्वदधीनजीवितां विनिकीर्य क्षणभिन्नसौहृदः।
   नलिनीं क्षतसेतुबन्धनो जलसंघात इवासि विद्रुतः।।
4. कृतवानसि विप्रियं न मे प्रतिकूलं न च ते मया कृतम्।
   किमकारणमेव दर्शनं विलपन्त्यै रतये न दीयते।।
5. स्मरसि स्मर मेखलागुणैरुत गोत्रस्खलितेषु बन्धनम्।
   च्युतकेशरदूषितेक्षणान्यवतंसोत्पलताडनानि वा।।
6. हृदये वससीति मत्प्रियं यदवोचस्तदवैमि कैतवम्।
   उपचारपदं न चेदिदं त्वमनंग कथमक्षता रतिः।।[51]

तब तो वह रति अत्यन्त विह्वल होकर धरती पर लोटने लगी, जिससे उसके स्तन धूलि से धूसरित हो उठे। वह अपने बालों को बिखेर कर विलाप करने लगी और इस

प्रकार उसके विलाप से वह वनस्थली भी उसके इस दुःख में समान दुःख वाली-सी बन गयी। अपने अनुपम सौन्दर्य के कारण तुम्हारा जो शरीर विलासी पुरुषों का उपमान बना हुआ था, उसकी आज ऐसी दयनीय दशा हो गयी है और मेरा हृदय फिर भी नहीं फट रहा है। हाय! सचमुच स्त्रियां बड़ी कठोर होती हैं। हे प्रियतम, जैसे जल का प्रवाह बांध टूट जाने पर कमलिनी को छोड़कर भाग खड़ा होता है, उसी प्रकार तुम्हारे सहारे जीवन बिताने वाली मुझको छोड़कर और पल-भर में ही स्नेह का नाता तोड़कर तुम कहां चले गये हो ? हे प्रियतम, तुमने मुझे अप्रसन्न करने वाला कोई कार्य नहीं किया और न मैंने ही तुम्हारे प्रतिकूल कोई आचरण किया। तब फिर बिना किसी कारण के ही बिलखती हुई इस रति को तुम अपना दर्शन क्यों नहीं दे रहे हो। हे स्मर, एक बार तुमने मेरे सामने भूल से किसी अन्य स्त्री का नाम ले लिया था, जिस पर मैंने प्रणय-कोप करके तुम्हें अपनी मेखला से बांध दिया था और अपने कर्णाभूषण कमल से तुम्हारे मुख में ताडन किया था, जिससे उस कमल का पराग तुम्हारी आंखों में पड़ गया था और तुम्हारी आंख दुखने लगी थी। कहीं उसी प्रसंग को याद करके तो तुम नहीं रूठे हुए हो। तुम (कामदेव) कहा करते थे कि तुम (रति) मेरे हृदय में निवास करती हो। मैं अब समझ रही हूं कि यह तुम्हारा छल था। यदि ऐसा न होता तो यह कैसे सम्भव था कि तुम्हारे भस्मशेष हो जाने पर भी मैं (रति) कैसे इस प्रकार जीवित बची रहती।

उपर्य्युद्धृत सभी पद्य कामदेव के हरकोपानल से भस्म हो जाने पर रति की विलाप कामदशा के निदर्शक हैं। *कुमारसम्भव* के प्रायः सम्पूर्ण चतुर्थ सर्ग में यह तथा मरण कामदशा निरूपित हैं। इस सर्ग के पद्यों में विलाप या प्रलाप कामदशा तभी मानी जा सकती है जब यहां करुणविप्रलम्भ श्रृंगार की स्थिति मानी जाये। आचार्य अभिनवगुप्त, भोजराज, आचार्य विश्वनाथ एवं शिगंभूपाल द्वारा निर्दिष्ट परिभाषाओं तथा निर्देशों के अनुसार रतिविलाप करुणविप्रलम्भ का पोषक है और वहाँ वर्णित रतिदशा करुणविप्रलंभ के अन्तर्गत होने वाली कामदशाओं में से विलाप या प्रलाप दशा है :

7. रजनीतिमिरावगुण्ठिते पुरमार्गे घनशब्दविक्लवाः।
 वसतिं प्रिय कामिनां प्रिया- स्त्वदृते प्रापयितुं क ईश्वरः।।
8. अलिपंक्तिरनेकशस्त्वया गुणकृत्ये धनुषो नियोजिता।।
 विरुतैः करुणस्वनैरियं गुरुशोकामनुरोदितीव माम्।।
9. प्रतिपद्य मनोहरं वपुः पुनरप्यादिश तावदुत्थितः।
 रतिदूतिपदेषु कोकिलां मधुरालापनिसर्गपण्डिताम्।।
10. रचितं रतिपण्डित त्वया स्वयमङ्गेषु ममेदमार्तवम्।
 ध्रियते कुसुमप्रसाधनं तव तच्चारु वपुर्न दृश्यते।।[52]

वर्षाकाल में रात के सघन अन्धकार से ढके हुए नगर के मार्गों पर चलती हुई एवं मेघगर्जन को सुनकर भयभीत अभिसारिकाओं को अब उनके प्रियतमों के घरों तक पहुंचाने की सहायता तुम्हारे बिना कौन कर सकेगा। यह काले भ्रमरों की पंक्ति, जिसे तुमने पहले अनेक बार अपने धनुष की डोरी के स्थान पर प्रयुक्त किया था, इस समय अपने करुणाजनक स्वर में मुझ अत्यन्त शोकवाली हतभागिनी के साथ रो-सी रही है। अब तुम फिर एक बार उठकर अपना वही मनोहर शरीर धारण कर लो और सुमधुर कूजन में स्वभाव से ही निपुण इस कोकिला को आदेश दो कि यह प्रेमियों के मध्य रति की दूती का कार्य सम्पन्न करे। हे रतिपण्डित कामदेव, तुमने स्वयम् अपने हाथों से इन वसन्त ऋतु के पुष्पों द्वारा मेरा शृंगार किया था। मैं तो अब भी उन पुष्पाभरणों को धारण किए हुए हूँ, किन्तु तुम्हारा वह कमनीय शरीर नहीं दिखाई पड़ रहा है।

उपर्य्युद्धृत सभी पद्य कामपत्नी रति की विलाप कामदशा के स्पष्ट निदर्शक हैं। कालिदास ने कामदेव के शिव द्वारा भस्मीभूत कर दिये जाने पर रति के जिस विलाप को अपनी चातुरी से उपन्यस्त किया है, वह समग्र संस्कृत साहित्य में अप्रतिम है। यद्यपि यहाँ आलम्बन (कामशरीर) नष्ट हो चुका है, किन्तु जिस प्रकार के भावों का उद्रेक रति में हो रहा है, वह पूर्णरूपेण उसकी कामदशा को ही अभिव्यञ्जित करता है। इसलिए रतिविलाप में विप्रलम्भ शृंगार के चतुर्थ भेद करुणविप्रलम्भ की ही अवस्थिति मानी जायेगी। जैसा कि अभिनवगुप्त, भोजराज, विश्वनाथ तथा शिंगभूपालप्रभृति आचार्यों द्वारा प्रदत्त करुणविप्रलम्भ की परिभाषा तथा विवेचन से स्पष्ट है :

11. तमवेक्ष्य रुरोद सा भृशं स्तनसंबाधमुरो जघान च।
स्वजनस्य हि दु:खमग्रतो विवृतद्वारमिवोपजायते।।
12. इति चैनमुवाच दु:खिता सुहृद: पश्य वसन्त स्थितम्।
तदिदं कणशो विकीर्यते पवनैर्भस्म कपोतकर्बुरम्।।
13. अयि संप्रति देहि दर्शनं स्मर पर्युत्सुक एष माधव:।
दयितास्वनवस्थितं नृणां न खलु प्रेम चलं सुहृज्जने।।
14. अमुना ननु पार्श्ववर्त्तिना जगदाज्ञां ससुरासुरं तव।
बिसतन्तुगुणस्य कारितं धनुष: पेलवपुष्पपत्रिण:।।
15. गत एव न ते निवर्तते स सखा दीप इवानिलाहत:।
अहमस्य दशेव पश्य मामविषह्यव्यसनेन धूमिताम्।।
16. विधिना कृतमर्धवैशसं ननु मां कामवधे विमुञ्चता।।
अनपायिनि संश्रयद्रुमे गजभग्ने पतनाय वल्लरी।।[53]

रति वसन्त को देख छाती पीटती हुई और जोर से रुदन करने लगी। अपने सामने इष्ट बन्धुजनों को देखकर दु:ख का द्वार खुल-सा जाता है। दु:ख से भरी रति वसन्त को

सम्मुख उपस्थित देखकर बोली–हे वसन्त, देखो तो तुम्हारे प्रिय मित्र की यह क्या दशा हो गयी ? कबूतर के समान रंग वाली कामदेव के शरीर की इस भस्म को वायु कण-कण करके इधर-उधर बिखेर रहा है। हे कामदेव, तुम्हारा यह प्रिय सखा वसन्त तुम्हारे दर्शन के लिए उत्सुक है, अत: अब तो दर्शन दो। पुरुषों का प्रेम अपनी स्त्रियों में भले ही सुदृढ़ न हो, किन्तु अपने मित्रों के साथ तो अचल ही होता है। तुम्हारे निकट रहने वाले तुम्हारे इसी सखा ने तो देवों तथा असुरों सहित समस्त संसार को तुम्हारे कमलनाल की प्रत्यञ्चा तथा कोमल पुष्पों के बाण वाले धनुष का आज्ञाकारी बनाया था। हे वसन्त, तुम्हारा यह मित्र कामदेव वायु से बुझाये गये दीपक की भाँति अब वापस नहीं आने वाला है, मैं तो उस दीपक की बत्ती के समान हूँ जो अब इस असहनीय विपत्ति के शोकरूपी धूम को उगल रही हूँ। मुझे छोड़कर मेरे अर्द्धांग पति की हत्या कर दैव की प्रतिहिंसा केवल आधी सफल हुई, किन्तु हाथी ने जब आश्रयभूत वृक्ष को ही नष्ट कर दिया तब उसकी आश्रित लता भी अवश्य ही नाश को प्राप्त होगी।

उपरि निर्दिष्ट सभी पद्य कामपत्नी रति की अनेकविध विलाप (प्रलाप) कामदशा के ही अभिव्यञ्जक हैं। इन सभी पद्यों में कामदशा की अवस्थिति मानने के लिए यह आवश्यक है कि सम्पूर्ण रतिविलाप में विप्रलम्भ श्रृंगार के चतुर्थ भेद करुणविप्रलम्भ के अभिव्यञ्जन को स्वीकार किया जाये। अभिनवगुप्त, भोजराज, शिंगभूपाल तथा विश्वनाथ प्रभृति आचार्यो के मतों को देखते हुए हमें यह समीचीन प्रतीत होता है कि कुमारसम्भव का रतिविलाप करुणविप्रलम्भ का श्रेष्ठ निदर्शन है और यहाँ वर्णित रति की सभी कामदशाएँ उसी करुणविप्रलम्भ के अन्तर्गत स्थित मानी जानी चाहिए।

मरण

मरण कामदशा का निरूपण प्राय: तीन प्रकार से किया जाता है-1. मरण की हार्दिक अभिलाषा के रूप में; 2. मरणासन्न दशा के रूप में एवं 3. प्रत्युज्जीवनरूप मरणदशा के रूप में। इन तीनों ही रूपों में मरण कामदशा का उपनिबन्धन रतिविलाप में हुआ है। रतिविलाप के प्रसिद्ध पद्य 'हृदये वससीति...' को लक्ष्य कर आचार्य अभिनवगुप्त का मत 'रतिप्रलापेषु च श्रृंगार एव करुणस्य जीवितम्'[54] अत्यन्त सामीचीन है तथा वह सम्पूर्ण रतिविलाप में घटित होता है। इस प्रकार आचार्य अभिनवगुप्त के मतानुसार भी रतिविलाप में करुणविप्रलम्भ का सुष्ठु अभिव्यञ्जन हुआ है। भोजराज, विश्वनाथ महापात्र एवं शिंगभूपाल प्रभृति प्रसिद्ध आचार्यो द्वारा प्रदत्त परिभाषाओं और विवेचनों के आधार पर भी रतिविलाप करुणविप्रलम्भ का निदर्शन है।

1. परलोकनवप्रवासिन: प्रतिपत्स्ये पदवीमहं तव।
   विधिना जन एष वञ्चितस्त्वदधीनं खलु देहिनां सुखम्।।

2. अहमेत्य पतङ्गवर्त्मना पुनरङ्काश्रयणी भवामि ते।
चतुरैः सुरकामिनीजनैः प्रिय यावन्न विलोभ्यसे दिवि।।
3. मदनेन विनाकृता रतिः क्षणमात्रं किल जीवितेति मे।
वचनीयमिदं व्यवस्थितं रमण त्वामनुयामि यद्यपि।[55]

तुम अभी-अभी परलोक गये हो और मैं भी अभी उसी मार्ग पर आने वाली हूँ, जिससे तुम गये हो। विधाता ने मुझे उस क्षण मूर्च्छित करके बड़ी वञ्चना की अन्यथा मैं भी तुम्हारे साथ ही चलती, क्योंकि संसार के समस्त प्राणियों का सुख तो तुम्हारे ही हाथ में था। चतुर अप्सराएँ स्वर्ग में तुम्हें मोहित करेंगी उसके पूर्व ही मैं अग्नि में प्रवेश कर तुम्हारे समीप तुम्हारा अनुगमन कर रही हूँ तथापि वह लोकापवाद तो बन ही गया कि कामदेव के बिना भी रति कुछ क्षणों तक जीवित बची ही रही।

उपर्य्युद्धृत सभी पद्य रति की मरण की हार्दिक अभिलाषा-रूप अन्तिम कामदशा के व्यञ्जक है। पतिव्रता मदनवधू रति अपने प्रियतम का परलोक में भी अनुगमन करने के लिए तत्पर हैं। अपने विरहदु:खातिशय से वह यह भूल जाती है कि कामदेव भी दिव्ययोनि के हैं और रति स्वयं भी दिव्य है तभी तो वह कहती है कि स्वर्ग में अप्सराएं जब तक तुम्हें विलुब्ध न कर पायें, उसके पहले मैं तुम्हारे पास आती हूँ। यह भी संभव है कि रति किसी उच्चतर लोक का संकेत कर रही हो, किन्तु किसी भी स्थिति में वह मरण के लिए समुत्कण्ठित है, जिससे कामदेव के साथ उसका समागम हो। अतएव, यहां मरण कामदशा उपन्यस्त है।

4. तदिदं क्रियतामनन्तरं भवता बन्धुजनप्रयोजनम्।
विधुरां ज्वलनातिसर्जनान्ननु मां प्रापय पत्युरन्तिकम्।।
5. शशिना सह याति कौमुदी सह मेघेन तडित्प्रलीयते।
प्रमदाः पतिवर्त्मगा इति प्रतिपन्नं हि विचेतनैरपि।।
6. अमुनैव कषायितस्तनी सुभगेन प्रियगात्रभस्मना।
नवपल्लवसंस्तरे यथा रचयिष्यामि तनुं विभावसौ।।
7. कुसुमास्तरणे सहायतां बहुशः सौम्य गतस्त्वमावयोः।
कुरु संप्रति तावदाशु मे प्रणिपाताञ्जलियाचितश्चिताम्।।
8. तदनु ज्वलनं मदर्पितं त्वरयेर्दक्षिणवातवीजनैः।
विदितं खलु ते यथा स्मरः क्षणमप्युत्सहते न मां विना।।
9. इति चापि विधाय दीयतां सलिलस्याञ्जलिरेक एव नौ।
अविभज्य परत्र तं मया सहितः पास्यति ते स बान्धवः।।[56]

इसलिए हे वसन्त! इसके बाद तुम अपने मित्र का यह कार्य करो कि मुझ पतिविहीना के लिए अग्नि प्रज्वलित करके तुम मुझे पति के समीप तक पहुँचा दो।

चाँदनी चन्द्रमा के साथ अस्त हो जाती है और बिजली मेघ के साथ ही विलीन हो जाती है। यह तथ्य तो अचेतन भी समझते हैं कि स्त्रियों को अपने पति के मार्ग का ही अनुगमन करना होता है। अपने प्रियतम की इस उत्तम भस्म से अपने स्तनों को रंग कर मैं नूतनपल्लवों से रचित शय्या के समान धधकती हुई चिता की अग्नि में प्रवेश करूंगी। हे सौम्य! तुम हम दोनों के सुरत-समय में भी पुष्पशय्यादि प्रस्तुत कर सहायता करते थे। मैं हाथ जोड़कर तुमसे प्रार्थना कर रही हूँ कि तुम आज मेरे लिए शीघ्र ही चिता का निर्माण कर दो। जब चिता की अग्नि में मैं कूद पड़ूं तो तुम उसे दक्षिण की वायु चलाकर शीघ्र धधका देना, क्योंकि तुम्हें यह तो ज्ञात ही है कि कामदेव मेरे बिना क्षण-भर के लिए भी नहीं रह सकते। यह सब कर देने के बाद तुम हम दोनों को एक जलाञ्जलि देना, क्योंकि तुम्हारे मित्र कामदेव परलोक में तुम्हारे दिए इस जल को बिना बांटे मेरे साथ पीयेंगे।

उपरिनिर्दिष्ट सभी पद्य पतिवर्त्मगा पतिव्रता मदनभार्या रति के मरण की हार्दिक अभिलाषा-रूप मरण कामदशा के स्पष्ट निदर्शक हैं। पतिव्रता की परिभाषा के लिए मल्लिनाथ निम्नांकित स्मृति को उद्धृत करते हैं-

आर्तार्ते मुदिते हृष्टा प्रोषिते मलिना कृशा।
मृते म्रियेत या पत्यौ सा स्त्री ज्ञेया पतिव्रता।।[57]

वैसे तो सम्पूर्ण रतिविलाप अद्भुत है, किन्तु 'शशिना सह याति कौमुदी' इस पद्य को उच्च कल्पना एवं काव्यात्मक चारुता के कारण विशिष्ट महत्त्व प्राप्त है। इस पद्य से मिलता-जुलता भाव रघुवंश में द्रष्टव्य है-

शशिनं पुनरेति शर्वरी दयिता द्वन्द्वचरं पतत्रिणम्।[58]

मदनवधू रति चिता को नूतनपल्लवरचित शय्या-सरस-किसलयशयनीय मान रही है जहाँ बैठकर उन्हें प्रियतम-सान्निध्य शीघ्र सुलभ होगा। इस भाव से विपरीत भाव की कल्पना रघुवंश में उपलब्ध है-

नवपल्लवसंस्तरेऽपि ते मृदु दूयेत यदंगमर्पितम्।
तदिदं विषहिष्यते कथं वद वामोरु! चिताधिरोहणम्।।[59]

रति कामसखा वसन्त से प्रार्थना करती है कि वह काम और रति उन दोनों के लिए एक ही जलाञ्जलि द्वारा तर्पण करे, क्योंकि उन दोनों को साथ ही पान एवं भोजन सदैव अभीष्ट था जैसा टीकाकार वल्लभदेव स्पष्ट लिखते हैं-

आवयोर्हि सहपानभोजनं सदैवेष्टम्। पृथग्दानेन तु तद्दुर्घटम्।[60]

10. तदिदं परिरक्ष शोभने भवितव्यप्रियसंगमं वपु:।
रविपीतजला तपात्यये पुनरोधेन हि युज्यते नदी।।
11. इत्थं रते: किमपि भूतमदृश्यरूपं मन्दीचकार मरणव्यवसायबुद्धिम्।
तत्प्रत्ययाच्च कुसुमायुधबन्धुरेनामाश्वासयत्सुचरिताऽर्थपदैर्वचोभि:।।[64]

हे सुन्दरि! तुमको प्रियसंगम अवश्य प्राप्त होगा। अत: तुमको इस शरीर की रक्षा प्रिय-समागम के लिए ही करनी चाहिए। अपने शरीर को त्याग कर भविष्य के प्रियसंगमोत्सव से वंचित न बनो। जो नदी ग्रीष्म ऋतु में सूर्य की किरणों से शोषित होकर जलहीन हो जाती है, वही नदी पुन: वर्षा ऋतु में जल से भर जाती है। इस प्रकार, न जाने किस अदृश्य तत्त्व ने आकर रति के शरीर त्यागने के संकल्प को शिथिल कर दिया और उसी दैववाणी पर विश्वास स्थापन कर कामसखा वसन्त भी युक्तिपूर्ण वचनों द्वारा अपनी बन्धुस्त्री रति को आश्वासन देने लगा। ये दोनों पद्य भी रति की मरण कामदशा के अभिव्यञ्जक हैं। यद्यपि रति मरण की हार्दिक अभिलाषा रखती है, किन्तु आकाशवाणी सुनकर अपने शरीर-त्याग के संकल्प से विरत होती है। यहाँ प्रकारान्तर से कामदेव के प्रत्युज्जीवन का भी संकेत है। रति के लिए 'शोभने!' सम्बोधन उसके भावी सौभाग्य-लाभ का द्योतक है।

12. विधिना कृतमर्धवैशसं ननु मां कामवधे विमुञ्चता।
अनपायिनि संश्रयद्रुमे गजभग्ने पतनाय वल्लरी।।[62]

काम का वध करते समय क्रूर दैव ने मुझ अर्धांगिनी को जीवित छोड़कर वध का केवल अधूरा कार्य किया है, किन्तु विश्वासपूर्वक आश्रय देने वाले वृक्ष के हाथी द्वारा तोड़ दिये जाने पर उस पर आश्रित लता तो अवश्य ही गिरकर नष्ट हो जाती है। तात्पर्य यह है कि काम के मृत्यु को प्राप्त करने पर कामस्त्री का भी मरण अवश्यंभावी है। यहां रति की मरणासन्नदशा-रूप मरण कामदशा उपन्यस्त है। क्रूर दैव का अर्धवैशसम्-वध का अधूरा कार्य *रघुवंश* में भी द्रष्टव्य है जहां क्रूर विधाता इन्दुमती को समाप्त कर देते हैं तथा अज जीवित रहते हैं-

13. अथवा मम भाग्यविप्लवादशनि: कल्पित एष वेधसा
यदनेन तरुर्न पातित: क्षपिता तद्विटपाश्रिता लता।।[63]
इति देहविमुक्तये स्थितां रतिमाकाशभवा सरस्वती।
शफरीं ह्रदशोषविक्लवां प्रथमां वृष्टिरिवान्वकम्पयत्।।
कुसुमायुधपत्नि दुर्लभस्तव भर्ता न चिराविष्यति।
शृणु येन स कर्मणा गत: शलभत्वं हरलोचनार्चिषि।।

15. अथ मदनवधूरुपप्लवान्तं व्यसनकृशा परिपालयांबभूव।
शशिन इव दिवातनस्य लेखा किरणपरिक्षयधूसरा प्रदोषम्।।[64]

इस प्रकार, जब अपना शरीर त्यागने के लिए रति तैयार हो रही थी तब अकस्मात् आकाशवाणी हुई, जिससे रति को उसी प्रकार शान्ति प्राप्त हुई, जिस प्रकार सरोवर के सूखने से विह्वल शफरी को प्रथम वृष्टि से शान्ति मिलती है। हे कामप्रिये! तुम्हारा पति तुम्हारे लिए शीघ्र ही दुर्लभ नहीं रहेगा अर्थात् वह शीघ्र ही तुम्हें प्राप्त होगा। वह किसलिए शिव के नेत्र की अग्नि में शलभ की भाँति जल कर भस्म हुआ है, उसका कारण सुनो। इसके अनन्तर पतिवियोग के दुःख से कृशांगी रति शाप की अवधि के समाप्त होने की उसी प्रकार प्रतीक्षा करने लगी, जिस प्रकार दिन में निकले हुए चन्द्रमा की किरणों के अभाव से धुंधली एवं तेजोविहीन कला रात्रि के आगमन की प्रतीक्षा किया करती है।

उपरिनिर्दिष्ट सभी पद्यों में मरण कामदशा निरूपित है। यहां प्रत्युज्जीवन-रूप तृतीय प्रकार की मरण दशा का स्पष्ट संकेत है। यहाँ आचार्य विश्वनाथ महापात्र तथा रुद्रट द्वारा प्रदत्त निर्देशों के अनुसार प्रत्युज्जीवन रूप मरणदशा विद्यमान है।

यहाँ रतिविलाप से मरणकामदशाबोधक पन्द्रह उद्धरण दिये गये जो करुण विप्रलम्भ के अन्तर्गत विद्यमान रति की कामदशा के अभिव्यञ्जक हैं। यहाँ मरण कामदशा के तीनों प्रकारों का निरूपण उपलब्ध है।

अजविलाप

अनुस्मृति कामदशा

तव निःश्वसितानुकारिभिर्बकुलैरर्धचितां समं गया।
असमाप्य विलासमेखलां किमिदं किन्नरकण्ठि! सुप्यते।।[65]
(तव निःश्वसितानुवादिभिर्बकुलैरर्धचितां समं मया।
असमाप्य विकल्पमेखलां किमिदं किन्नरकण्ठि! सुप्यते।।)[66]

हे किन्नर के समान मधुरकण्ठवाली इन्दुमति! सुगन्धि में तुम्हारे निःश्वास की अनुकरण करने वाले इन मौलसिरी के पुष्पों से, मेरे साथ आधी गुंथी हुई विलास-मेखला को बिना पूरा किये हुए ही तुम क्यों सो गयी हो। इस पद्य की टीका में श्रीगदरुणगिरिनाथ लिखते हैं-

तवेति। निश्वसितानुवादिभिः निश्वाससमानगन्धैरित्यर्थः। समं सह। विकल्पमेखलां कादाचित्कमेखलाम्। किन्नरकण्ठीति। मेखलारचनसमये यत् बकुलकुसुम प्रशस्तिगानं तदनुस्मरणात् सम्बोधनमिति दक्षिणावर्तः।[67]

इस पद्य की टीका में अरुणगिरिनाथ, जो टीकाकार दक्षिणावर्तनाथ का मत उद्धृत करते हैं, वह प्रशस्त है। महाराज अज अपनी प्रिय भार्या इन्दुमती, जो वास्तव में हरिणी नामक अप्सरा थीं और शापवशात् धरती पर आकर इन्दुमती बनीं, के साथ कभी-कभी सुरभित बकुल पुष्पों से उनके लिए विलास-मेखला की रचना करते थे। उस समय वे बकुल पुष्पों की प्रशंसा में गान भी किया करती थीं। इसीलिए, उस समय का स्मरण करते हुए महाराज अज यहाँ इन्दुमती के लिए 'किन्नरकण्ठि' सम्बोधन का साकूत प्रयोग कर रहे हैं। इन्दुमती वास्तव में सुमधुर कण्ठ की स्वामिनी थीं, क्योंकि वह वस्तुत: मानुषी स्त्री न होकर हरिणी नामक देवांगना थीं और देवयोनि की होने के कारण उनके कण्ठ का सुमधुर होना स्वाभाविक था। अत: यहां अजगत अनुस्मृति कामदशा सुन्दर रूप से विराजमान है।

विलाप कामदशा

2. मदिराक्षि! मदाननार्पितं मधु पीत्वा रसवत्कथं नु मे।
अनुपास्यसि बाष्पदूषितं परलोकोपनतं जलाञ्जलिम्।।[68]

हे मत्तनयने! (इन्दुमति!) मेरे द्वारा पहले पी गयी स्वादिष्ठ मदिरा को पीकर तुम अब मेरे अश्रुओं से दूषित तथा परलोक में प्राप्त तिलयुक्त जलाञ्जलि का पान किस प्रकार कर सकोगी। यहाँ अज की विलाप दशा निरूपित है। यहाँ विलाप कामदशा तभी मानी जा सकती है जब अजविलाप में करुणविप्रलम्भ की अवस्थिति मानी जाय। इन्दुमती के लिए प्रयुक्त 'मदिराक्षि' सम्बोधन की विविध टीकाकारों ने अनेक प्रकार से व्याख्या की है। चारित्रवर्धन के अनुसार इन्दुमती पद्मिनी नायिका थीं, अतएव उनके नयन हर्षदायक थे तथा प्रान्तरक्त थे-

मदिरे हर्षदायिनी प्रान्तशोणे वा पद्मिनीजातित्वादक्षिणी नेत्रो यस्यास्तत्सम्बुद्धौ।[69]

टीकाकार हेमाद्रि के अनुसार इन्दुमती मदिरा नामक दृष्टिप्रकार से सम्पन्न थीं-

मदिराभिधमक्षि दृष्टिर्यस्या: सा तत्सम्बोधनं यथा संगीतकलिकायाम्-
स्निग्धार्द्धमुकुला कान्ता लम्भिता मदिरा तथा।
पञ्चैवात्र प्रतिज्ञाता: शौर्यादित्येन दृष्टय:।।
सौष्ठवेनापरित्यक्ता स्मेरापांगमनोहरा।
वेपमानान्तरा दृष्टिर्मदिरा परिकीर्तिता।।इति।[70]

जडता एवं मूर्च्छा कामदशा

1. स तथेति विनेतुरुदारमते: प्रतिगृह्य वचो विससर्ज मुनिम्।
तदलब्धपदं हृदि शोकघने प्रतियातमिवान्तिकमस्य गुरो:।।[71]

इन्दुमती विरह-व्यथित राजा अज का हृदय गाढ़ शोक से आपूरित है, जिसके कारण शब्दतः तो वे गुरु वसिष्ठ का उपदेश ग्रहण कर लेते हैं, किन्तु शोकसान्द्र उनके हृदय में वह उपदेश स्थान ग्रहण नहीं कर पाता। वस्तुतः राजा अज की यहाँ हृदयशून्यता अवस्था चित्रित है जो उनकी जड़ता कामदशा को पुष्ट कर रही है। इसी पद्य में व्याधि दशा भी प्रकारान्तर से मानी जा सकती है।

2. वपुषा करणोज्झितेन सा निपतन्ती पतिमप्यपातयत्।
ननु तैलनिषेकबिन्दुना सह दीपार्चिरुपैति मेदिनीम्।।[72]

चेतनाशून्य शरीर से गिरती हुई इन्दुमती ने पति अज को भी गिरा दिया। इन्दुमती के संज्ञाशून्य शरीर के गिरते ही उसे मृत जानकर अज भी मूर्च्छित हो पछाड़ खाकर गिर पड़े। तैलबिन्दु के टपकने के साथ ही दीपक की लौ भी निश्चय ही पृथ्वी को प्राप्त करती है। यहाँ निरूपित अज-दशा प्रकारान्तर से अज की मूर्च्छा कामदशा को व्यञ्जित कर रही है। इन्दुमती के प्रति गाढ़ राग उनकी मूर्च्छा का कारण है।

मरण कामदशा

1. स्रगियं यदि जीवितापहा हृदये किं निहिता न हन्ति माम्।
विषमप्यमृतं क्वचिद्भवेदमृतं वा विषमीश्वरेच्छया।।[73]

(विलाप करते हुए अज कहते हैं) यदि यह माला प्राणों का हरण करने वाली है तो हृदय पर रखी हुई यह मेरे प्राणों का हरण क्यों नहीं कर रही है? ईश्वर की इच्छा से कहीं विष भी अमृत हो जाता है और कहीं अमृत भी विष हो जाता है। मरणोत्सुक अज इन्दुमती के प्राणों का अपहरण करने वाली माला को अपने वक्षःस्थल पर रख रहे हैं, किन्तु फिर भी उनका प्राणान्त नहीं हो रहा है। यहाँ अज के मरण की हार्दिक अभिलाषा रूप मरण कामदशा अभिव्यञ्जित है। टीकाकार अरुणगिरिनाथ के अनुसार प्रस्तुत पद्य में निर्वेद, मरण, वितर्क तथा मति का क्रमशः उदय निरूपित है। यहाँ मरण से अभिप्राय मरणोद्यम से है।[74]

2. प्रमदामनु संस्थितः शुचा नृपतिः सन्निति वाच्यदर्शनात्।
न चकार शरीरमग्निसात्सह देव्या न तु जीविताशया।।[75]

राजा अज परम विद्वान् होकर भी अत्यन्त शोक से प्रिया के पीछे मर गये-इस लोकनिन्दा के भय से ही उन्होंने अपने शरीर को रानी इन्दुमती के शरीर के साथ नहीं जलाया, स्वयं जीवित रहने की इच्छा से नहीं। इन्दुमती के प्रति गाढ़ अनुराग वाले अज इन्दुमती के विरह को सहने में असमर्थ होने से प्राणत्याग कर देते, किन्तु लोकापवाद के भय से तथा नृपति के कर्त्तव्यों के पालन के प्रति निष्ठावान् होने से उन्होंने वैसा नहीं

किया। यहां भी पूर्वोक्त पद्य की भांति मरण की हार्दिक अभिलाषा रूप मरण कामदशा निरूपित है। इस पद्य की अतिसुन्दर व्याख्या टीकाकार अरुणगिरिनाथ ने प्रस्तुत की है–

> कथं तथाविधप्रेमातान्नानुमृतवानित्याह–प्रमदामिति। अनुसंस्थितः अनुमृतः। वाच्यदर्शनात् अपवादपर्यालोचनया। अयं भावः–अनुमरणलक्षण आत्मत्याग एव पापीयान्। ततोऽपि शुचा, धैर्यावसादप्रथनात्। तत्रापि प्रमदानिमित्तिकः रागान्धताख्यापनात्। विशेषतो नृपतेः, यतस्तदपाये लोकयात्रोच्छेदः यतश्च प्रजासुखपरतन्त्रेण तेन भवितव्यम्, न तु स्वसुखदुःखाधीनेनेति।[76]

सभी आचार्यों के मतों तथा रतिविलापस्थ एवं अजविलापस्थ कामदशाओं का विवेचन करने के अनन्तर निष्कर्षतः कहा जा सकता है कि करुणविप्रलम्भ शृंगार के द्वितीय अधिष्ठान विप्रलम्भ का ही एक बहुत सुन्दर एवं हृदयावर्जक भेद है।

संदर्भ

1. *शृंगारप्रकाश*, चतुर्विंश अध्याय
2. *काव्यानुशासन*, 2.30
3. *मेघदूत*, आशाबन्धःकुसुमसदृशं प्रायशो ह्यङ्गनानां
   सद्यःपाति प्रणयिहृदयं विप्रयोगे रुणद्धि।।
4. *नाट्यशास्त्र* (डॉ. पारसनाथ द्विवेदी-सम्पादित), षष्ठ अध्याय, पृ. 140
5. *नाट्यशास्त्र*, षष्ठ अध्याय, पृ. 152
6. *काव्यालंकार* (रुद्रट-प्रणीत)-12.5, 6
7. *सरस्वतीकण्ठाभरण*, 5.45
8. *भावप्रकाशन*, 4.57
9. वही, 4.60
10. वही, 4.70
11. *साहित्यदर्पण*, 3.187
12. *रसगंगाधर* (पं. बदरीनाथ झा सम्पादित), पृ. 151
13. *काव्यालंकार*, 14.34
14. *सरस्वतीकण्ठाभरण*, 5.45-46
15. वही, 5.50
16. *नाट्यशास्त्र*, षष्ठ अध्याय, पृ. 152, 154
17. *रसार्णवसुधाकर*, 2.220, पृ. 222
18. *साहित्यदर्पण*, 3.209
19. वही, 3.209 पर वृत्ति
20. *शृंगारप्रकाश* (डॉ. वी. राघवन, अनुवादक डॉ. प्रभुदयालु अग्निहोत्री) पृ. 63
21. *साहित्यदर्पण*, 3.209 पर वृत्ति

22. *करुण रसः सैद्धान्तिक एवं प्रायोगिक उपलब्धियां*, पृ. 190
23. *रसार्णवसुधाकर*, 2.219 पर वृत्ति
24. *रसार्णवसुधाकर*, 2.219, 22 के अनन्तर वृत्ति
25. *शृंगारतिलक*, 2.1, पृ. 44
26. *रसकलिका*, *रसार्णवसुधाकर*, पृ. 275 में उद्धृत
27. *साहित्यदर्पण*, 3.190
28. वही, 3.194 के अनन्तर वृत्ति
29. वही, 3.205, 6
30. *उत्तररामचरित*, 3.44
31. *रसगंगाधर*-प्रथमानन, पृ. 142
32. वही, पृ. 142
33. वही, पृ. 142
34. वही, पृ. 143
35. *नाट्यशास्त्र*, षष्ठ अध्याय, पृ. 141
36. वही, पृ. 145, 146
37. रघुवंश, (नन्दार्गीकर सम्पादित) 8.95
38. वही, (अरुणगिरिनाथ टीका सहित, 8.93 तथा प्रकाशित टीका, पृ. 65)
39. वही
40. *ध्वन्यालोक*, 3.20 की वृत्ति
41. *नाट्यशास्त्र*, 24.190, *शृंगार*. 2.27, *नाटक*. पृ. 238, *भा. प्र.*-4. 102, *उज्ज्वल*. - *शृंगारभेद*, 42
42. *उज्ज्वलनीलमणि*, शृंगारभेद, 43
43. *नाट्यशास्त्र*, 24.191, *शृंगार*. 2.28, *नाटक*. पृ. 238, *भा. प्र.*-4.103, *सा.* द. 3.193
44. *शृंगारतिलक*, 2.29, 30
45. दशरूपक, 4.21 पर अवलोक
46. *साहित्यदर्पण*, 3.194
47. वही, तृतीय परिच्छेद, पृ. 236
48. वही
49. वही
50. *नाट्यशास्त्र*, षष्ठ अध्याय, पृ. 114, 15
51. *क़ुमारसम्भव*, 4.4, 9
52. *कुमारसम्भव*, 4, 11, 15, 16, 18
53. वही, 4, 26, 27, 28, 29, 30, 31
54. *नाट्यशास्त्र*, *अभिनवभारती*, षष्ठ अध्याय, पृ. 115
55. *कुमारसम्भव*, 4.10, 20, 21
56. वही, 4.32, 33, 34, 35, 36, 37

57. वही, 4.33 पर मल्लिनाथ टीका में उद्धृत
58. *रघुवंश*, 8.56
59. वही, 8.57
60. *कुमारसम्भव*, 4.37 पर बल्लभदेव, टीका
61. वही, 4.44, 45
62. वही, 431
63. *रघुवंश*, 8.47
64. *कुमारसम्भव*, 4.39, 40, 46
65. *रघुवंश*, 8.64
66. वही, (अरुणगिरिनाथ, टीका, सहित), 8.62
67. वही, (अरुणगिरिनाथ, टीका, सहित) 8.62 की प्रकाशिका टीका
68. वही, 8.68
69. वही, 68 के नोट्स में उद्धृत, पृ. 763
70. वही, 8.68 के नोट्स में उद्धृत, पृ. 763
71. वही, 8.91
72. *रघुवंश*, 8.38
73. वही, 8.46
74. वही, 8.46 पर अरुणगिरिनाथ, टीका द्रष्टव्य
75. वही, 8.72
76. वही, 8.70 पर अरुणगिरिनाथ, टीका

21

आचार्य अभिनवगुप्तनिरूपित रसप्रक्रिया

दशरथ द्विवेदी

यस्तन्मयान्हृदयसंवदनक्रमेण द्राक् चित्रशक्तिगणभूमिविभागभागी।
हर्षोल्लसत्परविकारजुषः करोति वन्देतमां तमहमिन्दुकलावतंसम्।।

हिरण्यवर्णा, सद्यःस्नाता युवती के समान सुवर्णरथारूढ[1] उषा की मधु-मधुर स्मित से विमुग्ध, निरभ्र प्रसन्न दुग्ध धवल चन्द्रिका वितानतले निष्पन्द, निःशब्द त्रिविष्टप को सुखद विश्राम की निद्रा में निमग्न कराने वाली निशावधू की उद्दाम मादकता से आप्यायित,[2] पुरोहित अग्नि की तपःपूत मृदूच्चण्ड अर्चियों का अनुभवी,[3] समान सुन्दर वृक्षाधिवासी दो सुपर्णों की फल के भोगाभोग से समुत्पन्न सौन्दर्यश्री का द्रष्टा[4] कालक्रम से विष्णु के परम पद में मधूत्स का उत्साही, परमसत्ता के रसस्वरूप – 'रसो वै सः', का भोक्ता, 'आनन्दं ब्रह्म' का अपरिमित सुख लूटने वाला, क्रान्तदर्शी वैदिक कवि रस का कितने समीप से कितनी विविधताओं और कितनी बारीकियों से साक्षात्कार करता था इसकी कल्पना आज के भौतिक प्राणी से केवल अनुमानित हो सकती है, अनुभूत नहीं। चराचर जगत् का विध्वंसी यन्त्र-मानव निषादविद्धाण्डजदर्शनोत्थ[5] शोक के पल्लवांश का भी आस्वाद पा सकेगा क्या? वैविध्यपूर्ण चित्रजगत् में परमसुदर स्रष्टा से सृष्ट धरती पर सुलभ सुच्छायाम्भोज मकरन्दवत् त्रिवर्ग की धर्मादिपूर्वक ही सेवन करने की ऊर्ध्वबाहु विरावपूर्वक अवधीरित सम्मति से विषण्ण महामति व्यास की-भगवान् वासुदवो हि कीर्त्यतेऽत्र सनातनः – विरसावसान मनोव्यथा की रमणीयता का आनन्द सहजगम्य है क्या? और फिर काल की असीम सीमा में भारतीय सौन्दर्य चेतना की सतत

गतिशील भंगिमा को आचार्य भरतमुनि ने एक दिन में ही पहचान लिया था, सांगोपांग उपन्यस्त कर दिया था, इसकी न कल्पना की जा सकती है न मुनि ने ही स्वीकार किया है। *नाट्यशास्त्र* में इसे स्वयं वह स्वीकार करते हैं। अभिनवगुप्त के वचन भी इसमें प्रमाण हैं[6]। देवों का शान्त[7] चाक्षुष क्रतु नाट्य सार्ववर्णिक पंचमवेद[8] है। वर्तमान *नाट्यशास्त्र* के प्रणेता भरत थे किन्तु रस के आचार्य तो नन्दिकेश्वर ही[9] थे। द्रुहिण, दत्तिल, कोहल आदि आचार्यों के नाम *नाट्यशास्त्र* में सादर उपात्त हैं।[10] स्पष्ट है कि भरतमुनि ने अपने पूर्ववर्ती आचार्यों के मतों की सम्यक् जानकारी प्राप्त की थी, परिशीलन किया था और तब अपने ग्रन्थ का प्रणयन किया था।

नाट्य को रसस्वभाव होना चाहिये।[11] रसस्वभाव होने के कारण ही नाट्य को रस का पर्याय ही माना गया – तेन रस एव नाट्यम्।[12] नाट्यमेव रसः।[13] नाट्यगत समस्त वस्तु रसानुगत होती है। इसीलिये रसों की विवेचना के पूर्व आचार्य ने लिखा – नहि रसादृते कश्चिदर्थः प्रवर्तते।[14] लोक के सुख–दुःखात्मक स्वभाव का भावानुकीर्तन ही नाट्य है।[15] यह नाट्य सभी का विश्रान्तिजनक है।[16] विश्रान्ति की अवस्था आनन्दमयी होती है। सभी रस आनन्दमय होते हैं।[17] नाट्य में साक्षात्कारकल्प अनुभूति होती है। इसीलिए संदर्भों में दशरूपकों को प्रशस्य माना गया है : सन्दर्भेषु दशरूपकं श्रेयः।[18]

प्रकृत में अभिनवाचार्य प्रतिपादित रस का विवेचन अपेक्षित है। मेरी दृष्टि में इस विवेचन के तीन पक्ष हैं (1) भरत (2) भरतेतर आचार्य और (3) अभिनवगुप्त निरूपित रस विचार। द्वितीय पक्ष में उन सभी मतों की समीक्षा अपेक्षित है जो ध्वनि या व्यञ्जनावृत्ति को स्वीकार नहीं करते। ऐसे आचार्यों में अभिधावादी विद्वानों के अतिरिक्त वे आचार्य भी आते हैं जो काव्य में रस की प्रधानता या अलक्षणीयता को स्वीकार करते हैं, पर उसकी अभिव्यञ्जना होती है, नहीं मानते। ऐसे में वक्रोक्तिजीवितकार कुन्तक और अनुमितिवादी शङ्कुक से लेकर महिमभट्ट तक आते हैं। यहाँ आचार्य अभिनवगुप्त के रसस्वरूप पर ही विचार करना समीचीन होगा।

अभिनवगुप्त आनन्दवर्द्धन के अनुयायी हैं। आनन्दवर्द्धन ने ध्वनि को काव्य की आत्मा – काव्यस्यात्मा ध्वनिः, माना और रस, वस्तु, एवं अलंकार त्रिविध प्रधान ध्वनियों में रस को ही प्रधान स्वीकार किया। अलंकार वादियों के अभाव – भक्तिवाद का खण्डन कर आपने अभिधादित्रतयोत्तरवर्ती ध्वनि व्यापार को मानकर रस को सर्वथा व्यंजनावृत्तिगम्य ध्वनि स्वरूप स्वीकार किया। अविवक्षितवाच्य और विवक्षितान्यपरवाच्य ध्वनियों में आपने रस को विवक्षितान्यपरवाच्य ध्वनि के एक भेद असंलक्ष्यक्रम व्यंग्य ध्वनि के रूप में प्रतिष्ठित किया जो – स्वप्नेऽपि न वाच्यः की स्थिति में होता है। *ध्वन्यालोक* की *लोचन* टीका में अभिनवगुप्त ने यथास्थान ध्वनि का समर्थन किया और प्रतिपक्ष मतनिरासपूर्वक रस का निरूपण भी किया। अभिनवगुप्त रस विवेचन में अपने पूर्ववर्ती आचार्यों की भूमिका को नकारते नहीं हैं क्योंकि सोपान तो वही है। आप

की रस विवेचना शैवागम प्रभावित मानी जाती है। दर्शन पर अधिक बल न देते हुए मैं संक्षेप में यहां अभिनवगुप्त की रस-क्रिया का विवेचन करूंगा।

अभिनवगुप्त दशरूपकों में रस को प्रत्यक्षायमान मानते हुए भी काव्य को भी दशरूपकात्मक ही मानते हैं, *अभिनवभारती* के प्रारम्भ में और *नाट्यशास्त्र* के षष्ठ अध्याय की टीका में तथा *लोचन* में भी उन्होंने इस तथ्य को स्वीकार किया है।[19] नाट्य और रस के विषय में अभिनवगुप्त की दृष्टि को जानने के लिये *नाट्यशास्त्र* के द्वितीय अध्याय के प्रारम्भ में उनकी भावना को देखना आवश्यक है।

> *ब्रह्मेव कविः, शक्र इव प्रयोजयिता, भरत इव नाट्याचार्यः कोहलादय इव नटाः, अप्सरस इव सुकुमारोपकरणं, स्वातिरिवानद्धवित्, नारदवद्गीतज्ञः, सुरक्षितो मण्डपः, इन्द्रोत्सव सदृशः प्रयोगकालः, प्रशान्तरागद्वेषादिकाः सामाजिकाः, देवतापूजनपूर्वक प्रयोगः।*[20]

इन पंक्तियों में रसापादनार्थ कवि, प्रयोक्ता, नट, गीतादि विधान, प्रेक्षागृह, प्रयोगावसर और सामाजिक की भूमिका को प्रधानोपकरण माना गया है। इसलिए अभिनवगुप्त के रस विवेचन में इनकी प्रमुख भूमिका है। कवि नाटक एवं काव्य का प्रजापति है। 'शृंगारी चेत्कविः' आदि आनन्दवर्द्धन की उक्ति के अनुसार कवि का रसिक और विदग्ध होना आवश्यक है। रसों की भावना में कवि, नट और सामाजिक तीनों की हृदय व्याप्ति होनी चाहिए। जब तक कवि और नट दोनों में उससे प्रयुज्यामान काव्यादि द्वारा सामाजिक में अपने हृदय में परिव्याप्त रस-विकास[21] से प्रफुल्ल उद्दाम चमत्कार पवित्रता न हो जाय तब तक कोई भी प्रयोग उपादेय नहीं हो सकता।

सोत्साहपरिषदाकृतसम्मानस्य सम्यक् प्रयोगनिष्पत्तिः।[22] इत्यादि कथनों द्वारा अभिनवगुप्त ने सामाजिक की भूमिका को भी रसप्रीति में प्रमुख माना है। इसलिए वह बराबर अधिकारी पात्र विमलप्रतिभानहृदयः[23] की चर्चा करते हैं। काव्याभ्यास प्राक्तन पुण्यपरिपाक से जो सहृदय हो जाते हैं, काव्यार्थ की प्रत्यक्ष भावना करने में वे ही समर्थ होते हैं।[24] जो स्वभावतः निर्मलमुकुरहृदय हैं, सांसारिक्रोध-मोहादि से वे सामान्यतः पराभूत नहीं होते, साधारणीभूत रसनात्मक चर्वणागम्य रसस्वरूप नाट्य उन्हीं को स्फुट होता है। इसलिये रसानुभूति के लिये योग्य प्रमाता या अधिकारी का होना आवश्यक है।

अधिकारी प्रमाता के साथ ही सृजन में लीन अपार काव्यजगत्-प्रजापति कवि का भी प्रजापति समान होना आवश्यक है। वर्णनानिपुण होना ही कविकर्म की इयत्ता है क्योंकि ऐसा कवि स्वयं रस समाहित होता है-कविगतसाधारणीभूतसंविन्मूलश्च काव्यपुरःसरो नटव्यापारः, सैव च संवित् परमार्थतो रसः।[25] जब तक कवि परिपूर्ण घट के समान स्वयं छलकता नहीं तब तक परमार्थ सार का प्रकाशन संभव नहीं-यावत्पूर्णो न चैतेन तावन्नैव वमत्यमुम्।[26] कविगत साधारणीभाव ही काव्य में, सामाजिक में संक्रान्त होता है। इसमें उसकी प्रतिभा ही प्रधान है। अपूर्ववस्तुनिर्माणक्षमा प्रज्ञा ही प्रतिभा

है। रसावेश की विशदता से परिपूर्ण सुन्दर काव्यनिर्माण की शक्ति ही उसकी विशेषता है। वह प्रतिभा ही परमभट्टारक भगवान् शिव की शक्ति है जिसके उन्मीलन मात्र से क्षण में ही विश्व का उन्मीलन हो जाता है - यदुन्मीलनशक्त्यैव विश्वमुन्मीलति क्षणात्। यही चिति है, आत्मा है। कविप्रतिभा विश्वप्रतिभा का ही एक रूप है। जो शिवस्वरूप उन्हीं का तृतीय नेत्र है।[27] इसलिए विश्व प्रतिभा स्वरूप कवि जब कोई सर्जना करता है तो वह अपूर्व रसाविष्ट शिवात्मक स्वात्मविश्रान्तिस्वभाव स्वतन्त्र शिव-ब्रह्मानन्द स्वरूप होता है जिसमें कवि-नट-श्रोता समानरूप से निमग्न होते हैं-नायकस्य कवे: श्रोतु: समानोनुभवस्तत:। इस प्रकार अभिनवगुप्त के अनुसार रसानुभूति के लिये प्रतिभायुक्त कवि, तन्निर्मित उदात्त रचना और योग्य प्रमाता का होना आवश्यक है।

रस के विषय में अभिनवगुप्त की दार्शनिक पृष्ठभूमि को संक्षेप में *अ.भा.* के आधार पर जान लेना चाहिये। प्रथम तो यह कि शिव स्वयं स्थायी है-स्थायी शिवश्चेतसि तेन वृत्ति: कृता।[28] व्यभिचारिभूत वही स्थायी त्रिनेत्रशिव प्रबुद्ध कवि, तथा नट के हृदय में, आनन्दोन्मुख जन प्रमाता में, अन्त: प्रकाश विभावरूप, महानुभाव रसमात्रमूर्ति, प्रसन्न हृदय प्रकाशित होते हैं।[29] चित्तिशक्ति गणों की भूमि विभाग भाजन वही संवाद क्रम से तन्मय सहृदय जनों को हर्षोल्लसित परमानन्द से युक्त करते हैं। षट्त्रिंशकात्मक जगत् जिनकी आकाशाभास संचित् का रूप है, स्वयं शब्दार्थ[30] स्वरूप उससे भी परे वह शिव स्वतन्त्र, नित्य, विमर्श, आनन्द,[31] आत्मविश्रान्त स्वभावाह्लाद युक्त है। वह स्वयं रसस्वरूप है। रस ही अभिनवगुप्त का प्रतिपाद्य है। शक्ति, ज्ञान, क्रिया, आनन्द और चित्तिस्वरूपा अपनी पांच प्रमुखशक्तियों से वह नाना क्रीडाएँ करते हैं। प्रतिभापरपर्याय अपनी चित्तशक्ति से ही वह जगदुन्मीलन निमीलन करते हैं। वही - गर्भीकृतान्तर्विश्व: निखिलवाच्यवाचककलाप:[32] है। इसलिए रसभोग अन्त:प्रकाश आनन्दस्वरूप शिव की अवस्था है।

रस प्रक्रिया में अभिनवगुप्त कहते हैं, जब कोई विमल प्रतिभानशालीहृदय प्रमाता, 'ग्रीवाभंगाभिरामम्' या 'उमापि नीलात्मक मध्यशोभि' आदि वाक्यों को पढ़ता या सुनता है तो वाक्यार्थ प्रतीति के अनन्तर उसके मन में उस चित्र की एक प्रत्यक्षात्मक प्रतीति उत्पन्न हो जाती है। काव्य की शक्ति अभिनय या अभिव्यंजना की महिमा ऐसी होती है कि इस मानसी प्रत्यक्ष प्रतीति में देश-काल-पात्र आदि का भान नहीं रहता या उसका परिहार हो जाता है। उस प्रतीति में देश-काल आदि विवर्जित केवल भय, या रति मात्र की प्रतीति होती है। ऐसे में स्व-पर, भीताभीत, शत्रु, वयस्य, मध्यस्थ की अवस्थायें विलुप्त हो जाती हैं। सुख, दु:ख, हानि-लाभ जैसे विघ्नाधायक बुद्धि से भिन्न निर्विघ्नप्रतीति मात्र एक ही रस, विभावाद्यनुसार, भयानक, शृंगारादि हृदय में प्रवेश करता हुआ-सा, आंखों में नाचता हुआ-सा प्रतीत होता है। इस प्रतीति में आत्मस्वरूप का न तो अत्यन्त परिहार रहता है न ही विशेष भान।[33] रसानुभव के विषय में डॉ. पाण्डेय

का मन्तव्य है कि इसके दो तल हैं। प्रथम में विषय साक्षात्कार होता है, द्वितीय में अन्तर्मुखता होने से स्थायी का भी लोप होकर प्रमाता-प्रमेय का द्वैत लुप्त हो जाता है।

रसावेश की उपर्युक्त पंक्तियों को और आगे बढ़ाते हुए अभिनवगुप्त कहते हैं कि जीवात्मा शिव का ही प्रकाश[34] है, तत्स्वरूप है। इसलिए वासना के स्तर पर सभी का अनादिसंवाद है। वासनासंवाद ही अविघ्ना संविद् है। उपर्युक्त जो मृगादिविषयक साधारणीकरण की बात कही गयी थी वह परिमित नहीं होती, अपरिमित होती है। नटादि सामग्री ही भयादि का परिपोष करती है। देश-काल-पात्रदि जो काव्य में अर्पित होते हैं, परस्पर में रस प्रतिबन्धक होते हैं, किन्तु अभिनयादि के कारण उनका अपसारण होने से साधारणीकरण का भाव पैदा हो जाता है जिसमें सभी सामाजिक को एकघन रस प्रतीति होती है। आवरण भंग होने से परमानन्दमय प्रकाशघन शिवाद्वैत की अवस्था[35] होती है, किन्तु योगियों की अवस्था से विलक्षण और लोकोत्तर होती है। रस की अविघ्ना संवित् में चित्त चमत्कार, तज्जन्य, कम्पपुलकादि देखे जाते हैं। वह संपूर्ण तृप्ति या भोगावेश की दशा होती है। इसको साक्षात्कारात्मक मानस अध्यवसाय, संकल्प, स्मृति कुछ भी कह सकते हैं। इसका यह तात्पर्य हुआ कि प्रमाता सहृदय को अपने स्थायी का बोध नहीं होता। विभावादि उसके स्थायी को उद्‌बुद्ध कर इस प्रकार नायक-कवि-नटादि से अभिन्न कर देते हैं जैसे साधना के स्तर पर मलापसार होने पर आत्मा-शिव से अभिन्न हो जाती है -स्वप्रकाश, आनन्द घन। रस की साक्षात्कारात्मिका प्रतीति का एक और उदाहरण 'रम्याणि वीक्ष्य मधुरांश्च निशम्य शब्दान्' आदि को प्रस्तुत कर अभिनवगुप्त ने स्पष्ट रूप से यहां दुष्यन्त की एक स्मृतिमूलक रति का उदाहरण दिया है। विमलप्रतिभान साक्षात्कृत आस्वाद्य इस स्मृति में - सकृतकृतप्रणयोऽयं जनः का जो प्रेम, रति है वही व्यंजित हो रही है। इसमें जो आनन्द की अनुभूति किसी भी सहृदय को होती है वह न लौकिक होती है, न मिथ्या, न अनिर्वाच्य, न लोकतुल्य तथा न आरोप रूप। इसकी चरम परिपुष्टि में देश, कालादि का कोई नियन्त्रण नहीं होता। वीतविघ्नग्राह्य रसनीय भाव ही रस है।[36] सकलविघ्नविमुक्ता संवित्ति ही चमत्कार, निर्वेश, रसना, आस्वाद, भोग, समापत्ति, लय, विश्रान्ति आदि शब्दों से कही जाती है।

रसावेश में सात विघ्न गिनाए गये हैं - (1) प्रतिपत्ति में अयोग्यता (2) स्वगत-परगत नियम से देशकाल विशेष से आविष्ट होना (3) निज सुख-दुःखादि से विवश होना (4) प्रतीति उपाय की विकलता (5) अस्फुटता (6) अप्रधान योग (7) संशय योग। इनके अपसारणार्थ - लोक संवेदनीय सामान्य या उदात्त प्रख्यात चरित कथा का संयोग, रंगविधान - नटादिवेशभूषा - भाषादि माध्यम से साधरणीकरणोपाय, गीतातोद्य, गणिका, विदूषकादि का प्रयोग किया जाता है। अप्रतीति अस्फुटत्व के निवारणार्थ ही नाटक में लोकधर्मी, वृत्ति, प्रवृत्ति रूप अभिनय जोड़े जाते हैं। कवि को रस की प्रधानता के प्रति सावधान रहना चाहिए और प्रधान भाव के आनुषंगिक पुरुषार्थो

का अंगांगिभाव से प्रयोग करना चाहिए। प्रायः एक ही अनुभावादि कई स्थायी के हो सकते हैं – प्रेक्षक में संशय उत्पन्न हो सकता है। अभिनवगुप्त का कहना है कि इसीलिए आचार्य ने प्रत्येक के अनुभावादि का पृथक् उल्लेख करके सूत्र में सामान्य रूप से किया और संयोग पद जोड़ा जिसका भाव है कि जिसका जिस भाव से सम्बन्ध है वही-वही विभावादि उसका है। इससे संशय निवारण हो सकता है।[37]

स्थायी के विषय में आपका कहना है कि प्राणी निम्नलिखित[38] संवेदनाओं से ही परिव्याप्त है – रिरंसा (रति), परोपहास (हास), संताप (शोक), कोप (क्रोध), अशक्त (भीरु-भय), विषय विमुखता (जुगुप्सा), जिगीषुता (उत्साह), उदिताश्चर्य (विस्मय) और जिहासा (निर्वेद)। ये संवेदनाएं किसी में कम होती हैं किसी में अधिक। इसलिए मुख्यतः नौ स्थायी और उतने ही रस हैं। जहाँ तक निर्वेदादि व्यभिचारी भावों का प्रश्न है, वे अनित्य होते हैं। समुचित विभावादि के अभाव में उनका जन्म ही नहीं होता। उत्पन्न हुए भी तो हेतु के समाप्त होते ही विलीन हो जाते हैं। उनका संस्कार भी नष्ट हो जाता है। किन्तु उत्साहादि स्थायी अपने कर्तव्य की समाप्ति के अनन्तर भी संस्कारतया बने रहते हैं। स्थायी में इन व्यभिचारी भावों की स्थिति माला के सूत्र में ग्रंथित विभिन्न मणियों जैसी होती है। सभी को एकसाथ बाँधने के कारणभूत स्थायी से उपकृत ये व्यभिचारी अपनी उदयास्तमयी शतसहस्र विचित्रताओं से भासित भी अपने संस्कार सौन्दर्य को बिना निविष्ट कराये उसको मध्ये-मध्ये चित्रित और प्रकाशित करते हुए शबलित सौन्दर्याधान करते हैं। विभाव रत्यादि के उद्बोधक होते हैं। उनके अभाव में व्यभिचारियों के नाम भी नहीं रहते।[39]

सभी रस सुखप्रधान होते हैं,[40] क्योंकि, सभी की संवित् चर्वणारूप एकघन प्रकाशस्वरूप आनन्दसार (शिवस्वरूप) होती है। दुःख में चंचलता और रजोवृत्तिता होती है। इसलिये जो लोग रस को सुख-दुःखात्मक मानते हैं, अभिनवगुप्त की दृष्टि से वह उचित नहीं है।

रससूत्र की व्याख्या में अभिनवगुप्त का कहना है कि जो प्रमाता स्थाय्यात्मक पर चित्तवृत्ति के अनुमान या अभ्यास में पटु है उन्हें ही चर्वणात्मक रसादिरूप अर्थ का प्रत्यक्ष होता है जो अलौकिक निर्विघ्नसंवेदनात्मक चर्वणागोचरस्वभाव होता है। योग से तात्पर्य सामाजिक की बुद्धि में वासनात्मक रूप में स्थित स्थायी भाव के सम्यग्योग, एकाग्रता, तन्मयीभाव तथा साधारणीकरण से है। लोक के कारणादि हेतु काव्य-नाटक में अलौकिक होते हैं, केवल प्राच्य संस्कारोपजीवनता के लिये वे विभावादि कहे जाते हैं किन्तु वे स्वयं में उस दशा में अलौकिक ही होते हैं। स्वसंवेदन स्वरूप चर्वणात्मक रस तात्कालिक होने के कारण चर्वणातिरिक्तकाल में नहीं रहता है। स्थायी रूप होने पर भी रस स्थायिविलक्षण है।[41] विभावानुभाव तो व्यक्त रहते हैं स्थायी कभी भी वाच्य नहीं होते, इसीलिए सूत्र में उनका ग्रहण नहीं किया गया, क्योंकि वे सर्वथा व्यंग्य,

चर्वणास्पद हैं। अतः शंकुकादि का स्थायी की प्रतीति को अनुमिति मानना ठीक नहीं है। मम्मट ने इसी मत को अपनी भाषा में अभिव्यक्त किया है जिसका अनुगमन रुय्यक, विद्याधर, विद्यानाथ के ग्रन्थ की टीका रत्नावली, कुछ विशेष व्याख्यानपूर्वक हेमचन्द्र, वेदान्तानुसारीरूप में पण्डितराजजगन्नाथ ने भी किया है। शिव प्रसाद भट्टाचार्य,[42] नोली, रामचन्द्र शुक्ल, नगीना पारिख, नन्ददुलारे बाजपेयी, डॉ. नगेन्द्र आदि आधुनिक विचारकों ने भी इस पर प्रभूत प्रकाश डाला है।

रस की अलौकिकता के सन्दर्भ में अभिनवगुप्त ने स्पष्ट किया है कि रसप्रतीति लौकिक प्रत्यक्ष, अनुमान, शब्दादि प्रमाण, स्वसंवित्तिज्ञानपरक तटस्थ योगी के प्रत्यक्ष तथा विषयोपरागशून्य शुद्धास्वात्मानन्दलीन परयोगी के प्रत्यक्षज्ञान से सर्वथा विलक्षण होती है। उपर्युक्त प्रतीतियों में अर्जनादि, विघ्नान्तरोदय, अस्फुट विषयावेशजन्यविवशताएँ रहती हैं जिनमें सौन्दर्य नहीं होता। हाँ, रस में स्वात्मैकगतत्व नियम का अभाव होता है क्योंकि रस सर्वसाधारण होता है। स्वात्मा का अनुप्रवेश होने से परगत तटस्थ योगी की तटस्थता का भी रस में अभाव है। विभावादिसाधारणीकरण द्वारा संप्रबुद्ध समुचित निजवासना का जो रत्यादिरूप होती है, उसका अनुप्रवेश होने से अर्जनादि विघ्नों का भी उदय नहीं होता। इस प्रकार रस अलौकिक है।[43] विभावादि रसनिष्पत्ति के कारण नहीं हैं क्योंकि वैसा होने पर उनकी बोध समाप्ति पर भी रस बना रह सकता है। रस के पूर्व से प्रमेय जैसा सिद्ध न होने के कारण विभावादि उसकी ज्ञप्ति के कारण नहीं है। चर्वणोपयोगी उनमें विभावादि का व्यवहार भी अलौकिक होता है।

रस्यमानता ही रस का प्राण है। अतः वह प्रमेय नहीं है। रस सूत्र में निष्पत्ति का अर्थ रस नहीं रस की रसना है। रसनैकप्राणतारूप में उसकी निष्पत्ति कही जा सकती है। रसना व्यापार को न प्रमाण व्यापार कह सकते हैं न ही कारक व्यापार। रस की रसनीयता स्वयं में अप्रमाण भी नहीं है क्योंकि शिवात्मक होने से वह स्वसंवेदन सिद्ध है। यह रसना एक विचित्र प्रकार का बोध होने पर भी बोधान्तरों से विलक्षण है क्योंकि उसके उपाय विभावादि लोकविलक्षण होते हैं। यह रसना विभावादि के योग से निष्पन्न होती है इसलिए उस प्रकार के स्वसंवेदनसिद्ध रसनैकगोचर लोकोत्तर रसादि रूप अर्थ निष्पन्न होता है। भरतसूत्र का तात्पर्य यही है-तेन विभावादिसंयोगाद्रसनातो निष्पद्यतेऽतस्तथाविधरसनागोचरो लोकोत्तरोर्त्थो रस इतितात्पर्य सूत्रस्य।[44]

अन्त में साररूप में अभिनवगुप्त का मन्तव्य है कि, नाटकादि में मुकुट आदि के माध्यम से प्रथमतः रामादि की बुद्धि का आच्छादन हो जाता है। प्राक्तनसंवित् संस्कार के कारण भी काव्यबलादानीत नट में रामबुद्धि नहीं रह जाती। उभयदेशकाल का परित्याग हो जाता है। रत्यादि की प्रतीति के रूप में रोमांचादि पहले से देखे गए रहते हैं। उससे ही नाटक में भी सामाजिक में रत्यादि की प्रतीति होती है। इस प्रतीति में रत्यादिवासना के कारण स्वात्मा भी अनुप्रविष्ट रहती है। यह प्रतीति न तटस्थ, न नियत

रूप में और न ही नियतपरात्मैक रूप में होती है। यही कारण है इसमें अर्जन, द्वेष, दु:खादि की बाधा का उदय नहीं हो पाता। सन्तानवृत्त्या सभी की संविदभिन्न है। इसलिए उस संविद् से साधारणीभूत या साक्षात्कृत रति ही श्रृंगार बन जाती है। यह साधारणभाव विभावादियों के माध्यम से उत्पन्न होता है। रससूत्र विषयक अभिनवगुप्त का यह निष्कर्ष है – *अयमत्र संक्षेप: ... तेन साधारणीभूता सन्तानवृत्तेरेकस्या वा संविदो गोचरभूता रति: श्रृंगार, साधारणीभावना च विभावादिभि:*।[45]

अभिनवगुप्त द्वारा विवेचित रस का पानकरसन्याय से सहृदय प्रमाता द्वारा उपभोग किया जाता है। भरतोक्त षाडवशब्द वाच्य अलौकिक पाकरस में जल के समान प्रबन्धनिर्वाह्य, विशेषकर दशरूपकानुप्राण रस में स्थायी की ही रसरूप में अभिव्यंजनात्मकता होती है। व्यजंन विभावस्थानीय होता है, चिंचाहरिद्रादि अनुभावस्थानीय और गुडादिद्रव्य व्यभिचारिस्थानीय होते हैं।

यह भी ध्यान देने योग्य है कि कविनिबद्ध नटादि द्वारा अभिनयों से प्रत्यक्षकल्पता को प्राप्त कराए गए विभावादियों से झटिति ही अविघ्नात्मक रस का भोगावेश हो जाता है। गमनक्रियावत् पर्यन्त में रसना क्रिया न होकर प्रथमावसर में ही हो जाती है – *कविनोपनिबद्धैर्नटेन साक्षात्कारकल्पतामानीतै: अविघ्नभोगात्मक रस उत्पद्यते झटित्येव। न गमनक्रियावत् पर्यन्ते रसनत्त्यिा निष्पद्यते अपितु प्रथम एवावसरे*।[46] इस प्रकार पुमर्थोपयोगी, रसनाधिक्यवशात् भरत ने आठ रसों की नाट्य में संस्तुति की है। इस सबका पर्यवसान मोक्ष (निर्वेद) में होता है, पर रसनाधिक्य न होने से नाट्यसन्दर्भ में उसको आचार्य ने उचित नहीं माना।

एक प्रश्न उठता है कि अभिनवगुप्त की रसप्रक्रिया में सार्ववर्णिक नाट्य जो रसापरपर्याय है जिसका प्रमाता विशिष्ट ही हो सकता है सभी अधिकारी होंगे क्या? स्वयं वह सार्ववर्णिक पद की व्याख्या में कहते हैं – अधिकृतानामनधिकृतानामपि सुकुमाराणां व्युत्पत्तिदायी। विशिष्ट प्रमाता के कथन और इस कथन में विरोध नहीं है क्या? स्वयं तो नहीं 'अन्येतु' के द्वारा वह इसका समाधान करते हैं– अश्रुतशास्त्रणामपि संवादादविचलकार्याकार्यसिद्धि:।[47] इस प्रकार पुन: वह छल से रस को प्रत्यभिज्ञादर्शन की भूमि में पहुंचा देते हैं। अस्तु –

यस्मिन्निगूढपरमार्थमबुध्यमाना: संसारनाट्यरसभावमुपाश्रयन्ते।
बुद्धवा पुनर्मुहुरहो निजमेवयान्ति तत् पूर्णधाम शिवतत्त्वमहं प्रपद्ये।।

सन्दर्भ ग्रन्थ

1. *नाट्यशास्त्र: अभिनवभारती*, बड़ौदा सं. 1956
2. *ना.शा.*, B.H.U. संस्करण, 1975
3. *ध्वन्यालोक*, *लोचन*, चौखम्बा, सं. 1997

4. *काव्यालंकारः*, भामह, विहार रा.भा. पटना, 1962 (काव्या.)
5. *काव्यादर्श*, मिथिला विद्यापीठ, 1957 (काव्या.)
6. *काव्यालंकार सं.*, लघुवृत्ति, प्रा.वि.सं. मन्दिर, 1925
7. *काव्या. सू. वृत्ति*, चौखम्बा, 1971
8. *वक्रोक्तिजीवितम्*, दशरथ द्विवेदी, वि.वि.प्र. वाराणसी, 1988 (व.जी.)
9. *वक्रोक्तिजीवितम्*, डॉ. के.सी. कृष्णमूर्ति, 1977
10. *अभिनवरससिद्धान्त*, दशरथ द्विवेदी, वाराणसी, 1984
11. *अभिनव का रस विवेचन*, डॉ. नगीना पारिख, वाराणसी, 1984 (अ.र.वि.)
12. *मतिमन्थन*, डॉ. गंगादत्त शास्त्री, 1972
13. *स्वतन्त्रकलाशास्त्र,* Vol. I : डॉ. के.सी. पाण्डेय, 1967
14. *व्यक्तिविवेक*, चौखम्बा, 1964 (व्य.वि.)
15. *नाट्यदर्पण* : सं. डॉ. नगेन्द्र, दिल्ली, 1961 (ना.द.)
16. *काव्यमीमांसा*, चौखम्बा, 1964
17. *सरस्वतीकण्ठाभरण*, काव्यमाला, 1934 (स.कं.)
18. *शृंगारप्रकाश*, मैसूर, 1955 (श्रृं.प्र.)
19. *भोजराज़ शृंगारप्रकाश* : डॉ. राघवन्, 1963 (भो.श्रृं.प्र.)
20. *काव्यप्रकाश*, बा. बोधिनी, 1965
21. *एकावली*, बाम्बे सं. सीरीज (एका.)
22. *प्रतापरूद्रयशोभूषण*, रत्नावली बाल मनोरमा सीरीज़ - 1950 (प्र.रू.य.)
23. *काव्यालंकार* : रुद्रट, चौखम्बा, 1966
24. *रसगंगाधर*, चौखम्बा, 1964
25. *अग्निपुराण*, आनन्दाश्रम, 1957
26. *चन्द्रालोक*, चौखम्बा, 1938
27. *भा. साहि. शास्त्र* : गं.त्र्यं. देशपाण्डे, बाम्बे, 1960
28. *काव्यशास्त्र*, डॉ. भगीरथ मिश्र, वाराणसी, 1975
29. *भा. सौन्दर्यशास्त्र की भूमिका* : डॉ. फतह सिंह, 1967
30. *कविराज प्रतिभा*, सं.सं.वि.वि., वाराणसी, 1987 (क.प्र.)
31. *कला और साहित्य की दार्शनिक भूमिका* : डॉ. अवस्थी, शिवशंकर, 1983 (क.सा. दा.भू.)
32. *महिमभट्ट*, डॉ. बी.एम. चतुर्वेदी, 1968
33. *कृष्णचैतन्य*, संस्कृत पोयटिक्स, 1918 (सं.पो.)
34. *काव्यतत्त्व समीक्षा*, डॉ. एन.एन. चौधुरी, 1959 (का.त.स.)
35. *डॉ. चारुदेव अभिनन्दन ग्रंथ*, डॉ. कृष्णमूर्ति, लेख पृ. 76, 1974
36. *दि एस्थेटिक्स एक्सपीरियन्स एकार्डिंग् टु अभिनवगुप्त*, आर. नोली, रोम, 1956
37. *स्टडीज इन इन्डियन पोयटिक्स*: डॉ. शि.प्र. भट्टाचार्य, 1964 (स्ट.इं.पो.)
38. *दशरूपक*, डॉ. रमाशंकर त्रिपाठी, वाराणसी, 1973 (द.रू.)

39. *साहित्यदर्पण*, चौखम्बा, 1955 (सा.द.)
40. *स्टा.रि. इन वेद*, डॉ. जे. खोद्रा
41. *पोयटिक ब्यूटी आफ ऋग्वेद*, डॉ. एम.के. वर्मा

संकेत

ऋ.	–	ऋग्वेद
भा.सौ.शा.	–	भरतीयसौन्दर्यशास्त्र
रामा.	–	रामायण वाल्मीकि कृत
ध्व.	–	ध्वन्यालोक
स्टा.रि.वे.	–	स्टाइलिस्टिक रिपीटीशन इन वेद
पो.व्यू.वे.	–	पोइटिक ब्यूटी ऑफ़ ऋग्वेद
अ.भा.	–	अभिनवभारती
ना.शा.	–	नाट्यशास्त्र
का.मी.	–	काव्यमीमांसा
अ.स.	–	अलंकारसर्वस्व
का.प्र.	–	काव्यप्रकाश
अ.र.सि.	–	अभिनवगुप्त रससिद्धान्त
का.सा.सं.	–	काव्यालंकारसारसंग्रह
ल.वृ.	–	लघुवृत्ति
अ.पु.	–	अग्निपुराण
का.सू.वृ.	–	काव्यालंकारसूत्रवृत्ति
ए.इ.अ.	–	एस्थेटिक्स इक्सपीरियन्स एकार्डिंग टू अभिनवगुप्त
स्व.क.शा.	–	स्वतन्त्रकलाशास्त्र
के.सी., कां.चं.पा.	–	कान्तिचन्द्र पाण्डेय
र.ग.	–	रसगंगाधर
म.मं.	–	मतिमन्थन
प्रत्य.	–	प्रत्यभिज्ञादर्शन
पारिख	–	डॉ. नगीना पारिख

पाद टिप्पणी

1. ऋ0, *उषस् सूक्त* 3/61/4/51 आदि, 1.113.7; 5.80.5; 1.123.10
2. वही, ह्वयामि रात्रिं जगतो निवेशिनीम्
3. वही, 1.1.1 वैदिक कवि की सौन्दर्यसाधना के लिए द्रष्टव्य; डा. फतेह सिंह की *भारतीय सौन्दर्यशास्त्र की भूमिका* तथा जे. खोंदा *स्टा.रि.वे.*; डॉ. एम.के. वर्मा – *पो. व्यू.वे.*

4. वही. द्वा सुवर्णा सयुजा सखाया .... अभिचाकशीति।। 1/164/20
5. मा निषाद प्रतिष्ठां त्वमगमः शाश्वशीःसमाः। रामा. 1/2/15, तथा कालिदास-*रघुवंश* 14/70; शोकः श्लोकत्वमागतः। आनन्द, *ध्व.* 1/5
6. सदाशिव-ब्रह्म-भरतमत त्रयविवेचनेन ... विहितमिदं शास्त्रम्, न तु मुनिविरचितमिति... प्रयुक्तम्। *अ.भा.*, पृ. 9, कोहलादिभिरेतैर्वावात्स्यशाण्डिल्यधूर्तिलैः। एतच्छास्त्रं प्रयुक्तं तु नराणां बुद्धिवर्धनम्।। ना.शा.
7. महाकवि कालिदास, देवनामिदमामनन्ति मुनयः शान्तं क्रतुं चाक्षुषम्। *मा.नि.* 1/4
8. तस्मातसृजापरं वेदं पंचमं सार्ववर्णिकम्। ना.शा. 1/12
9. रूपकनिरूपणीयं भरतः, रसाधिकारिकं नन्दिकेश्वरः। *का.मी.*, पृ. 2, राजशेखर
10. *अ.भा.*, पृ. 9 तथा षष्ठाध्याय
11. *नाट्यनाम्* ... वस्तु रसस्वभावम्। *आ.भा.*, पृ. 3
12 *अ.भा.*, पृ. 267
13. वहीं, पृ. 290
14. विस्तार से द्रष्टव्य, मेरी पुस्तक *अभिनव रस सिद्धान्त की भूमिका*
15. योऽयं स्वभावो लोकस्य सुखदुःखसमन्वितः। सांगाद्यभिनयोपेतः नाट्यभित्यभिधीयते।। *ना.शा.* 1/119 तथा त्रैलोक्यस्यास्य सर्वस्य नाट्यं भावानुकीर्तनम्।
16. ... विश्रान्तिजननम् काले नाट्यमेतद्भविष्यति। वही 1/114
17. सर्वे अमी सुखप्रधाना ... आनन्दसारत्वात् ... इति आनन्दरूपता सर्वरूपरसानाम्। *अ.भा.* पृ. 282
18. काव्यं तावन्मुख्यतो दशरूपकात्मकेव ... तत एवोच्यते - सन्दर्भेषु दशरूपकं श्रेयः (वामन काव्या) यत्तु दशरूपकं, तस्य योऽर्थस्तदेव नाट्यम्। वहीं 291
19. *अ.भा.*, पृ. 36, पृ. 291, लोचन पृ. 186
20. *अ.भा.*, पृ. 47 तथा पृ. 16
21. यावन्निजहृदयरसविलसद्विकस्वरनिर्वारचमत्कारपवित्रता न जाता भगवत इव तावाच्छिक्षाशतैरपि वैचित्त्यमनाहार्यम्। *अ.भा.*, पृ. 22
22. *अ.भा.*, पृ. 18
23. *अ.भा.*, पृ. 279
24. ये काव्याभ्यासप्राक्तनपुण्यहेतुबलादिभिः सहृदयाः। वहीं पृ. 289, ये स्वभावतो निर्मलमुकुरहृदयाः ...तेषामेव...साधारणरसनात्मकचर्वणाग्राह्यो रससंचयः। वहीं पृ. 291, सहृदयत्वं हि हृदयस्य कविहृदयतादात्म्यापत्तियोग्यतैव। पृ. 1328 (*का.हि.वि.सं.*), येषां काव्यनुशीलनाभ्यासवशाद्विशदीभूते मनोमुकुरे वर्णनीयतन्मयीभवनयोग्यता ते स्वहृदयसंवादभाजः सहृदयाः। *ध्व.*, पृ. 38
25. कविगतसाधारणीभूतसंविन्मूलश्च काव्यपुरस्सरो नटव्यापारः, सैव च संवित् परमार्थतो रसः। वहीं पृ. 294, डॉ. के. कृष्णमूर्ति, *ध्वनि एण्ड रस, चा.अ.गं.*, पृ. 486
26. हृदयसंवादतन्मयीभवनत्मात् आस्वाद्यमानतां प्रतिपन्नः... रसपरिपूर्णकुम्भोच्चलनव-चित्तवृत्तिनिःष्यन्दस्वभाव वाग्विलापादिवत्। *ध्व.लो.*, पृ. 86, 87, कृष्णमूर्ति वहीं 486

27. रसानुगुणशब्दार्थचिन्तास्तिमितचेतसः। क्षणं स्वरूपस्पर्शोत्था प्रज्ञैव प्रतिभा कवेः। साहि चक्षुर्भगवस्तस्तृतीयमिति गीयते। यया साक्षात्करोत्येष भावांस्त्रैलोक्यवर्तिनः। *व्य.वि.*, पृ. 453–53
28. *अ.भा.*, पृ. 341, 342
29. स्थायी प्रबुद्धहृदये व्यभिचारिभूतःऽकामाकुलासु जनतासु महानुभावः। अन्तर्विभावविषयो रसमात्रमूर्तिः श्रीमान्प्रसन्नहृदयोस्तु ममत्रिनेत्रः।। *अ.भा.*, पृ. 342
30. यस्तन्मयान्हृदयसंवदनक्रमेण द्राक् चित्रशक्तिगण भूमिविभागभागी। हर्षोल्कसत्परविकारजुषः करोति वन्देतमां तमहमिन्दुकलांवतंसम्।। षट्त्रिंशकात्मकजगद्गगनावभाससंविन्मरीचि चयचुम्बितबिम्ब शोभम्।। *अ.भा.*, पृ. 1
31. आनन्दः स्वातन्त्र्यं स्वात्मविश्रान्तिः स्वभावाह्लादः प्रधान्यात् (तन्त्रसार)। गंगादत्त शास्त्री, *मति.मं.*, पृ., 102
32. *तन्त्रालोक, म.मं.*, पृ. 102 तथा डॉ. के.सी. पा. पृ. 167–206
33. *अ.भा.*, पृ. 279
34. आत्मैव सर्वभावेन स्फुरन्ती वृत्तिचिद्विभुः। *म.नं.*, पृ. 101, प्रकाशस्वरूपता चित्शक्तिः। प्रकाशश्च अनन्योन्मुखविमर्श अहमिति। प्रत्य. वहीं म.मं.
35. श्रीमत्परमशिवस्य पुनः विश्वोत्तीर्णविश्वात्मकपरमानन्दमयप्रकाशैकघनस्य अखिलं अभेदेनैव स्फुरति। वहीं *म.मं.*, पृ. 101
36. *अ.भा.*, पृ. 279–80। द्रष्टव्य – डॉ. सुरजनदास स्वामी का लेख-*अभिनवगुप्तप्रतिपादित रसस्वरूपम् – प्रिन्सिपल्स ऑव् लिटरेरी क्रिटिसिज्म इन संस्कृत-पोयटिक्स*-सं. डॉ. रामचन्द्र द्विवेदी, पृ. 250,251
37. *अ.भा.*, पृ. 280–82
38. जात एव जन्तुरीयतीभिः संविद्भिः परीतो भवति। *अ.भा.*, पृ. 282, 83
39. वहीं पृ. 283। एते व्यभिचारिणः विद्युदुन्मेषनिमेषयुयुक्त्यैव स्थायिसूत्रे भव्यतां प्रकटयन्त्रः तिरोदधन्तश्च त द्वैचिभावहन्ति। *अ.भा.*, पृ. 308। निर्वेदग्लानिशलंकाख्याः... (त्रयस्त्रिंशद्व्यभिचारिणः)। *ना.शा.* 6.18.21
40. तत्र सर्वेऽमीसुखप्रधानाः। स्वसंविच्चर्वणा रूपस्यैकघनस्य प्रकाशानन्दस्वरूपतत्वात्।। वहीं पृ. 282। शृंगारहास्यवीराद्भुतशान्ताः सुखमयाः। अपरे पुनरनिष्टविभावाद्युपनीतात्मनः करुणरौद्रःबीभत्सभयानकाश्चत्वारः दुखात्मनः। रामचन्द्रगुणचन्द्र, *ना.द.*, पृ. 290। प्रकाशविमर्शात्मा संवित्स्वभावः परमः शिवो भगवान् स्वातन्त्र्यादेव रूद्रादिस्थावरान्तप्रमातृरूप तयानीत्लसुखादिप्रेमैकरूपतयैष स्वातन्त्र्यमहिमा प्रकाशते। प्रत्य. वहीं *म.मं.*, पृ. 107 तथा *कविराज प्रतिभा*, पृ. 25.268
41. *अ.भा.*, पृ. 284, *का.प्र.*, पृ. 95, *एकावली*, पृ. 86–90, *रत्नपणः पृ.प्र.रू.य.*, पृ. 154–58, काव्यानु. तथा इत्थंचानिनवगुप्तमम्मटभट्टादिग्रन्थस्वारस्येन भग्नावरणांचिद्विशिष्टो रत्यादिः स्थायीभावो रसः। ... रत्याद्यवच्छिन्नेनभग्नावरणा चिदेव रसः। *र.गं.*, पृ. 87–96
42. एस.एस. भट्टाचार्य – *स्टडीज इन इंडियन पोएटिक्स*, पृ. 39–53, ए.दू.ए.उ. , पृ. भूमिका 1–32, *पारिख*, पृ. 1–120

43. *अ.भा.*, पृ. 285, *का.प्र.*, पृ. 90, 91, रसगंगा आदि, द्रष्टव्य और एन.एन. चौधरी का *काव्य तत्व समीक्षा*, पृ. 190-214 जयदेव कृत रसविवेचनादि दृष्टव्य चन्द्रायेव-*पंचममूख* तथा *राकागम टीका*
44. वही, *अ.भा.*, पृ. 285। पाश्चात्य समीक्षा के आलोक में भारतीय रस-मीमांसा और मोक्ष की अवधारणा हेतु द्रष्टव्य, कृष्ण चैतन्य का-*संस्कृत पोएटिक्स*, पृ. 118-160 तथा 289-386
45. वही, *अ.भा.*, पृ. 285,86
46. वही, *अ.भा.*, पृ. 305
47. वही, *अ.भा.*, पृ. 12। वैष्णवसम्प्रदायानुसार-रस मीमांसा-प्रेक्षणीय है। द्रष्टव्य, एस. भट्टाचार्य, *स्ट.इं.पो.*, पृ. 52

22

Text of Bharata's Rasasūtra

Rewa Prasad Dwivedi

[1]

Bharata's *Nāṭyaśāstra/veda* (NS) is the base of Abhinavagupta's (AG) *rasa*-theory. Twofold text is running on its *rasa-sūtra* :

1. विभावानुभावव्यभिचारिसंयोगाद् रसनिष्पत्तिः[1] and
2. विभावानुभावव्यभिचारि-परिवृतः स्थायी रसनाम रसतां लभते।[2]

In support of the first, Abhinavagupta himself says :

तेन स्थायिप्रतीतिः, [सा] अनुमितिरूपा/ [सा च] न रसः।
अत एव सूत्रे स्थायिग्रहणं न कृतम्/तत् प्रत्युत शल्यभूतं स्यात्।।[3]

In the *Locana* on *ध्वन्यालोक* 1.18 AG, repeated the same idea and said: परकीया न चित्तवृत्तिर्गम्यते इत्यभिप्रायेण विभावानुभावव्यभिचारिसंयोगाद् रसनिष्पत्तिरिति सूत्रे स्थायिग्रहणं न कृतम्, तत् प्रत्युत शल्यभूतं स्यात्।।[4]

For the second one, several statements are available in AG's works : *Locana* and *Abhinavabhāratī* (AB). In *Locana* AG says:

रसध्वनिस्तु स एव योऽत्र मुख्यतया विभावानुभाव्यभिचारि संयोजनोदित-स्थायिप्रतिपत्तिकस्य प्रतिपत्तुः स्थाय्यंशचर्वणा-प्रयुक्त एवास्वाद प्रकर्षः।।[5]

Even Bharata severally speaks of स्थायी भाव in his NS, for example:

1. शृंगारो नाम रतिस्थायिभावप्रभव: — page 300
2. यद्ययं रतिप्रभव: शृंगार: कथमस्य करुणाश्रयिणो भावा: — page 308
3. हास्यो नाम हासस्थायिभावात्मक: — page 312
4. करुणो नाम शोकस्थायिभावप्रभव: — page 317
5. रौद्रो नाम क्रोध स्थायिभावात्मक: — page 319
6. वीरो नामोत्तमप्रकृतिरुत्साहात्मक: — page 324
7. भयानको नाम भयस्थायिभावात्मक: — page 326
8. बीभत्सो नाम जुगुप्सास्थायिभावात्मक: — page 328
9. अद्भुतो नाम विस्मयस्थायिभावात्मक: — page 329
10. शान्तो नाम शमस्थायिभावात्मक: — page 332
11. कथं स्थायिन एव भावा रसत्वमाप्नुवन्ति — page 349
12. स्थायिभावा रसत्वमाप्नुवन्ति — page 349
13. विभावानुभावव्यभिचारिपरिवृत: स्थायी भावो
    रस-नाम/तां लभते — page 349
14. यथा नाराणां नृपति: शिष्याणां च यथागुरु:।
    एवं हि सर्वभावानां भाव: स्थायी महानिह।। — page 350
15. बहूनां समवेतानां रूपं यस्य भवेद् बहु।
    स मन्तव्यो रस:[6] स्थायी शेषा: संचारिणो मता:।। — page 379
16. विभावानुभावयुतो ह्यंगवस्तुसमाश्रय:।
    संचारिभिस्तु संयुक्त: स्थाय्येव तु रसो भवेत्।। — page 379
17. स्थायी सत्त्वातिरेकेण प्रयोक्तव्य: प्रयोक्तृभि:। — page 379
18. नानाभावार्थसंपन्ना: स्थायिसत्त्वाभिचारिण:।
    पुष्पावकीर्णा: कर्त्तव्या: काव्येषु हि रसा बुधै:।।[7] — page 80

[2]

Now the question why then स्थायी is not mentioned in the रससूत्र by Bharata himself. AG's reply in this regard is no reply as he (AG) himself has gone against his own statement.

Among other replies natural and simple is one wherein term रस is meant for both स्थायी and रस as well. स्थायी transforms into the taste of *rasa*. Consequently even in the stage of *rasa*, *sthāyī* does not cease its स्थायित्व. The term *rasa* in the *rasa-sūtra* is presenting the sense of both *bhāva* and रसत्व as well. Now the problems are solved. This interpretation flashes to mind when one goes through the text of NS carefully.

[3]

Now the questions about *sthāyī* are as follows:

1. Why is it alone called *sthāyī* ? Why does it not fall into the category of संचारी or व्यभिचारी ?
2. What is the nature of their संचार, व्यभिचार and स्थेमा ? Why are they all not संचारी alone as they being mental state?
3. How can a momentory feeling reaches the stage of स्थायी ?

To solve the above questions one has to fix the duration of time and place of experience : for how much time the experience of *bhāve* goes on and where does the experience happens to be ? Rhetoricians have already been answering these questions. Majority of them is of the opinion that it is the artistic experience which decides the span of time and scale of place of any art. Rhetoricians say some emotions are स्थायी as they are felt throughout the work. For example, शोक is experienced throughout the *Uttararāmacaritam* or *Rāmāyaṇa*. If the *Uttararāmacaritam* is staged for three hours, all these three hours are full of pathos. Same is the case with the *Rāmāyaṇa*. If *Rāmāyaṇa* is enacted for ten days each days we are full of pathos.

The place of artistic production is none else but the heart or intellect of the spectator. Think over the intensity and depth of the emotion of pathos as to up to which degree they are felt or experienced or enjoyed.

These thinkers are of the opinion that the sense of लज्जा (shyness) or जड़ता are not experienced with the same intensity, depth and frequency as the feeling of love and sorrow. Aestheticians see the semblance of ocean, which makes all other things absorbed into it:

विरुद्धैरविरुद्धैर्वा भावैर्विच्छिद्यते न यः।
आत्मभावं नयत्यन्यान्/त्याशु स स्थायी लवणाकरः।।[8]
चिरं चित्तेऽवतिष्ठन्ते सम्बध्यन्तेऽनुबन्धिभिः।
रसत्वं ये प्रपद्यन्ते प्रसिद्धाः स्थायिनोऽत्र ते।।
सजातीयविजातीयैरतिस्कृतमूर्तिमान्।
यावद् रसं वर्तमानः स्थायिभाव उदाहृतः।।[9]
रत्यादयः स्थायिभावाः स्युर्भूयिष्ठ विभावजाः।
स्तोकैर्विभावैरुत्पन्नास्त एव व्यभिचारिणः।।[10]

In his *Rasagangādhara* (RG), Paṇḍitarāja tries to define the स्थायी at the end of discussion as follows:

1. आ प्रबन्धं स्थिरत्वादमीषां भावानां स्थायित्वम्।[11]
2. वासनारूपाणाममीषां मुहुर्मुहुरभिव्यक्तेरेव स्थिरपदार्थत्वात्।
   व्यभिचारिणां तु नैव, तदभिव्यक्तेर्विद्युदुद्द्योतप्रायत्वात्।[12]

In his *Kāvyanuśāsana* with his own *Viveka Tika* हेमचन्द्र reproduces almost all these delicacies of रस, स्थायी, संचारी as given by AG in AB and *Locana* in detail.[12] For *rasa*, हेमचन्द्र writes:

विभावानुभावव्यभिचारिभिरभिव्यक्तः स्थायी भावो रसः[13] In its वृत्ति he repeats again the same idea. He says सामाजिकानां वासनारूपेण स्थितः स्थायी रत्यादिको भावः ... साधारण्येन गोचरीक्रियमाणश्चर्व्यमाणतैकप्राणो विभावादिभावनावधिः[13a] कवि सहृदयै रस्यमानो रसः।

Earlier to Hemacandra, Mammaṭa had also put स्थायी भाव in his treatment of *rasa* in *Kāvyaprakāśa*:

कारणान्यथ कार्याणि सहकारीणी यानि च
रत्यादेः स्थायिनो लोके तानि चेन्नाट्यकाव्ययोः
विभावा अनुभावास्तत् कथ्यन्ते व्यभिचारणिः
व्यक्तः स तैर्विभावाद्यैः स्थायी भावो रसः स्मृतः।।[14]

In his वृत्ति on the above statement Mammata repeats the idea of *sthāyī*:

लोके प्रभेदादिभिः स्थाय्यनुमानेऽभ्यासपाटववतां
सामाजिकानां वासनात्मतया स्थितः स्थायी रत्यादिकः .... शृंगारादिको रसः

In the treatment of his predecessors too Mammaṭa could not forget स्थायी:

1. विभावैः कारणैः रत्यादिको भावो जनितः प्रतीयमानो रसः। (लोल्लटः)
2. रामोऽयमिति प्रतिपत्त्या ग्राह्ये नटे स्थायित्वेन संभाव्य
   मानो रत्यादिभावः रसः। (शंकुकः)
3. काव्ये नाट्ये च भाव्यमानः स्थायी भुज्यते (भट्टनायकः)[15]

In the *साहित्यदर्पण*, Viśvanātha also gives room to स्थायी भाव in the definition of *rasa*. He says:

विभावेनाऽनुभावेन व्यक्तः संचारिणा तथा।
रसतामेति रत्यादिः स्थायी भावः सचेतसाम्।।[?]

Then why Bharata could not incorporate स्थायी in his रससूत्रः विभावानुभावव्यभिचारिसंयोगाद् रसनिष्पत्तिः so also if स्थायी in not needed as declared तत् प्रत्युत शल्यभूतं, then why did the ancient rhetoricians, quoted above, try to include the same in the *sūtra*. In the *rasa* theory of AG, this knot still remains are uncut.

[4]

In the tenth century itself Bhoja (AD 1000) of Dhārānagarī, Dhār of the present day, took up this problem and showed the way of solution very satisfactorily. This solution is available in the eleventh chapter of the *Śṛṅgāraprakāśa* (SP). Two new things he adopted for it. First, he uprooted the sense of स्थायी from all the emotions. Accordingly, for him, all the emotions are merely संचारी and each of them reaches the stage of स्थायी if given suitable situation. Second, it is only spirit or ego or अहंतत्त्व or आत्मा which holds the reality called स्थायित्व. *Ātma* alone turns into *rasa* and then आस्वादयिता or कर्त्ता becomes one and identical with the आस्वाद्य or कर्म in artistic taste. In this procedure there is nothing which remains to count as स्थायी. In the form अहं we are facing भावऽ alone which are in every respect संचारी. Where could be, therefore, found the separate entity which could be called स्थायी. It is only hypothesis that one considers this or that emotion as stable. The reality is that soul alone fits in the rank of stable.

So far as रति, शोक, etc. are concerned they too are संचारी. At the same time, *rati* must be called प्रेमन्. In it neither male nor female is needed to cast as counterparts. This is the cosmic love spread over up to the beasts and creepers. After, सीताहरण, deers left the दर्भ from their mouths, मयूर left their dance and trees were pouring flowers. When Sita left the *āśrama* everything was sorrow-striken:

नृत्तं मयूराः कुसुमानि वृक्षा दर्भानुपात्तान् विजहुर्हरिण्यः।
तस्याः प्रपन्ने समदुःखभावमत्यन्तमासीद् रुदितं वनेऽपि।।

रघुवंश XIV. 6.9

It was all due to प्रेमा. *Rati* is here, obviously a sort of cosmic love.

Bhoja admits that the terms रस, अभिमान, अहंकार and शृंगार are synonyms like घट, कलश, etc. It is all nothing else but जीवात्मा which is one with ब्रह्म, ईश्वर, शिव or the ultimate reality whatsoever. When it desires to create the Universe it is full of *bhāvana*, i.e. perspiration. It is only after this *bhāvana* that the state called शृंगार is developed and from this *Śṛṅgāra* all the emotions whatsoever come out. This *Śṛṅgāra* is an absolute *rasa* with the taste of mere प्रेमन्, under which the emotions called रति, शोक, उत्साह so also निर्वेद, ग्लानि, etc. could easily be involved. Bhoja develops this theory of *rasa* as under–

सत्त्वात्मनामलधर्मविशेषजन्मा/जन्मान्तरानुभवनिर्मित वासनोत्थः।
सर्वात्मसंपदुदयातिशयैक हेतु/र्जागर्तिकोऽपि हृदि मानमयो विकारः।।

There is a विकार termed as मान in the human individuality. It is generated by the अमलधर्मविशेष created by the impressions of previous births. It inspires the आत्मसंपद् in its super degree. This मान is *rasa*: रसोऽभिमानोऽहंकारः शृंगारः शृंगारइति गीयते।

About this अभिमान or मान, Bhoja opines:

अप्रातिकूलिकतया मनसो मुदादेर्यःसंविदोऽनुभवहेतुरिहाभिमानः।
ज्ञेयो रसः सरसनीयतयात्मवृत्ते रत्यादिभूमनि पुनर्वितथा रसोक्तिः।।

It is the वृत्ति (आनन्द) of आत्मन् which in enjoyed and which gives birth to the *rasa*. In this रस what is felt is मुदादि the result of अभिमान. Why is it so ? Said in reply मनसः अप्रातिकूलिकतया, due to the absence of non-accordance with the mind; on the other hand, the subject of *rasanā* is आत्मशक्ति and not so-called *rati*, etc. Here we may recall the fact that *rasa* is Śiva and everything needed for its निष्पत्ति i.e., विभाव, अनुभाव and संचारी भाव are termed as शक्ति in the Agamic tradition. It is therefore good to accept विभावदि as शक्ति and आत्मशक्ति. AG himself calls the विभावादि as शक्तिः

यस्तन्मयान् हृदयसंवदन-क्रमेण
द्राक् चित्र-शक्तिगण-भूमिविभागभागी।

हर्षोल्लसत्परविकारजुषः करोति
वन्देतमां तमहमिन्दुकलावतंसम्।।[17]

In the language of dramaturgy *rasa* is termed as काव्यार्थ, शिव, रस and इन्दुकलावतंस and शृंगार is the synonym of *rasa*. *Bhāvas*, 49 in number, are all the time active to surround and elevate the शृंगार, i.e., रस. AB says:

रत्यादयोऽर्धशतमेकविवर्जितता ये
भावाः पृथग[18] *विविध-भाव-भुवो भवन्ति*
शृंगारतस्तमिह ते परिवारयन्तः
सप्ताच्चिर्षं द्युतिचया इव वर्धयन्ति।।

Bhāvas are the output of *rasa* like the lustre of fire. Here the element of संयोग of *rasa sūtra* and संयोजना of विभावादि is clear. In AB, AG says:

1. भावसंयोजना-व्यंग्य-परसंवित्ति-गोचरः।
   आस्वादनात्मनुभवो रसः काव्यार्थ उच्यते।।[19]
2. नन्वेवं कथं रसतत्त्वमास्ताम् (पृ. 277AB) ? उच्यतां
   परिशुद्धतत्त्वम्। उक्तमेव मुनिना न त्वपूर्वं किंचित्।
   तथा ह्याह काव्यार्थान् भावयन्तीति। तस्मात् काव्यार्थो रसः।।[20]

Now strikes the notion of *bhāvanā*. Bhoja makes difference between रस and भाव by saying:

आभावनोदयमनन्यधिया जनेन
यो भाव्यते मनसि भावनया स भावः।
यो भावनापथमतीत्य विवर्त्तमानः
सोऽङ्कृते हृदि परं स्वदते रसोऽसौ।।

Bhāva is enjoyed in mind through the means of keen concentration called *bhāvanā*. *Rasa* is that which comes forward only after the business of *bhāvanā* is over. That too in the heart full of अहंकार, the अहंभाव or ego. Here the element termed as अहम् is given importance. This अहं is nothing but आत्मतत्त्व, soul, self, as it is called. Taking अहंभाव in it, it becomes free of *bhāvanā*. Earlier it was mixed with *bhāvanā* that was residing in mind, after the operation of which nothing else could be felt. It is an experience of everybody. *bhāvanā* is noticed even by AG as he gives stress to तन्मयीभवन, a stage wherein nothing else is observed = वेद्यान्तरस्पर्शरहित।

[5]

Bhoja and Abhinava did not know each other. It is, therefore, thought that there where many canons of the *rasa* process. Abhinava follows the one which was followed by Bharata in his NS. On the other hand, Bhoja has gone upward and tried to adopt the Vedic theory of human development: सोऽकामयत एकोऽहं बहुस्याम्. Though Bharata is also a follower of Veda, yet, Bhoja's understanding of Vedic methodology is transparent and untouched or not disfigured with the ideas of later tantras.

Dr. V. Raghavan has summed up the *rasa* theory of Bhoja on pages 451-453 of his thesis 'Bhoja's *Śṛṅgāra Prakāśa*' (1978). It, however, is not free of his likes and dislikes, the latter being prominent. A rexamination or review of his assessment is very much needed.

Leaving aside the details what little I tried to say here is that the *rasa sūtras* of different canons were mingled in the NS long ago and the *sūtra* running with स्थायी is a later development of the first one running without स्थायी. So far as Abhinavagupta is concerned he followed the first but could not leave aside the latter one. In the नाटयानुशासन V the *Rasasūtra* of Bharata is discussed in detail–

मुनेर्यद् रससूत्रत्वेनास्ति वाक्यं प्रसिद्धिभाक्।
रसनिष्पत्तिसूत्रं तद् विशेष्यस्याऽपरिग्रहात्।। 40।।
शुद्धे रसे तु सर्वेषां भावानामस्ति वर्जना।
वैशेषिका रसा ये वै तेषां स्याद् भावसंयुतिः।। 44।।
किन्तु तेष्वपि शुद्धोहि रसः पार्यन्तिकः, स चित्।
स्पन्दो वा स्यात् स्फुरत्ता वा निर्दिशेषौ हि तौ शिवे।। 45।।
भुक्त्वा भोगान् समान् अन्ते स्वापमाप्नोति चेतना।
तत्र भोक्तारमेवाऽसौ भुंक्ते भोज्यत्वमागतम्।। 46।।
अयमेव रसः शुद्धो महारस इतीर्यते।
विरामः करणग्रामस्यासौ चिन्मात्र-संप्लवात्।। 47।।
कलास्वानन्दरूपेयं कला सत्या चिदात्मनः।
इयमेव रसः सर्व द्वन्द्वोतीर्णः समाधिना।। 58।।

समाधिरेष केषांचिद् व्यक्तिर्व्यंजनमेव वा।
यद्यपि व्यज्यनमानस्य स्पर्शमि लभामहे।। 59।।
व्यक्तौ तटस्थता काचित् प्रभातुरभिवीक्ष्यते।। 60।।[21]

संदर्भ

1. Bharata's *Nāṭyaśāstra*, Baroda edn., 1956, p. 272.
2. Ibid., p. 349. रसतां is printed as रसनाम. Though this is not a *sūtra*, yet can be cultivated and treated as *sūtra* easily.
3. Ibid., p. 284. See also Hemacandra's *Kāvyanuśāsana Viveka*, p. 78, Nirnayasagar edn., 1934.
4. *Dhvanyālokalocana*, Chaukhamba edn., 1940, p. 156.
5. Ibid., p. 179.
6. रस-स्थायी is the other reading given in the printed NS. The term श्रृंगार is to be explained in Bhoja's context.
7. There are the passages merely from NS VI and VII. References are taken from Baroda edn., 1954.
8. *Daśarūpaka* IV 34.
9. *Rasa Gangādhara* (RG), p.37, 1947, Nirnayasagar edn.
10. *Sangītaranākara* quoted in RG, by Paṇḍitarāja Jagannātha.
11. RG, p. 37, 1947, Nirnayasagar edn.
12. *Kāvyānuśāsana* by Hemacandra.
13. Hemacandra's *Kāvyānuśāsana* 2.1.

13a. 'भावना' reading is very much important, corresponding to the भावना of भोज. In Mammata's *Kāvyaprakāśa* 'विभावादिजीविताविधि:' is the reading printed in the editions : B.O.R.I. Poona, 1950; with the commentary of चण्डीदास edited by Prof. S.P. Bhattacharya, Calcutta, 1933; माणिक्यचन्द्रसंकेतयुतं, Poona, 1921; टीकात्रयोपेतं, 1976. Allahabad, and others.

14. *Kāvyaprakāśa* IV. 4-5.
15. Ibid., IV. 4-5 वृत्ति.
16. *Sāhityadarpaṇa* III. 1.
17. AB on NS 1.1.
18. 2-3. Josyer edn. of S., p. 436. In the edn. of HOS, 1998, p. 674 runs the text पृथक्-विध-विभावभुव: and श्रृंगारतत्त्वमभित:. It is irrelevant unlike the text given by Josyer adopted here by us.
19. (I) The verse is quoted in AB, p. 277 of Baroda edn., 1956 but in disfigured shape. The reading given here is available in महिमभट्ट व्यक्तिविवेक, p. 70, Chaukhamba, 1964. In AB, संयोजना is taken as संवेदना but संयोजना corresponds with the text of रससूत्र of NS.

    (II) The verse is not available in NS. In AB, भाव word is missing and संयोजनाव्यंग्य is taken as 'संवेदनाख्य (ख्यया) व्यंग्य'.

20. काव्यार्थ term is used by Bharatamuni himself and adopted in the same sense by AB. काव्यार्थो रसः should be understood as रसः काव्यार्थः also.
21. *Nāṭyanuśāsana*-V, 1996, Kalidasa Academy, Varanasi.

Contributors

Prof. V.N. Jha
Director, Centre of Advanced Study in Sanskrit, Ganesh Khind, Pune - 411 007

Prof. H.N. Chatterjee Sastri
175, Santoshpur Avenue, Calcutta - 700 075

Prof. Vidya Niwas Mishra
M/3 Badshah Bagh Colony, Fatman Road, Behind Kashi Vidyapeeth, Varanasi - 221 002

Prof. Rekha Jhanji
Department of Philosophy, Panjab University, Chandigarh - 160 014

Dr. S. Ranganath
Department of Sanskrit, N.M.K.R.V. College of Women, Jayanagar, Bangalore, Karnataka

Prof. Anupa Pande
Professor and Head, Department of Art History, National Museum Institute, Janpath, New Delhi - 110 011

Prof. Kamalesh Datta Tripathi
F/4 Jodhpur Colony, Banaras Hindu University,
Varanasi - 221 005

Dr. Biswanarayan Shastri
'RITAYAN', Nabagiri Road, Changmari, Guwahati - 781 003,
Assam

Dr. V. Kutumba Sastry
Head, Department of Sanskrit, Pondicherry University,
Pondicherry

Prof. Radhavallabh Tripathi
Head, Department of Sanskrit, Harisingh Gour University,
Sagar - 470 003, Madhya Pradesh

Dr. Amiya Kumar Mishra
16/A/5B, D.P. Road, Allahabad

Prof. Ramakant Sharma Angiras
1605, Sector 44B, Chandigarh

Dr. Kalanath Shastri
Manju Nikunj, C/8 Prithviraj Road, Jaipur - 302 001, Rajasthan

Prof. Rajendra Mishra
Department of Sanskrit, Himachal Pradesh University,
Shimla - 171 005

Prof. Damodar Ram Tripathi
Head, Department of Sanskrit, Kumaon University,
Nainital - 263 001

Dr. Hariram Mishra
4A/3, J.L. Nehru Road, Tagore Town, Allahabad, U.P.

Prof. Rahasbihari Dwivedi
Head, Department of Sanskrit, Rani Durgavati
Vishwavidyalaya, Jabalpur - 482 001, Madhya Pradesh

Dr. Prakash Pandey
Ganga Nath Jha Kendriya Sanskrit Vidyapith,
Chandra Shekhar Azad Park, Allahabad - 211 002

Prof. Navjiwan Rastogi
Department of Sanskrit, Lucknow University,
Lucknow - 226 007, Uttar Pradesh

Dr. Sushma Kulshreshtha
KC/12B, Ashok Vihar, Delhi - 110 052

Prof. Dashrath Dwivedi
Department of Sanskrit, Gorakhpur University,
Gorakhpur - 273 009, Uttar Pradesh

Prof. Rewa Prasad Dwivedi
28, Mahamanapuri, Varanasi - 221 005